There is a Providence that protects idiots, drunkards, children and the United States of America.

— *Otto von Bismarck*

You can always count on Americans to do the right thing . . . after they've tried everything else.

— *Winston Churchill*

America makes prodigious mistakes, America has colossal faults, but one thing cannot be denied: America is always on the move. She may be going to Hell, of course, but at least she isn't standing still.

—*E. E. Cummings*

Intellectually I know that America is no better than any other country; emotionally I know she is better than every other country.

— *Sinclair Lewis*

In America the biggest is the best.

— *Roy Lichtenstein*

Europe was created by history. America was created by philosophy.

— *Margaret Thatcher*

The greatness of America lies not in being more enlightened than any other nation, but rather in her ability to repair her faults.

— *Alexis de Tocqueville*

America is a large, friendly dog in a very small room. Every time it wags its tail, it knocks over a chair.

— *Arnold Toynbee*

So this is America. They must be out of their minds.

— *Ringo Starr*

Also available from **mental_**floss

The Mental Floss

HISTORY
of the
UNITED STATES

★ ★ ★ ★ ★ ★ ★ ★ ★ ★ ★ ★ ★

THE (ALMOST) COMPLETE AND (ENTIRELY) ENTERTAINING STORY OF AMERICA

Erik Sass

with *Will Pearson* and *Mangesh Hattikudur*

HARPER

NEW YORK · LONDON · TORONTO · SYDNEY

HARPER

A hardcover edition of this book was published in 2010 by Harper-Collins Publishers.

THE MENTAL FLOSS HISTORY OF THE UNITED STATES. Copyright © 2010 by Mental Floss LLC. All rights reserved. Printed in the United States of America. No part of this book may be used or reproduced in any manner whatsoever without written permission except in the case of brief quotations embodied in critical articles and reviews. For information address HarperCollins Publishers, 195 Broadway, New York, NY 10007.

HarperCollins books may be purchased for educational, business, or sales promotional use. For information please e-mail the Special Markets Department at SPsales@harpercollins.com.

FIRST HARPER PAPERBACK PUBLISHED 2011.

Designed by Emily Cavett Taff

The Library of Congress has catalogued the hardcover edition as follows:

Sass, Erik.
   The Mental floss history of the United States : the (almost) complete and (entirely) entertaining story of America / Erik Sass with Will Pearson and Mangesh Hattikudur.
      p. cm.
   Includes index.
   ISBN 978-0-06-192822-2
   1. United States—History. 2. United States—History—Humor. I. Pearson, Will. II. Hattikudur, Mangesh. III. Mental floss (Durham, N.C.) IV. Title.
   E179.S25 2010
   973—dc22

                                     2010038509

ISBN 978-0-06-192823-9 (pbk.)

            18   19   20   WBC/LSC   10   9

Contents

Acknowledgments

Erik would like to thank his parents, Karen and Stephen, for their enthusiastic, uncritical approval of everything he has ever written, and his brother Adam for his sense of the absurd. He would also like to express his gratitude to his history teachers, especially Mary-Therese Pasquale-Bowen, Col. Dan "D.A." Allen (Ret.), and Duke University professors Malachi Hacohen, Kent Rigsby, Kristin Neuschel, and Peter English. He also owes thanks to friends who contributed their expertise to this book, including Justin Schwab, on the American Revolution and Civil War; Alan Quillian, on medicine; Zeke Roeser, on personal computers and the Internet; and Greg Valentine on finance and economics, as well as Ben Osborne and Will Drake for their thorough reviews, and Sandy Wood and Kara Kovalchick for their fun facts. Needless to say, any errors in the text are his own. Last but not least, Erik would like to express his gratitude to Will Pearson and Mangesh Hattikudur for founding mental_floss and making his undergrad history degree a paying proposition, confounding the predictions of well-meaning family and friends.

Introduction

Americans are patriotic people: a 2008 poll showed 72 percent believe the USA is "the best nation in the world." But it turns out that "patriotic" and "historically knowledgeable" can be two different things: in recent surveys, almost half of Americans didn't know that the Constitution gives Congress the right to declare war, while one-quarter of high school students said Columbus set sail after 1750 and a third couldn't say in which century the American Revolution occurred.

Why is that, when there are so many amazing, fascinating, weird, unbelievable but still true facts and stories? Probably because some history books—and some history teachers—just aren't putting the "fun story" into "fundamental history." The truth is, learning about American history doesn't have to be a death-march through dusty dates, dreary details, and dead dudes in wigs. America is an amazing place, and it's all in the history, baby. How did rum and tobacco save the colonies? When did geopolitics hinge on a large rodent? Who made the first potato chip? What was the worst accident during a U.S. nuclear test? Who invented rock-and-roll? Did the CIA really support Osama bin Laden? Does internet dating really work?

You'll find all the answers in this book—plus plenty of other weird, intriguing, and downright incredible facts omitted by the average high school history course. Of course, there's absolutely no way a single volume can cover *all* the stuff you're supposed to know about American history, but we promise this book contains most of the stuff you *really* ought to know . . . along with crazy trivia and terribly ironic quotes perfect for breaking the ice at cocktail parties, wedding receptions, blind dates, armed stand-offs, and other awkward situations.

Prehistory, Puritans, Plantations, and Pirates

(23,000 BCE–1715 CE)

"Begin at the beginning" is tricky advice when you're talking about American history. Do you start with the arrival of the first human beings? The first native civilizations? The first European contact? The first permanent European settlement? But we'll give it a shot.

The first human inhabitants of North America arrived during the last Ice Age, when hunter-gatherers from northern Asia followed tasty wooly mammoths across a land bridge connecting Siberia to Alaska. Several waves of nomads may have crossed from Asia to North America between 23,000 BCE and 9000 BCE, at which point the Ice Age ended, the polar ice caps melted, and sea levels rose about 400 feet, submerging the land bridge and isolating the nomads in North America.

Over thousands of years their descendants migrated south, crossing 10,000 miles of incredibly varied terrain to reach the southern tip of South America no later than 8000 BCE. Spreading out across tundra, forests, grasslands, swamps, deserts, and jungles, they gradually formed separate linguistic and cultural groups. By one count, there are still about 2,000 native languages spoken in the Western Hemisphere, the vast majority—about 1,450—in South America.

Around 4000 BCE, one Mesoamerican group, the Olmecs of southeastern Mexico, invented agriculture by domesticating maize (corn), leading to the first Native American civilization. The Olmecs are considered the "mother culture" of the civilizations that followed, including the Maya and Aztecs. The domestication of maize and another staple crop, the potato, triggered the formation of complex societies in the Andean region of South America, including the Nazca, Moche, Chimu, and Inca.

But native societies in what became the United States never attained the same level of complexity. Although some groups had large populations that supported craftsmen, royalty, and priests, they never developed systems of writing, so much of their history remains mysterious. Sources like oral histories, linguistics, and archaeology generally only go back about 3,000 years, leaving the period from 7000 to 1000 BCE pretty darn enigmatic. The arrival of Europeans added assault to mystery, with new diseases and brutality decimating the native population of the future United States, which dropped from an estimated 5–10 million in 1492 to 250,000 in 1900. This tidal wave of death wiped out whole cultures and languages, so long story short: we know a lot more about the relatively short period of European settlement in the New World than we do about the much longer native history that preceded it. Acknowledging this bias, we're mostly going to begin with the parts of the past we know more about—meaning European settlement to the present—because a book filled with "gosh, we dunno" probably wouldn't sell too many copies.

·············· **WHAT HAPPENED WHEN** ··················

23,000 BCE–9000 BCE Asian nomads cross the land bridge connecting eastern Siberia to Alaska.

100 CE Teotihuacan in Central Mexico has a population of 150,000+.

700 Mayan city of Tikal has a population of 100,000+.

900 Mayan civilization mysteriously disappears.

1002/3 Vikings led by Leif Ericson discover Vinland (Newfoundland).

1150 Chaco Canyon culture sites are abandoned.

1427 Aztec Empire is founded in Mexico.

1438 Inca Empire is founded in Peru.

October 12, 1492 Columbus makes landfall in the Bahamas.

1499 Amerigo Vespucci explores coast of South America.

1519 Aztec Empire is destroyed by Hernán Cortés.

1533 Inca Empire is destroyed by Francisco Pizarro.

August 28, 1565 St. Augustine, Florida, is founded by Spanish settlers.

1585 English colonists settle on Roanoke Island, Virginia.

1590 Roanoke colony is mysteriously abandoned.

May 14, 1607 English colonists found Jamestown, Virginia.

July 3, 1608 French colonists found Quebec.

December 18, 1620 Puritan Separatists (Pilgrims) found Plymouth, Massachusetts.

1625 Dutch colonists found New Amsterdam.

September 17, 1630 Puritans found Boston, Massachusetts.

1634 English colonists (including persecuted Catholics) settle Maryland.

1641–1666 Beaver Wars pit Iroquois against rival tribes, with European support.

May 18, 1642 French colonists found Montreal.

June 6, 1676 Nathaniel Bacon leads rebellion against royal governor in Virginia.

March 4, 1681 Royal charter granted to William Penn for Quaker colony in Pennsylvania.

LIE: *Columbus was the first to discover America.*

THE TRUTH: Columbus gets his own holiday for his so-called accomplishment, but there's no doubt he was late to the discovery game. The Vikings discovered America about 500 years before he got there, and it's likely that the Polynesians found it even earlier!

The seafaring Polynesians reached Fiji by 1300 BCE, Tahiti by 300 CE, and Hawaii by 400. Given their remarkable feats of navigation, it seems likely they reached the Americas as early as 500. In South America, they appear to have brought chickens to Peru.

The Viking case is as solid as a battle axe: Leif Ericsson, the adventurer who sailed from Greenland to Newfoundland in 1002 or 1003, made several trips and reported his adventures in "Vinland" in detail. The sheer numerical superiority of the local Native Americans eventually persuaded the Vikings to pack it in. They abandoned Vinland around 1015, and the American adventure became a thing of legend. No one is certain of the dates because, well, the Vikings were illiterate (or preliterate, if you want to be nice about it), but Leif's adventures were incorporated into oral histories that were passed down until they were finally transcribed in the twelfth or thirteenth centuries.

BREAST ASSURED

While the Vikings weren't in the New World for long, they did pick up some good stories. One saga tells of a Viking hunting party in Newfoundland surrounded by native warriors. The Viking men were inclined to withdraw, but Freydis, the pregnant half sister of Leif Ericsson, would have none of this cowardice. She charged the field, revealed her ample bosom, and slapped one of her breasts with the flat side of a sword—because that's how Viking ladies do it. The startled natives retreated without a fight. Can you blame them?

CONSTRUCTION SEASON

The Aztecs, Mayans, and Incas tend to get all the credit for building awesomely gigantic monuments. But it wasn't all teepees and totem poles up North: there was plenty of major construction afoot.

In the Midwest, a succession of "mound-builder" tribes or tribal confederations lived in clusters of villages along the main tributaries of the Mississippi River. They are best known for, yes, building earthen mounds, beginning around the tenth century CE, including Monk's Mound, a 100-foot-tall flattened pyramid covering almost 14 acres, in modern-day Cahokia, Illinois. Most likely, the tribes used these mounds like the ancient Mesopotamians and Central Americans did, as platforms to bring the priestly elite closer to the gods. Around the same time, the "Fort Ancient" culture in the Midwest was busy raising enormous structures in the shapes of animals. The largest of these, the Serpent Mound in Adams County, Ohio, is three feet tall, six feet wide, and more than 1,300 feet long. The last mound-building society disappeared in the sixteenth century—possibly destroyed by nomadic Plains tribes, newly mobile with the acquisition of horses from Spaniards.

In the Southwest, the Anasazi of modern-day New Mexico built multi-story stone structures (some as tall as four stories) that are still standing—and they didn't even use mortar or cement! At its height in the tenth and eleventh centuries, the Chaco Canyon proto-city probably had a population of 4,000–5,000 people, while the surrounding network of villages may have housed 25,000–50,000 people. Two hundred and fifty miles of roads, some of them paved with cobblestones, connected Chaco and the surrounding villages. No one knows why Chaco Canyon was abandoned around 1150, but there is evidence prolonged drought caused a famine. There may also have been violent upheaval; the oral histories of Navajo pueblo-dwellers recall Chaco as a place where "people got power over other people," suggesting exploitation and social unrest.

LIE: *Columbus realized he'd discovered a new land.*

THE TRUTH: You've probably heard that Columbus discovered America by mistake. That's fair. After all, Renaissance Europeans believed that creation had been fully revealed, so they weren't exactly expecting to find two giant continents hidden on the other side of the planet. Plus, Columbus had drastically miscalculated the circumference of the earth at 19,000 miles instead of 24,900 miles—he based his projections on the work of Pierre d'Ailly, a Catholic cardinal who used Roman miles (4,840 feet) instead of nautical ones (6,080 feet). Units, people!

★ *In 1592, exactly 100 years after Columbus "discovered" the New World, the English Parliament passed a law setting the "statute mile" at its current length of 5,280 feet.*

Thus when the *Niña*, *Pinta*, and *Santa Maria* made landfall in the Bahamas on October 12, 1492, Columbus naturally assumed he had hit Asia. Sure, he saw no sign of the silk and pepper he was looking for, but he did find some people to call "Indians," with a small (but still worth it) amount of gold to steal. In 1493 his patrons, Ferdinand and Isabella of Spain, sent Columbus back across the ocean. He was given a sweet new title, Admiral of the Ocean Sea, and instructed to rob the place—wherever it was—blind. The admiral was then to serve as governor of whatever was left.

This is where an understandable mistake turns into bullheaded stupidity. On the four return expeditions from 1493 to 1502, it gradually dawned on *everyone but Columbus* that the land they were exploring wasn't the East Indies. This suspicion was supported by a whole bunch of evidence, including the testimony of natives who insisted, again and again, that they'd never heard of China, Japan, India, silk, pepper, elephants, or any of that nonsense.

Amerigo Vespucci, dispatched in 1499 by the king of Portugal as quality control, wrote in his first report that "these regions . . . may rightly be called a new world," and was later honored by having his name stamped on the place. But Columbus scoffed at his colleague. He dismissed the locals as "bestial men who believe the whole world is an island," and forced his crew, under threat of corporal punishment, to sign an affidavit declaring they'd discovered Asia. Obstinate till the very end, Columbus died in 1506, still believing he was right.

CHAINS YOU CAN BELIEVE IN

Geography wasn't the only subject Columbus failed at: he was also a terrible governor. In fact, he was so bad that Ferdinand and Isabella called him back to Spain in chains in 1503 to answer charges of corruption and brutality. In 1546, the Dominican monk Bartolomé de las Casas wrote:

> On the island of Hispaniola, of the above three million souls that we once saw, today there be no more than two hundred of those native peoples remaining . . . The Spaniards have shown not the slightest consideration for these people, treating them (and I speak from first-hand experience, having been there from the outset) not as brute animals—indeed, I prayed to God that they might treat them as well as animals—so much as piles of dung in the middle of the road.

The monarchs found Columbus not guilty (raping and pillaging had kind of been the whole point), but ordered him into retirement.

LIE: *The Puritans came to America to establish religious freedom.*

THE TRUTH: The Puritans came to America to escape other people's religious freedom. The story starts in 1593, when radical Protestant "Separatists" emigrated from England to Holland, where they could live in peace, without being hung or jailed for religious nonconformity. That led to a new problem for the Puritans: the easygoing Dutch allowed people to practice all sorts of crazy religions, including Judaism, Catholicism, and eventually even atheism—the horror! Meanwhile, the Protestant Dutch didn't observe the Sabbath with the same zeal as the Puritans and also permitted drinking, gambling, music, dancing, and "mixed company" in social settings—all big Puritan no-no's.

Worried that their children were being "Dutchified," the Separatists hopped the Mayflower out of Holland on September 16, 1620. Remembered as "the Pilgrims," they headed for northern Virginia but wound up in what is now Massachusetts, where they founded Plymouth, the first Puritan colony in the New World. The first years were fairly disastrous, with half the colonists dying in the first winter of 1620–1621—but it was still better than living near dancing, drinking gamblers. Separatists were so eager to get away from Holland and England that two more boatloads arrived in 1623 and 1627, offsetting the attrition.

Inspired by the "success" at Plymouth, about 20,000 non-Separatist Puritans left England for Boston, the first settlement of the royally chartered Massachusetts Bay Colony, beginning in 1628. But the fledgling theocracy of the non-Separatists proved just as intolerant as that of the Separatists. When the free-thinking Roger Williams suggested detaching church from state—a step that would technically allow the practice of other religions—he was banished. Williams went on to found Rhode Island in 1635, while fellow rebel Thomas Hooker led his more relaxed followers out of uber-strict Boston to Connecticut in 1636. Shortly thereafter, the Puritan elders exiled Anne Hutchinson for criticizing their authority, much as Puritans had criticized the Catholic and Anglican clergy. It seems that Puritans, in addition to disapproving of laughing, smiling, dancing, and touching, did not have a sense of irony. Good times.

But the bigger point is that traveling across the ocean in search of isolation didn't solve any of their problems. Like religious ideologues everywhere, the Puritans of Massachusetts were surprised when new immigrants and their own children didn't share the same enthusiasm for the doctrine. In 1691, King Charles II accelerated the breakdown of Puritan society when he changed the colony's royal charter so that property ownership, not membership in a Puritan church, became the basis of men's voting rights. He also amended the charter to include protection of religious dissenters. Looking back, the old-fashioned Puritans might have regretted the move overseas.

BONUS LIE: "THE THIRTEEN COLONIES"

Like the rest of us, you probably bought the ol' Thirteen Colonies story, but it's not an accurate depiction of colonial America for most of its history. In 1606 King James I chartered just two companies to settle North America, the Virginia Company of London and the Plymouth Company. As settlements were founded, each new city was recognized as it own colony: for example, Connecticut act ally contained 500 distinct "colonies" (c "plantations") before they were merged into a single colony in 1661. Sometimes colonies were mashed together into mega-colonies, like the short-lived, super-unpopular Dominion of New England, which incorporated Massachusetts, Rhode Island, Connecticut New Hampshire, and Maine from 1686 to

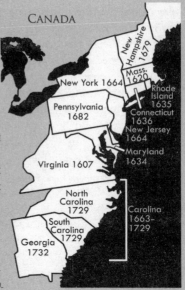

1691, plus New York and New Jersey from 1688 to 1691 for good measure. Colonies also split, like Massachusetts, which spawned New Hampshire in 1679. And some colonies weren't really colonies at all: while it's often listed as one of the Thirteen Colonies that rebelled in 1775, Delaware wasn't technically a colony or a province. Designated "the Lower Counties on the Delaware," it had its own assembly but fell under the authority of the governor of Pennsylvania until it declared itself an independent state in August 1776. So technically, there were just 12 colonies in 1775 and 13 states in 1776.

Good Witch Hunting

Was it mass hysteria, backlash against loosened social restrictions, or dark sorcery that fueled the Salem Witch Trials? Let's start with a little background. The infamous witch trials actually took place not in Salem Town, but in Salem Village, a small farming colony outside Salem Town. The place was "the sticks," as they say, with a population of about 90 adult male landowners (and their families), compared to Salem Town's 330 adult men. In keeping with the age-old divide between country and city folk, the conservative farmers from Salem Village viewed the big city as a den of sin and vice, while the cosmopolitan merchants of Salem Town looked down on their country cousins as ignorant hicks. Meanwhile, the increasing population of Salem Town put pressure on the farmers, as town streets pressed outward, and land grew increasingly scarce.

> ★ Salem Village sent a request to Britain for permission to incorporate as a town, but it was returned with the rejecting message "The King Unwilling." In 1757 the determined residents ignored His Majesty, calling the new town Danvers, and added the king's three-word message to the bottom of the town seal.

Unsettled by economic pressure and the feeling that society was evolving beyond their control, the farmers of Salem Village were all too ready to believe accusations of witchcraft, still widely feared in Europe. And of course, accusations of witchcraft are always a convenient way to dispose of women who are viewed as too smart, too independent, too strange, or too annoying. Many of the victims of the Salem Village witch trials matched this description, with a suspiciously high number of single women, some of them widows, who were highly visible for doing business in Salem Town. Plus, there was an added incentive: the rules for hunting witches gave the accuser part of a convicted witch's property.

The hysteria began when a group of teenage girls, led by the pastor's daughter, accused 156 people from 24 towns and villages of witchcraft. The girls claimed that these "witches" were casting spells and inflicting demonic possession on them. They were apparently inspired by the pastor's black female slave, Tituba, whom he'd brought to Massachusetts from the West Indies, and who frightened the girls with tales of voodoo.

When the deputy constable of Salem Town, John Willard, suggested the girls were making the stories up to get at personal enemies, they accused him of witchcraft too; he was one of 19 found guilty of bizarre charges and executed. Another of the 19 was George Burroughs—a Harvard graduate who hadn't lived in Salem for almost a decade, but who was brought back from Maine, tried, and executed after saying the Lord's Prayer correctly . . . because his accuser said the Devil spoke the correct version for him. Obviously.

Oddly enough, the few people who actually were practicing "witchcraft"—Tituba, another slave from the West Indies named Candy, and Dorcas Hoar, a white woman who dabbled in the occult—were all set free after a brief time in jail.

·········· **OTHER PEOPLE'S STUFF** ·····················

Location, Location, Location

After purchasing the entire island of Manhattan from uncomprehending natives for the legendary $24 worth of cheap trade goods, the Dutch couldn't get too upset when the English robbed them of the island in turn. The first Dutch settlers arrived on Governor's Island (just south of Manhattan Island) in 1624. They named it Noten Eylandt, or the "Island of Nuts." The following year, Fort Amsterdam was constructed on the southern tip of Manhattan Island, the purchase of which was finalized in 1626. By 1655 there were about 2,000 people living there—only half of them Dutch—making the city something of a metropolis. (Back in 1640, Boston was the biggest city, with 1,200 inhabitants.)

> ★ Manhattan Island was named for an Algonquin tribe known as the Manhattans, who "sold" it to the Dutch colonial governor, Peter Minuit, in 1626 for "trinkets" said to be worth $24. Some historians believe that the items were mistakenly given to a group of Canarsie natives who lived not in Manhattan, but what is now Brooklyn.

Dutch religious tolerance made New Amsterdam a haven for Spanish and Portuguese Jews fleeing oppression (which is basically redundant), Huguenots (French Protestants), and even Catholics (well, sort of). As far as trade, the spot was perfect for a number of reasons, including its proximity to the Hudson River, a highway for native trappers bringing beaver pelts from the interior. The trade route was protected by another Dutch colony, Orange (later Albany), about 200 miles upriver. At the same time, Manhattan itself was easily defended from native attack by the Hudson and East rivers, and later a defensive wall built just outside town (Wall Street).

Unfortunately for the Dutch, all of these advantages also attracted the attention of the British, who seized New Amsterdam in 1664 during the Second Anglo-Dutch War. The Dutch reclaimed it, but in 1673, the Brits seized it again in the Third Anglo-Dutch War. The Brits were smart enough to continue policies of religious tolerance and boosting commerce, and business went on pretty much as before—the only real change was that the British and Dutch elite began to intermarry, forming a new Anglo-Dutch governing caste called the Knickerbockers. (And oh yeah, under British law women could no longer own property. Sorry ladies).

It's All About the Beavers

The British and the French have never liked each other—ever—and their period of cohabitation in the New World was certainly no exception. The two imperial powers had totally different outlooks and delighted in annoying each other. The one thing they could agree on, however, was beavers—specifically, how awesome their fur was when they weren't wearing it anymore.

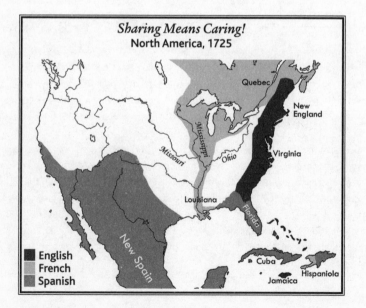

In fact, English, Dutch, and French colonial policy was largely shaped by competition for control of the international beaver market. To secure beaver access, each nation allied itself with different native tribes, whom they courted with gifts of money, alcohol, and firearms. The French got things started in 1609 by aligning themselves with the Huron and Algonquin, two fierce groups living in central Ontario and New England, respectively. The Algonquin and Huron had long battled the nearby Mohawks, and the French were happy to take advantage of existing hostilities and join the fight. The Mohawks, themselves a fairly fierce group of people living in what is now eastern New York State, had friends of their own. Together with the Seneca, the Cayuga, the Oneida, and the Onondaga, the Mohawks formed the Iroquois League—a defensive alliance that may date back to the twelfth century.

While the Iroquois League could field a formidable army, it suddenly found itself at a disadvantage against the Huron and Algonquin, who were now being armed with muskets by the French. That's where the English jumped into the fray, soon joined by the Dutch, who found a profit in running guns to the Iroquois in the 1640s. Now the Iroquois turned the tables, driving the Hurons from their homeland with a series of fierce attacks from 1645 to 1652.

MORE THAN JUST A PRETTY PELT

Europeans were big fans of beavers long before North America was settled. In fact, they had hunted European beavers to the brink of extinction by the sixteenth century—partly for their soft, glossy fur and partly for castoreum, a rather nasty secretion from the beaver's nether regions that doubles as a painkiller. (Certain Native American tribes still use beaver testicles in lieu of aspirin; how humans discovered this use for beaver bits is anyone's guess.)

Just as they had in Europe, the English, Dutch, and French set about killing every beaver they (or native trappers) could lay their hands on. In 1624 the Dutch colony of New Amsterdam shipped 400 beaver pelts to Europe. Two years later, the figure topped 7,000, and by 1671, it had climbed to about 80,000. Measuring dead beavers by the ton, the French recorded 45 tons of pelts delivered by native trappers in 1685, 75 tons in 1687, and 400 tons in 1689—by which time they'd managed to flood the European market. In fact, the last shipment ended up rotting on the docks in Montreal.

With this kind of treatment, it's not surprising that the total number of North American beavers dropped from perhaps 60 million before European contact to about 100,000 at the beginning of the twentieth century. Since then, prudent wildlife management policies have returned the population to about 10 million across the United States. But Americans are still trapping the poor little delightfully soft critters—about 15,000 in Ohio alone from 2000 to 2005.

This wasn't the end of the "Beaver Wars." The Hurons split into two groups, with one heading east into Quebec, and the other moving southwest into the Ohio River Valley—prime beaver-hunting ground, which was already attracting the interest of the English and French. The Huron's continued hatred of the English and their Iroquois allies gave a leg up to the French, who gained control over most of the American Midwest. Meanwhile, the Iroquois tightened their grasp on the northeastern beaver trade by wiping out two smaller native confederations—the Erie Nation in Ohio in 1657 and the Susquehannock Nation in Pennsylvania in the 1670s. (It seems the Europeans weren't the only ones practicing genocidal policies in the New World.) The pelt-driven warfare continued into the eighteenth century, as the French found new native allies and the Iroquois found themselves increasingly at odds with Dutch and English settlers.

★ *The Susquehannock people were also known as the Conestoga. In the mid-eighteenth century, craftsmen in the Pennsylvania town of Conestoga developed a large-wheeled covered wagon by that name. Pioneers traveling west commonly used these Conestoga wagons, and the cigars smoked by the drivers became known by the nickname "stogie."*

King Philip's War

Unsurprisingly, as European settlers encroached more and more on native land, tensions between natives and colonists frequently boiled over into open hostilities. One of the most destructive conflicts was King Philip's War, from 1675 to 1676. The war pitted white colonists in New England (along with their native allies from the Mohegan and Pequot tribes) against a coalition of native tribes led by the Wampanoag, whose chief, Metacom, was known to English colonists as "King Philip."

Half a century before the war, Metacom's father, Massasoit, had helped the first English settlers establish Plymouth, Massachusetts, in 1620, by providing emergency food aid that helped them survive the winter (the origin of the Thanksgiving celebration, when colonists and natives feasted together in 1621). More white settlers showed up over the following decades, establishing dozens of new towns across what are now Massachusetts, Rhode Island, Connecticut, and Maine, pushing native tribes off their land.

After the death of Massasoit in 1661, Metacom's older brother Wamsutta became chief of the Wampanoag but died in suspicious circumstances during a diplomatic visit to Plymouth colony. Coming to power in 1662, Metacom had obvious reasons to distrust white colonists. In December 1674, a Christian native missionary, John Sassomon, told the governor of Plymouth colony that the chief was organizing a native alliance against the white settlers. Sassomon was murdered by Metacom's henchmen as punishment for disloyalty. The enraged Puritans hanged three natives for Sassomon's murder in June 1675—which in turn enraged the natives. With everyone good and enraged, fighting broke out between Plymouth settlers and the local Pokanoket tribe and spread quickly to involve whites and natives all over New England.

In proportional terms, King Philip's War turned out to be one of the most destructive conflicts in American history, claiming the lives of about 800 colonists and 3,000 natives. The colonists finally won by sheer brutality, foreshadowing hundreds of years of native losses; in another sign of things to come, both sides employed tactics that would today be described as "ethnic cleansing," focusing on wiping out enemy villages. While male colonists were usually killed, women and children were sometimes kidnapped and held for ransom, as recounted in the "Narrative of the Captivity and Restoration of Mrs. Mary Rowlandson." Rowlandson, a young female colonist with a newborn child, described an attack on February 10, 1675:

> the bullets flying thick, one went through my side, and the same (as would seem) through the bowels and hand of my dear child in my arms . . . the Indians laid hold of us, pulling me one way, and the children another, and said, "Come go along with us"; I told them they would kill me: they answered, if I were willing to go along with them, they would not hurt me.

Triangular Trade
How to Screw Three Continents at Once!

By the time they arrived in America, the English were masters at screwing their subjects (see: Ireland). The settling of North America gave England a vast new canvas to work on, and the only thing that changed in the seventeenth century was the scale of the extortion. In its perfected form, the scheme became known as the Triangular Trade, because it linked three areas: Europe, the Americas, and Africa. As the trade evolved, the shape eventually became more of a squished baseball diamond, but if you keep your eye on the ball, you'll notice the American colonists got screwed every time.

The organizing principle of the British Empire was mercantilism, a philosophy that called for enriching the home country by accumulating stocks of precious metals. The rules of the game: First, the home country always had to export more than it imported, so it could stockpile gold and silver at the expense of its trading partners. Second, the government had to encourage and develop manufacturing in the homeland, since manufacturers could charge more for exported finished goods than they paid for imported raw materials. Third, foreign competitors were to be locked out of the market if they threatened domestic industries.

With these basic ground rules in place, the Brits were able to bilk their American colonists coming and going. In the early seventeenth century, agents for the Virginia Company could buy tobacco at 3 shillings per pound in Virginia and sell it for 8 shillings per pound in London, a 165 percent markup. British merchants could buy codfish from New England fishermen for about 12 shillings a quintal (which weighed about 110 pounds) and then sell it in Spain for 36 shillings a quintal, a markup of 200 percent. Beaver pelts purchased from native trappers for 12 shillings a pelt were sold in London for about 45 shillings, for a 205 percent markup.

Meanwhile, American colonies weren't allowed to sell their cotton, tobacco, timber, fish, grain, or beaver pelts to anyone besides British merchants—even if foreign buyers offered better prices. Mercantile policy also discouraged the development of colonial industries like clothing manufacturing, because they might compete with British businesses. The colonies were supposed to export raw materials to Britain at low prices and import manufactured goods at artificially high prices—and that was all.

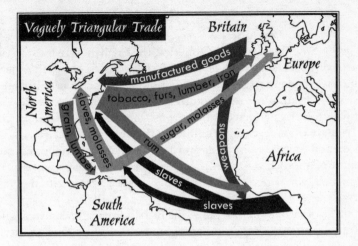

Vaguely Triangular Trade

Britain · Europe · North America · Africa · South America

manufactured goods · tobacco, furs, lumber, iron · slaves, molasses · grain, lumber · rum · sugar, molasses · weapons · slaves · slaves

Imports were no better. One of the best examples is the slave trade, which supplied indispensable labor for agriculture beginning in 1617. In addition to obviously victimizing the slaves themselves, the slave traders of the Royal Africa Company—who enjoyed a monopoly—gouged their customers. In 1690, male slaves were bought for an ounce of gold from the chiefs of coastal tribes in West Africa and then auctioned in the American colonies for an average of 20–25 pounds, a markup of 300 percent to 400 percent.

And for an extra dollop of irony, sometimes the over-priced imports were based on the colonists' own low-cost exports. Hats were manufactured in Britain using beaver pelts from the North American colonies, with hatters buying the pelts on the cheap and then selling the hats back to American colonists for more than double the price. By the mid-eighteenth century, American colonists were paying three to four times what British subjects in the homeland paid for items of clothing. But rest assured—the British government was screwing the regular people of Britain too, by forcing them to pay hugely inflated prices for goods they could get cheaper elsewhere, especially popular colonial commodities like sugar, tobacco, and rum.

Being Broke

One of the rawest of raw deals in history was indentured servitude, a cruel scam in which entrepreneurs offered to pay the costs of passage to America (about 10–15 pounds) for ambitious but broke young men and women seeking a better life. Roughly 75 percent of the early colonists arrived in America this way. Other indentured servants were convicts sentenced to hard labor or victims of large-scale kidnapping schemes. (One professional kidnapper claimed to have sent 800 people to America.) In exchange for passage, they had to work as field hands or domestic servants for a specified length of time, after which they would be free to claim a plot of land and go into business for themselves . . . supposedly.

But like a well-written mobile phone contract, the problems were all in the fine print and hidden fees. Once the indentured servants arrived in America, their masters were obligated to provide only the bare minimum in food, lodging, and clothing. Not coincidentally, the masters also ran a profitable sideline selling provisions on credit, which forced the laborers to borrow money just to eat, thus keeping them in debt and indentured. Life was hard for everyone in the early colonial period, but it was especially hard for these folk. Over half the young men and women who came to America as indentured servants died before they earned their freedom.

> ★ Two young men who worked as indentured servants would go on to become presidents of the United States: Millard Fillmore and Andrew Johnson.

The use of indentured servitude declined with the rise of slavery, which it strongly resembled: indentured servants could be bought and sold, were forbidden to marry, and could be hung for running away before their term was over. The key difference, of course, was that their period of indenture was (technically) supposed to end at some point.

While not quite indentured servants, the colonists who settled Georgia were pretty close. In fact, Georgia was founded as a debtors' colony for indigent men from England—a good 20,000 of whom were freed from debtors' prison by James Oglethorpe, the colony's founder, just before he obtained the colonial charter in 1732. It worked out for the crown because the new colony (the last of the 13 to be chartered) provided a buffer for the rich royal domain of South Carolina against the fierce Creek native tribes in Florida and Alabama. The state's charter, signed by George II, is a little long-winded but refreshingly honest about its motives:

> [M]any of our poor subjects are, through misfortunes and want of employment, reduced to great necessity, insomuch as by their labor they are not able to provide a maintenance for themselves and families; and if they had means to defray their charges of passage, and other expences, incident to new settlements, they would be glad to settle in any of our provinces in America where by cultivating the lands, at present waste and desolate, they might not only gain a comfortable subsistence for themselves and families, but also strengthen our colonies and increase the trade, navigation and wealth of these our realms.

Being a Slave

People of all races have been captured, bought, and sold in virtually every part of the world for most of human history. Slavery was practiced enthusiastically in Europe by the Greeks and Romans, and in the medieval period, the Vikings, Venetians, Genoese, and Mongols trafficked in slaves from Britain, Central Europe, and the Slavic tribes of the Balkans and Ukraine—in fact, the word "slave" comes from "Slav." But the European supply of slaves began drying up when the Catholic Church banned the enslavement of Christians in the tenth century, and by the fifteenth century, Europeans were looking for a new source of slaves. They didn't have to look very far.

Like various other groups, Africans had been kidnapped and sold as slaves in Europe and the Middle East ever since the Classical period. However, it wasn't until the mid-fifteenth century that the Portuguese hit on the idea of buying slaves on the west coast of Africa. A half-century later, the European discovery of the New World opened up a huge new market.

Modern African slavery was qualitatively different from the earlier versions. In the "good ol' days," the institution of slavery had a certain twisted fairness, as anyone of any race was liable to be enslaved: prisoners of battle, civilians on the losing side of a war, someone out for a walk. Slaves were also recognized as human beings—even if they weren't always treated that way. In Roman times, well-educated slaves could become trusted business advisors or personal tutors to the children of nobility. In contrast, by the 1400s, Europeans were only allowed to enslave "heathen" Africans, who were considered subhuman and treated like animals. They were transported from Africa to America in horrific conditions, jammed aboard slave ships in holds that didn't allow them to stand up straight, receiving only the bare minimum of food and water. In the seventeenth century, it wasn't uncommon for ships to lose a quarter of their human cargo to disease and starvation during the course of the Atlantic crossing.

The distinction between white men and African slaves was codified in British colonial law beginning in the late seventeenth century. To keep slaves ignorant and docile, white masters were forbidden to teach them to read or write. To prevent rebellion, slaves were forbidden to gather in groups or speak to each other in their native language, sometimes on penalty of death; likewise, runaway slaves could be hung or severely beaten. Children born to slaves were also slaves themselves, making the servitude heritable and giving masters an incentive to promote breeding (even though slave marriages weren't recognized—slave families could be broken up, with spouses and children sold to different masters in faraway places).

★ *The Fugitive Slave Act of 1793, signed into law by President George Washington, not only gave owners the right to capture their own escaped slaves from any American state or territory, but also established that children born to an escaped slave were also property of the owner.*

But there were still some ethical dilemmas to be solved. By the eighteenth century, most African slaves had been converted to Christianity, and European theologians decided that Africans did in fact possess immortal souls. But slave owners laid these issues to rest with some questionable theological reasoning: the souls of Africans might be equal in spiritual value to those of Europeans, they conceded, but they were paired with a "primitive" spirit that demanded "guidance" from superior Europeans to achieve salvation. The preposterous logic insisted that slavery was good for slaves.

> Slaves are no more at Liberty after they are Baptized, than they were before ... The liberty of Christianity is entirely spiritual.
>
> —Bishop William Fleetwood

·············· **MADE IN AMERICA** ·····················

Rum Punch

Rum wasn't invented in America, but it proved so popular in the colonies that it should qualify as an all-American drink.

> Upon all the new settlements the Spaniards make, the first thing they do is build a church, the first thing ye Dutch do upon a new colony is to build them a fort, but the first thing ye English do ... is to set up a tavern or drinking house.
>
> —Captain Thomas Walduck, 1708

It wasn't the flavor; by all accounts, the batches produced in the seventeenth century (called "kill-devil" by British colonists on Barbados) were incredibly nasty and dangerous. That's not surprising, considering that the liquor was invented as a way to get rid of an industrial byproduct—molasses, a thick, sticky brown goo that had to be drained from sugar crystals during the refining process. At first no one knew what to do with the stuff, but sometime in the first half of the seventeenth century, someone realized that molasses contains enough sugar to allow fermentation; with a little tinkering, you could turn it into booze.

But not delicious booze: one early imbiber called it a "fiery spirit," another "a hot, hellish, and terrible liquor." If this sounds unappealing, consider that distillers might throw a dead animal or animal dung into the "wash" to speed up fermentation. They also used lead pipes in the construction of their stills, sometimes resulting in lead poisoning among heavy imbibers—which was mostly everyone. In Barbados each colonist drank an average 10 gallons of rum per year, while North American colonists averaged 3 gallons per year. That this foul liquor could quickly become the most popular drink in the American colonies is evidence, above all, of the miserable conditions prevailing there, especially among poor colonists who came as indentured servants. Despite the occasional case of blindness or death, rum got you drunk enough to forget your miseries, at least temporarily—and when you woke up the next morning, you could start forgetting all over again.

Of course this was incredibly bad for your health. In 1639, a visitor to Barbados recounted men getting so drunk they passed out on the ground, where they were eaten alive by land crabs, and in 1707, a visitor to Jamaica estimated that rum killed over 1,000 colonists a year on that island alone (out of a total population of 7,000 white colonists). Colonial legislatures tried to control the sale and consumption of rum, with laws passed in Bermuda (1653), Connecticut (1654), Massachusetts (1657), and even Barbados itself (1668)—but with human misery trumping the law, rum continued making great if somewhat unsteady strides.

★ *Etymologists are uncertain about the exact origin of the word "rum," but most believe that it is a shortened form of the English word "rumbullion," meaning a fracas or uproar (and possibly related to "rumpus").*

Distilleries were established on Staten Island in 1664 and in Boston in 1667, fed by molasses imported from the Caribbean plantations; these drastically lowered the price and increased the level of intoxication to new highs (or lows, depending on your point of view). In fact, rum played an integral part in the development of the American colonies, as businessmen in New England invested their rum profits in new industries like textile manufacturing. Meanwhile, on the frontier, fur merchants used rum (and other hard alcohol) to buy furs from native trappers, despite—or maybe because of—its catastrophic impact on Native American society.

★ *Before the invention of rum, early colonists on Barbados experimented with other uses for molasses. One of the more innocuous suggestions called for mixing molasses with eggshells and horsehair to make mortar (as in cement). Somewhat more alarming were the practices of injecting molasses into the urethra as a cure for syphilis in both men and women and using it in enemas to combat intestinal complaints.*

Sticks and Stones

Contemporary sports like football and mixed martial arts might seem brutal, but they can't hold a candle to early Native American competitions. Take lacrosse. The sport originally combined religious devotion and combat training, and it served as a substitute for actual warfare among the Native American tribes of eastern North America. In fact, its original name in the Mohawk language means "little brother of war."

In many ways this is an apt description. Instead of the usual 10 players per team, opposing sides could number in the hundreds. Goals were separated by anywhere from 500 yards to several miles (compared to the 110×60 yard field of modern lacrosse), and there were no sideline boundaries, meaning players could range as far as they wished. A match could last all day, following a night of ritual chanting, dancing and prayers; afterward there might be another celebratory feast with more of the same.

The game was also dangerous. Injuries were inflicted before the matches began, with medicine men using ritual blades to make shallow cuts on the bodies of players—adorning them with their own blood as well as special paint made from ash and natural pigments. Then, during game play, hundreds of warriors would crowd around the ball, trying to scoop it up with sticks resembling large wooden spoons or paddles; these also served as weapons during the fierce struggle for possession of the ball, leading to stab wounds and broken limbs (and death, if the limb happened to be someone's head).

As a non-violent (well, less-violent) substitute for war, lacrosse helped settle disputes between tribes that might otherwise boil over into real armed conflict. This included property disputes: every player had to make a wager before the game started, a wager as small as a piece of jewelry or as big as a family. Through wagers, a lacrosse match could be used to settle the disputed possession of a woman or some other piece of property.

Nonetheless, like so many other native customs, lacrosse was roundly condemned by early European observers, beginning with French missionaries who saw a version of the game played by the Hurons in the 1630s. But the sport was so dynamic and entertaining that white settlers eventually adopted their own version. One slightly less judgmental missionary, Jean de Brebeuf, is credited with coining the European name for the sport, noting that the stick used to carry the ball resembled the ceremonial "crosier," a staff of office carried by high-ranking Catholic officials. In 1867 the rules of modern lacrosse were standardized by a Canadian dentist, W. George DeBeers, who probably enjoyed steady business as a result.

Lighting Up

It may not be our most admirable innovation, but tobacco is an all-American weed. In fact, without it, the permanent settlement of Virginia and indeed America itself might never have happened.

Virginia was colonized by poor men drawn from the dregs of England's southern ports. Desperate to leave their stations, they founded Jamestown in 1607 as the first permanent English settlement in America. By 1610, cold, starvation, and raids by the neighboring Powhatan tribe had carried off all but 65 of the 500 original settlers. Even after more settlers arrived the next year, Jamestown was still hanging by a thread. Most of the reinforcements were dead, with more colonists falling to native attacks. Lord De La Warr himself fell ill and returned to England. What could possibly save the colony?

Enter tobacco. The American weed gave the squalid little collection of shacks an economic reason to exist. The first Virginia tobacco was actually a hybrid of a local strain, cultivated casually by the neighboring native tribes, and a strain from Spanish Guyana (located just north of Brazil). The local strain was hardy enough to survive outside of the tropics, but it was too harsh, while the Guyanese variety was smoother. The hybrid version grew well in the southern "Tidewater" coastal region and the "Piedmont" (foothills) that separated the Tidewater from the Appalachian Mountains farther inland.

★ *Like molasses, tobacco was a favorite ingredient in suppositories or enemas prescribed by seventeenth-century physicians for a wide range of maladies. (And no, this is not why the discarded tips of cigars and cigarettes are called "butts.")*

The highly addictive crop quickly became very marketable. From 2,500 pounds in 1616, Virginia's tobacco exports soared to 17,500 tons in 1720—a 1.4 million percent increase! Tobacco exports constituted over 80 percent of the total value of all colonial

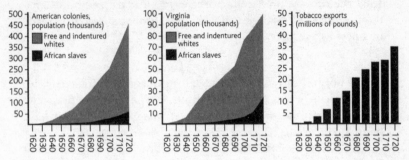

exports in the seventeenth century. The first law passed in the American colonies—approved by the Virginia legislature in 1619—set the minimum price for tobacco (three shillings). In the seventeenth and eighteenth centuries, tobacco served as a substitute for money, called "country money" or "country pay," and shop owners and small-time farmers cultivated small patches of tobacco just to have some petty cash.

JUST LIKE IN THE MOVIES

Like the Puritan settlers of New England, the first English colonists in Virginia probably would have been wiped out completely were it not for charitable natives. The starving inhabitants of Jamestown were particularly indebted to Pocahontas, the daughter of chief Powhatan, who was the "emperor" of a tribal confederation covering eastern Virginia. According to one colonist, John Smith, Pocahontas saved him from execution by her father's men and later brought provisions to the colonists, which allowed them to survive harsh winters in 1607–1608. To repay her kindness, in 1613 two colonists kidnapped Pocahontas and demanded the release of several English prisoners held by Powhatan (along with a ransom). Embittered by her father's failure to ransom her promptly, Pocahontas converted to Christianity and married a colonist named John Rolfe in 1614. In 1616 Pocahontas and Rolfe visited England, where she was treated as royalty and introduced to King James I. English hopes for converting the Virginia tribes died with Pocahontas, who succumbed to disease shortly after leaving England to return to the New World in 1617. Today many of Virginia's (and America's) oldest families proudly claim descent from Pocahontas through her son, Thomas Rolfe.

After Sir Walter Raleigh brought the first batch of tobacco to Europe's virgin lungs in the late sixteenth century, most people in England consumed tobacco in the form of snuff—powdered tobacco sometimes mixed with dried flowers or spices. Users could also place chewing tobacco against their gums or smoke it in long, slender clay pipes based on designs borrowed from Native Americans. There were numerous attempts to control and even eliminate tobacco use in England, beginning with James I, who issued a "counterblaste" against the "noxious weed" in the form of a pamphlet detailing its health drawbacks. In Turkey tobacco use could bring the death penalty in the 1630s, and in Russia the first offense brought deportation to Siberia; the second, execution. But none of these had much effect: tobacco was so habit-forming that users would risk death just to get their fix.

★ *In 1624 Pope Urban VIII threatened to excommunicate snuff users—not because snuff was habit-forming, but because the act of sneezing was considered too close to "sexual ecstasy."*

While they had barely scratched out a living before discovering tobacco, the first Virginia colonists became incredibly wealthy, and their success attracted thousands of imitators. Predictably, trouble followed.

········· **PROFILES IN SCOURGES** ·········

Nathaniel Bacon (c. 1647–1676)

Over the seventeenth century, the success of Virginia's tobacco planters attracted increasing numbers of poor but ambitious young Englishmen. Enticed to the New World by the promise of endless free land, these new colonists were surprised to find that all the good land had already been claimed. The new recruits soon pressured Governor William Berkeley to push farther west and displace various native tribes, most notably the formidable Susquehannocks. But Berkeley knew the Susquehannocks would not be happy about this. So to avoid violence, he tried to contain English settlement within the current colonial borders.

This proved futile. Defying Berkeley, the unhappy colonists formed unofficial militias and attacked Susquehannock villages along the border, massacring native men, women, and children. The Susquehannock retaliated by doing the same to white settlements. The enraged colonists now demanded firm action from Berkeley, who, under orders from the king not to antagonize the natives, had to refuse. It was at this point that Nathaniel Bacon stepped forward for his brief, and not entirely honorable, moment in the spotlight of history.

> ★ William Berkeley served as Virginia's governor for a total of 27 years—far longer than any person since.

A charismatic rabble-rouser, Bacon began respectably enough. Appointed to the Virginia colony's council by Berkeley, Bacon became bitter when the governor refused to allow him to attack the main Susquehannock villages. Accusing Berkeley of corruption, in 1676 Bacon organized his own personal 500-man militia—a motley collection of former and escaped indentured servants, freedmen, and runaway slaves. They began attacking neighboring natives—but not the Susquehannock (they weren't picky). Instead they turned on two other nearby tribes, who had previously enjoyed peaceful relations with the English.

Berkeley arrested Bacon and jailed him, but his followers sprang him from prison almost immediately. Surrounded and outgunned, the governor was forced to agree to Bacon's demand of new elections for the colonial assembly, elections that swept Bacon and his followers into power. Bacon turned out to be a violent nut with a real reform agenda—one that included genocidal policies. During the brief period he ruled Jamestown, the assembly granted freed indentured servants the right to vote, wrote a Declaration of the People of Virginia, and prepared to mount expeditions to wipe out the nearby native tribes once and for all. Before Bacon's rebels could really accomplish anything, however, troops loyal to the governor attacked Jamestown, forcing Bacon's army out. A few months later, the rebels returned and—perhaps at Bacon's order—burned Jamestown to the ground.

> That old fool has put to death more people in that nude [empty] country than I did here for the murder of my father.
>
> —Charles II of England, on Nathaniel Bacon

After a promising start, Bacon's rebellion rapidly lost steam. The coup de grâce came with Bacon's death from dysentery, apparently the result of an epic infestation of body lice—basically, he died from a really bad case of crabs.

Blackbeard (c. 1680–1718)

Who was the man behind the beard? No one is sure of his real name—either Edward Teach, Edward Thatch, or Edward Drummond—but one thing's for sure: the man was a big fan of violence and theft. Blackbeard's father was a privateer—in essence, an officially licensed pirate—who raided Spanish shipping on behalf of the British government in the closing years of the seventeenth century. Young Edward took up the same calling, following his father's bloody, drunken footsteps through the West Indies and the Spanish Main (the north coast of South America).

When the war with Spain ended, Blackbeard was out of a job, as all privateering licenses were revoked by King George I, who now wanted peace with Spain. But like many privateers, Blackbeard simply ignored the change in British foreign policy, which had only been an excuse to steal things in the first place. He could get along just as easily without a license—actually life would be even easier, since the list of potential targets now included British ships and settlements.

Even among heavyweights like Bartholomew "Black Bart" Roberts, Henry Morgan, and Ned Low, Blackbeard stood out for his daring and extraordinary capacity for cruelty. With his flagship, *Queen Anne's Revenge*, he captured two other ships and formed a pirate fleet crewed by several hundred that terrorized the Atlantic and Caribbean for two bloody years, 1716–1718. For the climax, in May 1718 Blackbeard laid siege to the port of Charleston. There, he captured ten ships and a group of leading citizens, whom he held for ransom. This audacious attack on one of the largest cities in colonial America served little purpose beyond putting Blackbeard firmly on the

---

LADIES IN RAIDING

Two of the most successful pirates during this era were women—Anne Bonny and Mary Read, who joined the crew of John "Calico Jack" Rackham. When they were finally captured in 1720, Bonny and Read put up a better fight than Rackham, who was plastered. As he was marched to the gallows, Bonny supposedly bid Rackham adieu with the comforting words: "I am sorry to see you here Jack, but if you had fought like a man, you need not be hanged like a dog." Read later died in prison, but Bonny—who avoided execution because she was pregnant—was ransomed by her father and died an old woman with eight children.

British most-wanted list. But then Blackbeard was never known for being rational.

What Blackbeard lacked in sanity, he made up for in creativity. Before going into combat, he would braid slow-burning cannon fuses or pieces of hemp into his enormous beard and tricorne hat, creating a wreath of smoke and sparks to look like "a Fury from Hell," if not "the Devil" himself. On one occasion, when business was slow and his crew was getting restless, he supposedly shot two of them in the legs so they "would remember who he was." On another slow day, figuring they were all going to hell anyway, Blackbeard proposed turning the ship into an imitation inferno with pots of burning sulfur belowdecks to see who could stand their impending fate the longest (surprise: it was him). Over his prolific career, he supposedly accumulated 14 wives, scattered around various Caribbean islands and the Carolinas, forcing the last to prostitute herself to his officers.

This general craziness helped terrify enemy crews into submission (after all, that's how he treated his friends), but it failed to protect him from the government. Blackbeard had allegedly struck secret deals with the governor of North Carolina, Charles Eden, and high-ranking officials in New York, who allowed him to plunder far and wide in return for a cut of the loot—but when Blackbeard became too big a liability, they sold him out. Eden granted Blackbeard a royal pardon, knowing it would lull the pirate chief into letting his guard down—then the governor of Virginia, Alexander Spotswood, sent two ships to attack him. Blackbeard destroyed one, but the commander of the other sneakily hid his crew belowdecks to lure Blackbeard on to the offensive. After a fierce battle, Blackbeard's throat was slit by a British sailor; the body was beheaded, and the head was posted on a stake by the Virginia shore as a warning to other pirates. By some accounts, in the final battle, Blackbeard was shot or stabbed 25 times before actually dying.

13 size, in acres, of the Monk's Mound in Cahokia, Illinois

100 height, in feet, of Monk's Mound

197 height, in feet, of the Great Pyramid in the Aztec capital, Tenochtitlan

80,400 number of human sacrifices supposedly made by the Aztecs to consecrate the Great Pyramid in 1487

4,700 population of English colonies in America, 1630

250,000 population of English colonies in America, 1690

7,289 number of English colonists sent to Virginia, 1607–1624

1,249 number of these still alive in 1624

30,000 male colonists in Maryland, 1704

7,000 female colonists in Maryland, 1704

85 percent proportion of Maryland colonists who were indentured servants

16 average age of marriage in Maryland, 1704

150 cost, in pounds of tobacco, of a "mail order" wife in Virginia in 1621

40 average life expectancy of white colonists in the seventeenth century

2,000 population of African slaves in North America, 1650

28,000 population of African slaves in North America, 1700

21.3 percent average mortality rate among captive Africans on British slave ships, 1619–1700

29.8 percent average mortality rate among captive Africans on Spanish slave ships, 1599–1700

10 percent average mortality rate among white colonists crossing the Atlantic, seventeenth century

50 percent proportion of white indentured servants who died before achieving freedom

20 average age of white indentured servants

10–15 average cost, in pounds, of a white indentured servant in the second half of the seventeenth century

15,000 total number of people engaged in piracy off the coast of North America, c. 1700

2

Don't Worry, Be Scrappy!

(1715–1815)

It's likely that up to 78 percent of American readers have heard of the "American Revolution"—something related to Washington's wooden teeth, tea brewed incorrectly in Boston Harbor, Paul Revere watching lamps in a distant steeple, bad people getting tarred and feathered, and Benedict Arnold doing something naughty.

While the Revolution may seem mundane—of course we had to declare independence! Taxation is bad!—on closer examination, it's pretty weird. For one thing, colonists still considered themselves Englishmen: all their complaints were based on customs and precedents established in the home country. There were also deep personal and economic connections between American revolutionaries and the evil British oppressors (who were basically indistinguishable from the colonists they were sent to govern). Indeed, about three in ten colonists remained loyal to King George III up through the end of the Revolution. But somehow, out of this strange brew of confused loyalties and competing ideologies, a new national identity arose. In other words, in their struggle to regain traditional British freedoms, the American colonists discovered—or decided—that they were, well, American.

Of course, that just included the white ones: in their fight for freedom and liberty, the colonists had no intention of extending this justice to the growing number of African (and African-American) slaves toiling on Southern plantations. The big increase in the slave population was thanks to a little invention known as the cotton gin, which made cotton production far more profitable, soon displacing tobacco as the main Southern cash crop. The rise of cotton led to continuing close economic ties between the United States and Britain well after the American Revolution, as British textile mills came to rely more and more on American cotton.

Not that everything was smooth sailing for the United States and its former colonial master: British stubbornness and American pride led to renewed conflict in the War of 1812, which is famous for its indecisive outcome. Although the United States lost almost every important battle during the war, it somehow came out ahead, securing its claim to the Northwest Territory (now the Midwest) and New Orleans, which opened the whole Mississippi basin to American settlers.

·············· **WHAT HAPPENED WHEN** ··················

1733 Molasses Act institutes tax on molasses but isn't strictly enforced.

1754–1763 French and Indian War (aka The Seven Years' War).

1763 Sugar Act enforces tax on molasses more strictly, leading to colonial protest.

1764 Currency Act forbids colonies to issue paper money; British taxes must be paid in gold or silver.

1765 Stamp Act levies tax on all official documents; Bostonians riot.

1767 Townshend Acts take control of judicial system and tighten customs enforcement, leading to more protests.

1773 Tea Act leads to widespread protests, Boston Tea Party on December 16.

1774 Parliament closes the port of Boston and tries to take direct control of Massachusetts.

September–October 1774 First Continental Congress agrees to a total boycott of British goods.

April 1–19, 1775 Paul Revere's ride; Battles of Lexington and Concord.

May 10, 1775 Ethan Allen and Benedict Arnold capture Fort Ticonderoga.

June 15, 1775 George Washington is unanimously elected commander in chief by Continental Congress.

July 1776 Revolutionary leaders issue the Declaration of Independence.

December 1776 Benjamin Franklin goes to France as the rebel ambassador.

June 1777 Marquis de Lafayette arrives in South Carolina.

September 1777 British defeat rebels at Brandywine Creek on September 11 and capture Philadelphia on September 26.

February 6, 1778 France declares war on Britain, joining war as an American ally.

September–October 1781 Main British army under Cornwallis surrenders at Yorktown.

March 1783 Unpaid Continental Army officers and soldiers in Newburgh, New York, plot a military coup.

September 3, 1783 The United States and Britain sign the Treaty of Paris.

August 1786–February 1787 Thousands of indebted Massachusetts farmers rise up in "Shays' Rebellion."

May–September 1787 Constitutional Convention meets in Philadelphia to draw up a new plan for national government.

April 30,1803 Thomas Jefferson purchases the Louisiana Territory from France.

August 14,1807 Robert Fulton launches the world's first successful steam-powered boat service.

January 1, 1808 Congress ends the slave trade with Africa; internal slave trade continues.

LIE: *The colonists rebelled against
the brutal tyranny of King George III.*

THE TRUTH: Unfazed by his occasional bouts of madness (talking to trees, etc.), the colonists actually hoped for a time that King George III might become an ally in their real struggle—against the British Parliament.

The problem with Parliament was that its rank-and-file members were inconsistent, greedy, and shortsighted. Having run up an enormous debt financing the French and Indian War, they squeezed the American colonies for cash and simply couldn't admit that things were starting to get revolutionary. They refused to hear American grievances and actively sabotaged negotiations hosted by their few reasonable colleagues. Finally, when the situation became violent, they overreacted and brought the hammer down on the American colonies—a move practically guaranteed to lead to partition.

> ★ Most depictions of King George III make him appear elderly, mostly due to the obligatory white wig worn by distinguished men of the era. But when the American Revolution broke out in 1775, the monarch was only 36 years of age. General George Washington was 43.

In 1700 colonists were already unhappy with mercantilist policies that enriched British merchants and manufacturers at the colonies' expense. But they tolerated these policies because, for an appropriate bribe, corrupt officials would gladly turn a blind eye to smuggling. This system worked through the end of the seventeenth century, but in the early eighteenth century, the cash-strapped British Parliament began levying taxes on whatever it could think of—beginning with a tax on molasses, passed in 1733. (This was especially loathed because it made rum more expensive, and you just don't mess with booze.) Above all, the new taxes angered American colonists because they were given no say in how the British Parliament decided that money should be raised or spent. This violated the 1689 British Bill of Rights, which said no subject of the English crown should be taxed without representation in the official legislature. But Parliament went ahead and granted itself the power to levy new colonial taxes—a power that members were thrilled to abuse.

The Molasses Act was followed by the French and Indian War (1754–1763), in which the British teamed up with the Iroquois to kick the French out of the New World once and for all. This proved to be more difficult and expensive than anyone expected, and Parliament "asked" (told) the colonies to make financial contributions for their own defense. True, the British had been urged into war by the colonists, including Benjamin Franklin, but Parliament was drinking too much of its own rum-flavored Kool-Aid. In addition to the expense, the war highlighted the colonists' biggest complaint: Parliament refused to let the colonists settle in the newly acquired territories for fear of alienating native allies.

Forcing colonists to bankroll the defense of a place they were banned from inhabiting was probably not the brightest idea. Then Britain's Parliament escalated the aggravation by cracking down on smuggling and collecting customs revenues to the penny. This new, tighter administration succeeded in raising customs revenues from about 2,000 pounds a year in 1760 to 30,000 pounds by 1768. It also succeeded in provoking rebellion. The colonists became especially angry about British use of writs of assistance— open-ended search warrants that gave inspectors the right to go anywhere while investigating smuggling and customs evasion. Outraged, many colonial lawyers, including John Adams, asserted that writs of assistance were illegal under the 1689 Bill of Rights.

Parliament also dreamed up some new taxes to pay off the huge debt after the French and Indian War ended in 1763. Arriving during an economic depression, the Sugar Act of 1764 (the first new tax since the Molasses Act) enraged rich and poor colonists alike, sparking episodes of violence across the colonies. In protest, Samuel Adams led Massachusetts merchants in the first boycott of British goods. Boycotts continued to be a favorite tactic of the patriots as 1765 brought the Revenue Act, which continued the tax on molasses, and the Stamp Act, which required a duty be paid on all official documents, from attorney's licenses and land grants all the way down to newspapers and lowly playing cards (and dice, for good measure).

In response to growing disorder, in 1765 Parliament passed the Quartering Act, which required ordinary Americans to open their property to house thousands of British troops. These were the famous Redcoats—rowdy, poorly educated teenage boys and young men drawn from the British lower classes, who liked to drink, carouse, and "blow kisses to the local lasses." Farmers, merchants, and landlords feared for their property—and their daughters. When, perhaps unsurprisingly, colonists in New York declined the offer to play hosts, Parliament hit back by trying to suspend New York's colonial legislature and governor for almost four years, until the New Yorkers finally caved in 1771.

> Many people do not hesitate in supposing that most of the young ladies who were in the city with the enemy, and wear the present fashionable dresses, have purchased them at the expense of their virtue.
>
> —A wealthy merchant in Philadelphia, 1778

It turned out that randy, substance-abusing British youths weren't the precise instruments of policy needed to resolve colonial grievances, but Parliament seemed to be looking for a fight. In 1768 the Townshend Acts, a power grab intended to grant Britain control of the colonial judicial system, sparked violent protests in Boston (long notorious as the most rebellious colonial city, and, not coincidentally, also the drunkest). In response, the Brits piled more Redcoats into the city, which led to more clashes and the killing of an 11-year-old boy, Christopher Seider, on February 22, 1770. About two weeks later, on March 5, an angry mob of 400 Bostonians confronted a dozen Redcoats guarding the Boston customs house, first pelting them with gravel-filled snowballs before escalating to stones and empty bottles. The Redcoats lost their cool and opened fire, hitting 11 men. Six of these died in what has come to be known as the "Boston Massacre."

But what was happening with old King George III while all this was going on? During this period the king was still mostly sane and enjoyed a reputation as a kind-hearted ruler. More to the point, George III had the power to call and dismiss Parliament and appoint the prime minister who led it. So it wasn't all that crazy for the American colonists to hope George might step in and convince Parliament to act reasonably.

★ Erected in Bowling Green Park in Manhattan in 1770, a two-ton equestrian statue of George III was a frequent target of vandalism, none greater than the one that occurred on the date the Declaration of Independence was read aloud in New York City for the first time. On July 9, 1776, a band of patriots brought down the statue with ropes. About half the pieces were taken to the Connecticut home of General Oliver Wolcott, where they were melted down to form exactly 42,088 bullets.

And on a number of occasions, he actually did, beginning in 1766, when he helped his former prime minister, William Pitt, persuade Parliament to repeal the hated Stamp Act. Grateful colonists erected statues of George III and Pitt in New York City. In fact, every unpopular colonial tax on the books was eventually repealed at the king's request, or at least with his consent, except for one: the Tea Act of 1773.

The Tea Act—intended to shore up the failing East India Company by allowing it to dump thousands of tons of tea at discount prices—stirred fears that cheap British tea would wipe out both local merchants and smugglers trafficking in competing brands. In retaliation, colonial leaders, merchants, and smugglers organized a massive tea boycott. In New York and Philadelphia, ship captains were persuaded to sail back to England, while in Charleston the tea rotted on the docks. Boston, as usual, opted for a more violent solution: the Boston Tea Party, in which 50 colonists—not very convincingly disguised as tea-hating Mohawk Indians about 300 miles from home—dumped all the tea in Boston Harbor.

At this point, George III went from nice to nasty. It was one thing to protest taxes on paper, but destruction of property was a villainous crime. More importantly, George III wanted to keep his right to arbitrary taxation. In fact, that was the whole point of the Tea Act: George III said Parliament had to hang on to at least "one tax to keep up the right." His fury only grew when the people of Boston refused to pay for the ruined tea. In 1774 the king supported the passing of what the colonists called the "Intolerable Acts," which closed the port of Boston, seized control of the colonial government of Massachusetts, and once again forced Americans to quarter Redcoats in their barns and warehouses. So the colonies convened the First Continental Congress, where they agreed to a total boycott of British goods. It was on.

★ *Most historians believe that King George III suffered from a hereditary disease called* porphyria, *which causes psychiatric symptoms such as depression and delirium.*

Thus fatherly King George III became George the Tyrant, whose recent goodwill was quickly forgotten. According to the Declaration of Independence,

> The history of the present King of Great Britain is a
> history of repeated injuries and usurpations, all having

in direct object the establishment of an absolute Tyranny over these States . . . In every stage of these Oppressions We have Petitioned for Redress in the most humble terms: Our repeated Petitions have been answered only by repeated injury. A Prince, whose character is thus marked by every act which may define a Tyrant, is unfit to be the ruler of a free people.

BONUS LIE: INDEPENDENCE DAZE

Everyone knows July 4, 1776, was Independence Day—the day the rebellious colonies declared their independence from Britain. But it's not: independence was declared a few times, and the best candidate is actually July 2. Obviously it's too late to change the holiday now, but for the record, here's how it went down.

Wednesday, June 12–Thursday, June 27: With a British invasion of New York looming, the rebel Continental Congress in Philadelphia asks Thomas Jefferson to draw up a rough draft of the Declaration of Independence, followed by a second draft for review.

Friday, June 28: The second draft is read to Congress, followed by informal discussions.

Monday, July 1: Formal discussions of the second draft begin.

Tuesday, July 2: As the British invasion fleet approaches New York, Congress votes to declare independence from Britain.

Thursday, July 4: After more discussions, Congress approves the revised Declaration of Independence, which is printed by John Dunlap of Philadelphia.

Saturday, July 6: The Declaration is published in the *Pennsylvania Evening Post*.

LIE: *George Washington was one of history's great military minds.*

THE TRUTH: There's no question George Washington was a brilliant leader, whose intelligence and moral qualities were key to the success of the Revolutionary War and the newly founded United States. However, he was not a particularly good general—and he said as much himself.

History makes it clear that Washington was physically brave, even daring. In 1752, on the death of his father, the 21-year-old Washington inherited the post of district adjutant in the royal government of Virginia. Because he was familiar with the Ohio

Territory from surveying expeditions, in 1753 he was chosen to travel 200 miles to the French Fort of Le Boeuf (near modern-day Pittsburgh, Pennsylvania) to deliver a blunt message: get out. The sassy French not only refused but built another fort, Fort Duquesne, at the head of the Ohio River, igniting the French and Indian War.

★ *Growing up, George Washington celebrated his birthdate as February 11, 1733. When all British colonies adopted the Gregorian calendar in 1752, and the "New Year" was moved from March to January, his birthdate was recalculated as February 22, 1732.*

In April 1754, Washington returned to the area with a ragtag force of 186 colonial militiamen, some frontiersmen, and a few native warriors allied with the Brits. Following an ill-advised advance on Fort Duquesne, Washington retreated to a makeshift wooden palisade dubbed "Fort Necessity," which 700 French soldiers and native allies soon encircled. After some bloody but inconclusive fighting, it started to rain heavily, and Washington's troops couldn't keep their gunpowder dry. Luckily, the French were happy to let the Virginians return home, where Washington was pleasantly surprised to receive a note of thanks from the House of Burgesses for his brave leadership.

It got worse in 1755, when Washington joined a second British expedition, led by General Edward Braddock, for a second try at Fort Duquesne. The motley British force of about 2,100 was ambushed by a force of French guerrilla fighters and their native allies as soon as it crossed the Monongahela River. In the Battle of Monongahela on July 9, 1755, Braddock was killed, along with 500 of his troops, but Washington managed a fighting retreat that allowed most of the rest to escape. Once again, Washington made the best of a bad situation—but it still ended in running away.

LADIES LOVE GEORGE WASHINGTON

Washington wasn't always the old, white-haired patriarchal Founding Father that we know and love. At six feet three inches, the young Washington had the ladies of pre-Revolutionary Virginia swooning. On closer introduction, they were enchanted by his magnetic gray-blue eyes and auburn ponytail. And he was ripped: modern experts who reconstructed Washington's appearance using techniques from forensic anthropology say he had a quarterback's physique, weighing 220 pounds with wide shoulders, a narrow waist, and muscular legs. Legs were a particularly important feature in colonial America, where styles favored breeches and knee stockings so women could admire men's calves. In 1759, at the age of 27, Washington's masculine wiles snared Martha Custis—the young, beautiful, and spectacularly wealthy widow of a Virginia planter.

> **Six feet high and proportionably (sp) made; if anything rather slender than thick for a person of that height with pretty long arms and thighs.**
>
> —George Washington's description of himself
> to a London tailor, 1763

Having played a key role in starting it, Washington sat out the rest of the French and Indian War. Two years into war, in 1756, he was assigned the tedious duty of maintaining "security" in the borderlands, and by 1758 he'd given up hope of a military career, focusing on his coming wedding to Martha Custis, a wealthy widow. So when Washington was appointed commander of the revolutionary forces in 1775, 17 years removed from active duty, he frankly advised the Second Continental Congress that he wasn't a very skilled or experienced military commander.

Then why did the rebels choose Washington, a man whose main contribution to military history thus far was successfully running away? Simple: he was the only prominent revolutionary with any military experience at all. Benjamin Franklin was many things—printer, inventor, diplomat, all-around genius—but he was not a soldier; John Adams was a lifelong bookworm and professional lawyer; Thomas Jefferson was also a lawyer when he wasn't busy being fabulously wealthy (or totally broke) and smart; and James Madison was a frail, philosophical gentleman who dabbled in law and politics.

> **I beg it may be remembered by every gentleman in this room, that I this day declare, with the utmost sincerity, I do not think myself equal to the command I am honoured with.**
>
> —George Washington, 1775

As commander by default, Washington went on to score important victories during the Revolutionary War, including Trenton, Princeton, and Monmouth. But there were at least as many defeats and "strategic withdrawals," including the Battles of Long Island, White Plains, Brandywine Creek, and Germantown. It's true he improved over time, in part by listening to good advice. In fact, the plan for the final victory that ended the Revolutionary War—the siege of Yorktown—was suggested to Washington by General Comte de Rochambeau of France.

Despite his mistakes and errors in judgment, of course, all anyone really remembers is Washington's eventual success. And his greatest military skills weren't strategic or tactical anyway. His real triumph was organizational: forming an army from scratch, procuring funds and supplies from a well-intentioned but totally unreliable Congress, and coordinating with his subordinate commanders—all through handwritten correspondence delivered by couriers on horseback.

☞ QUICK'N'EASY AMERICAN REVOLUTION ☜

The American Revolution saw the underdog colonists win an unlikely victory over the powerful British Empire—mostly because they just cared more.

Things started off well for the rebelling colonists: on April 19, 1775 Redcoats marched from Boston to Concord, Massachussetts, but Paul Revere rode ahead to warn the rebels, who gathered at the Lexington town green and defeated the Brits. On May 10, 1775 Benedict Arnold's Connecticut militia and Ethan Allen's Green Mountain Boys from Vermont stormed Fort Ticonderoga, then shipped their freshly captured cannons to George Washington for the siege of Boston. The cannons blocked the Royal Navy from supplying the Redcoats, who finally withdrew from Boston on March 17, 1776.

But the wheels were already coming off. In June 1775 the rebels mounted an ill-advised invasion of Canada, only to discover the Canadians wanted no part of the Revolution: the siege of Quebec ended in disastrous defeat on December 31, 1775. Meanwhile, after abandoning Boston, Admiral William Howe regrouped in Halifax, Nova Scotia, and returned to seize New York with 32,000 Redcoats on August 27–30, 1776. Howe then defeated Washington at the Battle of Brooklyn and again at White Plains,

New York on October 28. Retreating south, Washington scored two small victories at Trenton and Princeton, New Jersey—but the Brits still had the upper hand.

Hoping to divide and conquer, the Brits then tried to split the colonies along the Hudson River Valley and the Delaware River Valley, but only the latter succeeded: Admiral Howe sailed around the Chesapeake for a surprise attack on Philadelphia and defeated the rebels at Brandywine Creek on September 11, 1777. On October 4, 1777 Washington's push to retake the city was defeated at Germantown, and his desperate troops were forced to spend the winter at Valley Forge, Pennsylvania, without food or shelter. But they got a boost when Horatio Gates and Arnold stopped the British invasion of the Hudson Valley at Saratoga, New York, September 19–October 3, 1777.

The tide began to turn. In February 1778 Benjamin Franklin negotiated an alliance with France, and suddenly the Brits faced a blockade by the French Navy. Fearing they might be cut off up North, and hoping to consolidate loyalist support down South, the Brits withdrew from Philadelphia and took Charleston, South Carolina on May 12, 1780. The British general Lord Cornwallis scored a major victory over Southern rebels under Gates at Camden, South Carolina, on August 16, 1780, but then divided his army, leading to a rebel victory at Cowpens, South Carolina, on January 17, 1781. Alarmed, Cornwallis chased Nathanael Greene's forces across North Carolina and Virginia and defeated them at Guilford Court House, March 15, 1781.

Believing he'd secured the Southern colonies (nope) Cornwallis headed north to rest his tired troops and get supplies by sea at Yorktown, Virginia. On the advice of the French general Rochambeau, Washington scrapped a planned attack on New York City and instead rushed south to cut the Brits off on the Yorktown peninsula. The French Admiral de Grasse blockaded them by sea and 8,800 starving Redcoats were forced to surrender on October 19, 1781. The Brits called it quits soon after.

LIE: *The American Revolution pitted the Americans against the British.*

THE TRUTH: Loyalties during the American Revolution weren't as cut and dried as you might think. One British faction, the Whigs, were extremely sympathetic to the American patriots, and at least one-third of American colonists actually opposed the Revolution, remaining loyal to George III and Parliament.

In Britain, 1689's Bill of Rights had limited the king's power to tax his subjects. But the Whigs, a group of aristocrats and commoners opposed to royal power, also believed the king should no longer have the right to appoint the prime minister, and that he should be appointed by Parliament instead. Unsurprisingly, the king disagreed, reasserting the crown's right to appoint the prime minister in 1760. This angered the Whigs, who feared George III was trying to establish tyranny in Britain, and it made them natural allies of the American rebels (even while the latter were asking George for help against Parliament—it was complicated).

On the other side of the pond, the American colonists were hardly united in their opposition to British rule. According to John Adams, about one-third of the colonists were fervent supporters of the Revolutionary cause, one-third remained loyal to Britain, and one-third were neutral. So who made up the one-third of colonists that remained loyal to George III, and why were they so committed? In geographic terms, loyalists were spread throughout rural New York and New Jersey, as well as the southern colonies. Most stayed loyal for personal and professional reasons, including people with close family ties or financial connections to Britain. This could mean anyone from farmers to merchants to Anglican clergy. But being a loyalist was a risky proposition: those who admitted being pro-Britain on rebel turf had their property confiscated and ran the risk of being "tarred and feathered" (usually a fatal procedure). Or they'd just get the crap kicked out of them. Many loyalists fled the countryside for big cities held by the Brits, including New York, Philadelphia, Charleston, and Savannah, which was fine until the Brits called it quits in 1783.

> **America has chosen to be, in many respects to many purposes, a nation.**
>
> —U.S. Chief Justice John Marshall, 1821

Once the British left town, it became clear that not all of the loyalists were that loyal. Most swallowed their pride and stayed put, accepting their citizenship in the newfangled "United States" with quiet skepticism. Still, 62,000 hard-core loyalists (roughly one of every 40 colonists) left the new nation, with 46,000 heading to Canada (where New Brunswick was created as a home for 14,000 loyalist refugees), 9,000 fleeing for the Caribbean and

Bahamas, and 7,000 heading home to Britain. Later, expatriate loyalists helped keep Canada loyal to Britain despite American meddling.

> I never use the word "Nation" in speaking of the United States;
> I always use the word "Union" or "Confederacy."
>
> —former Vice President John C. Calhoun, 1849

So when exactly did Americans become, well, American? The Brits were probably the first to suggest that colonists were somehow fundamentally different—and not in a good way. Popular British opinion held that colonists had "degenerated to such a degree" that one Briton was equal to 20 colonists, and that they were "almost a different species from the English of Britain." With their pride wounded, colonists responded that they were indeed different from the British—but only because they were actually better. Benjamin Franklin asserted that American colonists were "much purer, much less corrupt" than the English who remained behind. However, he concluded with a plea to the British public to stop treating the colonists as "foreigners," indicating there was still some bond between the two nations.

Ultimately, it took British oppression and brutality during the Revolutionary War to sever the connection. It was the Brits' heavy-handed policies that not only alienated their colonies but united them around common grievances—the theme of Benjamin Franklin's famous "Join or Die!" cartoon from 1754. The fact that it was a conscious choice actually strengthened the new national identity, forever linking "American-ness" with the ideals of freedom and liberty.

★ *Ben Franklin's "Join or Die!" graphic reflected a common superstition at the time, claiming that a severed snake could come back to life if its sections were joined prior to sundown.*

Still, after the Revolution most people thought of themselves as citizens of their home state first and as "Americans" only second, while the states basically behaved as separate sovereign nations. The lack of effective central government made it pretty hard to do anything. The resulting crises eventually prompted the revolutionary leaders to write a new constitution—although nobody was quite sure what this plan for national government would look like.

THE TRUTH: Some of the Founding Fathers were big fans of democracy—but only some of them.

During the Revolutionary War, the states had (mostly) cooperated under the Articles of Confederation—an extra-loose, open-ended set of agreements that weren't even ratified until 1781, when the war was almost over. The Articles of Confederation had some major problems: most importantly, they didn't give the federal government the right to raise taxes. This made sense during an anti-tax uprising, but it also meant that the government would be perpetually broke.

It wasn't long before the resulting shortfall led to even more revolutionary fighting after the Revolution. In 1786 an ex-farmhand and Revolutionary veteran named Daniel Shays led a "debtors' rebellion" of poor, bankrupt farmers in western Massachusetts. Many Revolutionary veterans, including Shays and his rebels, had been given bonds for future payment or land grants in the western territories that never materialized. The veterans argued that if state governments were allowed to tax them and throw them in jail for defaulting on debts, they at least deserved to be paid by the federal government for their service during the war. "Shays' Rebellion" concluded with four dead and lots of arrests.

> I have been greatly abused, have been obliged to do more than my part in the war; been loaded with class rates, town rates, province rates, Continental rates and all rates ... been pulled and hauled by sheriffs, constables and collectors, and had my cattle sold for less than they were worth ... The great men are going to get all we have and I think it is time for us to rise and put a stop to it, and have no more courts, nor sheriffs, nor collectors nor lawyers.
>
> —A Massachusetts farmer and "Shays-ite," 1786

While everyone pretty much agreed on the need for a new national government, Shays' Rebellion put the spotlight on growing disagreement among the Revolutionary leaders about how much power "regular folks" should have. In the context of eighteenth-century political thought, it boiled down to a simple question: should white men who didn't own property be given the right to vote?

If the Founding Fathers looked to Britain, the answer was definitely "no." The right to vote for representatives to the British House of Commons extended only to landowning male British subjects, who were about 10 percent of the male population in 1750. If you were one of the "great, unwashed masses," you kept your mouth shut at the risk of getting beaten with a golden-handled cane. By comparison, America was far more democratic. About 75 percent of the male population of Rhode Island and Connecticut were eligible to vote because they owned land or livestock worth 40 pounds or more, equal to roughly $70,000 in 2008. But rules varied. Around the time of the Revolution, just 40 percent of New York's male citizens could vote for its governor.

During the Revolution, the swelling crowds of property-less (male) city dwellers agitated for the vote at the state level, usually with success—but the national electoral system was still up in the air. More than a decade after the Declaration of Independence, the Founding Fathers still weren't sure whether democracy was the way to go. At the Constitutional Convention in 1787, James Madison, Alexander Hamilton, and Gouverneur Morris expressed concern that poor people, given the right to vote, would simply become pawns of rich men who would pay them to vote a particular way. Even Thomas Paine—otherwise one of the most "democratic" Founding Fathers—argued servants shouldn't be allowed to vote, since they would just vote for whomever their masters chose. Other skeptics feared "democratic despotism"—that is, a rich dictator seizing power by promising to redistribute property to his poor followers.

> New claims will arise; women will demand the vote; lads from 12 to 21 will think their rights not enough attended to; and every man who has not a farthing, will demand an equal voice with any other.
>
> —John Adams, warning against expanding suffrage, 1776

But as dangerous as democracy seemed, the alternative was far worse. Aggrieved by the government's failure to pay them for their military service, Revolutionary War veterans had already flirted with another round of revolution during the Newburgh

Conspiracy of 1783, and denying them the right to vote might push them over the edge. So the Founding Fathers, encouraged by pro-democracy leaders like Thomas Jefferson, decided to bite the bullet and embrace universal (white male) suffrage, at least for elections to the lower house of Congress, the House of Representatives. There were still plenty of checks on popular sovereignty: the president was chosen by electors from an Electoral College, who were themselves elected by popular vote, and senators were chosen by state legislatures until 1913, when the Seventeenth Amendment to the Constitution provided for election by popular vote.

> Give the votes to the people who have no property,
> and they will sell them to the rich.
>
> —Gouverneur Morris, 1787

This didn't mean the new nation was out of the woods as far as uprisings were concerned. After Alexander Hamilton persuaded Congress to form the National Bank and assume the states' war debts in 1791, Congress raised a tax on whiskey to pay the debt—but as already demonstrated, you don't mess with America's booze. Poor farmers who made their living off whiskey in rural western regions refused to pay the tax, sparking the Whiskey Rebellion of 1794. Washington (now the country's first president) led an army 13,000 strong to restore order, and the rebellion subsided after a few months. But it was a stark reminder that America continued to face deep economic divisions.

$YMBOL MINDED

How did the word "dollar" come to be represented by "$"—a symbol with no apparent connection to any of the letters in dollar?

After the Revolution, the Founding Fathers were determined to dump the vestiges of British rule, including currency based on pounds, shillings, and pence. Instead of inventing a whole new system, however, they sensibly modeled their currency on that of another European power, Spain—partly because no one could confuse it with Britain's, and partly because gold and silver from Spanish colonies in South America and Mexico played a big role in international finance. The main denomination was intended to correspond in value to the Spanish *real de a ocho,* or piece of eight—the standard Spanish coin at this time. To mix things up a bit, the Founding Fathers called their version, with the same monetary value, a dollar, an old North European monetary unit from the German word *Taler,* a short form of *Joachimstaler*—a coin minted in the Joachimstal valley of Bohemia in the sixteenth century.

So where'd the $ sign come from? Well, nobody's sure, but there are a couple of possible explanations. One theory holds that it's a contorted version of the Spanish shorthand p^s, standing for *pesos*. Another theory says it's an 8 with a slash through it, referring to the Spanish piece of eight. Our favorite explanation: it's an abstract interpretation of an artistic detail on the Spanish *real de a ocho*, showing a banner wrapped around a pillar.

·················· **PROFILES IN SCOURGES** ··················

Benedict Arnold (1741–1801)

His name instantly summons images of betrayal by candlelight. But what exactly did Benedict Arnold do?

Before switching sides, Arnold was one of the best rebel officers. Representing Connecticut, in 1775 Arnold was co-commander with Ethan Allen of the expedition that captured Fort Ticonderoga, an important early rebel victory. In 1777, although outnumbered and outgunned, Arnold put up a fierce fight for Lake Champlain and then inflicted an impressive amount of damage before withdrawing at the Battle of Ridgefield, Connecticut. And during the climactic Battle of Saratoga, Arnold took two for the team: he was shot in the leg by a British bullet and was then crushed under his falling horse.

Yes, Arnold had all the makings of an American hero. But during the next five months, as he lay bedridden in excruciating pain, Arnold grew bitter. His grievances dated back to 1775, when his accomplishment at Ticonderoga was lost in a political battle between Connecticut, Massachusetts, and Congress over who would take credit for the victory (history favors Ethan Allen). Arnold then accepted two difficult commands refused by other officers, mounting a heroic resistance in both battles—but his accomplishments were ignored because these were technically defeats. In February 1777, following machinations by his political enemies, the Continental Congress passed over Arnold to promote a junior officer to major general. Although Arnold eventually received his promotion, Congress refused to restore the order of seniority—meaning Arnold was technically still subordinate to junior officers promoted over him.

To add insult to injury, Arnold now faced a smear campaign of rumor and innuendo by his political enemies in the Continental Congress. Actually, there was a good deal of truth in the whispered allegations. As military governor of Philadelphia, Arnold had made a series of insider business deals that would allow him to profit from supplying provisions to the rebel armies. When local merchants and politicians protested his corrupt dealings, Arnold demanded a court martial to clear himself of the charges. The court martial in December 1779 cleared him of all but two minor charges—but these two convictions still drew a rather nasty reprimand from Washington. Not long afterward, the accountants of Congress calculated that, after the expenses for his northern campaigns were tallied up, Arnold owed Congress 1,000 pounds (another snub from Ticonderoga).

Broke and upset, Arnold became involved in the loyalist underground through his marriage in April 1779 to 18-year-old Peggy Shippen, the daughter of a prominent loyalist judge. Over the next year, Arnold made contact with British spies in New York City, sometimes using Shippen's circle of pro-loyalist female friends to carry their secret correspondence. Arnold told the British about the locations of rebel troops and supplies. Eventually he agreed to a plan in which he would take command of the rebel fort at West Point on the Hudson River and then turn it over to the Brits. His fee for this service was to be 10,000 pounds—although he got greedy and upped the price to 20,000 pounds.

After taking command of West Point in August 1780, Arnold did everything in his power to weaken the fort's defenses, dispersing his troops and transferring supplies out of the fort. (His aides figured he was selling them on the black market.) But the whole plan was undone by Arnold's insistence on a personal meeting with his handler, British spymaster John Andre. After their meeting, rebel sentries searched Andre and found plans Arnold had sketched of the fort's weaknesses. Arnold fled aboard a British ship, Andre was hung, and Washington raced north to secure West Point.

But this was only the beginning of Arnold's career as a traitor. Recognizing his cunning and bravery, the Brits gave Arnold a series of substantial military commands, including a force of 1,600 Redcoats and loyalist irregulars that Arnold led on a devastating series of raids across Virginia and a fierce assault on the rebel port of New London, Connecticut, which he burned to the ground. Still, Arnold's new British superiors soon became wary of his alarming casualty rates. No one argued when Arnold left for London to give the prime minister his personal views on the war.

In the halls of power, however, Arnold found himself totally locked out of important decisions by the British officer elite. So from 1785 to 1792, Arnold busied himself losing money in a series of bad business deals in Britain and the Virgin Islands. He also had a number of alarming run-ins, including dueling with a member of Parliament and being burned in effigy by townsfolk in St. John. After organizing the British militias on various Caribbean islands, Arnold was rewarded for his service to the British government with land in Ontario, Canada. He died there in 1801, at the age of 60.

······················ **TRENDSPOTTING** ······················

Laying Out the Unwelcome Mat

Up until the end of the seventeenth century, most immigrants coming to the American colonies were either English or African: aside from the Dutch in New York and the Swedes in Delaware, there just weren't too many ethnicities around. This began to change in the early eighteenth century, when various non-English Europeans started to appear in large numbers. The two biggest groups were the Scots-Irish and the Germans; Anglo-Saxon Americans didn't exactly rush to set out the welcome mat for either.

The term "Scots-Irish" refers to a group—or actually a group of groups—with a rather complicated lineage. Unfortunately, like many shorthand terms, it is confusing and wrong, but it stuck.

After Queen Elizabeth conquered northern Ireland in the savage "Nine Years' War" (1594–1603), her successor, King James I, decided to stamp out Irish Catholic resistance by flooding the area around Ulster with English-speaking Protestants. The only problem with this plan was that no Englishmen would risk being skinned alive by Irish rebels. So James (who was also king of Scotland) invited troublesome Presbyterian Scots to move from England's border with Scotland to northern Ireland. The strategy was surprisingly effective: the English border calmed down, and the badass lowland Scots (descendants of Vikings) helped crush the Irish rebels. The Scots were eventually joined by Huguenot (French Protestant) refugees, enterprising Welshmen, and German Mennonites fleeing persecution in the Palatinate, all of whom would later (to their great puzzlement) be lumped together as Scots-Irish.

Although they were doing England's dirty work, as Presbyterians, the "Ulster Scots" were "the wrong kind of Protestants." English economic and religious discrimination breathed new life into long-standing grievances about the mistreatment of their ancestors. After English lords began confiscating their land without payment (also called stealing), from 1717 to 1775, about 200,000 dispossessed Scots-Irish fled to America, where they found that all of the best land along the coast had already been claimed by (surprise) the English. The first wave of Scots-Irish immigrants headed inland, divvying up the land in the foothills of the Appalachians, where the soil actually turned out to be pretty good. Later, waves of Scots-Irish moved farther inland until they reached the wild Appalachian Mountains, then fanned out along the "Great Wagon Road," eking out a living on small farms from western Pennsylvania to northern Georgia.

It would be hard to exaggerate just how much the Scots-Irish hated the English. They arrived in the colonies ready to rise up against British rule, and they formed the shock troops of the Revolution. Many of Boston's inhabitants were young, unemployed Scots-Irish men—a group with nothing to lose—while poor Scots-Irish frontiersmen in Appalachia, accustomed to self-sufficiency, were perfectly equipped to turn the countryside into a bloody morass of guerrilla warfare.

> **They swarm like the Goths and Vandals of old & will over-spread our Continent Soon.**
>
> —James Byrd II, on Scots-Irish immigrants, 1736

Because they came from Ireland, the Protestant immigrants were simply called "Irish" until the first half of the nineteenth century, when large numbers of Irish Catholic immigrants began to arrive in the United States for the first time. At this point, the proud Protestants began using the term Scots-Irish to distinguish themselves from the destitute Irish Catholics, whom their ancestors had helped oppress back in the old country not so long before. Meanwhile Anglo-Saxon American colonists disdained both groups—but at least everyone could still agree on hating the English!

The other main immigrant group was even more foreign, and thus even more disliked: German-speaking settlers from what are now Germany, Switzerland, and the Netherlands. These simple peasant farmers settled overwhelmingly in rural Pennsylvania, where they mostly tried to stay out of everyone's way. Once again inaccuracy reigned, as the new German settlers who began showing up around 1710 were all lumped together as "Pennsylvania Dutch"—a corruption of the closely related word *Deutsch*. The German immigrants came from all kinds of religious and geographic backgrounds, and most assimilated into the mainstream colonial culture; however, two groups of Swiss German Anabaptists— the Mennonites and Amish—preserved their cultural traditions by living in separate communities that embrace simplicity and reject technological conveniences.

> Those who come hither are generally of the most ignorant Stupid Sort of their own Nation . . . Why should Pennsylvania, founded by the English, become a Colony of Aliens, who will shortly be so numerous as to Germanize us instead of our Anglifying them?
>
> —Benjamin Franklin, on German immigrants, 1753

Ode to a Grecian Turn

During the Revolution, patriotic Americans started looking back to the liberty-loving Greeks as Classical role models. But identifying with these enlightened heroes of the past wasn't just an abstract mental exercise: it also sparked trends in architecture and clothing.

Examples of neo-Classical architecture are easy enough to find: just go to Washington, D.C., or visit any local government building from before 1900, and you'll see all the basic elements. The first big surge of neo-Classical architecture came with the so-called Federal Style (1780–1830), based on Roman architecture and simplified versions of Classical motifs used in Britain. This led to an offshoot called the Palladian style. The White House, Monticello, and the rotunda at the University of Virginia are all done in the Palladian style, partially because Thomas Jefferson was such a big fan of the look. (To be accurate, the Palladian style was actually a re-revival of an earlier, sixteenth century Venetian revival of Classical architecture.)

Beginning in the early nineteenth century, architecture influenced by ancient Athens became popular. The Federal Style soon gave way to the "Greek Revival," and famous buildings from this period include the U.S. Capitol, the Supreme Court, and the Bank of Pennsylvania. Eventually, the Greek Revival spread to more ordinary buildings and even private homes, and it remained the dominant architectural style in the United States through the first half of the nineteenth century.

Interestingly, the Classical look invaded American fashion too—especially when it came to women's clothing. Beginning around 1790, the simple, flowing neo-Classical lines replaced the elaborate gowns that had dominated the Revolutionary period. Ironically, the new style replacing the old "French look" was also plucked from fashion-forward France.

> We have imported the worst of French corruptions, the want of female delicacy. The fair and the innocent have borrowed from the lewd the arts of seduction.
>
> —A Bostonian, on neo-Classical clothing

At first the new line of clothing was considered too lewd for society. The best dresses were made of thin, sheer materials like silk, taffeta, and chiffon. And because there were fewer layers of fabric to shield women's bodies from wandering eyes, a prudish public frowned upon the clothes. But public opinion soon changed. After all, young women weren't going to let male stares and female disapproval dissuade them from showing off the new fashions!

These daring women complemented their silk dresses with jewelry inspired by Roman and Greek ornamentation, hairstyles based on Roman matrons', and accessories like silk kerchiefs printed with Egyptian patterns. One of the most visible adherents of the new style was Dolley Madison, wife of James Madison (who also served as First Lady in ceremonial functions for Thomas Jefferson, a widower). As the most-watched hostess in the country for 16 years, Dolley dazzled her guests with colorful, low-cut dresses, giving the costumes an ultra-chic Oriental twist with turbans decorated with ostrich feathers and jewelry.

Got Jesus?

One of the most significant long-term trends in American history is religious revivalism, which has produced several enormous surges in Christian evangelism. The first big Christian revival, or "Great Awakening," swept the American colonies in the first half of the eighteenth century, from around 1743 to 1755.

The causes of the First Great Awakening may have included a latent feeling of guilt that the colonies had strayed from the Puritan principles of their forefathers as they gained prosperity. With the spiritual stew already simmering, all America needed was a little more ecclesiastical kindling; this was provided by a young Anglican minister from England named George Whitefield, who toured the colonies in 1739–1740.

While the Anglican Church today may be perceived as, well, somewhat stodgy and boring, Whitefield was anything but: his electrifying sermons so moved his audiences that some critics deemed them sensational and even unseemly. Whitefield's warnings of eternal damnation and furious attacks on contemporary immorality struck fear and shame into his listeners, resulting in countless conversions on the spot. If this sounds familiar, that's because the First Great Awakening established the pattern for American evangelical Christian movements down to the present day.

After Whitefield's brief, stunning tour of the colonies, the cause was taken up by great American preachers like Jonathan Edwards, who together with Whitefield inspired a new generation of preachers. Methodist and Baptist preachers traveled the South, converting whites, freed blacks, and slaves, while across the country new churches were built to house growing congregations.

> There is nothing that keeps wicked men, at any one moment, out of hell, but the mere pleasure of God.
>
> —Jonathan Edwards, 1741

The Louisiana Wholesale Clearance

The biggest expansion of U.S. territory in history was an incredible deal—which, incredibly, almost didn't happen.

In 1803 Napoleon Bonaparte came into possession of a large chunk of real estate in the New World through some typical Corsican wheeling and dealing. This was actually business as usual for the American Midwest, which had changed hands a number of times in the previous half-century. After the French and Indian War, Britain had taken France's tree- and beaver-filled northern colonies in Canada but given the southern colonies to Spain—a weak, declining empire that could be counted on not to do anything rashly ambitious with them.

But the Spaniards were secretly determined to get something out of all that empty land. Fast forward to 1800, when King Charles IV signed the secret Treaty of Ildefonso, ceding the territory to France in exchange for a promise to help the Spanish king's son-in-law take the throne of a European principality. Napoleon was excited, envisioning a new French empire in the New World, with grain from the American Midwest feeding slaves in lucrative French sugar plantations in the Caribbean.

Stretching Our Legs
U.S. Expansion to 1804

NORTHWEST TERRITORY 1787

LOUISIANA PURCHASE 1803

OHIO 1803

KENTUCKY 1792

TENNESSEE 1796

MISSISSIPPI TERRITORY 1804

THIRTEEN-ISH COLONIES

But it was not to be: Napoleon's plans were derailed by a revolt of slaves and free blacks in the French colony of Saint-Domingue (modern-day Haiti), followed by the resumption of war with Britain in 1803, bringing the Royal Navy between France and its American possessions—just as France was about to get its paws on the Louisiana Territory. Disappointed but realistic, Napoleon decided to cash out and sell the whole thing to whoever wanted it (except for Britain—definitely *not* Britain).

The United States was the most logical buyer, and the deal should have been a foregone conclusion: the young republic stood to double its territory for the low, low price of $15 million (actually $11.25 million plus forgiving $3.75 million in French debt)—which works out to about $0.03 per acre. And as a bonus, they'd get New Orleans, which controlled access to the Mississippi River.

Amazingly, the deal faced substantial opposition in Congress, with the Federalists asserting, bizarrely and incorrectly, that the whole area was a useless desert. Thankfully, reason prevailed, in part because everyone was afraid that the territory might end up in British hands—not an implausible fear, as the Brits had nearby bases in Canada and Jamaica and attacked New Orleans (unsuccessfully) in 1814.

> This accession of territory affirms forever the power of the United States, and I have given England a maritime rival who sooner or later will humble her pride.
>
> —Napoleon Bonaparte, 1804

Realizing no one really knew what the heck he'd bought, in 1804 Jefferson dispatched two explorers—Meriwether Lewis and William Clark—to map the huge territory and assess its resources and potential. Congress, always cheap, complained about the excessive cost for the 33-person mission—$2,500—but ultimately agreed. Over two epic years, Lewis and Clark traveled over 8,000 miles, encountering three dozen native tribes and documenting over 100 new species of animal and 176 new species of plant. They were helped enormously by a French trapper, Toussaint Charbonneau, and his young native wife, Sacajawea, who acted as guides and translators for most of the expedition.

America's War of Dumb Luck

On the heels of one its finest moments, the newly minted United States proceeded to the distinctly less glorious War of 1812.

The American cause was fair enough: after the Revolution, the Brits reneged on their promise to evacuate forts in the "Northwest Territory"—covering Ohio, Indiana, Michigan, and Illinois. The Brits also had the obnoxious habit of stopping American ships on the high seas and kidnapping sailors, who were forced to serve with British crews. (The Brits claimed they were just reclaiming deserters from the Royal Navy.)

Having a just cause is a great start, but it doesn't substitute for an army, navy, or strategy. Even though the last American invasion of Canada during the Revolutionary War had been soundly defeated, the Americans decided to try again. They would liberate Canada from British rule, whether Canada liked it or not—and in fact, Canada did not like it, putting up a fierce resistance. Meanwhile the invading "militias" barely deserved the name; instead, they were angry mobs of frontiersmen scraped together with no real chain of command.

★ *The War of 1812 was poorly named, since little action occurred that year. Most of the fighting took place in 1813, a peace treaty was signed in 1814, and the deciding battle was fought in 1815 (before news of peace had arrived).*

After cleaning the American clocks up north, Britain took the fight to the United States, which was virtually defenseless. (The tiny U.S. Navy was vastly outnumbered by the Brits.) But it wasn't their aim to reconquer the United States; they just wanted to break heads. In August 1814 they burned Washington, D.C. They failed, however, to take Baltimore during an all-night bombardment in September (during which Francis Scott Key wrote the "Star-Spangled Banner"). The Royal Navy also enforced a strict blockade of American ports, inflicting serious damage on the U.S. economy. But the blockade was enormously expensive to maintain. Finally, in December 1814, with neither side making any progress toward its goals (whatever those may have been), America and Britain decided to call the whole thing off.

So how exactly did America manage to come out ahead? The Brits renounced their claims to the Northwest Territory, clearing the way for the first big surge of Western settlement. And there was a bonus: not knowing that a peace treaty had been signed in Paris three weeks before, the British attacked New Orleans in December 1814 but were roundly defeated by Andrew Jackson. So the Americans did score a victory in the end—after the war was over.

PIRATES OF THE . . . MEDITERRANEAN?

Not all of America's early wars were characterized by disastrous stupidity, and some were breathtakingly ambitious. For instance, if you menaced American merchants or damaged their property, the plucky little United States would send Marines to the other side of the world to complain, violently, in person.

Thomas Jefferson set the precedent in 1803 by sending a small force of Marines (possibly all the Marines there were) to the Mediterranean, where American ships were being harassed by the Barbary Pirates, based out of Tripoli. Technically vassals of the Ottoman Empire, by the early nineteenth century, these pirates barely paid lip service to the sultan in faraway Constantinople and preyed on the ships of any country that didn't pay them exorbitant "tolls."

Europeans were used to these fees as a cost of doing business, and Congress was prepared to foot bills of up to $30,000 a year—a considerable amount, considering that the total U.S. government revenues of the time were about $10 million. But Jefferson vehemently disagreed, pointing out that pirates are, well, not very trustworthy. And he was right: by the time Jefferson took office, the pasha of Tripoli alone was demanding $225,000 a year for "protection."

Seeing a chance to boost American prestige and fight pirates to boot, Jefferson dispatched naval squadrons to the Mediterranean beginning in May 1801. By August 1803 seven American ships—the better part of the U.S. Navy—were patrolling the North African coast with 800 men aboard. The duty was time-consuming and dangerous—not to mention way more expensive than just paying off the pirates.

Finally, in early 1805, General William Eaton and First Lieutenant Presley O'Bannon, the Marine commander, decided they'd had enough. To put an end to the menace, they convinced the pasha of Tripoli's brother—then in exile in Alexandria—to seize the throne. From March to May 1805, ten Marines, reinforced by a few hundred Arab mercenaries, marched across 500 miles of the Sahara Desert to mount a successful surprise attack on the Tripolitanian town of Derna.

Seeing a serious threat to his throne, the pasha of Tripoli moved to make peace with the United States, and the two sides signed the Treaty of Tripoli. The pasha rescinded his demands for tribute (except for one last ransom of $60,000 for the crew of the USS *Philadelphia*). Meanwhile, his brother's claim to the throne was conveniently forgotten.

A Ridiculously Long and Incomplete List of Things Ben Franklin Invented

We all remember Ben Franklin as a pretty bright guy who discovered some pretty important stuff. The real question is, what didn't this polymath genius invent?

1742: Observing the wasteful use of firewood in inefficient colonial fireplaces, he designed the Franklin Stove, which used its iron body to diffuse a much larger proportion of the heat. The stove enabled poor families to save money and be warmer in the winter.

1749: Noticing that lightning was attracted to metal and tall objects, Franklin hit on the idea of attaching vertical metal rods to the tops of tall buildings to attract the lightning, thus sparing the roof a direct hit.

1752: To prove that lightning was static electricity, Franklin carried out his famous kite experiment with the help of his young son William (nobody ever said he was a responsible parent). He conducted an electrical charge from a key along a wire into a primitive battery. Franklin and son were lucky to survive; in following years, a number of scientists who tried to replicate Franklin's experiment were killed by lightning.

★ *Franklin's kite was made of a thin silk handkerchief stretched across a handcrafted cedar crosspiece.*

1752: To allow his brother to urinate while suffering from kidney stones, Franklin invented the first flexible urinary catheter used in North America.

1763: Franklin, who had been appointed postmaster of Philadelphia in 1737, came up with the odometer. The complicated device composed of three interlocking gears was attached to the wheel of postal carriages in order to figure out the distances traveled by postal officers.

1770: He named and described the "Gulf Stream"—the giant Atlantic current circulating between the Gulf of

Mexico and the west coast of Ireland—and correctly identified it as the reason the voyage from Britain to America took longer along certain routes. British admirals ignored his findings and then came up with the same answer several decades later.

1784: Troubled by being both near- and far-sighted at the age of 78, Franklin improved spectacles by inventing the "bifocal."

1786: To reach merchandise on high shelves, he invented a pole with a claw at one end operated by handles at the other—a device still used at corner bodegas everywhere.

1787: Although he never actually built them, during one of his eight Atlantic crossings, Franklin came up with a design for watertight bulkheads that would help limit flooding below deck if a ship's hull was breached.

Along the way, he also helped develop America's first fire department and first library, as well as the concept of daylight savings time. But perhaps the most remarkable thing about Ben Franklin the inventor was his refusal to patent any of his ideas, so that the widest possible number of people could benefit from them.

> As we enjoy great Advantages from the Inventions of others we should be glad of an Opportunity to serve others by any Invention of ours, and this we should do freely and generously.
>
> —Benjamin Franklin's autobiography, published 1790

The Touch, the Feel of Cotton Gins

Benjamin Franklin wasn't the only American on the scene inventing useful things. In 1793, Eli Whitney came up with the cotton gin, a brilliant invention that—unfortunately—led to a resurgence of slavery in the United States. Like Ben Franklin, Whitney never profited from his invention, though it wasn't from lack of trying.

The cotton gin was a great labor-saving device, vastly speeding up the process for removing seeds from cotton (which used to be done by hand). But it was a mixed blessing: by freeing slaves from seed-picking duty, the cotton gin made them available for more fieldwork, so plantation owners could cultivate more land. This lowered the price of cotton, making woven textiles available to the masses, which increased demand. The machine fed a cycle in which plantation owners began buying even more slaves to grow and harvest the vital cash crop, which gave them money to buy more land and slaves, etc.

> ★ Another of Eli Whitney's contributions to society was his effort to streamline firearm production. He developed an early system of interchangeable parts that could be used to create multiple types of weapons, a tactic that later helped several industries (notably automobiles) develop quickly.

The big increases in the number of slaves and territory controlled by slave owners fueled fears in the North, where sentiment was already turning against slavery—foreshadowing the Civil War. All thanks to one machine!

As for Eli Whitney himself, he never got to enjoy the fruits of his epoch-making invention, thanks to his greediness. Instead of licensing the design (so other people could build their own cotton gins while paying him royalties), Whitney tried to keep a monopoly on the technology. He hoped to charge farmers and plantation owners exorbitant prices—up to 40 percent of the finished processed cotton. This caused so much resentment that competing knockoff cotton gins soon began springing up around the countryside. Whitney tried to stop these patent infringements, but at the time, patent laws were still evolving, as was the judicial system. Nonetheless, Whitney kept up the struggle until the lawsuits finally bankrupted him in 1797.

Bale Money
Two Telling Cotton Charts

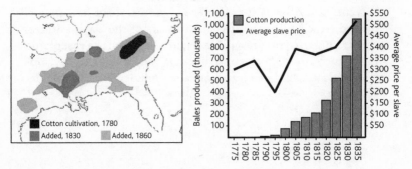

Full Steamboats Ahead

After James Watt patented the steam engine in 1765–1776, engineers and tech geeks everywhere set their minds to finding new ways to use steam power, including locomotives on rails and steam-powered vessels. A number of inventors built boats powered by steam engines, including Claude de Jouffroy, who demonstrated a paddle steamer in Paris in 1783; James Rumsey, a Virginian who launched a steamboat on the Potomac near Shepherdstown in 1786; John Fitch of Connecticut, who demonstrated his steamboat to members of Congress in 1787; and John Stevens, a New Yorker who built a propeller-driven steamboat in 1802. But none of the inventors were able to translate their designs into a viable business.

Enter Robert Fulton. In 1803 his first steamboat sank like a rock in the Seine River in Paris, France, but his second design for a steam-powered paddle-wheel boat performed perfectly. Returning to New York, Fulton built a new boat—the Clermont—with a stronger hull and areas for passengers and cargo. In 1807, Fulton and his wealthy soon-to-be uncle-in-law, Robert Livingston, launched the world's first steam-powered passenger service between New York and Albany. With a paddle wheel propelling it at four to five miles per hour, the 142-foot-long Clermont took just two and a half days to make the 300-mile round trip, compared to four days for sailing ships.

At first glance it might seem like Fulton won undeserved fame, reaching the prize after other men had cleared the way. But Fulton's achievement was real. Making steamboats commercially viable required cutting down on coal consumption and increasing the number of passengers who could be accommodated safely. To attract customers, Fulton also glammed up the experience: the price of the ticket for the overnight journey from New York to Albany included comfy beds and two meals.

In the years after Fulton launched his steamboat line, steam-powered vessels filled the rivers and coasts of the United States, making long-distance travel cheaper, helping open the vast plains of the American Midwest to settlers, enabling industrial development, and fueling the literary antics of Tom Sawyer and Huckleberry Finn.

250,000	European population of the American colonies in 1700
2.5 million	European population of the American colonies in 1775
1/20	ratio of colonial population to British population, 1700
1/3	ratio of colonial population to British population, 1775
2,000	British customs revenues from the American colonies, in pounds, 1760
30,000	British customs revenues, in pounds, in 1770
45	tons of tea dumped in Boston Harbor by American patriots, 1773
17,000	strength of the Continental Army commanded by Washington, at its peak
6,000	strength of French forces sent to help the rebels under Lafayette and Rochambeau
32,000	total strength of British forces in America, at their peak
50,000	total strength of Britain's standing armies around the world, 1775
1,500	number of native warriors provided to the British by their Iroquois allies
180,000	pounds of cotton produced in the Southern states in 1793
93 million	pounds of cotton produced in the Southern states in 1810
240,000	slave population of the 13 colonies, 1750
1,300,000	slave population of the Southern states, 1810
50,000	number of African slaves imported to Charleston, South Carolina, from 1804 to 1808
$240	cost of a slave imported from Africa, 1775
$390	cost of a slave imported from Africa, 1807
85 percent	proportion of slaves who were native-born in 1810
828,000	area, in square miles, of Louisiana Purchase in 1803
$15 million	cost, in dollars, of the Louisiana Purchase
$0.03	cost per acre, in dollars, of the Louisiana Purchase

14 number of American states formed from the Louisiana Purchase

23 percent their proportion of the current area of the United States

2/3 proportion of landless Virginian men who moved west to claim land in the 1790s

3

Drunk and Illiterate (and Not Just a Little Bit)

(1815–1850)

After winning the American Revolution and (mostly) not losing the War of 1812, the United States was suddenly the center of attention. The crowned heads of Europe were watching the newborn federation closely, praying that this weird experiment in nation-building and self-government would fail spectacularly. But they were disappointed. Far from degenerating into class warfare or regional rivalries, from 1815 to 1850 the United States pulled itself together and embarked on one of the greatest periods of territorial conquest in human history—settling the Wild West!

Still, the new country wasn't exactly a perfect union. It remained divided over slavery, having sidestepped the issue in the Constitution. Further, the westward push only exacerbated the conflict, as each new Western state threatened to change the balance of power in Congress. With fierce Northern abolitionists on one side and equally fierce pro-slavery Southerners on the other, something had to give. But for the time being, the young, carefree United States was happy to sweep the whole incendiary issue under the highly flammable rug.

Slavery wasn't the only question at hand. For example, what to do with all those Native Americans still living on Western land, which God had clearly set aside for white people? The settlers hit on a comprehensive solution—as their branding experts called it, "Manifest Destiny!" ("Mass murder?" "No: Manifest Destiny!") And in fairness to the settlers, many Native American tribes were also quite warlike. There were just fewer of them.

Before long, advances in steam power and mass production were transforming the big cities of the Northeast. Imported from Britain, industrialization raised the standard of living for a broad segment of society and set the stage for the rise of the United States as the world's biggest economy when it overtook Britain in the second half of the nineteenth century, thanks to its larger population and abundant natural resources. But the conditions were still far from ideal; many urban factory workers lived and worked in squalor. Additionally, these new industrial sweatshops employed ever-larger numbers of poor European immigrants, whose arrival triggered a massive wave of xenophobia and isolationism.

Meanwhile, American religious ferment gave rise to the Second Great Awakening, an evangelical Protestant revival that brought millions back to the old churches and also generated a new one: the Church of Jesus Christ of Latter-Day Saints, also known as the Mormon Church. The Mormons were a clean-living, hardworking crew, but some of their doctrine—particularly the practice of polygamy—raised eyebrows . . . followed quickly by torches, burning effigies, and pitchforks.

But probably the biggest development in early nineteenth-century America was the revolution in transportation and communications brought about by new technologies and investment in infrastructure, as railroads, canals, and telegraphs tied the states together like never before. With growing cohesion came a greater sense of national unity—but the feeling of pride inspired by this new American identity couldn't cover up the deepening divide over slavery.

·············· **WHAT HAPPENED WHEN** ··················

January 26, 1815 Andrew Jackson captures New Orleans.

January 17, 1821 Mexico invites Americans to settle in Texas and California.

1823 Joseph Smith Jr. is visited by the angel Moroni for the first time.

1825 Mexico bans slavery.

1828 Mexico tries to stop Anglo-American immigration to Texas.

1831 Nat Turner leads a slave rebellion in rural Virginia; Smith leads the Mormons to Kirtland, Ohio.

1832 Southern states pass harsh anti-literacy laws regulating slavery.

1833 Mexico repeals ban on Anglo-American immigration to Texas.

March 2, 1836 Texas rebellion begins.

March 3, 1837 Texas rebellion ends with Texan independence.

June 27, 1844 Smith is killed in a jail cell in Carthage, Illinois.

1845 Florida (March 3) and Texas (December 29) join the Union.

April 25, 1846 The Mexican-American War begins.

June 18, 1846 Americans stage the Bear Flag Revolt in California.

February 2, 1848 The Mexican-American War ends.

September 9, 1850 California joins the Union.

· SPECIAL REPORT · · · · · · · · · · · · · · ·

We've Got Issues
Slavery

In the first half of the nineteenth century, America was increasingly divided by one huge, ugly issue: slavery. Among other things, it complicated the young country's expansion in the west, where each new state threatened to change the national balance of power between pro-slavery and anti-slavery forces.

★ *East of the Rockies, slave state land covered an area of more than 850,000 square miles, while free states contained just 450,000 square miles.*

Even before the American Revolution, opposition to slavery was already entrenched in some areas of the North, particularly with the Quakers of Pennsylvania. This idealistic Christian sect, famous for egalitarian social views, began voicing opposition to slavery as early as 1688. And the Quakers weren't the only ones. During the Revolutionary War, Benjamin Franklin and Thomas Jefferson rallied the Continental Congress and orchestrated a ban on the overseas slave trade as part of the anti-British boycott. During the Revolutionary War, both sides promised emancipation to slaves who fought for their cause. Following independence, it seemed to some people that slavery was actually headed for extinction.

> **To bring men hither, or to rob and sell them against their will, we stand against.**
>
> —Quaker anti-slavery compact, 1688

But the invention of the cotton gin in 1793, followed by the invention of steam-powered looms for mass-producing cotton fabric, changed all of that. Suddenly slavery was far more profitable. People who wanted lots of cotton clothing were thrilled—the people hoping to escape from slavery, less so. From 1794 to 1807, new cotton plantations sprang up across the temperate Southern states, and the value of slaves increased, spurring the international and interstate slave trade.

This was bad news, not only for the slaves, but for the fledgling United States, which would pay for slavery with blood in the Civil War. Tensions began rising in the 1830s, as a new generation of Northern abolitionists—mostly Methodists, Baptists, Congregationalists, and New School Presbyterians—demanded immediate emancipation, believing they had a divine mission to abolish the "heinous sin" of slavery. Raising awareness with rallies where integrated choirs sang anti-slavery hymns, the abolitionists eventually succeeded in banning slavery in all of the Northern states. But the real goal was always abolition of slavery in the South—and not just for religious reasons. Threatened by competition from cheaper slave labor, Northern farmers and artisans resented the wealth of Southern plantation owners. The Northern elite also feared Southern political domination—"The Slave Power."

> **The Anti-Slavery movement . . . was at its commencement, and has ever since been, thoroughly and emphatically a religious enterprise.**
>
> —Charles K. Whipple, a Massachusetts abolitionist, 1856

Their fears were not unfounded. Although the North had a larger population, the big increase in slavery benefited the Southern states politically, thanks to the "Three-Fifths Compromise." This measure, demanded by Southern states as a condition for signing the Constitution in 1787, counted each slave as three-fifths of a white citizen when calculating proportional representation in the House of Representatives. While the slaves themselves couldn't

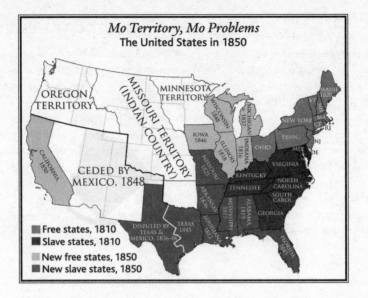

Mo Territory, Mo Problems
The United States in 1850

- OREGON TERRITORY
- MISSOURI TERRITORY (INDIAN COUNTRY)
- MINNESOTA TERRITORY
- WISCONSIN 1848
- MICHIGAN 1837
- MAINE 1820
- VT
- NEW YORK
- MASS
- CT RI
- IOWA 1846
- ILLINOIS 1818
- INDIANA 1816
- OHIO
- PENN.
- NJ
- CALIFORNIA 1850
- CEDED BY MEXICO, 1848
- MISSOURI 1821
- KENTUCKY
- VIRGINIA
- MD DE
- ARKANSAS 1836
- TENNESSEE
- NORTH CAROLINA
- SOUTH CAROL.
- DISPUTED BY TEXAS & MEXICO, 1836–48
- TEXAS 1845
- LOUISIANA 1812
- MISSISSIPPI 1817
- ALABAMA 1819
- GEORGIA
- FLORIDA

◼ Free states, 1810
◼ Slave states, 1810
◼ New free states, 1850
◼ New slave states, 1850

vote, their growing numbers gave an extra jolt of power to the white Southerners who could. In 1830 each Southern member of Congress represented about 40,600 actual citizens, while each Northern member represented 55,370 actual citizens. If you're scratching your head over this, you can guess how the Northerners felt.

The situation in the Senate was possibly even more dangerous. Since each new state received the same number of senators (two) regardless of population, there was an obvious incentive for both factions to create new states filled with their own sympathizers. The race got going after Thomas Jefferson's purchase of Louisiana from France in 1803, accelerated with the prospect of new states in the Missouri Territory, and kicked into high gear in 1848 after the American victory in the Mexican War opened vast new areas to settlement. As different parts of the country pursued their glaringly contradictory visions of Manifest Destiny, politicians tried to hammer out agreements to make the whole system a little less harebrained. The results were still ridiculous. For example, the Missouri Compromise of 1820 banned slavery above a certain line of latitude (36° 30′ N), except for Missouri, where slavery was allowed, but only as long as Maine was also admitted as a new free state to keep the balance of power. These congressional contortions foreshadowed worse conflict to come, especially as two parts of the Missouri Territory—Kansas and Nebraska—got in line for statehood.

Slave owners often tried to justify the institution of slavery by asserting slaves were actually happy to be slaves. This ludicrous claim was contradicted by a series of slave revolts, including about a dozen major uprisings or conspiracies in the eighteenth and nineteenth centuries. Regardless of whether they owned slaves or not, Southern whites lived in constant fear of a general uprising, especially as slaves made up more than half the population in some places. One of the most famous—and violent—slave revolts was led by Nat Turner, who rallied over 70 slaves and freed blacks and went on a rampage in Virginia, resulting in the murders of 60 white people on August 21–22, 1831. Turner's uprising was quickly crushed by the Virginia militia, which found and hung 56 blacks. (Meanwhile, angry white mobs lynched another 100–200.) But it stood out as proof of slaves' desperate misery, fueling abolitionist sentiment in the North.

·············· **LIES YOUR TEACHER TOLD YOU** ················

LIE: *The United States was strictly divided between the North and South.*

THE TRUTH: Okay. So we just traced the division that pitted North against South in the nineteenth century. But the familiar North-versus-South scenario overlooks the fact that there were actually three major territorial units in the nineteenth century: the North, the South, and the "Midlands," which, true to the name, occupied a huge area in between.

On maps, the North and South are neatly separated in the East by the Mason-Dixon Line, named after two surveyors—Charles Mason and Jeremiah Dixon—who laid down the famous border in 1763 to help resolve a territorial dispute between Maryland and Pennsylvania. But west of the Appalachians, things got blurry. Here pioneers had more in common with each other than with the North or South. This was partly due to the predominance of the Scots-Irish: although lots of other ethnicities were represented—including Germans, Swedes, and African-Americans (mostly freed slaves)—the Scots-Irish were the most numerous and adventurous group, leading expansion and shaping frontier culture with their traditions. Ignoring royal proclamations (did we mention they hated the English?), they began moving westward in the decades before the American Revolution, crossing the Appalachians through the Cumberland Gap and settling the fertile Tennessee and Ohio River valleys.

The Scots-Irish influence on the Midlands and America in general is pretty clear. Common Scots-Irish names include Alexander, Anderson, Carter, Clinton, Craig, Cunningham, Davison, Foster, Hamilton, Hall, Harrison, Jackson, Johnson, McDonald, Wilson, and Young. These settlers were fiercely independent to the point of belligerence, despising government and prizing self-reliance. They tended to be small-time farmers and avid hunters, drawn to the open land and wild game of the frontier. Literate and better-educated than most other frontiersmen, they clung to their local churches—except when there wasn't a local church (in which case they were known for carousing and rabble-rousing). Their cultural legacy includes square dancing to the music of fiddles and "jaw harps." After exposure to African-American music, they added guitars and banjos to their repertoire—in fact, Scots-Irish reels and jigs formed the basis of American bluegrass, folk, and country music.

But the differences between the Midlands and other parts of the country were based on economic as well as ethnic and cultural factors. In a time when "roads" were unpaved tracks in the wilderness, the Midlands were truly remote. Rivers like the Ohio, Tennessee, and Mississippi provided relatively fast transportation,

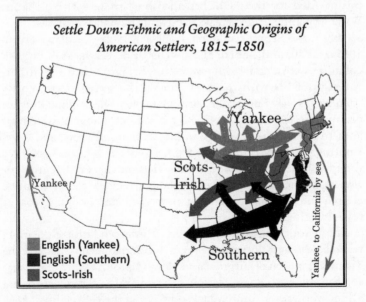

Settle Down: Ethnic and Geographic Origins of American Settlers, 1815–1850

Yankee

Scots-Irish

Yankee

Yankee, to California by sea

Southern

■ English (Yankee)
■ English (Southern)
■ Scots-Irish

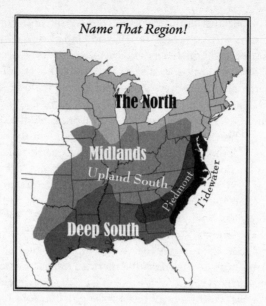

Name That Region!

but even with steamboats the journey from New Orleans to Louisville, Kentucky, could still take 25 days. This made it difficult to get agricultural produce to market before it spoiled. As a result, the Midlands never developed the huge plantations that arose in the South. Most farms remained small, with farmers focused on raising food for their families and some trade with neighbors. Without plantations, there wasn't really a demand for slaves.

While the Scots-Irish spread out across the Midlands from 1815 to 1850, to the north and south, the descendants of English colonists were also heading westward, bringing their very different ways of life with them. Up north, the settlers were mostly "Yankees"—New Englanders descended from the original Puritan colonists in Massachusetts, who fanned out across upstate New York to the northern parts of Ohio, Indiana, Illinois, and Iowa, entering Michigan and Wisconsin from the south. Here they founded orderly communities modeled on the small, conservative, egalitarian towns of New England, where life centered on the church and all important decisions were made by popular vote at town meetings.

To the south, the settlers were mostly descendants of the more relaxed, less morally uptight English colonists who'd settled the Tidewater region of Virginia and North Carolina. Part of the reason they were so relaxed, of course, was because slaves were doing all the work. After Andrew Jackson secured the U.S. claim to New

Orleans in 1815, ambitious young men from the lower echelons of the Tidewater aristocracy headed west to make their fortunes by establishing new (and bigger!) cotton plantations in Alabama, Mississippi, Louisiana, and Texas. The new plantations were concentrated in the southern parts of the states and along major rivers like the Mississippi, which provided cheap transportation for millions of bales of cotton.

LIE: *The Alamo was about defending liberty and freedom.*

THE TRUTH: The popular image of the Alamo—a glorious, desperate last stand for freedom—is one of the great American myths. Before an angry mob of Texans hunts us down, here's the real story: the roughly 250 Americans who died at the Alamo from February 23 through March 6, 1836, weren't defending liberty—they were protecting slavery.

> ★ *The word "álamo" is Spanish for a cottonwood tree.*

Although Texas was still part of Mexico in the decades following Mexico's War of Independence from Spain (1810–1821), it attracted more and more American settlers. Soon the Americans outnumbered the Mexicans, which was okay with the Mexican government—it had actually invited Americans to settle there in the hopes that they would control raids by native tribes, which they did. In fact, many Texans—led by Stephen Austin—actually wanted Texas to become a Mexican state.

The trouble started in 1829, when Vicente Guerrero, a hero of the Mexican War of Independence, was given dictatorial powers by the Mexican Senate, and horror of horrors, banned slavery throughout Mexico. This angered and alarmed American settlers who had moved to Texas specifically to establish Southern-style, slave-powered cotton plantations. Austin convinced Guerrero to grant Texas an exemption, and the move allowed everyone to sidestep this awkward issue . . .

At least, until Guerrero was toppled by Anastasio Bustamente— a far more ambitious dictator, who feared that Mexico was losing control of Texas. Bustamente was also determined to replace Mexico's relaxed federal system with a powerful central government. To strengthen his hold on Texas, Bustamente cut off all American immigration and raised taxes and tariffs on trade with the United States. This angered the Texans, but it wasn't too bad: the immigration restriction was repealed in 1833, and—since the government for the most part only pretended to collect taxes—the Texans only pretended to pay them.

> Dear Sir: We have received by the last mail a Decree
> Given by the executive of our Government Liberating all
> the Slaves in its territory . . . in the Name of God, what Shall
> we do? For God's sake advise me on the subject by the return
> of mail. We are ruined for ever Should this
> measure be adopted.
>
> —Letter to Stephen Austin from John Durst,
> a prominent Texan, 1829

The Texans' biggest fear was realized in 1835: two years after ousting Bustamente, General Antonio Lopez de Santa Anna extended the ban on slavery to specifically include Texas. With Stephen Austin leading the charge, the Texans rebelled.

Enter the Alamo. Overconfident after a few easy victories against smaller Mexican forces, the Texans foolishly divided their army. Leaving just a few hundred rebel troops to hold San Antonio, the remainder of the army made a futile attack on Matamoros, a city on the Gulf Coast hundreds of miles to the south. Santa Anna, after defeating a totally separate group of rebels in Zacatecas (he was not a popular dictator), headed north into Texas, taking San Antonio by surprise in February 1836. Frantically gathering supplies, 250 rebels took refuge in the Alamo, an old Spanish mission north of San Antonio, under the informal leadership of Davy Crockett and James Bowie.

> You may all go to hell, and I will go to Texas.
>
> —Davy Crockett, after failing to win reelection
> as U.S. representative for Tennessee, 1835

There was no way the rebels could break the siege—it was 1,500 Mexican troops to their 250—but there was no point in surrender either, as Santa Anna had announced that he would take no prisoners. In the end the defenders were (obviously) wiped out, but only after inflicting about 600 casualties on Santa Anna's troops. A Pyrrhic victory for the Mexicans, the Alamo crucially weakened Santa Anna, who then did himself no favors by dividing his reduced force to chase the fleeing provisional government of Texas.

Against all odds, on April 21, 1836, Santa Anna's Mexican cavalry was defeated in a record 18 minutes at the Battle of San Jacinto River by a smaller force of Texans in a desperate surprise attack. The Texans captured Santa Anna as he tried to flee through a nearby swamp. To buy his freedom, the humiliated dictator agreed to recognize Texas as an independent state. The Texans succeeded in upholding slavery, avoiding taxes, and all that other stuff. For the next nine years, the Republic of Texas existed as a nation unto itself, before joining the United States in 1845—needless to say, as a slave state.

LIE: *America has always welcomed immigrants.*

THE TRUTH: America has done better than most countries with its immigration policies. But welcomed? Not so much. If you're tempted to shout out something about the beautiful melting pot of our nation, we'd like to remind you of the "Nativist" political movements that preached virulent hatred of "un-American" immigrants—mostly Catholic Europeans—who began showing up in larger and larger numbers in the 1830s.

The biggest immigrant group of the era was Irish Catholic peasants. From 1820 to 1840, 220,000 Irish immigrants fled oppressive English landlords for America. They accounted for roughly a third of the total 742,000 immigrants arriving in that period. But Irish immigration really kicked into high gear when a potato blight destroyed the entire Irish potato crop in the late 1840s. As English landlords looked on indifferently, 1.5 million Irish starved to death, and another 1.6 million relocated. Immigrants went from less than 1 percent of the U.S. population in 1820 to around 10 percent in 1850. And with 961,719 Irish immigrants living in the United States in 1850, the Irish rose from less than 1 percent to about 4 percent of the total population (of 23 million).

> In the seventeenth century, Europeans were pressed to grow potatoes, which were hardier and offered more food per acre than most other crops. Farmers were asked (or forced) to plant potatoes in hopes of avoiding the famines that had plagued nations during wartime. The areas that depended most heavily on the potato crop—like Ireland—were those hardest hit by the famine of the 1840s.

That may not seem like a large percentage, but the Irish were highly visible in urban areas like New York, Boston, and Philadelphia, where they eventually made up a quarter of the population. Drawn to these cities by the initial stage of the Industrial

Revolution, the first Irish immigrants, despite their incredible poverty, saved enough money to bring over family members, who did the same in turn. Later immigrants often headed west, but still tended to gravitate to urban areas, contributing to the rapid growth of a new generation of cities, including Pittsburgh, Buffalo, Chicago, and St. Louis. They also settled almost exclusively in the North, in large part because the Southern slave economy offered few opportunities for unskilled, poor white laborers.

WHEN IRISH EYES ARE CRYING

So, where did all of this resentment for Irish folk come from? As with other immigrant groups, highly visible negative behaviors were exaggerated and combined with more fanciful fears to create a repulsive Irish stereotype. Some immigrants—especially young Irishmen—stood out for their unkempt appearance and rampant alcohol abuse, which resulted in public brawls, particularly after the emergence of Irish street gangs such as the 40 Thieves and the Roach Guards in the 1820s. Spurred by the miserable conditions, children of large immigrant families were often forced into panhandling or thievery, and young women turned to prostitution. The desperation shows in the numbers: in the 1840s, the notorious Five Points neighborhood of Manhattan contained 17 brothels and too many saloons to count. Just how bad was it? A Five Points tenement and flophouse for homeless Irish and African-Americans, known as the Old Brewery, was said to have witnessed a murder every night for 15 years from 1837 to 1852, when the Ladies' Home Mission Society finally bought the building and razed it.

> I do think I saw more drunken folks, men and women, that day than I ever saw before ... I would rather risk myself in an Indian fight than venture among these creatures after night.
>
> —Davy Crockett, on Irish immigrants in Five Points, 1834

The destitute Irish immigrants inspired an unprecedented wave of revulsion. According to official records, Irish immigrants were routinely classified as "colored," and caricatures in newspapers highlighted the supposed resemblance between Irish, Africans, and monkeys. In the popular imagination, the Irish were subhuman—filthy, congenitally stupid drunks who incited riots and wanted to turn America into a Catholic country ruled by the Pope. For a country where many equated religious freedom with Protestantism, this was a terrifying thought, especially because by

1850 there were 3.1 million Catholics living in the United States. Fear of "Papist" subversion fueled the anti-immigrant "Nativist" movement, which aimed to defend the "purity" of "Native Americans" (meaning Anglo-Saxon Protestants, not to be confused with *native* Native Americans) from "foreign pollution."

> There are several kinds of power working at the fabric of the republic—water-power, steam-power and Irish-power. The last works hardest of all.
>
> —U.S. newspaper, 1826

Anti-Irish violence flared up repeatedly in nineteenth-century America. Philadelphia was rocked by anti-Irish riots in 1844, after rabble-rousers spread rumors that Irish Catholics planned to remove copies of the Bible from public schools. A series of street battles in May between armed mobs left four Nativists and ten Irish dead; two Catholic churches and a number of associated buildings were also burned. In July, another Nativist mob gathered after learning Catholics had stockpiled weapons in a local church—ironically, in case it was attacked. When government troops arrived with cannons to disperse them, the Nativists brought their own cannons and began pelting the soldiers with stones. A pitched battle followed, leaving 19 dead. Amazingly, or perhaps not, grand juries blamed the Catholics for "inciting" these outbursts.

The Nativist movement also produced some popular but short-lived political parties that employed gangs to intimidate their rivals. Founded in 1843, the American Republican Party grew more radical under the influence of an anti-Catholic secret society, the Order of the Star-Spangled Banner. Soon, the party became better known by its nickname, the "Know-Nothings," stemming from the answer members gave when asked about their secret meetings. But after sweeping into power in local elections in 1855 in Chicago and Boston—both cities with large Irish populations—the Know-Nothings rapidly faded from the scene.

In 1856 the American Know-Nothing Party nominated former Whig President Millard Fillmore—who had been president during 1850–1853, after the death of Zachary Taylor—as its presidential candidate. He only earned eight electoral votes, behind Republican candidate John C. Fremont and Democratic winner James Buchanan.

Meanwhile, the Irish slowly worked their way up the social and political ladder. In New York the Irish gradually assumed control of the deeply corrupt Tammany Hall political machine, beginning in the 1830s. Reaching out to German, Jewish, and Italian immigrants, the Tammany politicians handed out crooked city contracts and public jobs (especially with the police) and arranged for the mass naturalization of immigrants, who then became voters. They also stood up for tenants against greedy landlords and helped workers organize unions. Just how corrupt were they? The most famous leader of the Tammany machine, Boss William M. Tweed is believed to have stolen about $200 million from New York City—the equivalent of $8 billion today.

············· **WHERE MY GODS AT** ·····················

Don't Hate Us Because We're Bountiful

Nowadays most people associate Mormons with Utah, but Utah was actually the last resort for the leaders of the Church of Jesus Christ of Latter-Day Saints. So what compelled them to make their home in the middle of a desert? Relentless persecution and attempted genocide, naturally.

From the beginning, the Church was viewed as a little, well, peculiar. Its founder, Joseph Smith Jr., was the son of a poor, semiliterate eccentric who moved his family 10 times in 19 years, drifting from Vermont to western upstate New York. Like his father, Smith was an amateur treasure hunter, who believed certain stones possessed magical powers for locating buried valuables. Meanwhile, his epileptic mother took him to intense religious revivals and shared her frequent visions. In 1819, at the age of 14, God the Father and Jesus Christ began speaking to Joseph Jr. as well.

The two sides of Smith's life came together in September 1823, when he told friends and family that an angel named Moroni had visited him and described a spot on a nearby hill where a buried box held mystical golden tablets. Smith said these tablets contained lost Christian scriptures, written by Moroni and his father Mormon around 400 CE, telling of a hitherto-unknown journey by Jesus Christ to the Americas. According to Smith, who dictated his translation of these tablets to followers, Jesus preached the gospel to native civilizations, which converted to Christianity.

The first round of persecution came when Smith refused to show the golden tablets to acquaintances who, having helped him on earlier treasure-hunting expeditions, now wanted part of his find as their own. Smith escaped by moving to his wife Emma's hometown in Pennsylvania in 1827, where he dictated the Book of Mormon to a schoolteacher named Oliver Cowdery. Their strange, secretive behavior attracted hostile attention from neighbors, prompting Smith to move back to upstate New York, where he and Cowdery finished their transcriptions. Smith was fated to follow this pattern for the rest of his short life, chased from place to place by neighbors suspicious of his unusual beliefs.

MR. AND MRS. SMITH (AND MRS. SMITH, AND MRS. SMITH)

By contemporary standards, Smith's beliefs were indeed pretty strange. For starters, Smith said the Book of Mormon "added to" and "confirmed" the New Testament, offending Protestants and Catholics alike with the implication that the Bible was somehow incomplete. Smith's stories of long-lost native civilizations seemed like outlandish fabrications, and the secrecy surrounding his revelations led many to label him a swindler and huckster. His view of the afterlife—in which every "saved" Mormon man will receive his own planet to populate with his progeny—and his later belief that dead people could be baptized posthumously were also considered sacrilegious.

But without question the deal breaker was polygamy. Smith secretly taught the elite inner circle that more children gave them more power in the afterlife. According to one count, he married 33 women himself, and before long, the practice spread to followers. In addition to going against Christian beliefs, polygamy also ran counter to the emerging Victorian romantic ideal, in which the wife submitted to her husband's authority, while he submitted to her moral guidance. Multiple wives would have less influence, since the man could withdraw his affections if one annoyed him. Despite that selling point, most men feared the rich and powerful would dominate the supply of marriageable women, while women feared that men would marry multiple wives as cheap labor, much as Southern plantation owners bought teams of slaves.

> I think no more of taking another wife than I do of buying a cow.
>
> —Heber C. Kimball,
> one of Smith's Twelve Apostles, 1857

Although the United States promised freedom of religion, it was hard to imagine a new, contradictory religion suddenly emerging and gaining followers. But the opening of the frontier and the incipient Industrial Revolution led to unprecedented mobility and economic upheaval, leaving people feeling disconnected and disoriented. These conditions triggered the Second Great Awakening, a huge religious revival, in the 1820s–1830s. In this context Smith's unusual ideas proved attractive to some people—especially spiritual individuals who found traditional Protestant sects unsatisfying. After Smith formally founded the Church in April 1830, his charismatic leadership attracted about 100 followers who gathered in upstate New York to be near him.

However, this growing community of spiritual seekers didn't get along with their more traditional Christian neighbors. Local newspapers condemned Mormonism as "extravagant delusion" and "abominable . . . blasphemy," with doctrines based on "ignorance and superstition." Smith himself was called "a real, unprincipled, villainous impostor."

In the face of this hostility, Smith led his followers on what turned out to be a circuitous path across the country, running from one angry mob after another and gaining thousands of converts along the way. They fled from New York to Kirtland, Ohio, to Independence, Missouri, where angry townspeople demanded Smith turn over his collection of four Egyptian mummies as repayment for debts, and where the state's governor issued the infamous "Extermination Order," which called for the citizens of Missouri to kill any Mormons they found. Most escaped to Illinois, thanks to the leadership of Brigham Young, Smith's energetic lieutenant, and settled on a swampy stretch of the Mississippi River in Illinois, which Smith optimistically named Nauvoo, an arcane Hebrew word meaning "beautiful." And aside from a couple of malaria epidemics, things went well enough at first . . . but in 1842 the trouble started again.

In Illinois more male church members began taking multiple wives, scandalizing non-Mormons. On top of all this, Smith's behavior was becoming increasingly erratic and grandiose: he declared his candidacy for president while also proclaiming himself king of the Kingdom of God. The last straw came when Smith proposed marriage to the wives of senior Mormons, turning their husbands against him.

In June of 1844, Smith tried to stifle growing dissent within the Church by destroying the printing press of a newspaper started by the ex-Mormon leaders. The move enraged non-Mormon neighbors, who saw the self-proclaimed "king" trampling on the First Amendment. Once again, angry mobs besieged the Mormons, and the governor of Illinois demanded that Smith give himself up and stand trial. On June 25, 1844, Smith agreed. Two days later an angry mob broke into the jail in Carthage, Illinois, and shot Smith to death.

Brigham Young, the new leader of the Church, now began planning what was in effect a Mormon exodus. From 1846 to 1852, Young organized the emigration of about 15,000 believers from Illinois to the Valley of the Great Salt Lake in what is now Utah. Along the way the Mormons cleared trails, built bridges, and established ferry services that were later used by non-Mormon pioneers. With new farms irrigated by mountain streams, the population of the valley swelled from 147 in 1847 to 40,000 in 1860. Salt Lake City became one of the main stopovers for pioneers headed to the Pacific coast, and in 1848 the Mexican-American War brought most of the West, including the Mormon territory, into the possession of the United States. The Mormons—who had always wanted to live peacefully alongside other Americans—were delighted. After all of that trouble, America came to them!

STATES OF DENIAL

The state of Utah, admitted to the Union in 1891, is just a fraction of the original proposed Mormon state covering three times Utah's territory: Deseret, which actually existed for two years from 1849–1851. Deseret (the word for "Honeybee" in the Book of Moroni, symbolizing hard work) covered the entire "Great Basin" between the Rocky Mountains and the Sierra Nevada range, including Utah and Nevada, most of Arizona, the eastern half of California, southern Oregon, and large chunks of Wyoming, Colorado, and New Mexico. This ambitious plan actually got some traction in Washington, D.C., and in 1849, President Zachary Taylor sent an emissary west with a proposal to combine Deseret and California into a single state. The plan came to nothing, and the promise of territorial status and eventual statehood spelled the end for Deseret: to gain federal recognition, the Mormon government voted to dissolve Deseret in 1851. However Deseret's General Assembly continued meeting as a kind of "ghost" government until 1872.

But Deseret isn't the only "almost state" in America's past:

The State of Franklin: In 1784, to pay off its Revolutionary War debt North Carolina's legislature voted, without consulting the inhabitants, to hand over the state's eight westernmost counties to the federal government. When finicky legislators decided to "re-annex" the territory just a few months later, the disgruntled settlers of the 45,000-square-mile area— many of them Revolutionary War veterans—voted to secede. Plan A was to gain admission to the Union as the new state of Franklin, but they missed statehood by two votes in Congress. Unfortunately there wasn't really a Plan B, so the territory entered administrative limbo. Nonetheless, the Franklinites proclaimed Greeneville the capital, wrote a constitution, elected a house of representatives and a governor, and established courts. But the area was poor (government officials were paid in deer hides) and Franklin's tiny militia couldn't protect it from native tribes. In 1790 Franklin agreed to become part of Tennessee, whose first governor was John Sevier—former governor of Franklin.

Republic of Madawaska: Literally a husband-and-wife operation, the Republic of Madawaska resulted from the fuzzy U.S.–Canada border after the American Revolution. In 1825 an American settler, John Baker, petitioned for his area of New Brunswick to become part of Maine and the United States; his wife Sophie Rice (later the "vice-president of the Republic") sewed an "American" flag which they flew on July 4, 1827. But Maine's legislature dragged its feet replying to Baker, who was considered a nuisance, so in August Baker and 14 other settlers declared themselves the Republic of Madawaska, a.k.a. American Aroostook. Great Britain, which still claimed the territory, arrested and jailed Baker for sedition; they also took Sophie's flag, which she promptly replaced. Ludicrous though it was, the incident touched a raw, patriotic nerve in the United States. Maine encouraged the Madawaskans to claim about 4,300 square miles of Canadian land for their "Republic," causing considerable alarm in Ottawa and Washington, D.C. After the Aroostook War (casualty: one pig), the U.S. and Britain divided the Republic of Madawaska in two. A version of Sophie's flag still flies over the city hall of Edmundston, New Brunswick, and the mayor of Edmundston also holds the title of "President of the Republic of Madawaska."

·········· **OTHER PEOPLE'S STUFF** ····················

So Long, and Thanks for All the States

In 1840 the United States measured just under 1.7 million square miles, making it five times the size of the Austrian Empire, then the largest state in Europe. By the end of the decade, it had grown to 2.9 million square miles, bigger than all of Europe. How did the young nation manage to add 1.2 million square miles, containing untold treasures in minerals, timber, and arable land, in just ten years? Well, it's a safe bet no one gave it to them.

Of all the countries in history that have been robbed, Mexico was neither the most nor least deserving. On one hand, it had been the legitimate, acknowledged owner of the western part of North America all the way up to Oregon and Colorado since 1540, when the conquistador Francisco Vazquez de Coronado first claimed the area for Spain. On the other hand, Mexico never really "did" anything with the place. In 1821 the entire Mexican population of Alta California—a vast region incorporating modern-day California, Nevada, and most of Arizona and Utah—was just 3,270, while Texas held just 2,500, with few if any "Anglos" in either territory. By 1836 there were about 30,000 Anglos in Texas versus 3,500 Mexicans. In California, by 1850 there were 60,000 Anglos versus about 7,000 Mexicans (along with about 1,000 African-Americans and 22,000 foreign immigrants).

But all of this is beside the point: America was going to take the land either way, because it was Manifest Destiny. Texas had been easy: the Texans did all the fighting in the Texan War of Independence, 1835–1836, and then voted to join the United States in 1845. But President James Polk wanted more. The Mexican-American War of 1846–1848 was supposedly about Texas, but in reality it was a gambit to pluck California and additional territory. In 1845, before the war even started, Polk dispatched a paramilitary unit led by John Fremont to infiltrate California from the east and a U.S. naval squadron to take the Pacific ports from the west. Californians formed their own state, the "Bear Flag Republic," and entered the Union as a free state in 1850.

YOU COULD SEE RUSSIA FROM YOUR HOUSE

Fort Ross, located about 90 miles north of San Francisco, marked the southernmost limit of Russian territory in North America. It was founded in 1812 by the Russian-American Company as an agricultural colony to feed Russian fur trappers in Alaska. With a population of 250 at its peak, Fort Ross was actually the central hub for a number of even smaller outposts as far south as Bodega Bay and the Farallon Islands, located 40 miles north and 18 miles west of San Francisco, respectively. The Russians dismantled the colony in 1841. But Mexico was still worried about the threat of Russian expansion into their land, so they invited Anglo-American settlers to California as a buffer against Russian expansion from Alaska. The Mexican government also considered inviting Chinese colonists and Irish famine refugees to California.

★ *Taxonomists still disagree on the identification of the now-extinct California grizzly—the bear depicted on the flag of California—as a unique species.*

THE LITTLE DOCTRINE THAT COULD

In 1823 President James Monroe probably never expected his little doctrine would become such a long-lasting or important part of American foreign policy—and world history. Following successful wars of independence in South America and Mexico, the Monroe Doctrine stated that the United States wouldn't permit European powers (Spain and France, this means you!) to reacquire territory in the New World—posing as the protective older sibling of the new Latin American republics. It was all bluff: the adolescent United States had just demonstrated in the War of 1812 that it was mostly no match for much larger European militaries outside its own borders (or inside them, for that matter). But the Monroe Doctrine proved surprisingly effective, even when America was still shrimpy, because it had the tacit support of Britain, which had a Royal Navy to actually enforce its will. Of course, the Monroe Doctrine wasn't quite as idealistic as it seemed: as soon as the United States was powerful enough, it stole a big chunk of Mexico for itself, and has made a habit of intervening in Latin America up to the present day.

In truth, Mexico was lucky it didn't lose more. Congressional East Coast Democrats wanted to annex the entire country, and Polk himself proposed annexing the less-populated northern territories down to the port of Tampico on the Gulf of Mexico. But the move was blocked by John C. Calhoun and Southern Democrats, who opposed extending America's borders to include Mexicans on racial grounds.

The long-term effects of the Mexican War are incalculable, but we'll give it a shot: Mexico lost 525,000 square miles of land to the United States, representing over half its total territory. As a result, it became even more committed to preserving the rest. The sense of victimization by the United States united Mexico's native peasants with its white and Creole elite, who closed ranks against the Anglo invaders from the north. On the American side, in addition to giant new territories for settlement, the war gave the United States a foothold on the Pacific, opening vast Asian markets to American trade—but it also aggravated the disagreement about slavery as new states lined up to join the Union.

Repatriate Games

As tension over slavery simmered, the growing number of freedmen—former slaves who earned enough to buy their freedom or were "manumitted" by kindly owners—became a highly visible reminder of the issue that America was resolutely ignoring. In the

South, slave owners were alarmed by the presence of freedmen, fearing they would encourage resistance or rebellion among the population that remained enslaved. In the North, even progressive whites still held racist views, and many doubted that whites and freedmen could live together in peace. In a rare moment of harmony, some Northerners and Southerners agreed on a plan: persuading the freedmen to "repatriate" to Africa.

While this plan was (sort of) well-intentioned, in retrospect it was pretty disgraceful. Basically, the sentiment was: "We appreciate all your hard work, but we changed our minds, so pack your bags! You're going back to your own country, or at least, somewhere on the same continent."

With this goal in mind, in 1816 a university teacher named Robert Finley founded the American Colonization Society (ACS), which raised money to send freedmen, along with a small amount of start-up capital, back to Africa. In 1820 the first ship sailed from New York City to Sierra Leone and then headed south to lay claim to a stretch of forbidding jungle inhabited by unfriendly native tribes. In less than a month, yellow fever claimed the lives of one quarter of the 88 freedmen, along with the three white ACS officials who accompanied the expedition.

However, over the next few years the settlement, christened "Liberia," was reinforced by hundreds more settlers, and in 1822 they founded the capital city of Monrovia, named in honor of President James Monroe. The early colonists accomplished a great deal, surviving disease, establishing farms, fighting off native attacks, and ending the slave trade from that region. By 1828, roughly 1,200 immigrants had settled in Liberia, including many sent from British and French colonies in the Caribbean. By 1838, there were 2,638 African-American settlers living in several small towns along the coast.

Ironically, the African-American settlers in Liberia treated the native Africans just as badly as the European colonialists did. Ultimately, the "Americo-Liberians" pushed the borders of their colony north and south to include 600 miles of African coastline and then ventured into the densely forested interior, where they clashed with hostile native tribes. Taking the natives' land with deceptive treaties, forbidding the use of alcohol, turning tribes against each other—it's hard to imagine why the Americo-Liberians weren't welcome. To this day, Liberian society is divided into two classes: people belonging to the native African tribes, who tend to be economically exploited and excluded from political power, and the wealthy elite, made up of descendants of the Americo-Liberian settlers.

Fashion to the Max

If you're into giant dresses, hats the size of hula hoops, and balloons on your biceps, the Romantic Era was the time for you. Taking a cue from London and Paris, between 1825 and 1845, American women of the middle and upper classes turned their backs on the slim, diaphanous styles of the previous decades in favor of a big new look.

> ★ *The invention of photography in the mid-nineteenth century led to more exacting standards in art and fashion, since near-perfect images could be widely produced.*

At the center of the Romantic style was a new silhouette, which widened the hem so that dresses became bell-shaped, with the bottom spanning three or four feet. And to support this considerable circumference, dresses were reinforced with horsehair and extra padding, especially (ahem) toward the rear. In fact, women had to wear up to a dozen starched cotton petticoats just to fill out the skirts. Capacious "beret" sleeves were accentuated with masses of lace and ruffles around the shoulders; as styles approached cartoon-like proportions, eventually the sleeves too had to be supported with whalebone stays or leather padding. Meanwhile, the waist of the dress was much lower than its neo-Classical predecessor, allowing the voluminous lower half of the dress to blossom out from a narrow waistline. And we do mean narrow: after a couple decades of relative freedom in the neo-Classical period, the "natural" waist of the Romantic period meant women once again had to wear constricting corsets to achieve the desired shape.

> Heaven save the ladies, how they dress! We have seen more colours in these ten minutes, than we should have seen elsewhere, in as many days. What various parasols! what rainbow silks and satins! what pinking of thin stockings, and pinching of thin shoes, and fluttering of ribbons and silk tassels, and display of rich cloaks with gaudy hoods and linings!
>
> —Charles Dickens, on the women of New York City, 1842

The sleeves and skirts weren't the only items expanding: the fairly compact turbans and bonnets from the turn of the century were replaced by hats of prodigious width, ornamented with ribbons, bows, baubles, feathers, flowers, and palm fronds until they looked like small topiaries.

Although colors became more muted as the Romantic period went on, in the first half of the nineteenth century, dresses could be quite distracting—with floral and geometric patterns embroidered in silk or velvet. These fashions might sound over-the-top nowadays, but if you think of them in all white, you'll recognize an outfit that's still with us today: the archetypal wedding dress, which became standard after Queen Victoria wore it to her wedding in 1840.

THE END OF ROMANCE

At the end of this period, bold, practical women, fed up with the sheer enormity of Romantic fashions, began wearing "bloomers"—large, billowy pantaloons—doing away with the need for petticoats. Although they were considered scandalous by some, bloomers were actually based on styles borrowed from the Ottoman Turks, giving them an exotic (and therefore more respectable) lineage.

Book Learnin'

As American literature blossomed in the first half of the nineteenth century, plenty of citizens were unable to appreciate the country's literary accomplishments. In 1800 about 33 percent of white American men and women couldn't read. In the Northern states, about 25 percent of the white population was totally illiterate, compared with 40 percent in the Southern states. This regional difference was attributable in part to the mostly rural character of Southern society, which tended to be poorer and geographically dispersed, making it difficult to establish primary schools; poor farmers also relied on their children as an important source of labor. In the North, literacy rates were aided by the high population density in New England and its tradition of primary schooling since Puritan times (only to read the Bible, of course).

As more primary schools were established, especially in the North, literacy increased significantly, but a large part of the population remained functionally illiterate (meaning they might be able to read simple text but couldn't write). By 1840, the functional illiteracy rate for white Americans was about 13 percent—still not great, but a major improvement from 1800.

> **Almost one-quarter of the men applying for marriage licenses were unable to write their names.**
>
> —Virginia Governor David Campbell,
> on Virginia literacy, 1839

Reflecting the social hierarchy of the time, literacy rates were especially low among women and African-Americans (both slaves and freedmen). In 1840 white women were almost twice as likely to be illiterate as men in both the North and South. Among African-Americans, anti-literacy laws actually forbade white masters to teach their slaves to read. In 1860, W.E.B. DuBois estimated that only about 5 percent of the African-American slave population had any degree of literacy. Counting everybody—white, black, male, female, free, enslaved—one-quarter of the American population was completely illiterate in 1840.

QUICK LIT

After two centuries following the English example in all things writerly, American literature exploded (in a good way) in the first half of the nineteenth century. There are so many deservedly famous authors in this period there's no way to do justice to them all, but here's a cheat sheet to three of the best:

Ralph Waldo Emerson (1803–1882): The seed of literacy was planted in New England, and one of its most impressive flowers was Ralph Waldo Emerson, who founded "transcendentalism." A profound genius with an intensely private character, Emerson was outspoken in his support of the individual's right to be him- or herself. In an 1837 address at Harvard called "The American Scholar," he called for a completely new, open, and objective approach to the world; some called the speech "The American Intellectual Declaration of Independence."

Nathaniel Hawthorne (1804–1864): A descendant of Puritan New Englanders, Hawthorne had a melancholy sensibility that resonated with the deep forests and often grim history of the region. Considered a leader of the literary movement called Dark Romanticism, his most famous work by far is the *Scarlet Letter,* published in 1850, which tells a story of illicit love, martyrdom, and redemption in Puritan times. The protagonist, Hester Prynne, is seduced by the town's minister, Arthur Dimmesdale, when her husband is lost at sea, and her transgression is revealed to all when she bears his child. As punishment, Prynne is forced to wear a red "A," for adulterer, for the rest of her life. Nonetheless, she refuses to betray Dimmesdale, who bears his guilt in anguished silence—but there's a twist (no, we're not going to tell you what it is).

Herman Melville (1819–1891): Considered by some to be the greatest author in American history, Melville's life was fully as adventurous as his novels. As a young man, he went to sea several times when sailing ships still ruled the waves. In 1841 he joined the crew of an American whaling ship, sailed around the world, deserted in Polynesia, and lived for a time among people reputed to be cannibals. His famous novel, *Moby Dick*, published in 1851, drew on his experiences in telling the story of Captain Ahab, who circles the globe obsessively searching for a mysterious white sperm whale that had ripped off one of his legs. High school English classes have been giggling at the word "sperm" ever since.

Libation Nation

Americans didn't invent the practice of habitually drinking far too much, but they did come up with the idea of alcoholism as a disease process: in 1784 Benjamin Rush, a Philadelphia physician (and signer of the Declaration of Independence) wrote a short treatise with a typically lengthy name, "An Inquiry into the Effects of Ardent Spirits upon the Human Body and Mind, with an Account of the Means of Preventing, and of the Remedies for Curing Them." A perceived rise in the level of drunkenness after the Revolution spurred renewed interest in Rush's work and led eventually to the founding of "Temperance Societies" beginning in 1789.

The most popular drink in the nineteenth century was whiskey—an "all-American" liquor borrowed from Scotland and Ireland which replaced rum during the British blockades in the American Revolution and War of 1812. So how much alcohol did Americans actually consume? Reliable figures are scarce, but in 1790 the people of the United States consumed three gallons of hard liquor for every man, woman, and child (they didn't even bother counting how much beer and wine was consumed). That equals about 750 shots per person per year. By 1830 per capita consumption had grown to five gallons, about 1,250 shots per year. When you factor out (most) women and children, who tended to drink less, it would appear that in 1830 5.5 million American males over the age of 10, of all races, drank an average eight shots per day!

The Rail World, Season I

After the War of 1812, the United States was transformed by a
revolutionary new form of transportation imported from Britain. In addition to allowing individuals more mobility than ever
before, railroads were tools of industry, linking resources, factories, products, and people at incredibly low cost.

Railroads were actually part of a larger transportation revolution that swept America from 1815 to 1850. They were preceded by
a network of canals linking rivers, lakes, and bays, including the
famous Erie Canal, the Chesapeake & Ohio, and the Ohio & Erie.
Like railroads, canals enabled individual mobility, the shipment
of agricultural goods, and increased industrial production—just at
lower speeds. Although railroads eventually replaced canals in the
second half of the nineteenth century, throughout the first half
they often worked together.

The first successful American railroad was the Delaware & Hudson, launched in 1829, which carried coal from mines in northeast

Keeping Tracks
U.S. Railroads 1835–1850

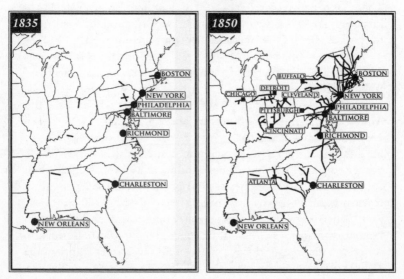

Pennsylvania to a nearby canal for shipment to urban markets. The second successful railroad, the Baltimore & Ohio, opened for business in 1830 and connected Baltimore, Maryland, to the Ohio River at Wheeling, Virginia (later West Virginia). The B&O—yes, of Monopoly fame—carried coal from western Virginia to industrializing Northeastern cities via Baltimore and carried finished goods in the opposite direction to the growing populations in Ohio and the other Midwestern states. In 1832 another railroad, the Camden & Amboy, provided a transit corridor running up the center of New Jersey, helping connect New York to Philadelphia and Baltimore.

Railroads followed America's volatile industrializing economy, including relatively slow growth following big busts like the Panic of 1837, followed by the Depression of 1838–1843 (resulting from rampant Western land speculation and bank failures). But even during the worst years, the U.S. railroad network expanded, jumping from under 30 miles in 1830 to over 9,000 miles in 1850.

The expanding canal and railroad networks not only allowed the settlement of vast new agricultural areas in the American Midwest—they also spurred the growth of a new generation of cities that served as collection and distribution hubs and soon rivaled the old colonial port cities in wealth and population. By 1850 Chicago (incorporated in 1833) had a population of 30,000, while Buffalo (incorporated in 1832) grew to 42,000. The transportation boom, industrialization, and the rise of new cities were concentrated in the Northeast and Midwest. The South experienced the same trends but on a smaller scale: for example, Atlanta (founded in 1837 to collect and ship cotton to Charleston and Savannah by rail) had only grown to 2,500 by 1850.

·················· **MADE IN AMERICA** ··················

Speedy Boats

Americans have always had a connection to boats—everyone arrived on them, after all—and the first half of the nineteenth century was a golden age of American seafaring, when U.S. shipyards revolutionized international commerce with a new kind of sailing ship: the super-fast clipper.

> ★ *The term "clipper" probably comes from the colloquial term for a fast horse, which could "go at a good clip."*

The first ships to go by this name were Baltimore clippers—small, fast schooners that weren't ideal for traveling the open ocean but sailed the Chesapeake Bay before the American Revolution and later served as privateers raiding British commerce during the War of 1812. But the classic ship was the bigger Yankee clipper, distinguished by multiple masts with large square sails, giving it an enormous surface area of canvas to catch the wind, paired with a slender, narrow hull with a "forward-raking" bow—a ship designed for maximum speed. The most famous builder of Yankee clippers was Donald McKay, who owned a shipyard in East Boston that turned out some of the best-known ships, including the *Flying Cloud, Bald Eagle, Great Republic, Lightning, Champion of the Seas*, and *Sovereign of the Seas*—the fastest sailing ship ever built up to that point, with a record speed of 25.5 miles per hour in 1854.

With a limited amount of room in their slender holds, clipper ships came to dominate passenger traffic and shipping for high-value cargoes like mail, tea, and spices; freight rates were simply too expensive for more mundane goods like timber, coal, or cotton. After the California Gold Rush began in 1849, these ships played a crucial role in the settling of the West Coast, carrying gold-hungry American and immigrant prospectors from East Coast ports all the way around South America to the land of golden opportunity. Thanks to clippers like the *Flying Cloud,* it now took less than 90 days to make a 16,000-mile journey that previously took sailing ships 200 days.

During the 1830s–1840s, American-made clipper ships were sought after by merchants of every nation, as embarrassed British shipbuilders found themselves outclassed by their upstart Yankee cousins. Eventually the Brits caught up, building world-class clippers of their own in the 1850s—but by this time, the sun was already setting on the age of sail, thanks to the arrival of cheaper (and far less romantic) oceangoing steamships.

Red, White, and Baseball

While its popularity has waned somewhat in recent decades, baseball still carries the cachet of the all-American pastime—a thoroughly patriotic sport. But much like most other sports, it's based on older games that were revised and juiced up by Americans in the early nineteenth century.

Baseball was probably derived from a ball game played in Irish towns and villages since the fifteenth century, called "rounders." By the eighteenth century, rounders incorporated many of the basic elements of modern baseball: two opposing teams face off, with one in the field and one "at bat," and successive batters try to hit a small ball and then make the "round" of four bases to score. Three strikes and you're out!

During the 1820s–1850s, Irish immigrants brought rounders with them to the New World, where local variations developed in cities with big Irish populations. In one variant, the Massachusetts game, the batter started out standing halfway between home plate and first base, and the opposing team could "out" someone by throwing the ball at them (ouch!)—but runners weren't required to stay on the baselines, meaning there was an element of "tag" in the game. Another variant, the Philadelphia game, incorporated the familiar diamond-shaped field and decreed nine players to a team.

However, it was the New York game that prevailed, as codified in the "Knickerbocker Rules" drawn up by Alexander Cartwright, a volunteer firefighter who founded the Knickerbocker Baseball Club, an amateur sports league for New York fire brigades. In 1845 the club decided to standardize the rules of New York's local "town game," giving the task to Cartwright and a committee of club members. The Knickerbocker Rules decreed nine innings and said any "knock" outside the lines of first and third base was a "foul ball." In 1858 they added a "strike zone," where a pitch would be counted as a strike even if the batter didn't swing, to prevent batters from simply waiting for an easy pitch. To prevent pitchers from throwing wide, in 1863 they added the "ball" rule, in which the batter gets an automatic "walk" to first base after four bad pitches, or balls.

Some elements of the New York game would still be unfamiliar to modern baseball fans. For several decades after 1845, the Knickerbocker Rules required underhand pitching. Until 1865, Knickerbocker Rules also allowed fielders to "out" the batter by catching the ball after one bounce—mostly out of concern for safety, since the game was still played without gloves or other protective gear.

Dancing Shoes

Tap-dancing and its cousins jazz dancing and "stepping" para-diddled into existence thanks to William Henry Lane, also known as "Master Juba," an African-American dancer who dominated the scene in the 1840s. Born to a free African-American couple in Providence, Rhode Island in 1825, at some time in his childhood he moved to the Five Points neighborhood of New

York City. Here the 5'3", light-skinned teenager learned to dance the jigs and reels of poor Irish immigrants—melding their precise footwork with African traditions.

In 1841 he hooked up with P.T. Barnum, the promoter and unapologetic swindler, who employed the 16-year-old Juba as an impostor for John Diamond, a white dancer in blackface who left Barnum's employment under a cloud. In time the deceit was revealed, but by then Juba was a star in his own right. His original dancing style, a forerunner of modern tap dance, quickly became the most popular part of the show. In 1842 he put on a show in a Five Points saloon for the visiting British author Charles Dickens.

> Single shuffle, double shuffle, and cross cut: snapping his fingers, rolling his eyes, turning in his knees, presenting the back of his legs in front, spinning about on his toes and heels ... dancing with two left legs, two right legs, two wooden legs, two wire legs, two spring legs — all sorts of legs and no legs.
>
> —Charles Dickens, 1842

In 1848 Juba toured Britain and was invited to perform for Queen Victoria at Buckingham Palace, the highpoint of his career. Tragically, despite his great success he never made that much money, and the combination of poverty and a physically exhausting schedule seems to have worn out his body by 1852. He was 27 years old.

·················· **BY THE NUMBERS** ·····················

6,184,477 free white population of Southern states, 1850

3,200,364 slave population of Southern states, 1850

1,920,218 number of white citizens these slaves "equaled" under the Three-Fifths Compromise

13,244,708 free white population of Northern and Western states, 1850

70,300 voters electing each Southern member of the House of Representatives, 1850

98,110 voters electing each Northern member of the House of Representatives, 1850

60,000 foreign-born (immigrant) population of the United States, 1820

2.25 million foreign-born (immigrant) population of the United States, 1850

200 number of major gang wars in New York City, 1834–1844

22 number of people killed in riots caused by fans of two rival actors at Astor Place in New York City, 1849

11,000 number of prostitutes in New York City, 1839

50,000 number of prostitutes in New York City, 1850

20,000 number of Irish who died aboard ships traveling from Britain to Canada, 1847

78 bushels of wheat shipped east by Chicago in 1838

2,000,000 bushels of wheat shipped east by Chicago in 1848

30–40 length, in days, of trip from St. Louis to New York City via the Ohio River, 1830

12–18 length, in days, of trip from St. Louis to New York City via Chicago and the Erie Canal, 1850

24 number of delegates at Wisconsin's constitutional convention in 1847 who were born in New England, out of a total 69

66 percent proportion of Chicago's adult male population that was foreign-born, 1850

$6.50 weekly earnings of a man working in a textile factory in 1850

$2.50–$3.50 weekly earnings of a woman working in a textile factory in 1850

$10.37 weekly cost of living for a family of five in New York City in 1850

13–15 age most children began working in factories in 1850

10 percentage of the white population in the North who were functionally illiterate in 1840

19 percentage of the white population in the South who were functionally illiterate in 1840

4

Time for Your Bloodbath

(1850–1880)

If you had to sum up the Civil War in one word, "bloodbath" wouldn't be a bad choice. Easily the most destructive war in U.S. history, the Civil War claimed the lives of 620,000 Americans and laid waste to large parts of the country. But as the central catastrophe of American history, it still inspires debate: could the North and South have worked out some kind of compromise? And could the South have won with a different strategy? (Basically, no.)

After the war ended in 1865, the North tried to "fix" the South by making Southern whites as angry as possible. Unsurprisingly it didn't turn out too well. The decade-long phase known as "Reconstruction" stalled in the face of Southern opposition. Embittered whites rolled back the reforms that had extended political and civil rights to freed slaves. Meanwhile, hard-core Confederate veterans formed new paramilitary organizations, including the Ku Klux Klan, to scare blacks into submission.

Once the war was over, expansion in North America resumed without missing a beat, as the period after the Civil War saw a rapid development of the Western frontier, including the inauguration of the first transcontinental railroad and the purchase of Alaska. Further afield, all eyes turned to Asia after a U.S. fleet under Commodore Mathew Perry "opened" Japan to the world in 1854.

On the home front, with slavery abolished, social reformers turned their crusading energy elsewhere, leading to the so-called Progressive Movement, which tried to improve American society through charitable efforts and government intervention. The Progressives had their work cut out for them, as America's breakneck development brought industrial slums to cities across the Northeast and Midwest. The postwar "Gilded Age" saw growing wealth but also increasing social inequality as America began shifting from a mostly rural and agrarian land to a dynamic, urban nation centered on teeming industrial metropolises.

September 4, 1850 The Compromise of 1850 allows settlers in Utah territory to decide by "popular sovereignty" whether slavery will be legal there, while admitting California as a free state.

August 24, 1853 George Crum invents the potato chip in Saratoga Springs, New York.

May 30, 1854 The Kansas-Nebraska Act allows settlers in the Kansas-Nebraska territory to decide by popular sovereignty whether slavery will be legal there.

1854 Republican Party is founded.

1854–1858 Pro- and anti-slavery settlers battle each other in "Bleeding Kansas."

July 12, 1856 William Walker seizes control of Nicaragua.

May 1, 1857 William Walker is deposed as president of Nicaragua.

1858 Abraham Lincoln runs for one of two U.S. Senate seats in Illinois on the Republican, anti-slavery ticket, but loses.

October 16–18, 1859 John Brown leads a doomed raid on the federal armory at Harper's Ferry, Virginia, in an attempt to start a slave uprising.

1860 Democratic party splits into Northern and Southern factions, running two candidates for president; Lincoln wins on the Republican ticket.

December 24, 1860 South Carolina secedes.

April 12, 1861 The Civil War begins.

1862 The North suffers multiple defeats but scores its first big victory at Antietam on September 17.

January 1, 1863 Lincoln issues the Emancipation Proclamation.

July 1–3, 1863 Meade defeats Lee at the Battle of Gettysburg; the tide turns against the Confederacy.

1864 Lincoln appoints Grant the supreme commander of Union forces; Sherman devastates Georgia, South Carolina, and North Carolina.

April 1865 The Confederacy surrenders on April 9; Lincoln is assassinated on April 14.

1866 Radical Republicans in Congress take control of Reconstruction; Confederate veterans found the Ku Klux Klan.

1868 Arkansas, Florida, North Carolina, South Carolina, Louisiana, and Alabama are readmitted to the Union.

1870 Virginia, Mississippi, Texas, and Georgia are readmitted to the Union.

·················· **LIES YOUR TEACHER TOLD YOU** ··············

LIE: *A compromise could have averted the Civil War.*
THE TRUTH: The politicians tried really, really hard, but there was just no way around the basic dispute over slavery, and disagreement over tariffs just added fuel to the fire.

Tackling the smaller issue first, the tariff argument came down to money. The Southern plantation system made certain families spectacularly wealthy, but it also committed the region to a relatively simple agrarian economy. The main issue with this, of course, was that the Southern exports—cotton, rice, tobacco, cotton, indigo, and cotton—were all agricultural commodities requiring mass cultivation to be profitable.

> ★ When the Civil War erupted in 1861, two U.S. states—Mississippi and South Carolina—were home to slave populations that outnumbered their free citizens.

As the demand for cotton increased, competition between Northern textile mills and their British counterparts drove up cotton prices. Meanwhile, Northerners in Congress continued to pursue protectionist policies to encourage industry, including tariffs on imports, hoping to give a boost to the factories in their region. Southern congressmen, on the other hand, opposed tariffs because they feared their British and French customers would respond by slapping counter-tariffs on Southern cotton exports.

> Shall we sink down as serfs to the heartless, speculative Yankees, swindled by his tariffs, robbed by his taxes, skinned by his railroad monopolies?
>
> —Democratic newspaper editor

And that's exactly what happened. In 1828 Northern congressmen passed a protectionist tariff (nicknamed the "Tariff of Abominations" by the South) so outrageous that the British responded with a counter-tariff of their own. The tariffs doubly affected the South, hurting cotton sales while making imports of manufactured goods more expensive. If the Northerners got their way, Southerners would have to sell cotton to Northern factories at low prices and buy expensive Northern manufactured goods; in other words, the South would be a Northern vassal, playing the same role India did for Britain. (Southerners, reaching for their rifles, naturally took exception.)

For all the bitter controversy, the tariff dispute could probably have been settled without violence. But at the same time, Southerners were worried about growing abolitionist sentiment in the North. True, in 1838 William Lloyd Garrison's American Anti-Slavery Society had only 250,000 members (about 2.7 percent of the Northern population), but they were committed and well-connected, with a disproportionate influence in Protestant churches. More importantly, their opposition to slavery was uncompromising. Southerners especially detested Northern whites and free blacks who gave refuge to runaway slaves, accusing them of abetting the theft of property. Adding insult to injury, some Northern states passed "personal liberty laws," which protected fugitive slaves by prohibiting local law enforcement from apprehending them. In response, slave owners began hiring bounty hunters, and the whole situation escalated. Before long, abolitionists were helping runaway slaves to escape to Canada, where slavery had been abolished since 1834.

	Northern extremists (including Republicans and abolitionists)	Moderates (including Northern "Peace" Democrats and pro-Union Southerners)	Southern extremists and sympathizers (including Northern "Copperheads")
Slavery is ...	A wicked sin that must be abolished at once, before Christ's return.	Maybe good, maybe bad, but definitely not worth getting killed for either way.	An inalienable right, sanctioned in the Bible and integral to Southern society.
Possible remedies include ...	Remedy? We said abolish it. And no, we won't pay for a buyout.	The government could spend billions to buy out slave owners, if anyone will pay.	Meddling Yankees could mind their own damn business.
Future expansion ...	Cannot include any new slave states, period.	Should adhere to the original 36°30' border between slave and free states agreed to in 1820.	Should include slave states above the 36°30' border, if voters choose to allow it.
Tariffs on imports ...	Are critical to encourage industry by protecting against British dumping.	Should probably be repealed or lowered to avoid provoking foreign counter-tariffs.	Are a Yankee industrialist plot to provoke foreign tariffs on cotton exports.
States' rights ...	Don't include the right to secede (and we won't allow slavery to spread).	Allow slavery in new states if the people vote for it, but not secession.	Allow slavery in new states AND secession.
Secession is ...	Treason.	A tragedy to be averted at all costs (and probably illegal).	A second American Revolution.

It's no exaggeration to say that *Uncle Tom's Cabin, Or, Life Among the Lowly,* published in 1852 by Harriet Beecher Stowe, was one of the main causes for the Civil War, because it built sympathy among Northern whites for blacks suffering in servitude. Stowe's story portrayed the sufferings of a kindly old slave, Uncle Tom, and his loved ones under the oppression of plantation owner Simon Legree. With an emphasis on Christian virtues like humility, charity, and forgiveness (Harriet was the daughter of noted preacher Lyman Beecher), the book was the most powerful literary expression of the abolitionist movement. Banned in the South, *Uncle Tom's Cabin* sold 300,000 copies in the North in 1852–1853 alone. That number is even more impressive when you consider that each copy was probably read by eight to ten people, meaning that over 10 percent of the total U.S. population read the book.

> So you're the little woman who wrote the book that made this great war!
>
> —Abraham Lincoln's supposed greeting
> to Harriet Beecher Stowe, 1862

Under the weight of the combined economic and social pressures, Southern members of Congress became determined to spread support for slavery to new states. In fact, the admissions of Florida and Texas (1845) to the United States were explicitly intended to "strengthen slavery" and with it, the South, by adding Southern senators. But Southern expansion stalled after Texas, as there was little prospect of the underpopulated Southwest or Indian Territory (Oklahoma) becoming states anytime soon. Meanwhile, the North ushered in the free states of Michigan (1837), Iowa (1846), Wisconsin (1848), and California (1850). Northern states were also generally more populous.

To catch up, the South needed access to territories north of the Missouri Compromise line. A new measure, the Compromise of 1850, gave the South new hope. In return for admitting California as a free state, even though half of it lay "below the line," Northern politicians agreed to let settlers in Utah vote for themselves whether slavery should be legal there. The compromise also strengthened federal fugitive-slave laws and left open the status of slavery in the New Mexico Territory.

COMPROMISE, COP-OUTS, AND CONFUSION:
YOUR CONGRESS AT WORK

Compromise	Compromisers	Issue and "resolution"
Three-Fifths Compromise (1787)	James Wilson, Roger Sherman	Northern and Southern delegates to the Constitutional Convention agreed to count each slave as three-fifths of a person in calculating proportional representation. Neither side was happy: Southerners still felt threatened by Northern population growth, and Northerners were angry that slaves were used to boost white Southern representation.
Missouri Compromise (1820)	Sen. Henry Clay, Rep. John Taylor, Sen. Jesse B. Thomas	Northern and Southern members of Congress agreed to 36°30' as the border between slave states and free states as the West was settled—except for Missouri, which was admitted as a slave state in 1820 along with Maine as a free state, for balance. Confused? So were they!
Democratic Convention (1844)	James Polk	As Texas sought admission as a slave state, Democrats were divided over slavery's long-term prospects. Polk promised to admit Texas but then step down after one term so the two sides could duke it out over new states.
Compromise of 1850	Sen. Stephen A. Douglas	With the dispute still simmering, the compromise proposed by Illinois Sen. Stephen A. Douglas allowed California to enter as a free state in exchange for opening territories above the 36°30' line (namely, Utah) to slavery, if voters supported it (they didn't).
Kansas-Nebraska Act (1854)	Sen. Stephen A. Douglas	This deal allowed settlers to decide whether Kansas and Nebraska would be slave or free states, even though they were above 36°30', because Northern businessmen wanted to build a transcontinental railroad there.

This measure soon made way for the Kansas-Nebraska Act of 1854, when Congress decreed that the new territories of Kansas and Nebraska could also determine the legality of slavery on their own, through a popular vote. Moderate Northern congressmen like Stephen A. Douglas, the Democratic senator from Illinois, forged these concessions in the Kansas-Nebraska Act because they wanted to build a transcontinental railroad through Kansas and Nebraska. Besides, what could possibly be wrong with referring the issue to a popular vote?

As it turns out, plenty. The "slavery debates" in Kansas often featured guns, knives, ropes, pitchforks, and fire. From 1854 to 1858, about 10,000 pro- and anti-slavery partisans battled fiercely to control the fate of "Bleeding Kansas." It wasn't long before high-profile officials got involved. David Rice Atchison, a Democratic senator from Missouri, led the pro-slavery invasion in 1855. Meanwhile John Brown—a devout Christian and anti-slavery fanatic—rode from Ohio to Kansas with his seven sons, recruiting radical anti-slavery fighters along the way. In May of 1856, Brown's militia murdered five unarmed pro-slavery settlers near Pottawatomie Creek in Franklin County, Kansas. Over four years Bleeding Kansas claimed about 200 lives.

> We are determined to repel this Northern invasion, and make Kansas a Slave State; though our rivers should be covered with the blood of their victims, and the carcasses of the Abolitionists should be so numerous in the territory as to breed disease and sickness, we will not be deterred from our purpose.
>
> —Benjamin F. Stringfellow, in the newspaper *Squatter Sovereign*, 1855

Bleeding Kansas eventually entered the Union as a free state— but this was only the beginning. On October 16, 1859, John Brown charged back into the national limelight in spectacularly crazy fashion with an implausible plan to start a slave rebellion in Virginia. With 22 followers, Brown staged a daring (and suicidal) raid on the federal armory at Harper's Ferry, now located in West Virginia, to obtain weapons for a rebel slave army that he really, really hoped would materialize to fight with him. It didn't. Unfortunately for Brown, the only crowds that surfaced were local militias, along with some spectators. The militias surrounded the arsenal and cut off all escape routes, and after a two-day siege, Marines led by U.S. Army Colonel Robert E. Lee assaulted the arsenal and killed 10 of Brown's followers. Five rebels escaped, but Brown was captured alive along with six of his followers. Over the next few months, all seven were convicted of treason and hanged.

ABRAHAM LINCOLN IN 90 SECONDS

Born in a log cabin in central Kentucky on February 12, 1809, Abraham Lincoln was a son of the early American frontier. In 1816 the family moved to neighboring Indiana, in part because Lincoln's father, Thomas, disapproved of slavery. In typical frontier fashion, his family relocated again to Illinois in 1830, where Lincoln got a job carrying goods on raft-like "flatboats" on local tributaries of the Mississippi River. Lincoln had less than two years of formal schooling but managed to teach himself about a wide range of subjects, and by 1837 he was practicing law in Springfield, Illinois.

Although he didn't hunt or fish, Lincoln was an accomplished outdoorsman, whose height and strength made him a formidable wrestler. This came in handy in his early political career: during his first, unsuccessful candidacy for the Illinois General Assembly in 1832, one of Lincoln's supporters was being harassed by a heckler at a rally—so Lincoln picked up the man by his collar and the back of his pants and literally threw him out of the meeting.

Lincoln didn't win that election, but he did get elected to the Assembly in 1834. In 1837 he stated his opposition to slavery for the first time, publicly voicing a long-held private belief. His first stint in national politics, as a congressman from Illinois, wasn't all that promising: an old-school Whig, he alienated his constituents by arguing that the Mexican War of 1848 was unconstitutional, and he didn't run for reelection.

Meanwhile his first love, Ann Rutledge, died of typhoid fever in 1835; following a rocky courtship and at least one canceled wedding, in 1841 Lincoln married Mary Todd, the daughter of a wealthy Kentucky slave owner. After giving up his seat in Congress, Lincoln focused on his legal practice (even arguing a case before the U.S. Supreme Court) and raising a family. But in 1854 he finally came out of political retirement to oppose the Kansas-Nebraska Act, which would extend slavery to new states.

That year he helped orchestrate an alliance with remnants of the Whig Party, dissenting Democrats, and various "Free Soil" groups to form the Republican Party. In 1858 Lincoln lost his bid for the Senate seat held by Illinois Democrat Stephen

A. Douglas, the author of the Kansas-Nebraska Act, but became famous for his brilliant oratory in their debates.

> A house divided against itself cannot stand. I believe this government cannot endure, permanently, half slave and half free. I do not expect the Union to be dissolved—I do not expect the house to fall—but I do expect it will cease to be divided.
>
> —Abraham Lincoln, 1858

Brown's ill-fated raid cast a pall over the presidential election of 1860, heightening Southern suspicions about Abraham Lincoln, the Republican candidate. Lincoln claimed that he only wanted to prevent slavery from spreading to new states, but Southerners were convinced that he wanted to eliminate slavery everywhere. During the campaign, Southern politicians and newspaper editors warned that the South would secede if Lincoln were elected—but Northern voters viewed these threats as bullying. In fact, the secession talk played right into Lincoln's hands: plenty of Northerners who were indifferent to slavery were horrified at these Southern tactics and the idea of dividing the Union. Indeed, the threat of secession split the Democratic Party into Northern and Southern factions, which ran separate candidates—Douglas in the North and John C. Breckinridge, a zealous pro-slavery candidate, in the South. Ironically, by splitting the Democratic vote, they helped their worst fear come true: Lincoln won.

But this is where we get back to our original point: with the idea of Southern secession on the table, Congress moved into crisis mode. Moderates on both sides tried frantically to work out a compromise, led by legislators from Kentucky, Missouri, and Maryland, who feared—correctly—their border states would be torn apart if the conflict turned violent. In December 1860, John J. Crittenden, a senator from Kentucky, proposed constitutional amendments reinstating the 36° 30' boundary, prohibiting Congress from making any law regulating slavery, and providing compensation for owners of runaway slaves. Both houses of Congress created committees to finesse these proposals, but Republicans refused to allow slavery in any more states—which, after all, was their entire political platform.

On December 20, 1860, a state convention in South Carolina formally voted to secede from the Union. South Carolina was followed in January 1861 by Mississippi, Florida, Alabama, Georgia, and Louisiana. Texas seceded on February 1. Still, last-minute efforts to work out a compromise continued. In February of 1861, state legislators in Virginia invited all of the states to a "Peace Conference," but this too failed: Northern attendees, anticipating military action against the secessionists, refused to tie President Lincoln's hands before he took office on March 4, 1861. On April 12, troops of the new Confederate States of America bombarded the federal garrison at Fort Sumter on an island in Charleston harbor. The Civil War had begun.

LIE: *Lincoln protected civil liberties.*

THE TRUTH: There's no question that Abraham Lincoln was one of the greatest presidents in U.S. history. He's venerated for winning the Civil War, saving the United States, and freeing the slaves. But protecting constitutional liberties wasn't one of his strong points. In fact, he placed more temporary restrictions on civil liberties than any other president. Modern legal scholars and historians are sympathetic to Lincoln because of the problems he had to tackle: the country was tearing itself apart, and Lincoln believed extreme measures were justified to put it back together. But this took him into some iffy areas, constitutionally speaking.

Lincoln's most controversial orders suspended the basic right of habeas corpus. At the time, habeas corpus guaranteed the right of any U.S. citizen held prisoner by the federal government to appear before a judge and petition for release. Typically a court issued a "writ of habeas corpus" requiring the jailer or warden to bring the prisoner before the court within a certain amount of time, along with official documentation showing legal authority to hold the prisoner. The Constitution allowed that habeas corpus could be suspended in times of rebellion or foreign invasion. This meant that the federal authorities could arrest and detain dangerous individuals indefinitely, without charges, for as long as the state of emergency lasted. But the Constitution was vague about who should wield this tremendous power. Could it be suspended by a simple majority vote in Congress? Or a two-thirds vote? Lincoln had his own answer: presidential decree. It's no surprise that the president used his power to press the issue, but that didn't make it constitutional. On the other hand, the constitution gave so little guidance on the topic that it wasn't exactly *un*constitutional either.

> The privilege of the Writ of Habeas Corpus shall not be suspended, unless when in Cases of Rebellion or Invasion the public Safety may require it.
>
> —Section 9 of Article I of the U.S. Constitution

With serious reservations, Lincoln first suspended habeas corpus in Maryland on April 27, 1861. (It remained suspended until the Supreme Court restored habeas corpus in all states in 1866.) Lincoln was afraid that Maryland's pro-slavery state legislature might vote to secede and join the Southern Confederacy, thus cutting the Washington, D.C. train line off from the Northern states. So in 1861, federal troops arrested Baltimore's mayor and chief of police, as well as nine members of the state legislature who were suspected of favoring secession. They also arrested newspaper editors and businessmen, some of whom were held for a year without charge.

There were immediate challenges to Lincoln's authority. In fact, the Supreme Court ruled that Lincoln had acted illegally, asserting that only Congress could suspend habeas corpus. But Lincoln ignored the ruling, pointing out that Congress wasn't in session at the time. Henceforth, cases involving the suspension of habeas corpus would usually be heard by military commissions, meaning Union officers got to decide whether to restore liberty to prisoners they considered despicable traitors . . . and you can guess how that usually turned out.

Multiple defeats suffered by Union forces in 1861–1862 sparked more dissent in the North, which in turn brought more restrictions on personal liberty. Habeas corpus was suspended again. But this time it was to keep Northerners in line while the government was trying to enforce the draft.

Many Northerners—especially, anti-war Democrats—were increasingly unhappy with Lincoln, and opposition to his tactics reached fever pitch after he issued the Emancipation Proclamation on September 22, 1862. Before long, these Northern Democrats were playing on white resentment, saying there was no reason whites should fight and die for African slaves. Poor Northerners were also outraged by a "commutation fee" that allowed rich men to duck out of military service for $300. Draft riots erupted in New York, Massachusetts, Vermont, New Hampshire, Ohio, Indiana, and Iowa, with entire cities rebelling against the federal government. On March 3, 1863, the Republican-dominated Congress passed the Habeas Corpus Indemnity Act, stating that "during the present rebellion, the president of the United States, whenever in his judgment the public safety may require it, is authorized to suspend the privilege of the writ of *habeas corpus* in any case throughout the United States or any part thereof." Armed with this unambiguous authority, Union officers were instructed to suppress the riots and imprison dissidents, whoever they were—even members of Congress.

On May 5, 1863, Clement Vallandigham—a Democratic congressman from Ohio who discouraged constituents from joining the war effort and called for the removal of "King Lincoln"—was arrested, denied habeas corpus, tried by a military commission, and sentenced to two years in prison for "uttering disloyal sentiments." This time the Supreme Court refused to review the sentence of the military commission. Lincoln averted a PR disaster by shipping Vallandigham across the lines to the Confederacy, where he obviously belonged.

Vallandigham was afforded an unusual bit of clemency due to his high profile. But Lincoln kept dozens of newspaper editors jailed and didn't commute their sentences. In effect, this meant that the suspension of habeas corpus was essentially a suspension of the First Amendment. As press censorship escalated, it especially targeted Northern Democrat ("Copperhead") newspapers that opposed the war. Official censorship measures included denying journalists telegraph service, denying publishers postal service for circulation, and closing newspaper offices. Unofficially, paramilitary groups of Union soldiers on leave destroyed printing presses and roughed up Copperhead journalists.

★ *The Copperheads were nicknamed after the venomous North American snake* Agkistrodon contortrix, *but Democrats embraced the moniker and even wore Liberty Head pennies as badges.*

Altogether, around 300 out of a total 3,000 newspapers were censored during the course of the Civil War, including some well-known titles still in operation today, such as the *Cincinnati Enquirer, Iowa Constitution*, and New York's *Daily News*.

> **Good! We'll have dispatches from hell before breakfast.**
>
> —Union General William Tecumseh Sherman, on being told (incorrectly) that three newspaper journalists had just been killed

LIE: *The South could have won the Civil War.*

THE TRUTH: The South started the Civil War with better troops, better generals, and better morale than the North, but in the end it didn't matter, because the North had more. More what, you ask? More *everything*.

Before we give you the gloom report, it's only fair to give Dixie its due and explain why Confederate leaders thought they had a fighting chance. Many of the best officers in the U.S. Army were Southern. Out of a total 1,108 U.S. Army officers in 1860, 270 resigned to join the Confederate Army, and of these, 184 were West Point graduates. More importantly, they included a large proportion of the mid-career lieutenants and colonels with actual command experience. This was especially true of the elite cavalry, where four out of five regimental commanders left to fight for the South (most notably Robert E. Lee). Meanwhile, most Southern rank-and-file soldiers, coming from rural backgrounds, owned their own guns and had hunting experience, unlike urban Northerners. Fighting for their homes, the rebels were also more gung ho in general: 100,000 rebels enlisted in March 1861, versus 92,000 volunteers in the North, even though the Southern population was considerably smaller.

> **But for these startling defections, the rebellion never could have assumed formidable proportions.**
>
> —War Department report to Congress, 1861, after so many West Point graduates fought for the Confederacy that the U.S. Senate debated closing the academy

Yet the Confederacy had problems before the first shot was fired. There was widespread opposition to secession in certain areas—especially the Upland South areas like Tennessee, Arkansas, western North Carolina, and what became West Virginia. Unlike plantation owners in the Deep South, the whites in Appalachia—largely the descendants of Scots-Irish settlers—had no financial stake in slavery and tended to be more ambivalent. Most of the poor "dirt farmers" saw no reason to fight for the right of the wealthy to own slaves. These feelings essentially mirrored the sentiments of poor whites in the North, who saw no reason to fight to free the slaves. Likewise, Kentucky and Missouri declared their neutrality before being invaded by both Confederate and Union forces in 1861. Meanwhile, counties in northern Alabama and eastern Tennessee tried to secede from the Confederacy and rejoin the Union. Some succeeded: West Virginia seceded from Virginia to form a new Union state in 1863, and the citizens of Winston County, Alabama, declared themselves the Republic of Winston and defied Confederate authority to the end of the Civil War, helping Union forces with local scouts.

> I hope to have God on my side, but I must have Kentucky.
>
> —Abraham Lincoln, 1861

Nonetheless, the Confederacy's early military superiority allowed it to inflict a series of humiliating defeats on poorly led, untrained Northern troops. At this stage the Union resembled a heavily tranquilized badger: comically helpless, but when the tranqs wear off, watch out!

Confederate leaders knew their only hope of success lay in scoring so many victories early on that the North became demoralized. And they had enough military experience to guess that if the war dragged on, the North would have time to marshal its huge economy and crush the South.

And that's what happened. In 1860 Northern cities were home to 86 percent of the nation's industry. That year Northern states produced 25 times as much iron, and Pennsylvania alone produced nine times as much coal as the entire Confederacy. So once the North got its act together, it put that might to use, churning out a huge navy to blockade the South, cutting off cotton exports and ruining the Southern economy. The North also had more than twice the length of railroads and nine times the length of telegraphs in 1860—huge advantages in mobility and communications.

★ *One of the railroad workers who physically strung the telegraph lines from Pennsylvania to Virginia was future millionaire philanthropist Andrew Carnegie.*

Putting the Union's strength to use took some time: as rebel troops schooled Union forces again and again, Lincoln desperately shuffled through commanders, fully aware of the discontent building up in the North. From 1861 through 1864, the Army of the Potomac—the main Union force in the key mid-Atlantic region—had five different commanders: Irvin McDowell (1861), George B. McClellan (1861–1862), Ambrose Burnside (1862–1863), Joseph Hooker (1863), and George Meade (1863–1864).

THE BRITISH AREN'T COMING!

Occasionally, historians entertain the idea that the South might have won if the British had stepped in to help the Confederates. The theory generally goes that if Robert E. Lee had won at Gettysburg, the Brits would have stepped in, giving the South a boost with their powerful navy. It's true some British officials considered the idea in the early part of the war, but the scenario is implausible at best. The Royal Navy was formidable, but British fleets were spread around the globe. Meanwhile, the Union Navy grew rapidly, surpassing the Royal Navy in size by 1865. Although Union ships and crews couldn't match the Brits, they were concentrated in one place.

The British were also afraid that the North might retaliate by invading Canada, requiring costly defensive measures. Furthermore, the Confederacy's "trump card"—British industry's need for Southern cotton—wasn't much of a trump card at all. The Brits had alternative cotton sources in Egypt and India. Last but not least, Queen Victoria—then at the height of her power—had worked for decades to enforce an 1833 decree banning slavery in most of the British Empire, and many of her subjects would have objected to helping slave owners.

Meanwhile, Robert E. Lee assumed supreme command of the Confederate armies and pressed the Southern advantage with a daring invasion of central Pennsylvania—the only major military action on Northern soil. But Lee lost his gamble, meeting defeat at Gettysburg in July 1863, and from there on things looked grim: the badger was fully awake and very, very angry.

In 1864 Lincoln promoted Ulysses S. Grant to supreme command. Grant was fresh from victories in the West, where he had split the Confederacy by conquering Tennessee and Mississippi. Although he wasn't a brilliant battlefield strategist like his opponent, Robert E. Lee, he made full use of the Union's advantages in population, transportation, and communication to pin Southern armies and overwhelm them with sheer numbers. And he was tenacious, hounding Confederate armies constantly with little regard for Union casualties. During his bloody pursuit of Lee across northern Virginia, Northern newspapers gave him the nickname "Butcher Grant."

The end result of the Civil War was the total impoverishment of the South, thanks partly to the Union's policy of "hard war," implemented most thoroughly by William Tecumseh Sherman on his March to the Sea. After helping Grant capture Chattanooga, Tennessee, in November 1863, Sherman captured Atlanta in September 1864, ordered all of the residents out, and burned the city to the ground. He then led 98,000 Union troops across Georgia to the port of Savannah, relying on "forage" for supplies—i.e., stealing anything that wasn't bolted down and burning the rest.

> General Grant is a great general. I know him well. He stood by me when I was crazy, and I stood by him when he was drunk; and now, sir, we stand by each other always.
>
> —Sherman, 1864

☞ QUICK'N'EASY CIVIL WAR ☜

The Big Picture: There were two major "theatres" or areas of operations during the Civil War: the Eastern theater (focused on the area around Washington, D.C., and the Confederate capital, Richmond) and the Western theater, where Union and rebel forces

vied for control of divided states like Missouri, Kentucky, Mississippi, and Tennessee.

It all started in the east: after the Union garrison at Fort Sumter in Charleston Harbor surrendered in April, the first Union march on Richmond ended in total defeat at Bull Run, Maryland, July 21, 1861.

To the west, both sides invaded Kentucky in September–November, 1861. Union forces from Illinois invaded Missouri, and by the end of 1861, they basically controlled both states. In 1862, Union forces under Ulysses S. Grant began splitting the Confederacy by conquering the Mississippi River Valley and Tennessee, culminating in a bloody victory at Shiloh, Tennessee, April 6–7. With Commander David Farragut's capture of New Orleans on April 29, 1862, Union forces were poised to cut the Confederacy in two. Confederate Gen. Braxton Bragg tried to turn the tide by invading Kentucky, and scored a victory at Perryville, October 8, 1862, but failed to follow up. His later push to retake Tennessee ended in defeat at Stones River, December 31.

Meanwhile, back east, the Union was schooled by rebels under Thomas J. "Stonewall" Jackson, who won five battles in the Shenandoah Valley from April–June, 1862. Union forces chasing Jackson were mauled again at the Second Battle of Bull Run, August 28–30, 1862. George McClellan (Lincoln's general of the hour) chased Robert E. Lee's Army of Northern Virginia into Maryland, where Lee fought him to a draw at Antietam, September 17, 1862. Desperate for a victory before year's end, Lincoln ordered Ambrose Burnside to attack Richmond. Bad idea: the Army of the Potomac was badly beaten by Lee's Army of Northern Virginia at Fredericksburg, Virginia, December 11–15.

> If General McClellan does not want to use the army, I would like to borrow it for a time.
>
> —Lincoln, 1862

On January 1, 1863, Lincoln issued the Emancipation Proclamation freeing the slaves, but he still needed a victory for political support. Gen. Joseph Hooker marched on Richmond but was badly beaten by Lee at Chancellorsville, VA, April 30–May 6; however Lee lost Jackson, his best commander, to friendly fire. The Union got a much-needed boost when West Virginia voted to secede from Virginia and (re-)join the Union on June 20. Hoping a victory on Northern soil would break Union morale, Lee crossed the Mason-Dixon Line into Pennsylvania, but was defeated by Gen. George Meade at Gettysburg on July 1–3. And on July 4, over in the Western theatre, Grant captured Vicksburg, Mississippi—completing the division of the Confederacy. But a Union invasion of Georgia was repelled at Chickamauga, September 19–20.

Desperate to find a commander who would attack Lee and regain control in the east, Lincoln promoted Grant to overall commander of Union forces. Grant's first major attacks in the Overland Campaign were repulsed at the Battles of Wilderness, Spotsylvania, and Cold Harbor, May 31–June 12, 1864. But Lee was slowly forced back, and Grant laid siege to Petersburg, VA—key to Richmond's defenses.

Meanwhile Grant's right-hand man William Tecumseh Sherman invaded northern Georgia and captured Atlanta on September 2, 1864. Forced out of Atlanta, Confederate Gen. John Bell Hood counter-invaded Tennessee to distract Sherman but met defeat at Franklin, November 30, 1864. After burning Atlanta in November 1864, Sherman marched southeast through Georgia to the Atlantic Ocean, with his troops laying waste to everything in their path.

Sherman then turned his march north from January–March 1865, devastating South Carolina and North Carolina, where he joined forces with Union troops arriving by sea. He encountered fierce resistance from Confederate troops under Joseph E. Johnston, but sheer Union numbers forced Johnston to retreat west. He finally surrendered to Sherman at Durham Station, North Carolina, on April 26.

Things came to a head in Virginia around the same time: after ten months Grant crushed rebel defenses at Petersburg in March, and Lee was forced to abandon Richmond on April 2 (during the retreat it burned to the ground, probably mostly by accident). Grant chased Lee across Virginia until he finally surrendered at Appomattox, April 9.

· **SPECIAL REPORT** · · · · · · · · · · · · · · · ·

Reconstruction Derby

As the Civil War drew to a close, Congress was completely dominated by Northern Republicans, including a number of "Radical Republicans"—fierce abolitionists who made no secret of their loathing for the South. However, the Radical Republicans were mostly kept in line by Abraham Lincoln, who enjoyed enormous moral authority and prestige after leading the Union to victory. Lincoln, a moderate Republican, favored relatively lenient treatment for the South, including a quick end to military occupation and speedy readmission of ex-Confederate states to the Union.

But Lincoln's assassination by John Wilkes Booth on April 14, 1865, let the Radical Republicans out of their cage. Lincoln's successor, Vice President Andrew Johnson, was a former senator from Tennessee and the only Southern senator to stay in Congress after secession. This gave him enough credibility to serve as Lincoln's V.P.—but not to deal with the rabidly anti-Southern Radical Republicans once Lincoln was gone.

While Johnson proposed continuing Lincoln's lenient policies for Reconstruction, the Radical Republicans demanded the South be punished for slavery and secession. The rift widened quickly, beginning with Johnson's amnesty for the vast majority of Confederate soldiers (excluding only those above the rank of colonel) on May 29, 1865. The first open congressional rebellion came after Johnson allowed Southern states to hold elections to Congress in September–October 1865.

In December 1865 the Radical Republicans simply refused to admit Southern representatives into the 39th Congress. This meant there was no real opposition in 1866 when the Republicans passed the Thirteenth Amendment abolishing slavery and created a Joint Committee on Reconstruction—signaling their intention to take control of Reconstruction in the not-too-distant future. Next, they moved to renew and expand the Bureau of Refugees, Freedmen, and Abandoned Lands, better known as the Freedmen's Bureau, originally created in March 1865 to protect and advance the interests of freed slaves. They also passed the Civil Rights Act, granting full citizenship to the freed slaves.

These idealistic acts were sure to raise tensions in the South, where whites bitterly resented the growing power of former slaves. Still hoping for national reconciliation, Johnson vetoed both acts, which needless to say enraged the Radical Republicans, who overrode Johnson's veto of the Civil Rights Act—the first time Congress had passed a major law over a presidential veto. Their aggressive moves triggered a wave of race riots across the South, with scores of freedmen killed by angry white mobs.

Southern resistance in turn angered Northern voters, who returned an overwhelming Republican majority to Congress in November 1866. In March 1867 Congress passed the First Reconstruction Act—again over Johnson's veto—taking control of the Union occupation and administration of Southern states. This marked the end of "Presidential Reconstruction" and the beginning of "Congressional Reconstruction"—though a better name for it might be "Military Reconstruction," as the Republicans basically treated the South like a foreign country under military occupation.

The Reconstruction Act divided the former Confederacy into five military districts, took the vote away (again) from many ex-Confederates, and made state governments subject to Union military commanders. This second-class status continued until the states gave black adult males the vote and ratified the Fourteenth Amendment, which guaranteed the rights of citizens to equal protection under the law. Johnson protested these harsh tactics but was basically rendered powerless when Congress impeached him in February 1868 (coming within one vote of actually removing him from office). And in November the Union military hero Ulysses S. Grant won the presidential election with the explicit support of Radical Republicans, promising a hard line on Reconstruction.

Under the Reconstruction regime in the late 1860s and early 1870s, freedmen voted for the first time, while many Southern white men were disenfranchised for taking part in secessionist activities. As a result, large numbers of African-American representatives were elected to Congress for the first time in U.S. history. To help secure this promising step toward political equality, in February of 1869 Congress passed the Fifteenth Amendment, declaring that "race, color, or previous condition of servitude" cannot be used to bar citizens from exercising their right to vote; it was ratified by the states a year later. Then the Republican Congress declared war on the Klu Klux Klan, which had sprung up in resistance to Reconstruction. In the fall of 1867, the KKK began "night-riding" to intimidate blacks in rural Tennessee—the first known instance of organized, large-scale racial persecution by the secretive group. In April of 1871, Congress passed the Ku Klux Klan Act, allowing Grant to suspend habeas corpus to fight the KKK in South Carolina.

But these early signs of progress proved fleeting. After a decade of Reconstruction, it became clear the federal government would never be able to crush entrenched white resistance across the South. The Northern states lacked the political will to maintain a large army of occupation in the South indefinitely, and when the occupation finally ended, embittered Southern whites reasserted their traditional control of the region by excluding freedmen from political and civil life.

Eventually the Republicans just gave up, effectively cutting loose Southern blacks, as part of one of the dirtiest political deals in U.S. history—and that's saying something. In 1876 the Republican candidate Rutherford B. Hayes lost the popular vote, but the election was still up in the air because of disputed counts in Florida, Louisiana, and South Carolina. Realizing the Republicans were probably going to steal the election anyway, Southern Democrats cut a secret deal giving Hayes these states, and the presidency, in exchange for withdrawing Union troops from the South. In the process, they were screwing over their own candidate, Samuel J. Tilden, but as a New York Yankee and former War Democrat, he was almost as bad as any Republican.

·············· **PROFILES IN SCOURGES** ····················

Nathan Bedford Forrest (1821–1877)

One of the Confederacy's most brilliant cavalry commanders, today Nathan Bedford Forrest is mostly remembered for one thing: being a racist cracker. Forrest sealed his legacy when he served as the first "Grand Wizard" of the Ku Klux Klan. In truth, he was a lot more complicated than that.

Compared to most of his fellow officers, Forrest came from a remarkably humble background. The firstborn son of a poor blacksmith in Chapel Hill, Tennessee, at the age of 13, he saved his mother from an attack by a panther. On his father's death in 1838, the 17-year-old Forrest became head of the family and legal guardian of 11 younger siblings. Three years later, he went into business in Mississippi with his uncle, who was soon killed by two local rivals. Forrest killed both of his uncle's murderers and went on to great success as a plantation owner and slave trader based out of Memphis. With stints as a steamboat captain and a professional gambler, by the time the Civil War began in 1861, Forrest was worth $1.5 million, making him one of the richest men in the South.

Planters were legally exempt from military service, but in 1861 Forrest enlisted in the Confederate Army as a private and was quickly elevated to colonel on account of his wealth. In fact, he was asked to recruit his own special cavalry regiment, "Forrest's Tennessee Cavalry Battalion," which became one of the elite units of the Confederate Army. The battalion included 45 of Forrest's slaves, whom he promised to free if they would fight with him in the war. (He freed them all in late 1863, before the war was over.)

Personally, Forrest was fearless and ferocious, killing 31 men over the course of the Civil War, many in hand-to-hand fighting. In April 1862 at the battle of Shiloh—not realizing he had become separated from his men—he charged into a brigade of Union soldiers by himself and then incredibly managed to escape by using an enemy soldier as a human shield.

But there was more to Forrest than just the physical bravery. Although he had no formal education and almost no military training, he surprised everyone with his inborn genius for cavalry combat. He was especially skilled at using the mobility and speed of horse-mounted troops to outmaneuver and surprise opposing commanders. And he had plenty of tricks up his sleeve: he once duped a much larger force of Union cavalry into surrendering by making his own army appear bigger than it was. (He had his troops circle a hill several times within sight of Union lines.) He won battle after battle and was eventually promoted to major general in December 1863.

In 1865, as the war became an increasingly desperate attempt to evade Union armies, Forrest fought on, leading his dwindling army in a last-ditch defense of Tennessee and Alabama. But on learning that Robert E. Lee had finally surrendered at Appomattox, Virginia, Forrest decided to lay down arms as well, asking his troops to "cultivate friendly feelings towards those with whom we have so long contended . . ."

This all contrasted sharply with another part of Forrest's legacy. On capturing Fort Pillow in central Mississippi in April 1864, Forrest's men massacred Union soldiers, including many African-Americans, which historians have interpreted as an early expression of racial animosity. After the war, Forrest joined the Ku Klux Klan, a paramilitary organization formed by Confederate veterans to resist Reconstruction. The first goal of the Klan was to regain control of state governments across the South by 1867. After trying to persuade African-Americans to vote for old-school Confederates (good luck!), the Klan soon turned to violence, intimidating African-American voters to prevent them from going to the polls. Meanwhile, as one of the South's great Civil War heroes, Forrest was elevated to Grand Wizard of the shadowy group.

★ *Mississippi's Fort Pillow was not named after a head cushion, but after General Gideon Johnson Pillow.*

All of this certainly reads like an indictment of Forrest—but there is some evidence to the contrary. Take the massacre at Fort Pillow: according to some sources, Forrest ordered his troops to kill the Union soldiers as they tried to surrender—but others say he begged the Union soldiers to surrender and was ignored. After the battle, Forrest arranged for wounded African-American prisoners to be transported to a Confederate military hospital to receive medical care. And although his political opponents implicated him in the Klan's turn to violence, Forrest publicly denounced the violence and ordered the Klan to disband as a result. In 1875 he was invited to address an African-American civic group, the "Jubilee of Pole-Bearers," where the mistress of ceremonies presented him with a bouquet of flowers "as a token of reconciliation, an offering of peace and good will." After explaining his motives in fighting for the Confederacy, Forrest spoke in favor of civil equality for African-Americans, calling for their admission to professions from which they had been excluded.

> This is a proud day for me. Having occupied the position I have for thirteen years, and being misunderstood by the colored race, I take this occasion to say that I am your friend . . . We were born on the same soil, breathe the same air, live in the same land, and why should we not be brothers and sisters. . . . I want to elevate every man, and to see you take your places in your shops, stores and offices.
>
> —Nathan Bedford Forrest, in an address to
> African-American civic leaders, 1875

John Wilkes Booth (1838–1865)

A vain, shallow man, John Wilkes Booth struck out against the North when it was too late to have any effect on the outcome of the war. In fact, he succeeded in making things (much) worse for his beloved South, which is why he's still remembered today as a Great American Dingbat.

Booth was born on May 10, 1838, the ninth child in a well-known family of actors. His early upbringing more or less guaranteed an unstable personality: his father, Junius, loved the spotlight but kept his family isolated in a primitive log cabin in Bel Air, Maryland. In addition to Junius's alcoholism, there's also evidence that he, as well as John and various siblings, may have suffered from bipolar disorder. In fact, in 1835 Junius threatened to kill

President Andrew Jackson in a letter. So it seems his son was just a crazy chip off an already unstable block.

In 1854 Booth briefly involved himself in political causes, traveling to Baltimore as an anti-immigrant "Know-Nothing Party" delegate. But he soon threw himself into acting, where he won fame as a master of the overwrought, melodramatic style then in vogue. Called "the handsomest man in America" and "a muscular, perfect man," Booth was more than just a rugged face: he also had an amazing memory, which allowed him to act in 83 different plays in one year. In 1860 he embarked on a national tour, appearing at popular theaters across the country. He even earned praise from Walt Whitman, who swooned over his New York performance!

After the Civil War began, Booth continued touring the North—evidently he wasn't so angry he couldn't stand Northern adulation. Along the way, he was actually in the same room as President Lincoln twice before the assassination, as a performer in plays at Ford's Theatre in November 1863. Booth earned a fortune as an actor, but he invested it foolishly and lost large amounts of money. He became more and more agitated as the tide of the Civil War turned against the Confederacy, and he raged against Lincoln to the point that his brothers stopped talking to him. Falling in with a shady crowd of Confederate sympathizers, Booth smuggled quinine for the Southern cause and cooked up a far-fetched plan to kidnap Lincoln and hold him hostage until the Union agreed to make peace. On April 11, he was in a small audience addressed by Lincoln from the White House balcony. Lincoln said he supported giving freed slaves the vote, which drove Booth into paroxysms of rage. With seven co-conspirators, Booth decided to assassinate Lincoln as the president watched a performance of the romantic comedy *Our American Cousin* at Ford's Theatre on the evening of April 14. The plan was more or less spontaneous, as Booth and his accomplices only learned Lincoln would be attending that morning.

> African slavery is one of the greatest blessings that God has ever bestowed upon a favored nation
>
> —John Wilkes Booth, in a posthumous letter

That evening, Booth—a regular at Ford's Theatre—had no problem getting access to the hallway behind the president's box. And because no one had ever assassinated the president before, there was no security detail. Booth simply stepped into the unlocked box and shot Lincoln in the back of the head with a .44-caliber Derringer as he sat next to his wife, Mary. Henry Rathbone, a major in the Union army who was sitting in the president's box, threw himself at Booth, but the assassin stabbed him and clambered over the railing to make his getaway. Booth injured his leg leaping from the balcony to the stage, but had the presence of mind to shout *sic semper tyrannis*," a Latin phrase meaning "thus always to tyrants" before making his exit. In the end Booth and a co-conspirator made it as far as a barn in southern Maryland, where Union troops found them hiding on April 26, 1865. When Booth refused to give himself up, the soldiers set fire to the barn, forcing Booth into an open spot, where one of the soldiers shot him in the neck. Booth died a few hours later on the porch of the farmhouse.

So what did Booth accomplish with his famous misdeed? Lincoln had always advocated a lenient policy for the Reconstruction of the South: he wanted to have all the Confederate states reincorporated into the Union by the end of 1865 and proposed relatively moderate requirements for readmission. Vice President Andrew Johnson was ready to carry out Lincoln's moderate plan—but after the assassination, he didn't have the authority or charisma to control Radical Republicans in Congress who took a much harsher approach, motivated in part by anger over Lincoln's assassination—so Booth's last act only made a bad situation worse for his beloved region.

> ★ Booth was far from alone in his Lincoln hatred; a Wisconsin editor named Marcus Pomeroy editorialized about the Great Emancipator in 1864: ". . . If he is elected to misgovern for another four years, we trust some bold hand will pierce his heart with dagger point for the public good."

· · · · · · · · · · · · · · · · WHERE MY GODS AT ·

A Haunted White House

In the second half of the nineteenth century, people from all walks of life in Europe and America became deeply interested in supernatural phenomena. In particular, many educated people believed they could contact the dead through "séances" facilitated by Spiritualist mediums. And this wasn't just considered spooky entertainment. In an age when modern medicine still involved generous application of leeches, death was both common-place and mysterious. One out of every hundred pregnant women died in childbirth—more in germ-filled hospitals—while 25 per-cent of newborn children died before the age of one. Meanwhile, diseases like cancer and tuberculosis carried off otherwise healthy adults seemingly at random.

Spiritualism was basically an entirely separate religion, com-plete with its own churches, weekly services, hymns, retreats, and charitable organizations. Although Spiritualists were monothe-ists, they often doubted the Old and New Testaments and em-braced a vision of God embodied in the Universe. Spiritualists also didn't believe that souls were rewarded or punished for their behavior in life: instead they imagined the afterlife divided into different spheres or astral planes through which the souls of the deceased could progress while striving to draw closer to the lov-ing spirit of God. Because this afterlife coexisted with the visible physical world, the spirits of the dead were all around, meaning that mediums with "the gift" could make contact.

Spiritualism first made headlines in upstate New York. In March 1848, two sisters, Kate and Margaret Fox, claimed to be able to communicate with a local murder victim in séances where witnesses heard the deceased "answer" questions with knocks. The Fox sisters quickly became local celebrities, gaining a follow-ing among free-thinking Quakers, who had a long tradition of religious nonconformity. Other famous Spiritualists in the sec-ond half of the nineteenth century were Cora Scott, a beautiful young woman who used mesmerism to induce trances, and Achsa Sprague, who gave trance lectures until her death in 1861.

Some of the most famous séances took place in the White House in 1863, when Mary Todd Lincoln invited the female me-dium Nettie Colburn Maynard to help her contact the spirit of her dead son Willie. Colburn's stories from the Lincoln séances include some fantastic occurrences: supposedly a grand piano began levitating when she played it, and another time a bench levitated with the president still sitting on it. Historians disagree on whether Lincoln actually took part in these séances, but it seems likely that he did on at least some occasions. Lincoln was extremely distraught over Willie's death: in the week following his funeral, on two occasions Lincoln visited the crypt where the em-balmed body was interred and asked for the coffin to be opened so he could look on his face again. Afterward, he often said that he could sense the presence of Willie's spirit in the White House.

Lincoln's Spiritual bent also expressed itself in premonitions and visions of his own death: throughout his life, Lincoln claimed that when he looked in the mirror, he could sometimes see his own dead face floating, disembodied, next to his living reflection. According to other sources, Lincoln also consulted Spiritualists seeking information about the future course of the war.

> Gentlemen, you may be surprised and think it strange, but when the doctor here was describing a war, I distinctly saw myself, in second sight, bearing an important part in that strife.
>
> —Abraham Lincoln, shortly before the election of 1860

·········· **OTHER PEOPLE'S STUFF** ················

Presidente for a Day

In the years before the Civil War, Southern expansionists had big plans to create a tropical slave empire encompassing the Caribbean and more. But when Northerners foiled those ambitions in Congress, some Southern adventurers decided to ignore the government and handle the task themselves. A good number tried to conquer Latin American territory with their own personal armies, launching literally hundreds of "filibustering" expeditions in the mid-nineteenth century.

> The time will come when the free navigation of the Amazon … will be regarded by the people of this country as second only in importance to the acquisition of Louisiana.
>
> —William L. Herndon, *Exploration of the Valley of the Amazon 1851–1852*

The most successful of the nineteenth-century filibusters was William Walker, a Tennessee native who made himself president of Nicaragua from 1856 to 1857. But as with most of his colleagues, Walker's megalomaniacal plans led him to ruin.

Born into a Nashville banking family, William Walker graduated summa cum laude from the University of Tennessee at the age of 14. After studying in Scotland, France, and Germany; earning a medical degree from the University of Pennsylvania (by 19); and beginning law school in New Orleans, Walker decided to drop his studies and became a journalist—which in Walker's case meant living the high life, fighting duels, and dabbling in international intrigue.

> ★ The term "filibuster" is based on the Dutch word for "pirate," vrijbuiter—also the origin of the English word "freebooter." In today's world, the word is more commonly used in the legislature for tactics taken by an opponent in order to delay or prevent action on a bill.

Walker arrived in San Francisco in June 1850, just a few months after the seedy boom town was officially incorporated on April 15, 1850. Taking a job as the editor of the *San Francisco Herald*, Walker became a local hero when Judge Levi Parsons, stung by critical editorials, charged Walker with contempt of court and threw him in jail. This flagrant violation of First Amendment rights sparked mass protests by the people of San Francisco, and it made Walker a celebrity. He tried to stay in the public eye after being freed, but he lacked the warmth and charm needed to win in politics. And anyway, his interests lay elsewhere.

In 1853 Walker led 45 desperate characters in a brazen attempt to seize Mexico's Baja Peninsula. Landing at La Paz, Walker declared the place the "Republic of Sonora" and proceeded to institute Louisiana laws, since he wanted to ensure that slavery remained legal. Back home, his dashing bravery captured the popular imagination, and most Americans appear to have supported Walker: plenty of Northerners still favored expansion, and even some anti-slavery, anti-expansion newspapers in New York and Boston caught the Walker bug.

But Walker's plans began to unravel with the arrival of reinforcements from San Francisco. Food supplies dwindled, and half the reinforcements deserted almost immediately. Alarmed, Walker doubled down by invading the main part of the Mexican state of Sonora, just across the narrow Gulf of Baja, with his 130 remaining troops. Following the Colorado River, they penetrated 200 miles before their supplies finally ran out. Another 50 men deserted, and Walker was forced to lead the sorry crew of would-be empire builders back to the Baja Peninsula, where they now found themselves harassed by local outlaws. After a humiliating evacuation and repatriation to California, Walker and his chief officers faced federal charges of violating neutrality laws. Luckily for Walker, he was acquitted by a sympathetic San Francisco court.

This meant his schedule was totally open in 1855, when Nicaraguan rebels asked him to help overthrow the government of Nicaragua. Walker jumped at the opportunity. After all, Nicaragua meant 50,000 square miles, with a population approaching 300,000, combined with good soil, plentiful fresh water, cotton, tobacco, rice, and indigo. And in the mid-nineteenth century, its strategic location made Nicaragua a crucial transit point for Americans traveling by sea from the eastern United States to California. Every month up to 2,000 U.S. citizens crossed Nicaragua via steamboats and stage coach, courtesy of Cornelius Vanderbilt's Accessory Transit Company (ATC). Since 1849, Vanderbilt had worked to build a canal across Nicaragua—and whoever wished to control Nicaragua had to have Vanderbilt's support.

Walker's invasion of Nicaragua went remarkably well at first. His private army of 58 men set sail for Nicaragua on May 4, 1855, and miraculously their leaky, old ship made it all the way to Nicaragua's Pacific port of Realejo without serious damage or loss of life. Walker then headed inland to the provincial capital of Leon, where his men received a warm welcome from their rebel hosts. After bolstering his army with about 100 native recruits, Walker sailed south to attack San Juan del Sur, the Pacific terminus of ATC's trans-Nicaragua transportation system, and roundly defeated a Nicaraguan force three times the size of his. This success attracted even more recruits, swelling the ranks of Walker's army to over 250. Fearing local toughs would desert if they didn't see some action (and loot), Walker and his men embarked on a passenger steamboat and steamed north through Lake Nicaragua to capture Granada, the enemy capital, in a bloodless predawn raid. And so Walker became master of Nicaragua. Seriously!

As military governor and then *presidente,* Walker freed Nicaragua's political prisoners and tried to reconcile with supporters of the former government. While he (shockingly) alienated regular Nicaraguans, he was recognized as the legitimate ruler of Nicaragua by U.S. President Franklin Pierce—a Northern expansionist and Southern sympathizer who favored the annexation of Cuba and Central America. Hoping to build economic and political ties with the United States, Walker also solicited investments from American capitalists—specifically former partners of Vanderbilt who were now his competitors, trying to replace the ATC's steam ferries and stagecoaches with a new trans-Nicaraguan railroad.

However, Vanderbilt—who was worth about $180 billion in today's U.S. dollars—was not a man to be trifled with.

> Gentlemen, you have undertaken to cheat me. I won't sue you, for the law is too slow. I'll ruin you. Yours truly, Cornelius Vanderbilt.
>
> —Cornelius Vanderbilt

There was only one way this could end: Vanderbilt organized a coalition of half a dozen Central American states opposed to Walker, raised a rebel army in Costa Rica, and toppled the filibuster's year-old regime. And just like that, Walker was forced to return to Mobile, Alabama, which he used as a base for an attempt to take over Honduras in August 1860. But by this time, his luck had run out. Walker was captured by British troops and was handed over to Honduran authorities for execution.

Your Kingdom for a Whale

In the eighteenth and nineteenth centuries, ships sailing from New England literally circled the globe in pursuit of mankind's eternal nemesis—the whale. By the early nineteenth century, they had the enemy on the run. The peak harvest came in 1840, when Yankee whalers brought in 11,593,483 gallons of whale oil to feed the American demand for lamp fuel. But as the supply diminished, the price went up, and even more whalers went into the business. From 1823 to 1846, the American whaling fleet increased from 203 to 736 ships, and they chased whales all the way from New England to the waters off Alaska; from there it was just a short trip down the Aleutian and Kuril island chains to the coast of Japan.

Thousands of miles away from their home base, it wasn't profitable or practical for Yankee whalers to return home whenever they ran out of food, water, or firewood. Luckily, Japan was a convenient source of all three. There was just one small issue: the Japanese were legally required to kill or arrest all foreigners who set foot on their soil. These extreme *sakoku* ("seclusion laws") were no joke: in 1837 an American merchant named Charles King tried to return three shipwrecked Japanese sailors and had his ship shelled for his trouble.

Everything changed, however, with the discovery of gold in California in 1849, followed by the admission of California to the

Union in 1850. Now that America owned real estate on the Pacific Ocean, the tantalizing prospect of trade with Asian countries seemed within reach. It was time for Japan to be a little friendlier, whether the Japanese liked it or not. An expedition by U.S. Navy Captain James Glynn to Nagasaki in 1849 achieved little—but yielded an important development, as Glynn advised Congress to use force the next time. Thus Japan received a surprise visit from Commodore Matthew Perry and four heavily armed steam-powered frigates on July 8, 1853.

Perry's demand was fairly simple: he wanted to drop off a letter from President Millard Fillmore requesting that Americans be allowed to trade in Japan, and that the Japanese help rescue and return American sailors in case of shipwreck. However, this was asking too much of the samurai officials at the Uraga harbor, who instructed Perry to continue on to Nagasaki. But Perry's instructions were clear. When the officials continued to refuse to let him deliver his letter, he demonstrated the superiority of modern American weaponry by destroying a few buildings with new, super-accurate Paixhans guns that fired exploding shells. The samurai sensibly relented and agreed to allow Perry to come ashore to deliver the letter, for one of history's more dramatic mail drops.

★ When Commodore Perry's four ships pulled into Edo (Tokyo) Bay in 1854, the locals had never seen steamships before. They feared that the vessels were "giant dragons puffing smoke."

The Japanese took abundant (absurd) precautions. Accompanied by dozens of sailors, on July 14 Perry was allowed to walk a short distance through the town of Kurihama to an official silk tent set up just for the occasion. To make sure the foreigners saw nothing of Japan, wood and silk screens were erected along the entire route, concealing practically everything but the cobblestone streets. To be on the safe side, the town was also guarded by thousands of samurai, brought in especially to make sure the Americans wouldn't somehow slip unnoticed into Japan. Once Perry arrived at the tent, neither of the Japanese officials present would speak to him—they were determined to adhere to the official rule against interacting with foreigners. The trio sat in uncomfortable silence for several minutes before an underling indicated—through mime—that Perry should place Fillmore's letter in an ornate box used for official documents.

After this incredibly awkward audience, Perry left for China with a promise to return for their reply in a year—giving the shogun's top officials plenty of time to totally freak out. As they raced to fortify the country's ports, the samurai realized that their armaments were woefully inadequate. Maybe cutting themselves off from the outside world for hundreds of years hadn't been such a good idea, after all. Reform-minded members of the elite decided that Japan needed new management. So in 1867 they installed a figurehead for their new government with the title Emperor Meiji. The new era brought a top-down social revolution that saw the importation of modern technology, breakneck industrialization, and the adoption of some outward trappings of Western culture. Known as the Meiji Restoration, in one incredible decade, Japan jumped from feudalism to an advanced industrial economy. But this didn't mean everything was peachy: although they ended up agreeing to Perry's demands, Japan's leaders weren't about to forget the fear and humiliation inflicted by the Westerners.

The Bargain Basement Sale on Alaska

Sometimes politicians don't know a good thing, even if it's been encrusted with diamonds and handed to them on a golden platter. Just consider the ambivalence over whether the United States should purchase Alaska from the Russian Empire in 1867. The deal, brokered by Secretary of State William Seward, almost fell through because Congress couldn't imagine a possible use for the territory, which many derisively dismissed as "Seward's Icebox."

As the global chess game between London and St. Petersburg unfolded, the Russians first offered to sell Alaska in 1859, motivated by concern that the Brits might swoop in and take the underpopulated territory for free. But the Americans hemmed and hawed, and then got distracted by the Civil War. The second time around, the Russian ambassador, Eduard de Stoeckl, had to distribute massive bribes to Congress just to make sure the deal went through. In the end, the United States paid $7.2 million for territory measuring 656,425 square miles, working out to just under $0.02 per acre, which increased total U.S. territory by about 20 percent. Americans only realized what an incredible deal they'd gotten after gold was discovered in 1896—followed by diamonds, platinum, nickel, copper, oil, and natural gas. (Not to mention timber, one of Alaska's biggest natural resources, which should have been enough reason to buy the place on its own.)

YOUR LANDMASS IS SO BIG

One of the most incredible things about Alaska is its sheer size, which is perhaps best communicated through "yo momma" jokes:

Alaska's so big . . . you could fit 75 New Jerseys in it!

Alaska's so fresh . . . it holds 32 percent of the total U.S. supply of freshwater! (980 cubic kilometers/year, out of a total 3,069/year)

Alaska's so rich . . . it's produced about 42 million ounces of gold to date! (1,305 tons, which would be worth $46.2 billion at today's values)

Alaska's so rugged . . . it has the tallest mountain in North America! (Mount McKinley, 20,320 feet)

Alaska's so forested . . . it has more trees than France (42 million acres), Germany (26 million acres), Italy (26 million acres), and Britain (7 million acres) combined (129 million acres total)!

> Except for the Aleutian Islands and a narrow strip of land extending along the southern coast the country would be not worth taking as a gift. . . .
>
> —Horace Greely, 1867

· · · · · · · · · · · · · · · · TRENDSPOTTING · · · · · · · · · · · · · · · · · · ·

Hoop Dreams

In the 1850s and 1860s, women's skirts reached such absurd proportions that they actually required hidden structural supports, in the form of cage-like wire frames. In the United States the first cage-frame support for skirts was patented in 1856 by W. S. Thompson. His "hoop" supports became wildly popular on both sides of the Atlantic, as women freed their legs from suffocating layers of wool or cotton petticoats. There were some drawbacks, however. On an unpracticed wearer, the wide, wiry undergarments could knock over furniture. Worse still, cheap, knockoff models were sometimes visible through the dress and audibly creaky. But the hoops were so much more comfortable that women from all walks of life wanted them: in fact, they were one of the first fashions widely adopted by both upper- and lower-class women.

After a certain point, however, skirts just couldn't get any bigger. (When you occupy more space than a dining room table, it's a good sign you should curb the trend.) Thus the new fashion, emerging from 1862 to 1864, called for skirts that were smaller in front while retaining the characteristic bell shape in back. This allowed women to wear much smaller hoop structures and eventually do away with them altogether in favor of bustles, which were less cumbersome while providing the same structure. Upper-class women might still wear the classic full bell-shaped skirts, but usually only for special formal occasions.

Meanwhile, the invention of synthetic dyes allowed women to go crazy with new, eye-catching colors and patterns—and they did. Most of the synthetic dyes from this period were developed by German chemists and their students in Britain and France, including mauve in 1856, magenta in 1858, several bright blue dyes in 1861, yellow in 1862, "Hoffman violet" and "Bismarck brown" in 1863, "Metternich green" in 1866, aldehyde green in 1869, and orange in 1876. Although the early dyes had some distinct limitations—the colors tended to run—they were so novel that dressmakers couldn't resist. In typical fashion-world style, the craze for color went through a push pull. The color rush in the 1860s led to a backlash in favor of muted colors in 1872, only to reemerge again in the late 1870s, and then be cast aside again in the early 1880s. Oh, fashion world, if only you could make up your mind.

·················· **MADE IN THE USA** ···············

A Chip Off the Old Potato

Potatoes are native to the Western Hemisphere, so it's only fitting that after conquering Europe, they migrated back to North America, where they achieved their most sublime incarnation—the glorious, greasy, salty chip.

In 1853, Saratoga Springs was a fashionable resort destination in upstate New York. Just five hours away from New York City by train, its mineral springs promised recuperation and relaxation for rich folks fleeing the filthy, squalid city. Today, however, the Springs are equally famous for being the birthplace of the potato chip, invented by George Crum, a part African-American, part Native American chef, employed by the luxurious Moon Lake Lodge.

Like many brilliant inventions, the first batch of potato chips resulted from a failed attempt to do something else. Crum's specialties were French fries, and he usually prepared them in the traditional thick-cut style, producing meaty wedges with the skin unpeeled. But on August 24, 1853, a particularly troublesome guest sent his fries back to Crum's kitchen, complaining they were too chunky. Crum obligingly produced another dish of more slender fries, but these too were sent back. Now completely riled up, Crum decided to create French fries that were so impossibly thin and brittle that the finicky guest wouldn't be able to spear them with a fork. To make sure they were inedible, he fried them for even longer and then coated them liberally with salt.

Of course the plan backfired, and the guest pronounced the dish delicious. Soon other diners wanted to sample the addictive chips. Before long "Saratoga chips" were packaged in portable paper bags and were being sold across New York and New England. In 1860 Crum opened his very own restaurant, where every meal started with a basket of potato chips.

Oil! The Early Years

In the mid-nineteenth century, the United States was powered by wood, waterwheels, coal, and whale oil. Of these, coal was clearly "the next big thing." But the period from 1850 to 1875 also saw growing interest in another form of fossilized organic matter: petroleum. "Rock oil," as it was called, could be converted to kerosene, and it worked terrifically as a replacement for whale oil, which was increasingly scarce and expensive. Additionally, in its unrefined form, petroleum worked as an excellent lubricant for steam engines, keeping pistons from overheating.

In the early days of the Industrial Revolution, only small amounts of petroleum were needed. This meant that the demand could be met easily enough from natural seepage—pools of oil that formed on the surface above subterranean deposits. But as the number of steam engines grew and kerosene became more popular, so did the demand for rock oil. Engineers had experimented with various well designs around the world in the 1840s and 1850s, but the first modern oil well—which became the model for all subsequent commercial oil wells—was drilled in Titusville, Pennsylvania, in 1859 by a freelance engineer named Edwin Drake. And though Drake's backers gave up on him, he eventually succeeded in hitting oil by using a steam engine to drill through 60 feet of topsoil, gravel, and bedrock.

★ Before they were pushed out of the Northeast, members of the Seneca tribe used "rock oil" seeping from the ground for various medicinal purposes.

The whole process was a whole lot more complicated than simply drilling a hole in the ground. The main problem was that as the drill passed through the gravel layer, the sides of the well kept collapsing. As the crumbling sides filled in the bottom, they impeded the drill's progress. To solve this problem, Drake hit on a genius idea: the "drive pipe." Composed of 10-foot segments connected by flexible joints, the pipe worked to hold back the mud and gravel. And though drilling through bedrock was labor-intensive and time-consuming, Drake finally struck oil at a depth of 69.5 feet.

In no time, Drake's well began producing 25 barrels of oil a day, and in just over a decade, the area around Titusville was producing 5.8 million barrels of oil per year, thanks to the copycat operations that sprang up almost immediately. Like many great minds in early American history, Drake neglected to file a patent for his invention. Oops!

Stop That Cow

Nasty and effective, barbed wire is a quintessential American invention: without it, the West might not have been won. Or at least, there would have been a lot more cows, horses, and miscellaneous livestock roaming free, with distraught ranchers in pursuit!

Called "the Devil's Rope," barbed wire substituted for more substantial fencing materials like wood or stone. While regular wire was an option, the average cow, weighing 1,000 pounds or more, was not deterred by "smooth" wire fences. Bulls, weighing up to a ton and armed with horns, were even less daunted. The difficulty of ranching without fencing quickly became a serious hindrance to Western expansion.

From 1857 to 1867, a handful of inventors "back East" experimented with wire augmented with small knots of sharp cut wire, but there wasn't much demand in the tree-filled eastern part of the country. Farther west, however, it was an idea whose time had come. Approximately 176 ranchers submitted some variation of the basic idea to Illinois patent offices, which set in motion an exciting legal free-for-all, with various patent holders trying to prove that barbed wire manufacturers were stealing their ideas.

In the end, the patent office chose Joseph F. Glidden's economical design, which produced the maximum number of sharp edges with the least amount of wire. And in 1874, Glidden sold half his patent to an enterprising Illinois hardware entrepreneur named Isaac L. Ellwood, who began manufacturing barbed wire by hand. Imitators produced close variants of the design, and small factories sprang up across western Illinois, all of them turning out barbed wire using manual labor. By 1884 the legitimate factories (there were still plenty of bootleg joints too) were manufacturing up to 100,000 tons of barbed wire a year. That's roughly 600,000 miles of barbed wire, or 40 times the circumference of the earth!

Touchdowns and Tight Ends

Early versions of a rugby-like game were probably being played in Wales in the medieval period, and there are records of "fute ball" being played in English villages in the twelfth century. These games were favorites of English boarding schools, where they provided schoolboys with an opportunity to beat each other senseless (like they needed an excuse). Some of these followed English colonists across the Atlantic Ocean.

At first both American and English football games were more mob happenings than sporting events, with rival "teams" of over a hundred players churning playing fields into muddy, bloody chaos. Unsurprisingly, the American strain was particularly popular on college campuses, with a Harvard tradition called "Bloody Monday" pitting sophomores against freshmen beginning in 1827, and another mob-friendly version called "ball-own" played at Princeton around the same time. (Injuries were common, and occasionally property was destroyed in drunken riot–celebrations, prompting Yale to ban football in 1860, followed by Harvard in 1861.)

However, in the eighteenth and nineteenth centuries, the American and English versions began slowly drifting apart, moving toward the football and rugby we know and love today, but continued to cross-pollinate. One of the basic elements of American football—the touchdown—was borrowed from rugby. The touchdown, or "try" in rugby, was introduced to American players in May 1874 during a series of matches between Montreal's McGill University and Harvard, played in Cambridge, Massachusetts; in the first game, they played American football, and in the second, rugby. Harvard players introduced the rugby touchdown to other college teams, and this quickly became the most popular version of the game.

In following years some finishing touches were added by Walter Camp, whose innovations as a Yale undergrad and alumnus earned him the title the "Father of American Football." Most notably, Camp formed the rival teams into two lines—"the line of scrimmage"—and added the center-quarterback "snap," which initiates play. From 1876 to 1887, he also reduced the number of players per team from 15 to 11, established the standard playing field size of 120 yards by 53 and one-third yards, and set the length of play at two 45-minute halves.

························ **BY THE NUMBERS** ················

781 number of pro-slavery votes cast in Lawrence, Kansas, 1855

253 number of anti-slavery votes cast in Lawrence, Kansas, 1855

232 number of legal votes cast in Lawrence, Kansas, 1855

128,300 number of "industrial establishments" in the United States, June 1860

110,274 number of those that were located in the North

$700 million amount of Union wartime expenditures "tainted with fraud"

20 percent proportion of total wartime expenditures this represented

300 miles of railroad destroyed in Sherman's "March to the Sea" through Georgia

12,000 square miles of Georgia devastated in the march

620,000 number of Americans killed in the Civil War

110,000	number of Union soldiers killed in action
93,000	number of Confederate soldiers killed in action
250,000	number of Union soldiers who died from injuries or disease
167,000	number of Confederate soldiers who died from injuries or disease
64 percent	percent of delegates to Louisiana's 1867 state constitutional convention who were African-American
61 percent	percent of delegates to South Carolina's 1867 state constitutional convention who were African-American
8 million	tons of coal consumed in the United States, 1850
46.6 million	tons of coal consumed in the United States, 1875
440,000	U.S. oil production in barrels,1859
10.9 million	U.S. oil production in barrels, 1875
20 percent	proportion of state budget spent by Mississippi on prosthetic limbs in 1866

Empire State of Mind

(1880–1910)

After the epic, futile spanking that was Reconstruction, a new equilibrium was established between the triumphant Northern states and their defeated (but not-at-all-repentant) Southern counterparts. With the passage of time, the majority of Americans on both sides seemed determined to put the Civil War behind them and move on. Veterans returned to their wives and fathered a new generation of children who had no personal experience of the war. And in many places, the only visible reminders of the Civil War were the unusual number of amputees in public life and military cemeteries sprinkled liberally across North and South.

Imbued with a grand "Progressive" vision from this optimistic period, ambitious men of every stripe turned their energies to science, medicine, law, business, politics, and religion, confident in their ability to truly improve the world. American scientists and inventors made technical advances that revolutionized everyday life. Riding the wave of technological progress, businessmen (The Rockefellers! The Carnegies!) built colossal companies whose unprecedented size allowed them to dominate the American economy— and not in a fun role-playing way.

Meanwhile, statesmen and their friends in the press reunited North and South in pursuit of an array of glittering imperial causes. The demise of slavery meant that the main political obstacle to settling the remaining Western territories and accepting them as states had been removed. Hundreds of thousands of Civil War veterans, African-American freedmen, and immigrants headed West to make their fortunes. America wasn't just interested in local real estate, and it wasn't long before the United States had seized Cuba, Puerto Rico, Hawaii, and the Philippines with the intention of creating its own European-style colonial empire. But being an imperial power turned out to be way more trouble than it was worth, and before long Americans soured on the project.

Nonetheless, great men of American finance and industry still had many "interests" in Latin American affairs, which the U.S. government obligingly protected with diplomacy, espionage, and outright invasion when necessary. One of the biggest projects in Central America was digging a canal across the narrow Isthmus of Panama, connecting the Pacific Ocean to the Caribbean Sea and thereby saving freight and passenger liners the month-long detour around South America. Meanwhile, another new American mega-corporation, United Fruit, effectively ruled large parts of Central America with the approval and assistance of statesmen and spies in Washington, D.C.

During this period, cities took the leading role in the U.S. economy. Foreigners continued to pour into the United States, but more of them settled in urban areas—a big change from the 1840s to 1870s, when huge numbers of Europeans (especially Germans) had flocked to the Midwest. The closing of the frontier in the 1890s meant there was less and less unclaimed land, and urban industry began to displace rural agriculture in the economy's top spot.

·············· **WHAT HAPPENED WHEN** ····················

January 10, 1870 John D. Rockefeller founds Standard Oil.

April 4, 1877 First telephone switchboard goes into operation in Boston.

April 24, 1877 U.S. troops withdraw from the South.

February 19, 1878 Thomas Edison patents the phonograph.

January 27, 1880 Thomas Edison patents the light bulb.

July 2,1890 Congress passes Sherman Anti-Trust Act.

1892 New York City and Chicago are connected by a telephone line; Andrew Carnegie forms Carnegie Steel.

1893 Henry Ford begins experimenting with automobile design; American sugar planters overthrow the Polynesian monarchy in Hawaii.

1894 New York City and Boston are connected by a telephone line.

1898 United States conquers Cuba, Puerto Rico, Guam, and the Philippines in the Spanish-American War.

1900	Wright brothers begin experimenting with gliders.
September 14, 1901	President William McKinley is assassinated.
1903	The Ford Motor Company is incorporated; Wright brothers make first powered flights in Kitty Hawk, North Carolina; Teddy Roosevelt supports revolution in Panama.
March 9, 1907	Indiana passes first state eugenics law in the United States
1908	Henry Ford introduces the Model T.
May 15, 1911	The Supreme Court orders Standard Oil broken up into 34 companies.

····················· **SPECIAL REPORT** ·············

We've Still Got Issues
Jim Crow Laws and National Reconciliation

As with any messy breakup, the reconciliation between North and South required distasteful sacrifices from both sides: defeated white Southerners had to accept the failure of their cause and the loss of their slaves, while victorious Northerners had to accept real limits on their ability to transform Southern society.

No one was particularly surprised by the failure of Reconstruction, considering the basic facts on the ground: the Southern economy remained focused on agriculture, and whites still owned virtually all of the land. As Southern Democrats returned to power, they brushed aside proposals to redistribute plantation land to freed slaves and instead created a new, re-branded system of slavery called "sharecropping." Landowners loaned African-Americans farmland in return for a cut of the harvest. Tenant farmers also had to pay their former masters to use their cotton gins to process their own crops. Thus African-American sharecroppers remained indebted and impoverished and could never save enough cash to buy their land.

> ★ Sharecropping continued well into the twentieth century. In fact, two of America's most heartfelt female vocalists—Tina Turner and Dolly Parton—were born to sharecropper parents.

While lack of property and education kept African-American tenant farmers poor, they were deprived of their political rights by the Ku Klux Klan, the White Leagues, and the Red Shirts—paramilitary groups formed by Confederate veterans to instill terror in former slaves. Eventually the White Leagues, described without irony as "the military arm of the Democratic Party," were incorporated into state militias and the National Guard, revealing the close connections between local governments and illegal thuggery. In the 1880s and 1890s, these mobs of white vigilantes were essentially immune from the legal system and used their power to lynch hundreds of African-Americans for supposed offenses like rape, "speaking rudely," and "making obscene gestures." Many victims were simply too successful or too outspoken—e.g., actually trying to vote—for poor whites who resented any competition.

Unwilling to revisit the issue of states' rights, the Supreme Court refused to overturn state laws enabling massive electoral fraud in 1875. Meanwhile in Congress, sympathetic Northern Democrats also opposed any attempt to enforce policies protecting freedmen, calling the attempts federal "tyranny" against the states.

To formalize the disenfranchisement of freed African-Americans, the resurgent Southern Democrats—or "Dixiecrats"—instituted requirements for voters, including literacy tests and poll taxes. Of course, both measures excluded poor whites too. In Alabama, the number of eligible white voters decreased from 232,821 in 1900 to 191,432 in 1903. When poor whites protested, legislators in some Southern states responded with "grandfather clauses," which said a man could vote if his grandfather had voted in 1867 (the year before freedmen got the vote). These tactics, upheld by the Supreme Court well into the twentieth century, effectively sidelined black voters. In Louisiana, for instance, the number of black voters fell from 130,000 in 1896 to 1,300 in 1904.

> ★ *After the turn of the century, the term "grandfather clause" became a standard term for any new law that offers exemptions to certain people based on prior standing or action.*

In 1883 the Supreme Court overturned the Civil Rights Act of 1875, which guaranteed equal treatment in "public accommodations," as an unconstitutional extension of federal power over the states. This emboldened Southern legislators to draft laws enforcing racial segregation in public places. These were known as "Jim Crow" laws (named for the main character in a satirical song about slaves from the 1830s). The new ordinances mandated the creation of "separate but equal" facilities for whites and African-Americans in schools, hospitals, public transportation, restaurants, bars, and virtually everywhere else. Both groups already lived and worked apart, so to some extent Jim Crow laws merely reinforced customary segregation. Still, the creation of legal barriers based on race made it even easier for the white majority to control and exploit African-Americans. And the creation of "always separate, but never equal" African-American schools further limited the prospects of children born to illiterate ex-slaves. In 1896 the legality of "separate but equal" segregation was upheld by the Supreme Court in *Plessy v. Ferguson*.

·············· **LIES YOUR TEACHER TOLD YOU** ··············

LIE: *The North was less racist than the South.*
THE TRUTH: The sad fact is that racism continued to be more or less the norm in late nineteenth-century and early twentieth-century America, and Northern states were no exception—they were just less honest about what they were doing.

Northern racism was evident before the Civil War, when whites instigated bloody race riots to protest not only the planned integration of public schools, but also proposals to build separate black-only schools. The fracas left most African-American children with no schools, period. Then, during the Civil War, anti-war Northern Democrats, known as Copperheads, urged whites to resist the draft with the virulent slogan "We won't fight for the nigger." The group played on the fears of poor immigrants worried about losing their jobs to free African-Americans.

After the war, Northern racists were galvanized by the increasing numbers of African-Americans migrating to Northern cities in search of factory jobs—a gradual increase at first, which began to accelerate after the turn of the century. This prompted a new wave of white opposition; while most Northern states had passed laws by 1890 to ban segregation in public schools, in reality most local school boards bitterly resisted integration.

★ *Braves slugger Henry "Hank" Aaron revealed that racism was more difficult to deal with during his time in Milwaukee than it was in Atlanta. In the South, it was more obvious and blatant, and thus easier to combat. In the North, it occurred "behind your back."*

The unofficial segregation was buttressed by economic discrimination. White employers generally hired white applicants
over black candidates when given the choice. Worse still, the
status quo was reinforced by threats from violent immigrant
gangs—especially Irish and Italians—who demanded jobs for their
"constituents." Corrupt political machines like the Tammany Hall
Democrats in New York City also steered city jobs and public contracts to white supporters. And although lynching was less common than in the South, bouts of anti-black violence erupted in
New York City; Baltimore; Cincinnati; Omaha; Philadelphia; and
Washington, D.C., between 1900 and 1910.

Despite all of this, African-Americans continued migrating
from the South. Northern cities simply provided more economic
opportunities than the rural South, where there was little prospect of employment outside of sharecropping.

LIE: *Immigrants came to America to participate in its capitalist economy.*

THE TRUTH: Most immigrants came to America for work on
whatever terms they could get it, but there were a good number
who weren't willing to settle for the capitalist grind. From 1880
to 1903, there was an influx of radical leftists who espoused ideologies like communism and anarchism—and most Americans didn't
want a dash of communism in their melting pot. Both groups drew
support from the ranks of immigrant factory workers who lived
and worked in miserable conditions. Eventually, public fears of
"bomb-throwing anarchists" prompted Congress to pass the Immigration Act of March 3, 1903, prohibiting immigration by "anarchists, or persons who believe in, or advocate, the overthrow by
force or violence, or of all government, or of all forms of law, or
the assassination of public officials."

These fears weren't groundless. Indeed, radical anarchists—most
visibly those from Germany, Italy, and Russia—were the nineteenth-
century equivalent of modern-day terrorist groups like Al Qaeda.
Forming autonomous cells, they pursued their fantastic vision of a
world without government through assassinations and indiscrimi-
nate bombings—dignifying terrorism as "propaganda of the deed,"
a term invented by the Russian group "People's Will." And they were
surprisingly successful. Two particular groups dominated these
threats in America—Germans before 1890, and Italians afterward.
(Otto von Bismarck lifted the ban on the Social Democratic Party
in 1890, giving left-wing Germans a political outlet—but when anar-

chists from the Italian Socialist party were excluded in 1892, they picked up the violence baton and ran with it.)

Despite the two groups' European origins, the most famous incident of anarchist agitation occurred in the United States: the "Haymarket Massacre." On May 4, 1886, Chicago police tried to break up a peaceful demonstration by factory workers in Haymarket Square. As the officers directed the crowd, someone threw a bomb. A cop died from the explosion, chaos ensued, and in the resulting violence, seven more police officers were killed. An unknown number of civilians (up to 50, by one count) also became casualties. And though it remains unclear just who did what—some of the police deaths were due to friendly fire—the incident became a rallying cry for anarchists and anti-anarchists alike. Anarchists were infuriated by the prosecution of eight of their own who helped organize the rally. (The fact that they were arrested on the trumped-up charges of "conspiracy to commit murder" only fanned the flames.) Seven were condemned to death, four were actually executed in November 1887, and a fifth committed suicide in jail.

The names of the defendants were enough to convince many Americans that anarchism was an immigrant conspiracy. Seven of the eight men prosecuted in the Haymarket incident were German immigrants, and the eighth, Oscar Neebe, was born in America to German immigrant parents. Eight years later, in July 1892, two German-speaking Lithuanian Jewish anarchists conspired to assassinate Henry Clay Frick, the operating manager for Carnegie Steel. To be fair, Clay was called the most hated man in

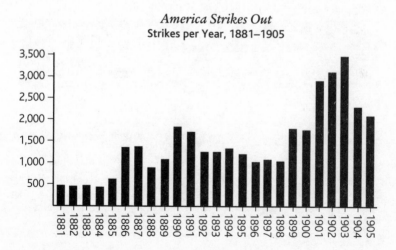

America Strikes Out
Strikes per Year, 1881–1905

America because of his brutal strike-breaking tactics. But the plan backfired, and instead of bringing support to the striking workers, the pair undermined the cause and only reinforced the public perception of the immigrant stereotype.

But those weren't the only terrorist acts on American soil. Perhaps the most disturbing anarchist terror plot was the assassination of President William McKinley by Leon Czolgosz on September 6, 1901. While not an immigrant himself, Czolgosz, born to Polish immigrant parents, was lumped together with other foreign malefactors as part of the "black anarchist" threat from abroad. Czolgosz encouraged the association, and his personal history would have been familiar to many immigrants: after going to work at the American Wire and Steel Company at the age of 10, he and his brothers were fired when other workers went on strike. From the ages of 16 to 18, Czolgosz worked at a glass factory in Pennsylvania. Not long after, he had a mental breakdown.

Thrilled and inspired by the recent assassination of Italy's King Umberto I, in late August of 1901, Czolgosz rented a room in Buffalo, New York. Then, on September 6, he snuck his .32-caliber revolver into the Pan-American Exposition, where President McKinley was scheduled to make an appearance. Somehow evading the security (three Secret Service agents were guarding the president, against his wishes), Czolgosz made his way to the front of the line and shot the president twice at point-blank range. After being severely beaten by the crowd, Czolgosz was convicted and sentenced to death on September 23; on October 29 he was electrocuted at Auburn Prison in upstate New York. Meanwhile, McKinley lingered for eight days before dying on September 14.

★ *Shortly after his execution, sulfuric acid was thrown on Leon Czolgosz's body in order to hasten decomposition. His remains were then diffused into the prison's soil.*

FROM PINKERTON TO BLACKWATER

Despite the name, most employees of the Pinkerton National Detective Agency weren't really "detectives." A more appropriate list of roles would include security guards, bounty hunters, and plain ol' thugs. Pinkerton founded the agency in 1855 to assist railroads threatened with labor outages, and Pinkertons were soon providing security for "scabs" brought in to replace striking workers at factories and mines across the Northeast. In this role, Pinkertons became hated symbols of industrial exploitation. These chaotic scenes often turned violent, with Pinkertons accused of beating and killing striking workers (who sometimes started the violence).

In the 1870s a Pinkerton detective, James McParland, infiltrated the Molly Maguires, a secret labor union/criminal group composed of Irish immigrants in the Pennsylvania coal mines. McParland helped bring down the secret Mafia-style organization—but it seems his employers shared information with vigilantes, probably in the pay of Pennsylvania industrialists, who murdered suspected members of the Molly Maguires as well as their families. The most notorious Pinkerton case, however, is the Homestead Steel Strike of 1892, near Pittsburgh, Pennsylvania, when violence left seven Pinkertons and nine strikers dead.

The Pinkertons were also forerunners of modern-day private security contractors hired by the government. They were sometimes given a huge amount of authority. In February 1861 Allan Pinkerton personally supervised Abraham Lincoln's security as he passed through hostile Baltimore en route to his inauguration in Washington. Pinkerton based his strategy in part on intelligence from a female spy, Kate Warne, who had infiltrated a group of alleged plotters. (She was an employee of his Female Detective Bureau, created to use "feminine wiles" in detective work.)

During the Civil War, Pinkertons provided security for the Union Army and carried out espionage for the United States in the Confederacy, including organizing "Loyal Leagues" of slaves, runaways, and freedmen as intelligence networks. In 1871 the U.S. Department of Justice hired the Pinkertons to investigate violations of federal law—basically employing them as a proto-FBI. At one point in 1909, Pinkerton employed 40,000 agents—larger than the 28,000 personnel in the U.S. Army.

But the growing power of the agency alarmed authorities. In 1889 Ohio outlawed the Pinkertons over concern they might serve as a private army, and over the next 10 years, 24 states banned armed guards—mostly targeting Pinkerton. After the Homestead Steel Strike, in 1893 Congress passed the Anti-Pinkerton Act, forbidding any government agency from employing them.

LIE: *America is (not) an imperialist nation.*

THE TRUTH: The United States is definitely not an imperialist nation, except when it is. Confused? One prime example of America behaving as an imperialist power, while simultaneously opposing imperialism, is the Spanish-American War of 1898.

As the vast territories of the American West were claimed and divided up in the late 1800s, the American public turned its attention to nearby territories like Cuba, Puerto Rico, and the Philippines (in this case, "nearby" means nearby China). The only problem was that all these islands belonged to Spain, which refused to sell them to the United States, even when America said "please." So the United States decided to take them.

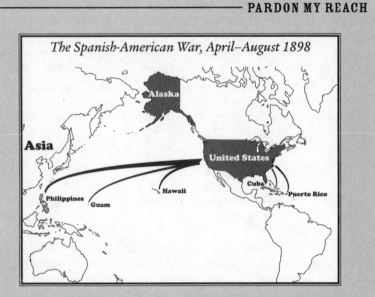

The Spanish-American War, April–August 1898

1890: Alfred T. Mahan advocates the conquest of Cuba, the Philippines, and Hawaii to project American naval power.

1892: Cuban exiles in the United States organize the Cuban Revolutionary Party with the goal of achieving independence; Filipinos form several armed revolutionary leagues to do the same.

1895: Cuban uprising against Spanish rule begins.

1896: The U.S. Congress votes to recognize Cuban independence; President Grover Cleveland warns the United States may intervene in Cuba; Filipinos revolt against Spanish rule.

1897: Newspapers owned by William Randolph Hearst and Joseph Pulitzer whip up anti-Spanish sentiment in the United States.

1898

> *January:* Spain grants some autonomy to Cuba.
> *February:* USS *Maine* explodes in Havana harbor, triggering pro-war sentiment in the United States.
> *March:* Commodore George Dewey is ordered to sail for the Philippines.

April: The U.S. Congress declares war on Spain; President McKinley enlists 125,000 volunteers.

May: Commodore Dewey arrives in Manila and defeats the Spanish navy.

June: Marines land in Cuba; Guam surrenders; American Anti-Imperialist League formed.

July: Teddy Roosevelt and the Rough Riders capture San Juan Hill, near Santiago de Cuba; Hawaii is annexed; Spanish forces in Cuba surrender.

August: The United States and Spain agree to a cease-fire; Manila falls to U.S. forces the next day.

September: First Congress of Philippine Republic meets to draw up a constitution.

October: McKinley insists on the annexation of the Philippines.

December: The United States and Spain sign formal peace treaty, giving the United States control of Puerto Rico, the Philippines, and Guam for $20 million.

1899

January: The United States refuses to recognize the new Filipino government.

February: The Filipino insurrection against the American occupation begins.

But this bully tactic wasn't a uniquely American concept. At the time, there was plenty of "taking" going on across the globe—Britain, France, and Germany were actively carving up Asia and Africa, conquering native peoples and booting out the earlier generation of colonial powers like Spain and Portugal. The growing power of European empires made America nervous, especially because Britain and France both had their sights on Cuba and the Philippines. To preempt the brutish and uncouth European imperialism,

SHE AIN'T HEAVY, SHE'S MY SISTER

If you're not clear on the United States' take on imperialism yet, consider Secretary of State James G. Blaine's "Big Sister Policy." This name was meant to convey American benevolence. Of course, as anyone with a big sister can attest, they're also bossy, hypocritical know-it-alls who humiliate you and take your stuff without asking, all while telling you it's for your own good. That pretty much sums up U.S. relations with Latin America in this period.

American politicians proposed that the United States pursue a policy of "enlightened" imperialism. (Sounds delightful, no?)

But there were other reasons America wanted to take Spain's stuff. In the second half of the nineteenth century, seafaring was revolutionized by the introduction of the steam engine, which replaced wind as the main source of power. However, this presented a new challenge. Coal took up a lot of space and limited the amount of cargo that ships could carry. So to make steam-powered shipping cost-effective, merchants and militaries needed networks of refueling stations. One near Asia would be particularly useful, but Cuba seemed like a nice option as well.

Still, the popular rationale for engaging in the Spanish-American War was that the United States was selflessly advancing the cause of liberty and freedom. And this sentiment was surprisingly genuine: Americans were empathetic to Cuban rebels in their fight for independence from Spain. Even before the uprising began in 1895, Cuban exiles in the United States were rallying financial and political support—a job made easier when Spain herded 300,000 civilians into concentration camps in Cuba, where 100,000 died of disease and starvation.

With public opinion firmly behind the rebels, all the United States needed was a reason to get involved. This didn't take long. In January 1898 President McKinley sent the warship USS *Maine* to Havana—supposedly to protect Americans living in Cuba but actually to intimidate Spain. On the evening of February 15, 1898, the *Maine* hit a Spanish mine, exploded, and sank in Havana harbor with the loss of 266 American sailors. The fate of the Spanish Empire was sealed as sensational newspaper accounts whipped public opinion into war frenzy around the rallying cry, "Remember the *Maine*, To Hell with Spain!" (Where would jingoism be without rhyming?) Of course, newspaper publishers like William Randolph Hearst had an interest in promoting conflict, since wars sold lots of papers.

> We are the ruling race of the world . . . ours is the blood of government; ours the heart of dominion; ours the brain and genius of administration.
>
> —Senator Albert Beveridge, 1898

SO GOOD IT HEARST

In an effort to amp up sales, William Randolph Hearst exaggerated the situation in Cuba just a tad by printing front-page stories of Spanish soldiers cannibalizing Cuban prisoners and strip-searching female American tourists in public. That kind of thing is why he's remembered as one of this era's over-the-top industrial titans. Hearst reveled in being able to control public opinion—but was above all a businessman. Born in San Francisco on April 29, 1863, he was the son of a wealthy miner who also owned several local newspapers. As a youth, Hearst was a mischievous troublemaker, getting himself expelled from Harvard for giving some of his instructors chamber pots with their names inscribed on the bottom. But as a publisher, he was a force of nature. In 1887 his father gave him control over *The San Francisco Examiner,* and Hearst soon went bicoastal with his acquisition of *The New York Journal,* followed by 28 other newspapers in major American cities, as well as a number of magazines. Indeed, he created one of the first truly national newspaper chains, with a daily circulation of 13 million reaching approximately 40 million readers—almost half the population in 1910—giving him unprecedented power to mold public opinion and influence events. This wasn't always a good thing, however, as he also pioneered sensationalistic tabloid journalism that tended to be long on emotion and somewhat shorter on facts. Of course, that's what sold newspapers. And he sold quite a few: in 1935 Hearst was worth about $200 million, equal to about $3 billion–$5 billion today.

> You furnish the pictures, and I'll furnish the war.
>
> —Newspaper publisher William Randolph Hearst,
> to illustrator Frederic Remington

Congress itself was still ambivalent about the whole imperial thing: on one hand a resolution introduced by Senator Henry M. Teller of Colorado renounced all U.S. claims to Cuban territory. But the imperialists also got their way: after the war, the U.S. military governor in Cuba, John R. Brooke, appointed provincial governors and mayors, and U.S. capitalists soon dominated Cuban industry and agriculture. By 1902, U.S. mining companies controlled 80 percent of Cuba's exports of copper ore, and by 1905, 10 percent of the land belonged to giant American-owned agriculture estates. Meanwhile, the right to vote was restricted to literate Cuban landowners, excluding the majority of Cubans and empowering the elite, who traditionally favored closer relations with the United States.

But Cuba was only one part of the imperial plan sort of endorsed by the American public. In four brief months, from April to August 1898, the United States also conquered the Spanish possessions of Puerto Rico, Guam, and the Philippines (paying a nominal fee to make it all look aboveboard). Like Cuba, the last was mostly a cakewalk, as American troops intervened on the side of native rebels who were already fighting for independence. Unlike Cuba, however, the Filipino rebels were not prepared to accept another foreign occupation.

> **Damn the Americans! Why don't they tyrannize us more?**
>
> —Manuel Quezon, a rebel commander, later the
> president of the Philippines

Over three bloody years, from 1899 to 1902, U.S. troops ultimately secured victory over the Filipino rebels. All told, the fighting claimed the lives of about 200,000 civilians—3 percent of the total population—through disease, starvation, and atrocities committed by both sides. (Much like regular imperialists, "enlightened" imperialists were also willing to herd hundreds of thousands of civilians into concentration camps.) On the other hand, outside the war zone, the American occupation was relatively relaxed, and U.S. forces aided development. In the Philippines, this meant building roads and telegraphs, ensuring clean water supplies, and controlling diseases like malaria, cholera, smallpox, and typhoid fever. The U.S. government also won hearts and minds in noncombat zones by buying 400,000 acres of land from the Vatican (which had received it as a pious gift from the Spanish crown) and redistributing it to local peasants.

ACT NOW AND GET A FREE CHAIN OF ISLANDS!

On June 20, 1898, U.S. Navy ships on the way to the Philippines seized the small but strategically located island of Guam. After capturing a few dozen Spanish soldiers, the squadron commander decided not to garrison Guam—so Frank Portusach, an American civilian who happened to be living there, temporarily served as the entire U.S. occupation force!

Following the "while we're at it" school of foreign policy, the United States also picked up Hawaii, even though it didn't belong to Spain. Actually the islands' Christian Polynesian monarchy had already been overthrown in 1893 by American settlers—mostly sugar plantation owners—who asked for U.S. Marines to help keep things under control. After four years as an independent republic, the settlers persuaded Congress to annex Hawaii as a territory in July 1898. The acquisition fit in nicely with America's other holdings, especially since the Philippines provided a cheap labor source for Hawaii's sugarcane plantations.

> We must have Hawaii to help us get our share of China.
>
> —President William McKinley, to Congress, 1898

All in all, American empire-building was a fairly halfhearted, wishy-washy affair. In Cuba, the Platt Amendment of 1899 withdrew U.S. troops and handed the authority over to a civilian government elected by Cubans. But it also prohibited Cuba from conducting most of its own foreign policy, gave America military bases on Cuban soil, and gave Congress the right to intervene on behalf of American economic interests—aka, the entire Cuban economy.

The Filipinos received fewer powers of self-government, but plenty of lip service. In 1901 President McKinley appointed a Philippine Commission that William Howard Taft oversaw as governor. In 1907 the Filipinos were finally allowed to elect their own representative assembly, which became the lower body of a two-part legislature, with the commission playing the senior role. In the racist fashion of the day, Americans were reluctant to turn authority over to the Filipinos out of prejudice, arguing "childlike" Asians were incapable of self-government.

> The Pacific is the ocean of the commerce of the future . . . The power that rules the Pacific, therefore, is the power that rules the world. And, with the Philippines, that power is and will forever be the American Republic.
>
> —Senator Albert Beveridge, 1898

·················· OTHER PEOPLE'S STUFF ···········

Good America/Bad America

The Spanish-American War signaled the emergence of a new, more aggressive approach to relations with Latin America, especially when debt was involved. And it was involved quite often. At the time, a number of Latin American regimes had borrowed money that they couldn't pay back from European financiers. This fueled American fears because European powers were in the habit of repossessing countries that defaulted on loans, and the United States wasn't exactly eager for Britain, France, or Germany to have a foothold in the Western Hemisphere. American anxiety only increased after a dozen Latin American nations defaulted on British loans in the 1870s. (The fact that the Brits bombarded a port in Honduras and seized a strip of Nicaraguan land soon after wasn't calming anyone's nerves.)

Determined to keep those wily Europeans out, President Teddy Roosevelt and his successor, William Howard Taft, laid out a "good cop, bad cop" foreign policy. On one hand, European lending would be replaced by American finance, referred to as "dollar diplomacy." On the other hand, the United States was happy to take control of countries that defaulted on European loans—by force if necessary—and manage their finances until those debts were repaid. The idea was to deprive Europeans of any excuse to intervene, and it was referred to as "gunboat diplomacy." This bad cop part of the plan was also a blatant violation of each country's sovereignty, but whatever: the United States figured that in time they'd get used to it. In the first two decades of the twentieth century, the United States assumed control of the Dominican Republic, Nicaragua, and Haiti (the young Assistant Secretary of the U.S. Navy, Franklin Delano Roosevelt, drew up a new Haitian constitution) and threatened similar measures against Honduras and Guatemala.

★ *Until coffee gained popularity, beer was the breakfast beverage of choice in most urban areas of the United States.*

Unsurprisingly, American financiers ended up controlling huge sections of the regional economy: for example, as part of debt restructuring, U.S. banks took possession of Nicaragua's national bank and railroads. The United States also intervened throughout Central America and the Caribbean to protect American property, prop up friendly rulers, and get rid of the unfriendly ones with a combination of cloak-and-dagger methods and open force. Once again, Nicaragua was a frequent beneficiary: in 1909, after President Jose Santos Zelaya became too friendly with European investors, an American mining company engineered a rebellion as a pretext for occupation by U.S. Marines. Zelaya was replaced by Adolfo Diaz, an executive from the mining company, who formally invited U.S. forces to occupy Nicaragua for over a decade. Not surprisingly, the United States happily accepted.

> ★ *The headquarters of the* Banco Nacional de Nicaragua *were technically located in Connecticut, where it was incorporated by American bankers. Meanwhile, the headquarters of* Ferrocarril del Pacifico, *the Nicaraguan national railway, were located in Maine!*

This was a typical approach, as America's distinctive form of "imperial*isn't*" favored indirect control through puppet regimes. It was cheaper than ruling a country outright, which required spending money on administration, infrastructure, sanitation, education, and other assorted amenities. Native leaders also inspired less popular resentment than gringo governors and could get away with harsher measures when resistance cropped up. (Plus, they could take the blame if anything went sour, as it often did.)

FOREIGN POLICY GOES BANANAS

Controlling so-called Banana Republics was often too taxing for U.S. policymakers, so they simply "subcontracted" the work out. Take United Fruit (now Chiquita). The company was formed by the 1899 merger of the Boston Fruit Company with the national railroad of Costa Rica, and was controlled by an American mogul, Minor C. Keith, who built the rail system in exchange for 800,000 acres of tax-free land. Keith's big idea—taking Asian bananas and growing them in Central America—proved to be a big success. In the 1890s he expanded his banana-railroad empire to include large parts of Guatemala, El Salvador, Nicaragua, Panama, Colombia, Venezuela, Brazil, Jamaica, and the Dominican Republic. The merger with the Boston Fruit Company, which controlled production in Cuba, formed the largest agricultural conglomerate in the world.

But there was competition. In 1899 Standard Fruit (now Dole) was founded by two Sicilian immigrants, Joseph Vaccaro, a New Orleans fruit wholesaler, and Salvador D'Antoni, a smuggler and gunrunner operating in northern Honduras. Taking a page from United Fruit's book, Vaccaro and D'Antoni soon dominated Honduras, building and controlling ports, railroads, and telegraph lines. And they didn't shrink from deceit and violence. Early on, for example, they raised money from Honduran investors in the port of La Ceiba—but in 1903, when the Honduran investors demanded their share of the profits, Vaccaro had the city hall of La Ceiba burned down, destroying the records of their investments. How you like *them* bananas?

A Man, a Plan, an American-Constructed Uprising

Probably the single biggest U.S. intervention in Central America involved the creation of a new country, Panama, in territory that used to belong to Colombia. This was the culmination of a long, drawn-out effort to build a canal connecting the Atlantic and Pacific oceans somewhere in Central America, where the distance between them was narrowest.

People had been talking about a "trans-Isthmian" canal as early as the sixteenth century, when a Spanish priest suggested building one with native slave labor. Similar plans received enthusiastic support from Thomas Jefferson and John Quincy Adams during their presidencies. The value was obvious: a very fast clipper ship took about 90 days to make the voyage from New York City around South America to San Francisco in 1850. But after the Panama Canal opened in 1914, steamships could make the trip in just 22 days. In addition to encouraging trade, this resulted in fewer shipwrecks—especially in the perilous Straits of Magellan—not to mention fewer shipboard deaths from disease and starvation. But huge obstacles (e.g., landslides, malaria, and pesky governments) kept the vision from being realized until the late nineteenth century, when they were finally vanquished by America's "can-do" attitude, along with some good old-fashioned manipulation.

Initially, the French seemed like the best bet to make the canal happen. In 1879 Ferdinand de Lesseps, the French engineer famous for building the Suez

HAPPY BELATED B-DAY, AMERICA!

In 1886 Ferdinand de Lesseps presented the speech that officially dedicated France's greatest gift to the United States, the Statue of Liberty. The Statue (whose full title is Liberty Enlightening the World) was originally supposed to be unveiled on the centennial of the Declaration of Independence, but the project ran into a number of delays. Besides engineering challenges, fundraising for the pedestal went slowly until newspaper publisher Joseph Pulitzer shamed readers into donating with scolding editorials. The internal structure of the 151-foot-tall statue was designed by Maurice Koechlin, the engineer who designed the Eiffel Tower for Gustave Eiffel. With the pedestal, the entire Statue of Liberty monument is 305 feet tall, and was the tallest structure in the United States when it was erected; Chicago's Home Insurance Building, completed in 1885, was 138 feet tall.

Canal, secured funding to build an enormously expensive canal that would cut through Panama's mountainous terrain at sea level. In 1888, however, Lessep's Panama Canal Company went bankrupt. Landslides and tropical diseases had bested French ambition.

Meanwhile, for at least half a century, America's attention had been focused on building a canal in Nicaragua. The country's low-lying terrain and network of navigable rivers and lakes made it feel like the better candidate. But the bargain-basement price of Lessep's Panama Canal Company proved irresistible, and in 1904 the U.S. government bought it for a song. And along with the fine price, America was happy to keep Lessep's half-built canal out of the other European nations' hands.

★ *The stretch of land upon which the Panama Canal was constructed lies at such an odd angle that ships heading from the Caribbean to the Pacific have to travel in a southeasterly direction.*

After the purchase, American engineers quickly set about working on a new, more realistic design for the canal. The final design incorporated three sets of locks to raise and lower ships across the isthmus. But even before construction began, there was a problem. The Colombian Senate refused to ratify the treaty giving the United States a 99-year lease on the Colombian territory where the canal was supposed to be built—not because of any misgivings about U.S. imperialism, but rather simple greed. They wanted another $15 million on top of the $10 million down payment that the United States had already agreed to. Unfortunately, they made a rookie mistake in underestimating Teddy Roosevelt. Possessing little patience for foreigners, and even less for Congress, "TR" refused to go back to Capitol Hill to wheedle more money for the canal. He had a better plan: why make a new treaty, when you can make a new country?

This proved surprisingly easy, thanks to the geographic isolation and rebellious character of the territory in question. Like other parts of the Central America hinterland, Panama was in a chronic state of just-about-to-rebel, needing only a little encouragement (along with some money and guns) to erupt. Simply start with one off-the-shelf uprising, throw in a naval blockade to prevent Colombia from sending troops, and *voila*—Panama! The United

States recognized Panamanian independence immediately, and in the next breath, the two countries signed a treaty giving the United States a lease on the same terms previously offered to Colombia.

But creating a new country was the easy part. It would take another 10 long years before the United States cut a canal across the 50 miles of mountainous jungle.

RUMBLE IN THE JUNGLE

The Americans faced the same challenges in digging the canal as their French predecessors, including malaria and yellow fever outbreaks. In fact, America's greatest accomplishment might have been in controlling these mosquito-borne diseases. The effort was led by Colonel William Crawford Gorgas, who declared an all-out war on the pests. Gorgas's methods induce cringes nowadays, but they worked: after ordering miles of the jungle leveled, he went after the mosquitoes' ability to reproduce by draining all the standing water in the country. Gorgas took no prisoners and every puddle, pond, and wetland was sucked dry. Any standing water that couldn't be drained was treated with pesticide and coated with a layer of petroleum, preventing new mosquito larvae from taking hold. Gorgas also ordered the fumigation of buildings and instituted a quarantine policy for sick individuals. Finally, he ordered workers' barracks enclosed with screens to keep out mosquitoes (well, white workers' barracks, anyway—black workers mostly slept in tents). The result: fever reduction and more construction!

························ **MADE IN AMERICA** ························

The Gibson Girls

Here's something you don't see every decade: in the last quarter of the nineteenth century, American women embraced a homegrown fashion trend! That's right. Instead of copping styles from Paris or London, the new feminine ideal was personified by "the Gibson Girl," depicted by the pen-and-ink illustrator Charles Gibson. Like other fashion movements, the Gibson Girl style had a definite look, but also reflected an attitude and a unique approach to the world. Gibson Girls were beautiful and glamorous, but they were also fun-loving and even a bit cheeky.

How could the drawings of one illustrator become the iconic images of an age? One word: print. With literacy levels steadily increasing and production and distribution costs simultaneously decreasing, newspapers became a daily habit for most educated people. Readers could choose from morning and evening editions, and news junkies often picked up both. The total circulation of daily newspapers increased from 3,566,395 in 1880 to 24,211,977 in 1909 (from 7 percent to 26 percent of the U.S. population). Meanwhile, the total number of monthly magazines increased from 1,167 in 1880 to 2,767 in 1910. Some big titles even boasted circulations over 1 million. These print publications, along with the advertisements within, helped create a mass culture—both shaping and reflecting the standards and expectations of all parts of life.

★ *Part of the increase in magazine readership from 1880 to 1910 was the result of the Postal Act of 1879, which reduced the mailing cost by establishing a lower second-class rate for magazines.*

It was in this context that Charles Gibson drew his satirical cartoons, with his "Girls" sometimes enchantingly ethereal, sometimes comical, but always beautiful. The stereotypical Gibson Girl was tall and trim, with a narrow waist. She had curves, a distinctive S-shaped profile with the help of a corset, and delicate facial features. Popular hairstyles, like the pompadour and bouffant, resembled more relaxed, free-flowing versions of Romantic hairdos; a few locks of a Gibson Girl's hair might trail carelessly for artistic effect.

Running errands during the day, the Gibson Girl was likely to wear a "traveling suit," including an embroidered blouse with a dark bowtie, a seersucker "outing" skirt, elbow-length satin gloves, and a straw "boater" hat decorated with flowers or ribbons. When she wanted to stand out in the evening, the Gibson Girl got a bit friskier, wearing elegant, low-cut gowns that revealed her shoulders, arms, and more than a hint of cleavage. Of course, she always had spectacular gem-encrusted earrings and necklaces to call attention to the aforementioned cleavage. Other elegant, must-have accessories included fancy silk fans, jeweled hatpins, and tiny silk handbags.

★ *If you're still trying to picture the archetypal Gibson Girl, two words capture the look: Mary Poppins. Yowza!*

The women Gibson idolized were a new breed, and much of their behavior—smoking, drinking, maintaining an active, sporty lifestyle—was viewed as unladylike. Some worked as shopgirls, priding themselves on financial independence. Others even traveled on their own, unaccompanied by men. Overall, guys were clearly nervous about the blurring of gender boundaries, fearing a female invasion of traditionally male domains. As a satirist, Gibson was an equally keen observer of men, and he loved playing off of their anxieties and befuddlement.

A Deeply Undesirable Movement

The dark side of the post–Civil War Progressive Era was the eugenics movement. To be fair, eugenics began in Britain and had a global following, but its first application on a big scale came in the United States. In fact, Americans were so good at eugenics that U.S. laws were used as models for the program established in Germany in the 1920s and 1930s by the Nazi regime.

Inspired by Charles Darwin's theory of natural selection, the doctrine held that "desirable" and "undesirable" human traits corresponded to "superior" and "inferior" genes inherited from ancestors. Eugenicists also believed that society was actively undermining the process of natural selection through benevolent institutions like public education, charity, and social welfare. These programs had the unintended consequence of enabling "inferior" individuals to have more children, reversing the natural order of things. With natural selection suspended, desirable traits were doomed to be overwhelmed by multiplying hordes of genetically unfit human beings.

Pointing to the success of American farmers who embraced "scientific" principles, eugenicists persuaded educated Americans that humanity could be improved if the country employed the same methods used in animal husbandry. In fact, the first organization to advocate eugenics was the American Breeders' Association, a group of professional livestock breeders. Bolstered by their success with cattle and poultry, they were quick to apply their learnings to the human population with their "Report on the Best Practical Means to Cut off the Defective Germ-Plasm of the American Population." But what exactly was this "defective germ-plasm" they hoped to eradicate from the human population? The catchall term included people with mental disabilities, epileptics, alcoholics, criminals, blind people, deaf people, people with congenital deformities, "paupers," the homeless, and anyone suffering from "immorality."

As the movement gained popularity in the 1880s, eugenics drew on a body of (supposedly) scientific literature produced by researchers at nonprofit organizations. Simultaneously, various groups were using these results to lobby for state and federal eugenics laws.

To gain political support, eugenics advocates exploited the American public's vague but deep-seated fears of contagion, sexual defilement, and racial impurity. To get a sense of how rapidly this movement progressed, take a look at Indiana—the first state to pass a eugenics law:

1879—Harriet Foster, a social scientist, presents a paper on "The Education of Idiots and Imbeciles," blaming inbreeding and inherited alcoholism for mental disabilities.

1881—Preacher Oscar C. McCulloch presents a "Study in Social Degradation," asserting a hereditary basis for vice and ignorance, based on questionable observations he made of farm families in rural Indiana.

1889—Their research is confirmed by the Board of State Charities.

1898—The Board advocates that all "defective" individuals be forbidden to marry, and that all "defectives" in the custody of state prisons and mental hospitals be sterilized.

1899—This agenda is quickly put into action at the Indiana State Reformatory by Dr. Harry C. Sharp, who sterilized about 500 inmates from 1899 to 1910.

1901—The governor signs a law putting "feeble-minded" women with no legal guardians into state custody to prevent them from reproducing.

1905—It becomes illegal for "imbeciles, epileptics, and those of unsound mind" to marry.

1907—The Indiana Eugenics Law is passed, mandating the sterilization of "criminals, idiots, rapists, and imbeciles."

Ultimately, about 2,500 people were sterilized involuntarily in Indiana. By 1914 similar eugenics laws had been adopted in 14 states, including New York, New Jersey, California, Michigan, and Iowa, and legislators were considering eugenics laws in 11 more. By the 1940s, 30 states had laws ordering sterilization of "feeble-minded" people who were "wards of the state." Altogether, approximately 65,000 Americans were sterilized.

> In this family history are murders, a large number of illegitimacies and of prostitutes. They are generally diseased. The children die young. They live by petty stealing, begging, ash-gathering ... this condition is met by the benevolent public with almost unlimited public and private aid, thus encouraging them in the idle, wandering life, and in the propagation of similarly disposed children.
>
> —Oscar C. McCulloch, "The Tribe of Ishmael: A Study in Social Degradation," 1881

But the American eugenics movement had another insidious legislative goal as well: to prevent the interbreeding of different groups. In the decades following the Civil War, Americans were particularly anxious about the influx of immigrants from southern and eastern Europe and the prospect of African-Americans mixing with whites biologically. In the fevered public imagination, the threat of race mixing overlapped with an increase in venereal diseases—especially syphilis—which were felt to damage the genetic stock of the human race. Eugenics advocates also appealed to American patriotism, drawing parallels between international competition and Darwin's theory of survival of the fittest. Eugenicists warned of dire results if the "blood" of the white race became "corrupted" or "polluted" by African blood, conveniently aligning social Darwinist pseudoscience with white fears of black men raping white women (or, even worse, consensual relations). In many states eugenics advocates simply had to reinstate bans from the colonial period on marriage and sexual relations between blacks and whites. By 1914, 30 states had laws prohibiting race mixing, with six states going so far as to amend their constitutions. Many of these statutes required couples who wanted to wed to produce proof of their racial purity, along with a form certifying that a doctor's examination and blood test showed no sign of genetic defect.

At the national level, Congress debated three constitutional amendments prohibiting interracial marriages, but none succeeded. When Congress did get around to passing eugenics laws, it focused on limiting immigration by "undesirables," including whole races and nationalities. Urged by lobbyists from groups like the Immigration Restriction League, the main targets were Slavs and Jews from Eastern Europe and Italians, who were supposedly less intelligent on average. In 1924 Congress invited Harry Laughlin—a former high school principal and the director of Eugenics Record Office—to testify on the subject of mentally defective immigrants. This led to the Immigration Restriction Act, effectively ending immigration until after the Second World War.

Nothing but the Blues

The traditions of African-American music stretch back to the arrival of the first slaves in the early seventeenth century, but since they never wrote down anything down, it's hard to know what it sounded like. Most of our information comes from descriptions left by white contemporaries, who noted that there were different kinds of music for different occasions. In the cotton fields, groups of slaves used work songs to set a pace that everyone could maintain, making sure no one fell behind and subtly managing the expectations of white overseers. Visitors to plantations also left accounts of groups of slaves dancing in circles to drumming or fiddle music accompanied by rhythmic clapping and stomping. On Sundays, in simple log cabin churches, slaves sang "anthems" (better known as gospel songs) whose Christian imagery expressed their suffering and hopes for freedom.

After the Civil War, newly liberated African-Americans could travel where they pleased for the first time, just as the South was being crisscrossed by new railroads. Riding the rails, itinerant black musicians were able to share local songs and styles and were also exposed to various kinds of white music, including Scots-Irish ballads that evolved into modern country music; in fact, there was a great deal of overlap between country music and the blues (evident in shared subject matter, tending toward complaints about S.O.B. bosses, lost dogs, and unfaithful women).

We'll probably never be able to pinpoint the exact time and place where the blues was born, but the new style seems to have emerged in the 1880s and 1890s in small rural towns that sprang up across the Deep South. A common feature of these towns was a "juke joint" offering liquor and music, sometimes sharing a roof with a small general store. The joints generally showcased a regular "in-house" musician, who lived nearby, as well as touring musicians ("wandering" might be more accurate), who visited from neighboring counties.

During this period, the most successful bluesmen would cover larger territories, visiting more towns and building their reputations until word eventually reached the region's small but growing cities, concentrated on the banks of the Mississippi River. After making a name in these small cities, it would be easy enough to hitch a ride on a paddle-wheel steamer heading upriver to St. Louis and points north. Thus the blues became popular in black communities throughout the Mississippi River basin, and anywhere else that could be reached easily by riverboats or tramp freighters. Musicians continued to innovate, and in the 1910s and 1920s, the original form—Mississippi Delta blues—spawned regional styles like Memphis blues (folksy, using banjos, washboards, and kazoos), St. Louis blues (incorporating elements of ragtime) and Texas blues (emphasizing guitar virtuosity, with more "swing").

★ *"The blues" is a shortened form of the term "the blue devils," the demons once believed to cause sadness and melancholy.*

No Bottles of Coke on the Wall

Yes, it's true: when the fizzy soft drink was first formulated, Coca-Cola contained small amounts of cocaine, which probably made it mildly habit-forming. But it turns out the early business dealings surrounding the "Pause That Refreshes" were far more nefarious than any of its ingredients.

In the decades after the Civil War, the United States was swept by a new wave of anti-alcohol activism. This was partially triggered by the return home of Civil War soldiers who had gotten a taste for drink to escape the terror and tedium of war. Temperance also absorbed the energies of Christian women who had previously focused their energies on the abolition of slavery. (Basically, it was "next on the list" of moral causes.) With concerned members of the clergy leading the way, the mostly female rank and file pushed for local and state laws controlling or prohibiting the sale of alcohol.

> There is some of the onerest men here that I ever saw, and the most swearing and card playing and fitin and drunkenness that I ever saw at any place.
>
> —A new recruit in the Union army,
> in a letter to his mother, 1861

That's how the city of Atlanta and Fulton County came to be no-booze zones in 1886. While most shopkeepers threw their hands up in despair, one proprietor in Columbus, Georgia, saw the ban as an opportunity. John Pemberton, who'd developed a "French Wine Coca" containing alcohol as a "patent medicine," now set about producing an alcohol-free version, to appeal to the health-conscious ladies of Atlanta. Pemberton also claimed his Coca-Cola could cure morphine addiction, depression, headaches, and erectile dysfunction. Interestingly, the alleged health benefits of Coca-Cola were attributed less to its caffeine or cocaine content than its carbonation, which was believed to be "restorative" in this period.

Selling for five cents a glass at soda fountains in pharmacies around Atlanta, Pemberton's beverage was a hit, and like every successful invention, it soon gave rise to a field of knockoffs and imitators. Eventually Pemberton, who was suffering from a morphine addiction, sold his Coca-Cola Company to Asa Griggs Candler, the maker of a rival beverage, who (this is important!) also bought the formula. On learning that Pemberton had also sold majority stakes in Coca-Cola Company to at least four other businessmen—he was a morphine addict, after all—in 1892 Candler decided to ditch the whole legal mess and create a new corporation, *The* Coca-Cola Company (note the important difference). If this all sounds a bit shady and illegal, well, it probably was: Candler supposedly forged Pemberton's signature on the 1888 bill of sale—and his decision in 1910 to burn the company's early corporate records doesn't exactly allay suspicion.

But as the old American saying goes: "Whatever!" The Coca-Cola Company now belonged to Candler, who proved to be a capable marketer. Fittingly, however, his best idea was actually somebody else's: in 1891 the Biedenharn Candy Company began bottling Coca-Cola in Vicksburg, Mississippi, and in 1899 two entrepreneurs obtained Candler's skeptical permission to open a proprietary Coca-Cola bottling operation in Chattanooga,

Tennessee. Bottling Coca-Cola allowed the beverage to expand into retail distribution, via general stores, as well as restaurants and hotels, which didn't always have soda fountains. Of course pharmacies continued to sell the fountain drink. Operated by "soda jerks," these were informally known as "dope shops" because of the cocaine content.

So how much cocaine did Coca-Cola actually contain in the good old days? Pemberton's original formula had five ounces of coca leaves for every gallon of syrup; this would produce 65 twelve-ounce cups of Coca-Cola, each containing 34 milligrams of cocaine (providing the cocaine was fully extracted from the coca leaves). For an adult man weighing 150 pounds, or 68 kilograms, that works out to 0.5 milligrams of cocaine per kilogram. While that's not a huge amount of cocaine (100 milligrams is a fairly small recreational dose) it's nothing to sniff at either: 0.5 milligrams per kilogram can produce feelings of euphoria, and long-term changes in dopamine levels in the brains of lab monkeys.

Thanks for Everything, Edison

In 1862, at the age of 15, Thomas Edison's first job was selling newspapers at a train station near his home in Mount Clemens, Michigan. While hawking papers one day, Edison saved a three-year-old boy, Jimmy Mackenzie, from a runaway freight car. The boy's father, the train station's telegraph operator, was so grateful that he trained Edison in telegraphy, beginning his lifelong love affair with technology (and especially electricity). Later, at his laboratory in Menlo Park, New Jersey, Edison went on to invent everything but the kitchen sink, including . . .

The Phonograph

Strange though it seems now, before Edison invented the phonograph in 1877, there was no way for human beings to capture and re-create sound mechanically. Edison changed all that by using precise mechanical motion to transcribe dynamic sound waves into a solid, three-dimensional object, which stored the information until he wanted to reverse the process. When Edison put it all together, a carbon fiber diaphragm vibrated in response to sound waves, causing a needle to move up and down, leaving a series of indentations on a rotating cylinder. By adjusting the needle and diaphragm, Edison could make the process flow backward, so that indentations on the cylinder caused the needle to move up and down, making the carbon fibers vibrate and thus producing sound—or rather, *re*-producing it. The phonograph stunned and delighted people the world over, and it earned Edison the nickname "The Wizard of Menlo Park."

★ *The first recorded sound on Edison's new invention was the inventor's own voice, reciting the nursery rhyme "Mary Had a Little Lamb." He later claimed that it was the first thing that sprang to mind. Edison didn't wish to make a grand announcement in case the device failed to work properly.*

The Light Bulb

In the nineteenth century, Americans and Europeans were still using lamps that burned whale oil or kerosene, but these were expensive and maybe not as safe as desired (sorry Chicago!). Inspired by Britain's "arc lamps," which worked by passing an electric charge through gaseous, ionized neon, argon, or mercury, in 1878 Edison hit on the idea of replacing the reactive gas with a thin filament. The challenge was finding a material whose chemical structure caused it to emit light when electrified, but also stood up to prolonged electric current without burning up. Part of the answer came from enclosing the filament in a glass vacuum bulb to limit exposure to oxygen. But Edison and his assistants still had to experiment with thousands of materials to find one cheap and durable enough to be practical. After more than a year of experimentation, he discovered that carbonized cotton fiber could produce light for 13.5 hours before burning out. Several months later he discovered that carbonized bamboo filament could last up to 1,200 hours. Nowadays, however, most filaments are made of tungsten.

The Movie Camera

Without movie cameras there would be no movies, no Hollywood, no glamour, no gratuitous sex and violence, no ludicrously overpriced popcorn—everything that makes America America. Thankfully two important elements were already in place when Edison came along: in the 1820s two Frenchmen, Joseph Nicephore Niepce and Louis Daguerre, had invented still photography, and in 1884 George Eastman had invented lightweight film, which replaced cumbersome metal plates. Eastman's invention allowed for a large number of photographic images to be produced using a smaller, more manageable medium. And this set the stage for Edison to give the job to someone else: his assistant William Dickson. With a general directive from Edison to apply the basic idea of the phonograph to photography, Dickson—a photographer himself—eventually came up with a system using strips of celluloid wrapped around a rotating cylinder. Together with Edison's phonograph, the kinetoscope could produce "sight, sound, and motion." Gratuitous sex and violence weren't far behind.

What Didn't Edison Invent?!

While we could go on and on about the things Thomas Alva worked on (A complete 3-story house with moldings and furniture that could be created from one single pour of concrete! Electric railroads! Underwater searchlights! A trick for camouflaging the Navy's ships!), we should probably give a few other great inventors their due. Here are a few other inventions from the period that we couldn't do without:

Telephones

Alexander Graham Bell was born in Edinburgh, Scotland, but his famous invention was conceived in Boston, Massachusetts, where he settled in 1871. (Well, sort of settled. He was actually commuting from Canada and is now hailed as a proud native son of Scotland, Canada, and the United States.) Bell was another one of those infuriatingly capable polymath eggheads, who showed off his Towering Genius at the age of 12 by inventing a labor-saving device for a local mill. By the age of 16, he had taught himself piano, ventriloquism, and sign language to talk to his mother, who was becoming deaf. He also translated instructions from a German inventor on how to build an "automaton" capable of rudimentary artificial speech. Later, he trained his family dog to growl on command so he could figure out how to manipulate the dog's lips and tongue to produce what sounded like human speech—standard stuff, really.

After a distinctly mediocre high school career, Bell took a job as a teacher, but then tragedy struck twice. Tuberculosis claimed the lives of one of his brothers in 1867, and then it took the other in 1870. When Bell also took ill, his parents dropped everything and moved from Scotland to Canada so their sole surviving son could recuperate. In Canada, Bell started hanging out with members of the Onondoga tribe, learned their language, and created a written language for them, for which they honored him with an honorary chieftainship. In 1871, at the age of 24, he was asked to train instructors for a school for deaf people in Boston.

Sometime in 1873–1874, Bell began working on a device he called a "harmonic telegraph" or the "electric speech machine," which would transmit sounds long distances using electric current. The basic idea was similar to telegraphy: a series of inputs on one end would be transmitted electrically and decoded at a distant location—but instead of a telegraph operator tapping a lever, a human voice would open and close the circuit using sound waves. There were some major challenges. At first, Bell thought he would need cables containing many more strands of copper than conventional telegraph lines. That's because his initial concept called for a group of electrical impulses traveling down separate wires, each triggered by a specific frequency, which then activated specific metal "reeds" on the other end.

But as Bell was assembling the first multi-reed model with the help of his assistant, Thomas Watson, Watson accidentally "twanged" one of the metal reeds. Bell heard the full range of tones created by the reed, rather than just one frequency, and he quickly realized that he could use a single reed instead of multiple reeds, and just one wire instead of many wires. Other obstacles remained, but ultimately, Bell hit on a novel solution that worked.

Soon Bell was giving personal demonstrations to various notables, including Queen Victoria, who declared it "most extraordinary." After founding the Bell Telephone Company in 1877, he continued improving the telephone to make it more practical. Meanwhile, work began on long-distance phone lines connecting Boston, New York, Baltimore, and Chicago. By 1886, 150,000 Americans owned telephones, and everyone else wanted one. We haven't shut up since.

★ *Ironically, Bell came to hate the constant ringing of his own home telephone and banished it from his study so he could think in peace.*

Plane Genius

Flying has been one of the most coveted superhero powers since the beginning of time. But attempts to get airborne tended to end pretty badly (see: Icarus, small children leaping off of tall objects, etc.). All of this changed, however, with the invention of the internal combustion engine by an Italian engineer, Pietro Benini, in 1856. The internal combustion engine operated on the same basic principle as the steam engine—raising and lowering pistons to turn wheels or propellers—but it made the process more efficient by replacing super-heated water vapor with flammable diesel or gasoline, providing far more horsepower from a much smaller unit. Further refinements made internal combustion engines even lighter, setting the stage for two enterprising bicycle geeks from Dayton, Ohio, to change the world forever.

In 1899 Orville and Wilbur Wright, two brothers who owned a bike shop and had mechanical experience with electric motors, began work on a "flying machine." They were inspired by Otto Lilienthal, a German inventor who built and flew gliders in the early 1890s, proving that a heavier-than-air object could stay aloft for quite some time, even without a source of power, if it had the right wing design. Basically, their idea was to put an internal combustion engine on a glider, allowing it to stay aloft as long as the fuel lasted. Sounds easy, right? Not really: as Lilienthal's tragic death in 1896 illustrated, this was a dangerous business, and it's kind of amazing that both Wright brothers lived to enjoy their success.

> ### Small sacrifices must be made!
> —final words of Otto Lilienthal, German aviation pioneer, after breaking his spine, 1896

With the more outgoing and ambitious Wilbur taking the lead, the brothers took a different tack from other would-be aeronauts. They focused on what they considered the real challenge: the difficulty of maneuvering a large, unstable object in midair. Plenty of other inventors had seen the potential of putting an engine on a glider to get airborne, but no one seems to have given much thought to the method of steering—or even more critically, getting back on the ground *safely*.

To develop an effective mechanism for controlling their flying machine, from 1900 to 1903, the Wright brothers performed a thorough battery of tests using gliders modeled on recent French and German craft. They incorporated the "double-decker" wing design favored by European inventors and Lilienthal's design for a curved-top cross-section to provide more lift. They also added their own innovation: a "front elevator," which was basically a forward-facing tail for steering and stabilization.

The brothers then journeyed to Kitty Hawk, North Carolina. There, for the next three years, they conducted over 1,000 gliding experiments aided by ocean breezes and the beach as a soft landing area. In the off seasons, they returned to Ohio, where they investigated air resistance, lift, and optimal wing design, using scale models and a homemade wind tunnel. Their experimentation was also sped along by their clever system for fastening various wings together using struts made of bicycle wheel spokes. This allowed them to test different configurations without having to rebuild their models every time.

In 1903, after perfecting a system for controlling midair maneuvers, the brothers decided it was time to add a propeller powered by an internal combustion engine. The 12-horsepower engine was built in just six weeks by Charlie Taylor, an employee at their bicycle shop. By casting the engine block out of lightweight aluminum, Taylor helped keep the Wright Flyer I remarkably light. In the end, the biplane had a 40-foot wingspan and tipped the scales at just 625 pounds. On December 17, 1903, unfazed by the freezing cold, the brothers made four short flights over the beach at Kitty Hawk, North Carolina, ranging in length from 120 to 852 feet, at an altitude of 10 feet, with an airspeed of seven miles per hour. The era of flight had begun.

···················· **PROFILES IN SCROOGES** ···················

In the second half of the nineteenth century, the phenomenal expansion of American industry allowed a handful of brilliant, ruthless businessmen to acquire more money, in relative terms, than any private individual before or since.

John D. Rockefeller (1839–1937)

The super-richest member of the super-rich club, John D. Rockefeller was the second child of a traveling elixir salesman. Resolving not to follow his father's ne'er-do-well example, Rockefeller nonetheless inherited his knack for creative deal-making and showed an entrepreneurial bent early in life: he earned extra money by raising turkeys and selling candy to local children. Soon he had enough cash to start making small loans to neighboring farmers. In 1855, at the age of 16, Rockefeller took a job as a bookkeeper for a dry goods store in Cleveland. There, he impressed everyone with his diligence, mathematical ability, and an intuitive grasp of the logistics involved in commerce—especially freight costs.

Four years later, he went into business for himself with a partner in produce distribution, and in 1863 they opened a small oil refinery to produce kerosene, which was rapidly replacing whale oil as the preferred fuel for lamps. In 1865 Rockefeller, now 26, bought out his partners, and a year later he joined forces with his brother, William, who built another oil refinery in Cleveland. The brothers luckily (or wisely) took up the oil business just before a prolonged boom, selling their kerosene in New York City and reinvesting their profits in the refining operation. Before long they owned the largest oil refinery in the world, and in 1870, the brothers created a new corporation, Standard Oil of Ohio. The duo borrowed heavily to acquire new competing refiners, but John was able to achieve substantial savings elsewhere by striking secret deals with railroads that gave Standard Oil rebates for its high-volume oil shipping business. These methods allowed him to drive competing companies into bankruptcy and buy them cheaply. Once under Standard Oil's control, the acquired companies participated in Rockefeller's shipping rebate scheme, giving him leverage to negotiate even bigger discounts with the railroads. By 1872 Standard Oil had acquired 22 of its 26 competitors in Cleveland, setting the stage for national expansion.

Rockefeller's achievements didn't just benefit his own bank account. By creating economies of scale, he could offer consumers better quality kerosene at a lower price. But after achieving dominance in kerosene refining, there was nothing left to do but take over other parts of the supply chain. In the 1880s, Rockefeller used the same ruthless tactics to methodically expand his control to new areas like oil prospecting and production, crude oil shipment, and kerosene retail sales. Eventually Standard Oil came to control 90 percent of the U.S. kerosene market, raising alarm in the general public about its dominance.

Opponents focused on the "trust" structure created by Standard Oil's attorneys in 1879, which allowed it to sidestep state laws preventing one corporation from owning stock in another. In 1892 Ohio state regulators went after Standard Oil, forcing separation of the core Ohio business from corporate branches in various states. Wily Rockefeller found ways to work around this "anti-trust" regulation, and Standard Oil was eventually reorganized as a national holding company based in New Jersey in 1909. However, it was about to run afoul of the federal government, thanks to the growth of a whole new industry: automobiles.

The prospect of giving Rockefeller control over the indispensable fuel for the automobile craze was too much for federal regulators. In 1911, Standard Oil of New Jersey—which controlled an astonishing 64 percent of the vastly expanded oil and gas business—became the target of federal prosecution under the Sherman Anti-Trust Act of 1890. The Supreme Court found that the company had engaged in anti-competitive . . . well, competition. The company was ordered dismembered, and today, the list of companies created from Standard Oil includes familiar names like Exxon, Mobil, Chevron, Amoco, and Conoco. However, things weren't all bad for Rockefeller. He got to keep his huge fortune as well as his stock in the new companies. Shortly after Standard Oil was broken up, his total worth was estimated at $900 million, or about 2.3 percent of U.S. GDP at that time. (Nowadays that would be equivalent to about $318 billion.)

> He [Rockefeller] couldn't walk down the aisle of his church without people asking for some money.
>
> —Peter Johnson, *The Rockefeller Century*

Andrew Carnegie (1835–1919)

Another ruthless entrepreneurial spirit, Andrew Carnegie played a key role in the rise of the United States as the world's leading industrial power. Thanks to the superior strength of steel, railroads required less maintenance, allowing them to expand to new areas; shipyards were able to turn out the biggest vessels in history, including giant passenger liners and cargo ships; and architects could transform the urban landscape with skyscrapers and suspension bridges.

Andrew Carnegie's family migrated from Scotland to Pittsburgh in 1848, when he was 13 years old. Like most other children from poor families, Carnegie went to work in a factory, working 12-hour days, six days a week in a cotton mill for a weekly wage of $1.25. In 1850 his uncle got him a job as a messenger boy for the Pittsburgh office of the Ohio Telegraph Company. Carnegie impressed his employer with his intelligence and work ethic, and by 1851 he was working as a telegraph operator. In 1853 he left this post to work as the personal secretary and telegraph operator for Thomas A. Scott, the president of the Pennsylvania Railroad Company (yes, the same one from the board game Monopoly) and soon became the boss of its Pittsburgh division. Meanwhile, beginning in 1855, Carnegie started investing in railroads, iron foundries, and steel mills, which used the new Bessemer process to cheaply produce large amounts of high-quality steel.

During the Civil War, Scott was appointed Assistant Secretary of War, with responsibility for the critical area of transportation. Scott brought his trusted lieutenant along, at the tender age of 26, to oversee military railroads and telegraph operations in the Eastern United States. Still tending his private investments, Carnegie founded a steel mill in Pittsburgh and made a fortune supplying the Union army's endless need for steel.

Most of this steel went to weapons, but in his official position, Carnegie noted that wooden railroad bridges were weak and unreliable and could use the steel as well. After the Civil War, Carnegie focused all of his attention on the steel business, taking over the Keystone Bridge Works and the Union Ironworks and marketing his steel to railroads as a replacement for rickety wood structures. Like Rockefeller, Carnegie used his growing dominance in steel production to negotiate lower shipping costs, and before long, he began expanding his empire to include the sources of iron ore, iron ore transportation, and sales and distribution. Beginning in 1886 Carnegie made a series of acquisitions of iron ore fields and rival companies, and in 1892 rolled them all up in Carnegie Steel—the world's largest producer of iron and steel at the time. But there was still more hugeness to come. In 1901, when Carnegie was 66 years old and planning his retirement, he was approached by the New York City financiers, John Pierpont Morgan and Charles Schwab, with a proposal to combine Carnegie Steel with its two main competitors, Federal Steel and National Steel, along with eight other companies. The result would be a colossal trust called U.S. Steel. In the end, Morgan and Schwab bought Carnegie Steel for $480 million. Carnegie's take was $225 million—slightly over 1 percent of U.S. GDP at the time.

Like Rockefeller, Carnegie devoted himself to philanthropic causes in later years, opening 3,000 libraries around the world, buying organs for 7,000 churches, building Carnegie Hall in New York City, donating to the Tuskegee Institute, and helping fund

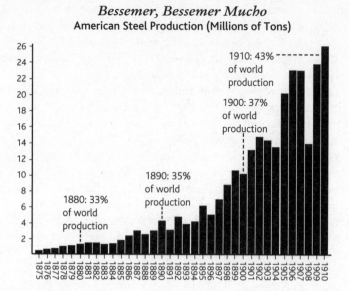

Bessemer, Bessemer Mucho
American Steel Production (Millions of Tons)

1910: 43% of world production

1900: 37% of world production

1890: 35% of world production

1880: 33% of world production

the establishment of both the University of Birmingham in the United Kingdom and Carnegie Mellon University in Pittsburgh. But like Rockefeller, Carnegie's philanthropy may have been intended to assuage guilt over the methods behind his success— or at least, regret about the reputation they earned him. Among other things, his name was always associated with the Homestead Steel Strike, a 143-day labor conflict between steelworkers and Carnegie Steel's management in 1892 that left 16 dead.

Henry Ford (1863–1947)

Henry Ford's accomplishments go way beyond simply founding the Ford Motor Company. His innovations in manufacturing and marketing revolutionized dozens of industries, raised the standard of living for billions of people around the world, and literally reshaped the landscape, all while securing America's position as the leading industrial power.

Born on a farm in Dearborn, Michigan, in 1863, the young Ford gained a reputation for being a technical whiz. As a child he fixed watches, and by the age of 16, he'd taken a job as an apprentice machinist in Detroit. By 19, Ford had returned to Dearborn to work on the family farm; but he found the work intolerably tedious. To pass the time, he tinkered with his father's small portable steam engine, and before long he was hired as a steam engine repairman. After marrying his wife, Clara, in 1888, Ford also opened a sawmill to supplement their income—but his brilliant mind was drawn to the new, more complex technologies transforming the United States and the wider world. In 1891 he took a job as an engineer with the Edison Illuminating Company, where he quickly worked his way up to chief engineer.

In 1893, Ford began experimenting with gas-powered internal combustion engines, and by 1896, he'd built his own rudimentary automobile, dubbed the "Quadricycle." After receiving encouragement from Edison himself, in 1899 Ford rounded up enough investors to create the Detroit Automobile Company, but his first attempt at automobile manufacturing failed, and the company went belly-up within two years. Ford blamed the high price of the vehicles. But he also noticed that consumers were deterred by the noisy engines, which many assumed were unsafe. After building two faster, quieter models, in 1902 Ford and his friend Alexander Malcomson launched a new company, Ford & Malcomson, Ltd., which was renamed Ford Motor Company in 1903.

This time around, Ford cleverly promoted his new vehicles by giving souped-up versions to race car drivers and sponsoring the Indianapolis 500. (Predictably, as soon as Americans had cars, they started racing them.) Then, in 1908, he introduced the Model T, which combined affordability with quality and a less noisy engine. The model became immensely popular, and immensely profitable for Ford—who maximized profits by implementing assembly-line manufacturing at his plant in Dearborn, Michigan. His innovative system used moving belts to carry parts and partially assembled machinery from station to station, where workers performed different tasks again and again. By having workers focus on performing just one task many times, instead of the complex process of assembling an entire vehicle, Ford was able to raise productivity, which in turn allowed him to offer his workers better wages than any other factory owner.

Like his fellow industrial barons, Ford left a mixed legacy, earning praise as a pioneer of industry, a generous employer (he was an early advocate of profit sharing and the 40-hour workweek), and a philanthropist. However, he also had some noteworthy flaws: like Carnegie, he employed thuggish security details to break up protests by striking employees, sometimes resulting in bloodshed. Ford is also remembered for his eccentric political views, which were colored by his surprisingly passionate anti-Semitism. During World War I, he claimed that Jewish war financiers sank the Lusitania to bring the United States into the war. Ford also became an admirer of Adolf Hitler—who returned the sentiment, telling an American reporter, "I regard Henry Ford as my inspiration." The German dictator even awarded Ford a medal and kept a portrait of Ford next to his desk.

······················· **BY THE NUMBERS** ·················

84 percent	voter turnout in South Carolina, 1880
18 percent	voter turnout in South Carolina, 1896
181,315	number of African-Americans eligible to vote in Alabama, 1900
2,980	number of African-Americans eligible to vote in Alabama, 1903
600,000	total number of white voters disenfranchised by Alabama, 1900–1941
500,000	total number of black voters disenfranchised by Alabama, 1900–1941
49,371,340	U.S. population, 1880
91,641,195	U.S. population, 1910
6,499,431	number of U.S. citizens/permanent residents who were born abroad, 1880
15,243,626	number of U.S. citizens/permanent residents who were born abroad, 1910
1,388,550	tons of steel manufactured in the United States, 1880
26,094,919	tons of steel manufactured in the United States, 1910
43 percent	proportion of world steel output this represented, 1910
1,912,000	population of New York City, 1880
4,767,000	population of New York City, 1910
$350 million	total cost of the U.S. Panama Canal project
21,900	death toll among workers on the French attempt to build a canal
5,600	death toll among workers in the American canal project
232,000,000	cubic yards of earth excavated in the American canal project
200,000	total number of Filipino civilian deaths during the rebellion against American occupation from 1899 to 1903

60,000 number of Americans sterilized under various
eugenics laws in the twentieth century

47,900 number of telephones in the United States, 1880

150,000 number of telephones in the United States, 1886

1,800 number of gas-powered automobiles in the
United States, 1900

458,000 number of gas-powered automobiles in the
United States, 1910

6

The United States of Amazing

(1910–1930)

For most of the world, the first half of the twentieth century was a horrible nightmare of violence and destruction, beginning with World War I (1914–1918). But for the USA, things were booming, and America did its best to stay aloof from all those Debbie Downers abroad. Alas, in the "modern" era, that turned out to be impossible.

Once roused into joining World War I, the United States poured its resources into the effort, providing a decisive surge of manpower that forced Germany and the other Central Powers to admit defeat. Afterward, the peoples of Europe (though not their leaders) looked to the United States to lead peace negotiations. Unfortunately for everybody, President Woodrow Wilson kind of screwed up the peace negotiations, and his successors did the same to international finance.

But let's stay positive. Back home, the postwar period was super, as continuing revolutions in science, technology, and manufacturing transformed American society and culture. More and more households owned things: cars, telephones, refrigerators, and best of all, radios! At the push of a button you could get the latest news, listen to a sporting event in another time zone, or even turn an isolated farmhouse into a dance hall. And there was plenty of new music to dance to. Jazz was part of a hip urban aesthetic with its own slang, fashion, art, and literature, created by poor African-Americans fleeing the Jim Crow South for Northern cities. Unfortunately, the refugees encountered a whole new set of problems, including drug abuse, crime, and—you guessed it—more racial discrimination.

The whole period shared this ambiguity. On one hand, the "Roaring '20s" was fueled by spectacular economic growth. Between the easy access to loans and all the fun new consumer must-haves, America was quick to indulge. But (*spoiler alert*) this was all leading to dangerous "bubbles" in the credit and stock and as the '20s roared on, storm clouds began appearing on the horizon.

Meanwhile, World War I established an ominous precedent by expanding the government's role in the economy and the lives of citizens, making Americans more beholden to their government. But at least we had jazz to keep us humming.

············· **WHAT HAPPENED WHEN** ····················

November 5, 1912 Woodrow Wilson wins first term as president, beating Teddy Roosevelt, who ran on the "Bull Moose" ticket.

August 1, 1914 World War I begins in Europe.

November 7, 1916 Woodrow Wilson wins reelection with slogan "He Kept Us Out of the War."

January 19, 1917 Zimmerman telegram, in which Germany urges Mexico to declare war on the United States, is made public.

February 1, 1917 Germany resumes unrestricted submarine warfare.

April 6, 1917 United States joins World War I.

July 3, 1917 First U.S. troops arrive in France.

January 8, 1918 Wilson outlines "Fourteen Points" for peace.

March 3, 1918 Bolsheviks make separate peace with Germany, Treaty of Brest-Litovsk.

March 11, 1918 First outbreak of influenza at Fort Riley, Kansas.

April–May 1918 Influenza spreads in French camps near Bordeaux.

November 11, 1918 Germany agrees to an armistice.

June 28, 1919 Treaty of Versailles is signed.

January 16, 1919 Eighteenth Amendment ratified, enacting Prohibition of alcohol.

August 18, 1920	Nineteenth Amendment ratified, giving women the right to vote.
March 3, 1923	Henry Luce launches *Time* magazine.
August 2, 1923	Warren Harding dies in office, is succeeded by Calvin Coolidge.
September 1, 1924	United States formulates Dawes Plan to regulate European debt repayments.
April 10, 1925	F. Scott Fitzgerald publishes *The Great Gatsby*.
July 10, 1925	Scopes Monkey Trial begins in Dayton, Tennessee.
October 22, 1926	Ernest Hemingway publishes *The Sun Also Rises*.
May 20–21, 1927	Charles Lindbergh flies across the Atlantic Ocean from New York to Paris.
October 6, 1927	"The Jazz Singer," starring Al Jolson, popularizes "talkies."
November 18, 1928	Mickey Mouse makes first appearance in Disney's cartoon "Steamboat Willie."
November 6, 1928	Herbert Hoover wins presidency with a promise of "A Chicken in Every Pot."

· · · · · · · · · · · · · · · · LIES YOUR TEACHER TOLD YOU · · · · · · · · · · · · · ·

LIE: *America has always stood by other democracies.*
THE TRUTH: Let's call a spade a spade. For most of its history, America hasn't given a darn about other democracies. There have been some heroic interventions—like World War I—but these were really just heroic justifications for protecting American trade (which America has always cared about). Over the decades, the "preserving democracy" excuse was only trotted out when the nation's leaders needed to rally public opinion. Thus it wasn't until trade was threatened that the United States discovered that World War I was putting Democracy in Danger.

To be fair, American isolationists had some good arguments against entering World War I. From the U.S. perspective, the arrogant Europeans had foolishly gotten themselves into the war through a ridiculous tangle of treaties. And the players weren't exactly defenseless: Britain stood at the head of the largest empire in history, French soldiers were considered the bravest in Europe, and Russia was really, really big. So the Allied powers didn't seem to need American help. Further, Germany was a multiparty democracy at the time, and millions of Americans were descended from German immigrants.

By 1915 public opposition to the war was mushrooming, and it spawned dozens and dozens of civic and religious organizations, many organized by Quakers and women. In a politically savvy, though not entirely truthful reaction to the broad-based feelings of opposition, President Woodrow Wilson won the 1916 election with the catchy slogan "He Kept Us Out of the War." Of course, skeptics noted that Wilson actually seemed to be preparing for war by expanding the U.S. Army, National Guard, and Navy, establishing the Army Reserve Officer Training Corps (ROTC), and giving himself authority over the National Guard in case of emergency.

★ *Woodrow Wilson's "He Kept Us Out of the War" slogan held true for barely a month into his second term; he was re-inaugurated on March 4, 1917. The United States declared war on Germany on April 6.*

But not everyone in the United States shunned the fight: America's political and economic elite favored intervention as early as 1915, knowing that key trade relationships with Britain and France would be ruined if they were defeated. After American trade with Germany was severed by the British blockade, trade with Britain and France grew even more important. During the war, American exporters supplied both countries with vehicles, fuel, food, and consumer goods, allowing the Allied Powers to devote their own industry exclusively to armaments—and American exporters were making out like bandits. Then bankers got in on the act: starting in 1915 American banks loaned Britain and France hundreds of millions of dollars to continue buying American goods. These war financiers feared that the debts might never be repaid if the Allied Powers lost. With so much trade and money at risk, these business interests were all the motivation that the United States needed to get in on the Allied action. But how would the politicians and elite get ordinary Americans on board?

Luckily, they had some help from the Germans. In the throes of warfare, German "U-boats" (from *unterseeboot* or "undersea boat") began by sinking British and French merchant ships and then started going after neutral ships and passenger vessels as well—especially those carrying armaments and supplies to their enemies. Before long, U-boat attacks had claimed the lives of hundreds of American civilians; the most infamous incident was the sinking of the Cunard liner RMS *Lusitania* on May 17, 1915. Indeed, the ship had been carrying arms—including 4.5 million rifle cartridges—but the huge number of civilian casualties (1,198 lives, including almost 100 children and 128 Americans) triggered a wave of anti-German sentiment.

★ *Upon its launch in 1907, the* Lusitania *was the largest ocean liner in the world.*

In response, Germany—which was wisely trying to avoid baiting the United States into the war—forbade attacks against neutral shipping and passenger liners. But the position didn't last: German civilians were suffering from the British blockade, and as the war dragged on, German hard-liners demanded a return to unrestricted submarine warfare against neutral shipping, American vessels or not. The German strategy almost worked: in the last two years of the war, U-boats sank 8.9 million tons of shipping, and the effort nearly starved Britain into surrender. But it also gave Wilson the support he needed to get Congress to declare war in April of 1917.

A few days after obtaining the declaration of war, Wilson established the Committee for Public Information (CPI), tasked with unleashing a barrage of propaganda to get Americans marching to the same tune. Guided by marketing all-stars from journalist Walter Lippmann (the Pulitzer prize winner who also introduced the concept of "Cold War") to Edward Bernays (considered the "father of public relations"), the CPI launched a propaganda blitz through every medium possible: newspapers, magazines, books, pamphlets, radio, movies, public events, and public school curricula. The campaign had two main thrusts: first, highlight the German brutality, and second, link the war effort to democracy instead of, you know, business interests. Here, the

German military again pitched in by effectively overthrowing the democratic government in January 1917. Once a military coup took over Germany, American sympathy for the nation waned, and the anti-war movement was promptly pushed aside to make way for the Great War.

> It all culminates in the fabrication of a system of all evil, and of another which is the system of all good ... It is not enough to say our side is more right than the enemy's, that our victory will help democracy more than his. One must insist that our victory will end war forever, and make the world safe for democracy.
>
> —Walter Lippmann, *Public Opinion*, 1922

QUICK'N'EASY WORLD WAR I

In a major dose of irony, WWI essentially resulted from a system of treaties created to keep the peace in Europe. After initially staying aloof, the United States was forced to join the fight because of economic ties with Britain and France (along with Russia, the main Allied Powers). U.S. industry and manpower helped bring the Central Powers—Germany, Austria-Hungary and the Ottoman Empire—to their knees.

1914: On June 28, Archduke Franz-Ferdinand of the Austrian Hapsburg dynasty was assassinated in Sarajevo—the capital of Bosnia, a province of Austria-Hungary—by a Bosnian Serb nationalist. Backed by Germany, Austria-Hungary declared war on the neighboring Kingdom of Serbia in August, triggering a counter-declaration of war by Serbia's ally Russia, followed by Germany, France, and Britain. Germany seemed unstoppable at first, scoring major victories over Russia on the eastern front and smashing through neutral Belgium to invade northern France on the western front. However, both fronts settled into trench warfare thanks to a badass new weapon—the machine gun—which could mow down hundreds of attackers.

1915: Both sides tried to break the stalemate of trench warfare with new tactics, especially poison gas, pioneered by the Germans. Germany conducted the first aerial bombardments of London with zeppelins and unleashed submarine warfare against Allied shipping. Meanwhile the Turks launched the Armenian genocide which eventually killed 1.5 million. Britain set up a naval blockade of Germany in March, and Italy joined the Allied Powers in April.

1916: Having failed to break the stalemate, both sides resorted to more human wave assaults which failed to achieve anything. The Somme saw the first experimental use of tanks by the British, who also introduced the draft in May. Meanwhile in August Kaiser Wilhelm II appointed a new top commander, Paul von Hindenburg, who took control of the entire German economy.

1917: The Allied Powers suffered a major setback as Russian armies mutinied and revolutionaries toppled Czar Nicholas II in February, leading to the collapse of the eastern front. However, the odds were evened by the United States joining the war on April 6, 1917, following renewed German submarine warfare and anger over the Zimmerman telegram (in which Germany encouraged Mexico to attack the U.S.).

1918: Following a second revolution by Lenin's Bolsheviks, the Bolsheviks made peace with Germany, allowing the Germans to shift over a million troops from the eastern front to the west. U.S. troops under John "Blackjack" Pershing help blunt the impact of the final German offensive. As the world was decimated by influenza, the Ottoman Empire signed an armistice on October 30, followed by Austria-Hungary on November 3 and Germany on November 11. All three soon collapsed as revolutions swept away outdated monarchies.

LIE: *Woodrow Wilson failed to achieve his goals because he was too idealistic.*

THE TRUTH: Things might have turned out better for Europe and the rest of the world if President Wilson had been a little *more* idealistic—or at least, more consistent.

When the smoke cleared after World War I, the United States had clearly bumped aside Britain as top dog. Wilson, dubbed by the press as "the most powerful man in the world" and "the Prince of Peace," was widely expected to forge a fair settlement balancing the interests of the victorious Allied Powers (Britain, France, and Italy) with those of the defeated Central Powers (Germany, Austria, and Turkey). This wasn't unreasonable. Although the

United States fought on the side of the Allied Powers, America's short involvement left its citizens relatively untainted by the bitterness permeating Europe. Thus, Wilson had room to present himself as an impartial mediator who could exercise a restraining influence on the victors. Plus, France and Britain both owed the United States billions of dollars and were hoping to renegotiate their enormous debts on more favorable terms, giving him leverage, if he chose to use it (in the end he didn't). The situation seemed ideal, especially since the Germans were already on board with Wilson's plan for peace—or so they thought.

In three addresses to Congress during 1918, Wilson outlined a framework for peace negotiations, consisting of "Fourteen Points" elaborated by "Four Principles" and capped by "Five Particulars." These included "absolute freedom of navigation upon the seas," implying the British blockade would be lifted; "no discrimination or favoritism between peoples," implying the United States wouldn't favor the Allied powers over Germany; and last but not least, "peoples and provinces are not to be bartered about from sovereignty to sovereignty," implying that Germany would retain its territorial integrity. This Powerpoint for Peace was consistent with Wilson's call for "peace without victory," meaning a fair settlement that didn't blame or punish the losers.

> **Mr. Wilson bores me with his Fourteen Points.**
> **Why, God Almighty has only ten!**
>
> —French Prime Minister Georges Clemenceau, 1918

Two days after Wilson made the promise about territorial integrity, the top German general, Erich von Ludendorff, instructed his staff to open negotiations for a cease-fire. Wilson had offered Germany peace with honor, and his generous terms were critical to von Ludendorff's decision: Germans wanted peace, but not at the price of German territory, which would dishonor the sacrifice of over 2 million German soldiers and the half a million German civilians who died. And while Germany was in bad shape, it wasn't finished—with Russia out of the war due to a Bolshevik uprising, the German army appeared capable of fighting on if necessary. By September 1918, roughly 1.4 million German soldiers were conducting a fighting withdrawal, inflicting huge casualties on a combined French, British, and American force of about 1.7 million.

Unfortunately, Wilson didn't stick to his promises. On October 29, 1918, Wilson's personal representative, Edward House, met secretly in London with French Prime Minister Georges Clemenceau and British Prime Minister David Lloyd George to secretly hear their "commentary" on the president's proposal. Their secret revisions basically gutted Wilson's most important promises, calling for the breakup of the Austro-Hungarian Empire, the creation of a new Polish state using a chunk of Germany, and the transfer of the province of Alsace-Lorraine from Germany to France. The Brits and French also demanded that the treaty include a statement of Germany's official "war guilt," a meaningless insult practically designed to make the Germans angry—but not as angry as the subsequent bill for the damages. The Allies figured something along the lines of $33 billion ($2.2 trillion in today's dollars) should do it, with payments scheduled until 1988.

After secretly saying goodbye to the two prime ministers, House sent a telegraph to Wilson summarizing the French and British revisions, so the president knew about them when the Allies agreed to begin armistice negotiations just a week later. But he neglected to inform the Germans about these incredibly important changes. It was a classic bait and switch. When the Germans finally did find out about the revisions in March of 1919, another promise to them was broken: instead of a negotiation between the Central Powers and the Allies, as Wilson had guaranteed, Germany and Austria were simply told to sign.

> When President Wilson left Washington he enjoyed a prestige and a moral influence throughout the world unequalled in history ... The disillusion was so complete, that some of those who had trusted most hardly dared speak of it ... Was the treaty really as bad as it seemed? What had happened to the President?
>
> —John Maynard Keynes,
> *The Economic Consequences of the Peace,* 1919

So the question remains: if the Germans objected to the final treaty, why didn't they just refuse to sign it and keep fighting? By this point, it wasn't an option. Six months had passed since the armistice took effect, and both sides were already demobilizing, sending exhausted, traumatized soldiers home as fast as they could. And by the time the German delegation arrived in Versailles to sign the treaty, the government of the new Weimar Republic was barely able to maintain order at home. The delegation had no choice but to sign under protest and then tell the German people they'd been duped.

A common response at the time was: so what? After all, the Germans had just imposed an incredibly unfair peace treaty on the Russians at Brest-Litovsk in 1917—so why should they expect to be treated any better? Besides, the whole war was pretty much their fault anyway, according to the Allies. But the deception was a big deal. It triggered a wave of outrage across the German political spectrum—left, right, and center—which almost never agreed on anything. If Allied diplomats didn't understand why this was a problem, then they'd just have to wait and see. It wouldn't be long.

To this day, nobody really knows what Wilson was thinking. It's possible he deliberately deceived the Germans—but the implication that he drew up an idealistic peace program as part of the biggest con job in history just seems too perversely cynical. Alternatively, it may have just slipped his mind; there are, in fact, questions about Wilson's mental health during this period. In April 1919, while in Paris, he suffered a minor stroke, which can change one's personality and cause disordered thinking. And there may have been earlier strokes that were covered up. But the most likely explanation is that he just deferred these unpleasant, complicated issues to the new League of Nations proposed by Britain: sure, the Germans would be wildly upset for a few years, but his successors in the White House could make sure the new international body addressed Germany's grievances.

★ *Woodrow Wilson never owned a dog while in the White House, but he and his wife kept a flock of sheep as pets (and natural lawn mowers). Their wool was auctioned to raise funds for the American Red Cross.*

That plan would maybe have worked had the United States actually joined the newly formed League of Nations, but partisan politics and senile dementia ensured the United States would never join the League. Without U.S. participation, the terms of the Treaty of Versailles were never revised—meaning Germany stayed angry, and indeed, got even angrier.

WHOLE LOTTA GOV

From 1910 to 1930, everything about America got bigger: population, industrial power, energy consumption, cars, buildings. All this growth was viewed as good for Americans and therefore, the world. But this period also saw remarkable expansion of government at the local, state, and national levels. This was partly due to the huge expansion of the American economy, whose growing complexity demanded more regulatory mechanisms. In December 1913, Woodrow Wilson signed the Federal Reserve Act, creating the Federal Reserve System (in essence, a new U.S. central bank) to provide liquidity in case of emergency. "The Fed" also assumed responsibility for controlling the money supply by raising or lowering interest rates on loans to private banks and determining the interest rates they charged for their loans. 1913 also saw the creation of a permanent federal income tax.

World War I accelerated the expansion: the government was suddenly tasked with coordinating industrial production, creating an army of over four million men, transporting them to Europe, and guaranteeing massive loans to European allies. Inevitably, the war spending ran up huge deficits, which most Americans accepted, because the war was an emergency. But once the war ended, America quickly discovered that shrinking government is like trying to get toothpaste back in the tube: although total government spending decreased sharply after World War I, the government's share of GDP ended up being almost twice as large (14.3 percent) as before the war (8.2 percent).

LIE: *Social progress began in cities*
and then filtered out to rural areas.

THE TRUTH: Sorry, city slickers! One of the most important social movements in American history—women's suffrage—got going on the frontier before taking root in cities.

As early as the eighteenth century, women (and men) had been advocating women's suffrage in Europe and America, but their numbers had remained small. That all changed, however, in the middle of the nineteenth century when their cause became intertwined with abolitionism. As female activists became major players in the movement to end slavery, they became increasingly frustrated by its slow progress—a hurdle they blamed on their inability to voice opinions directly through the ballot box.

While women's suffrage was discussed everywhere in the United States in the nineteenth century—most notably at the Seneca Falls Convention organized by Elizabeth Cady Stanton in upstate New York in 1848—the first real progress came on the Western frontier. In 1869 the Wyoming territory became the first political entity in the Northern Hemisphere to grant women the right to vote regardless of their professional or marital status. Following Wyoming's lead, women's suffrage movements won the right to vote from all-male state governments in Colorado in 1893, Utah in 1895, and Idaho in 1896. After the turn of the century, they were joined by Washington in 1910; California in 1911; Arizona, Oregon, and Kansas in 1912; Alaska in 1913; and Montana in 1914. Progress was considerably slower back East. In 1913 Illinois gave women the right to vote in presidential elections but not state elections. And it wasn't until 1917 that New York became the first Eastern state to grant women full suffrage. Finally, in 1919 both houses of Congress caught on to the 50-year old trend and passed the Nineteenth Amendment to the Constitution, giving women the right to vote.

★ *The first American woman to cast a vote in a public election was Wyoming's Eliza Swain, on September 6, 1870.*

So why were Western states so far ahead of the curve? The reason may have been economic—women were in short supply in many parts of the frontier, resulting in a scarcity of labor. In 1870 women made up just 19 percent of Idaho's population, 19 percent in Montana, 24 percent in Nevada, 21 percent in Wyoming, and 37 percent in Colorado. Or perhaps it was biological, as these were great odds for the ladies, but not so ideal for the menfolk. As the years progressed, lonely legislators hoped that giving women the right to vote would attract more women from back East as well as lure more immigrants.

> **As I am from a city farther east, where the best hands get only $5 per week, I think the wages, $7.50, here are very good, but the girls here do much more work.**
>
> —female worker in Denver, 1888

Back at the national level, one of the main reasons Congress finally passed the Nineteenth Amendment—nearly half a century after women had been given suffrage in Wyoming—was the war.

Wilson's claim that the United States fought to protect democracy sparked suffrage protests and a vigil for freedom in Washington, D.C. Meanwhile, America was also feeling the effects of events in Europe, where new postwar governments in Germany, Austria, Russia, and Poland had given women the right to vote in 1918. Even Britain had granted women limited suffrage by that point, and Congress was feeling the pressure.

····················· **TRENDSPOTTING** ··············

The Great American Road Trip

The 1920s kicked off the golden age of automobiles. The appeal was obvious: compared to horses, cars were faster, more reliable, required less care, and didn't leave large clumps of the brown stuff in the street. Henry Ford's assembly-line production made cars so cheap that practically every household could aspire to own one: the Model T fell from $850 in 1909 to just $290 in the 1920s. Meanwhile, larger vehicles revolutionized public transportation and distribution in American cities: buses carried the carless for a penny, while refrigerator trucks allowed more reliable delivery of fresh foods and ice.

> Imagine a motor car able to support on its roof the live weight of a 10,000 pound elephant!
>
> —Chrysler magazine advertisement, 1931

Autonation
The Rise of American Car Culture, 1905–1935

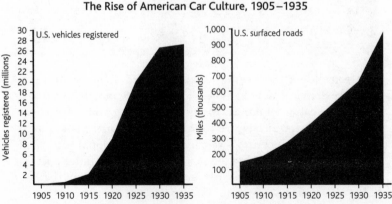

This new age of pistons and four-wheelers also brought with it a new custom: the road trip. Suddenly, families and groups of friends could tour states, regions, or even the whole country by automobile, stopping to see the sights and experience the local color. These early road trips weren't for the faint of heart. Most cars lacked insulation against the elements, and the stretches of road outside cities and towns were poorly constructed. At the time, American roads were still a patchwork of local streets, "post roads," privately maintained "auto trails," and private roads on farms and ranches; that remained the case until the late 1920s, when the first primitive interstate highways went into service. In fact, these new roads were paid for by taxes on gasoline—one of the few times Americans actually welcomed taxes. As one of Tennessee's top gas tax officers put it, "Who ever heard, before, of a popular tax?"

But it was clear, as a new America blossomed, that folks were keen to put their new cars to the road, exploring every inch of the country. The sudden increase in the number of people taking long-distance car trips, for business and pleasure, led to the emergence of a whole new world of commercial enterprises to serve them. One obvious necessity—fuel—was filled by roadside gas stations. America's first "filling station," built in St. Louis in 1905, was an independent business (read: not owned by Standard Oil). However, the second was built by Standard Oil in Seattle in 1907, beginning a trend of national chains owned by American energy companies. The number of U.S. gas stations in operation jumped from 25 in 1910 to 15,000 in 1920 and over 100,000 in 1930.

★ The first cross-country road trip was made in 1903 by H. Nelson Jackson, Sewall Crocker, and a dog, Bud, who traveled from San Francisco to New York in 63 days.

Meanwhile new businesses also offered lodging to long-distance drivers—"auto camps," basically early motels consisting of separate cabins or bungalows (or concrete "teepees," if you were feeling kitschy), which rented for a few dollars a night. Many auto camps, or "tourist courts," were located near national parks and recreation areas, reflecting the surge in interest in outdoor activities and sightseeing enabled by car ownership. During the late

1920s and 1930s, auto camps gave way to bona fide motels (that's "motor" + "hotel")—single structures, usually no more than one or two stories in height, offering hotel-like accommodations, including gross, vaguely mildewed towels. Like so many other twentieth-century lifestyle innovations, motels came from California: the first, the Motel Inn of San Luis Obispo, was built by Arthur Heineman in 1925.

Don't forget about food! Road-tripping builds an appetite, but in an era before effective health regulations, drivers were understandably leery of catching salmonella at some roadside greasy spoon. New national restaurant chains sprang up to meet this demand, offering travelers alimentary assurance with a standard menu and prominently displayed promises of cleanliness. The most famous of the new chains was Howard Johnson's. Beginning with a single soda shop and newsstand founded in Quincy, Massachusetts, in 1925, over the next three decades Howard Deering Johnson built an empire of roadside diners (with matching motels, beginning in 1954), which achieved iconic status with their bizarre orange roofs and glowing blue beacons.

HERE WE ARE NOW, ENTERTAIN U.S.

The 1920s wasn't just a golden age for automobiles. It was also the dawn of a new era of fun! New forms of entertainment quickly became cultural necessities. The widespread availability of radio receivers, based on the work of the Italian Guglielmo Marconi in the late nineteenth century, gave rise to radio broadcasts that carried news, music, talk shows, and serialized melodramas to millions of households across the United States. Meanwhile, beginning in the 1910s, record numbers of Americans went to silent movies, with almost 75 percent of the population attending a movie at least once a week by the end of the 1920s. Moviegoers were drawn by the first generation of Hollywood movie stars, including beauties like Mary Pickford, Louise Brooks, Clara Bow, and Lillian Gish, as well as comedians like Charlie Chaplin, Buster Keaton, and Harold Lloyd and dashing leading men like Douglas Fairbanks and the legendary Rudolph Valentino. The introduction of "talkies," beginning with "The Jazz Singer," starring Al Jolson (1927), took the movie craze to the next level.

Good Morning, Vladivostok!

Of all the odd, unexpected places occupied by American troops over the years, two of the weirdest have to be the Russian ports of Vladivostok and Archangelsk, located on the Pacific Ocean and the White Sea, respectively. So how the heck did U.S. troops end up there?

Following a successful coup in November 1917, Vladimir Lenin's communist Bolsheviks seized control of the Russian heartland in Eastern Europe. But the "Reds" still faced a loose alliance of "Whites" (Russian officers still loyal to the throne), "Greens" (nationalist and peasant armies fighting for independence), "Blacks" (anarchists), and various foreign POWs and volunteer fighters, who didn't get colored jerseys.

Fearing a Bolshevik victory might trigger revolutions in Western Europe, the British and French decided to nip the threat in the bud by helping Bolshevik foes crush the movement. Of course the two countries were a little overextended, what with World War I and all, so they looked to their new ally—the United States—to do the heavy lifting. President Wilson was skeptical, but in July 1918 he agreed to send 5,000 troops to Archangelsk and 8,000 troops to Vladivostok on the condition that their missions be limited to guarding Allied aid shipments.

By the time the American North Russia Expeditionary Force (nicknamed the "Polar Bears") arrived in Archangelsk, the Bolsheviks had already lifted the stockpiles, leaving the Americans twiddling their thumbs. So the British general in charge sent them into battle. The American force fought bravely, pushing the Reds back hundreds of miles, but ultimately, just like every other would-be Russia invader in history, they were frustrated by the nation's sheer size. Then the Russians—who were better prepared for winter fighting—launched a series of attacks forcing them back to Archangelsk. The U.S. troops were finally withdrawn after the ice melted in May 1919, by which time they'd suffered about 110 combat deaths and 70 deaths from disease (mostly influenza).

Meanwhile, the American Expeditionary Force Siberia arrived in Vladivostok in August of 1918. Their American commander, General William S. Graves, refused to take part in Allied attacks on the Bolsheviks, pointing out that this wasn't part of his mission. This saved his troops from combat. But during the two long years Graves and his troops spent guarding the eastern end of the

Trans-Siberian Railroad, they suffered all the miseries for which Siberia is famous: freezing temperatures, disease, and shortages of food and fuel. Their endurance earned them their own animal nickname, the "Wolfhounds," after their hardy canine mascot. The lucky ones got to take R&R in Vladivostok, a cosmopolitan city with electricity, streetcars, and, well, ladies of the night. The last Wolfhounds left Siberia in April 1920, having suffered 189 deaths from noncombat causes.

In the end, neither occupation achieved much of anything. The Bolsheviks' success and the aftermath—including the murders of millions of innocent people ordered by Lenin and Stalin—horrified the world and especially offended the staunchly capitalist United States, where anti-communism became the defining political ethos of the twentieth century.

The Loan Ranger

Most wartime loans to the European allies actually came from the U.S. government rather than private sources. In 1923 the Brits still owed the United States $4.66 billion, equal to one-quarter of the U.K.'s gross domestic product, while France owed about $3 billion. France and Italy also owed money to Britain, and thanks to the reparations agreement, Germany owed money to, like, everyone.

After the war, the Brits and French suggested canceling their debt, or at least lowering the interest, to help revive Europe's totaled economy. The American response, delivered by Wilson's successors, the Republican Presidents Warren Harding and Calvin Coolidge, was basically what you'd say to your broke cousin Eddie who owes you two grand: "That's a nice idea. Where's my money?" Counterintuitively, some forgiving and forgetting would actually have been more beneficial to the United States: putting cash in European pockets would have allowed them to buy more American imports, and the United States could have used its leverage to demand an end to protective tariffs. Renewed trade could also have tied Europe together, possibly averting another war. But the U.S. government wasn't interested in thinking the situation through. In fact, American diplomats were forbidden to even talk about canceling the debt.

★ At today's value, the combined postwar debts that Britain and France owed the United States would exceed $500 billion.

The problem with this strategy was that Britain's debt was merely the last link in a debt chain involving practically every country in Europe. The first domino fell in January 1923, when the Americans refused to allow any major revisions to the terms of Britain's debt, meaning Britain couldn't offer France easier terms. Of course the French refused to lower German reparations payments until they knew theirs would be lowered too. To drive the point home, in January of 1923 France declared Germany in default and sent troops to occupy the Ruhr Valley, a key German industrial region, with the intention of squeezing the cash out of local banks and industries.

> Borrowed money, even when owing to a nation by another nation, should be repaid. They hired the money didn't they? Let them repay it.
>
> —President Calvin Coolidge, explaining why he wouldn't forgive European debts, 1925

Unfortunately, the French squeezed too hard. German workers in the Ruhr went on strike, German businessmen refused to pay the French taxes, and on March 31, eleven German factory workers were killed in clashes with French troops. In August, the whole situation just got worse. The British demanded that the French pay at least enough to enable Britain to pay its debts to America, at the same time begging the French to stop extorting funds from Germany. The French replied that they'd be happy to reduce Germany's payments as soon as Britain reduced French debt, which . . . well, you get the idea.

Meanwhile, the German government, infuriated by the French occupation, had a brilliant idea for paying off its debts: print more money! This scheme triggered hyperinflation, and by November 1923, the average price of consumer goods in Reichsmarks was an incredible 260 million times what it had been in January of that year. (Around this time, cash had become so devalued that German housewives started using money to light their kitchen stoves.) In September, Bavaria revolted, and this was followed by a communist uprising in Hamburg. Martial law was declared, and in October of 1924, a new chancellor announced that Germany wouldn't pay further reparations without some kind of deal to get French troops out of Germany.

Finally, in 1924 the United States took action and proposed an awesomely ridiculous scheme that "solved" the problem. The "Dawes Plan" (named for Assistant Secretary of the Treasury Charles Dawes) called for billions of dollars in new American loans to Germany, which Germany would use to pay reparations to France, so France could pay Britain, and Britain in turn could pay America. The circular scheme ended up being just as futile as it sounds, since all the loans were basically wiped out by the Great Depression. No country benefited, and everyone suffered. Just canceling the debts really would have been the smarter move.

This would all be sort of comical, in a Three Stooges kind of way, except for the terrible long-term results. The French occupation of the Ruhr inspired a fresh surge of anger in Germany, multiplied by the economic meltdown that followed. As various groups vied to grab the reins in an unsteady German state, one crazy contestant rose to prominence. In 1923 a war veteran named Adolf Hitler led his tiny Nazi Party in a (failed) attempt to seize power in Munich. Thanks in part to the Dawes Plan, he'd be back.

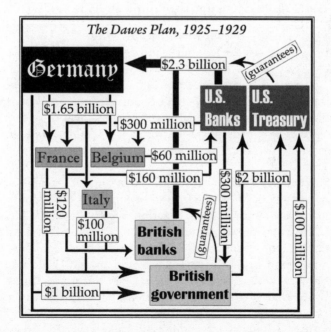

············· **WHERE MY GODS AT** ··················

Fundamentally Speaking

In the last decades of the nineteenth century, against the glorious backdrop of Gilded Age materialism, immorality, alcohol, prostitution, and violent crime, a new breed of evangelical Protestants emerged. Until then, most Protestant theologians had accommodated the growing field of science by interpreting Scripture metaphorically, but this hard-line group believed in "inerrancy"—interpreting Scripture as the literal word of God.

This new approach was first outlined by Dwight Lyman Moody, the son of a poor Massachusetts stonemason. In 1886 Moody established the Chicago Evangelization Society (later the Moody Bible Institute) and led huge conversion crusades all over America. Before long, "fundamentals" became the group's rallying cry for a return to "true" Christian faith, and around 1920 these activists were dubbed "fundamentalists." By this point, they were led by the charismatic William B. Riley, a Baptist from Minneapolis who founded the World Christian Fundamentals Association. After helping enact Prohibition, Riley went after "the new infidelity...modernism" and its "awful harvest of skepticism," as exemplified by Charles Darwin's theories. Riley homed in on Darwin, because he believed that his brand of skepticism especially threatened and contradicted the word of the Bible.

> When the Church is regarded as the body of God-fearing, righteous-living men, then, it ought to be in politics, and as a powerful influence.
>
> —William B. Riley

While Riley scorned evolutionary scientists, he reserved his harshest criticism for the "liberal" theologians who tried to accommodate evolution by interpreting the Bible figuratively. In an effort to counter the emerging beliefs, fundamentalists opened more than a dozen new schools across the country based around inerrancy. They also took to radio, believing it was the perfect medium to reach the masses. In 1923–1924 debates between fundamentalist John R. Straton and a liberal Unitarian minister named Charles Francis Potter were broadcast live from Carnegie Hall, with listeners voting for the winner by telephone. Not satisfied with airtime on "unchurched" radio, fundamentalists established their own stations, including the Bible Institute of Los Angeles's KJS (1922) and the Moody Bible Institute's WMBI (1925). In 1932 fundamentalists contributed 246 hours to Chicago's weekly total of 290 hours of religious programming; by 1935, 80 stations were broadcasting 400 fundamentalist programs nationwide.

The fundamentalists were encouraged by large, enthusiastic audiences whose presence seemed to confirm that they spoke for ordinary Americans. There's no question that they struck a chord with millions of people, especially in the South, West, and rural Midwest, where "the great commoner," William Jennings Bryan, persuaded five state legislatures to pass laws banning the teaching of evolution. But it turns out the fundamentalists fundamentally overestimated their support base . . .

Monkey See, Monkey Sue

The infamous Scopes Monkey Trial (*John Thomas Scopes v. State of Tennessee*) was a high-profile, unintentionally comical legal showdown over Tennessee's 1925 Butler Act, forbidding public schools "to teach any theory that denies the story of the Divine Creation of man as taught in the Bible, and to teach instead that man has descended from a lower order of animals." The act was named for John Washington Butler, a farmer and clerk for the Round Lick Association of Primitive Baptists (really), who ran for the state legislature after an itinerant preacher convinced him of the evils of evolution.

Encouraged by the American Civil Liberties Union, challengers to Butler's law chose John Scopes, a 24-year-old football coach and substitute science teacher at Rhea County High School in Dayton, Tennessee, to contest the law. The ACLU brought in Clarence Darrow, the country's leading criminal attorney, to match wits with William Jennings Bryan, who had suddenly agreed to act as the special guest prosecutor for the state of Tennessee. Both sides were eager to have the trial broadcast live on national radio, and the court case became a contest between opposing worldviews.

Over eight days Bryan argued that evolution wasn't fact but merely an unproven theory, since science couldn't explain the mechanism behind it. (DNA wouldn't be discovered until 1953.) Darrow argued that the meaning of "teach" was ambiguous: if students asked about evolution, could teachers explain the theory without necessarily endorsing it, or was it illegal to even mention the word? In a bizarre, fairly malicious move, Darrow also called Bryan to testify about his Christian beliefs and then pounced when he hauled out the King James Bible for reference, noting there are several versions of the Bible—which one did the law refer to?

After just over a week of media circus, the jury found Scopes guilty (he was), and the judge fined him $100, the minimum amount required by the law. Bryan and Riley preened while their followers celebrated the defeat of evolution—but the real victory went to their opponents, who carried public opinion, thanks to the radio audience. To their surprise, the fundamentalists were ridiculed in the press. The headlines also played on ever-present sectional tensions, depicting the South as a laughingstock. Newspapers noted that the presiding judge—a fundamentalist—opened proceedings with a toddler seated on his desk, began each day with a blessing delivered by a fundamentalist minister, and refused to allow the defense to explain the tenets of evolution to jurors. Meanwhile, the citizens of Rhea County were uncharitably portrayed as a bunch of toothless, whittling, banjo-plucking rubes. The verdict, according to political satirists of the day, was that Darrow had "made a monkey" out of Bryan.

Over the next few years "modernist" clergy defeated fundamentalists trying to take over evangelical churches. The group was further marginalized following the bad press surrounding Sister Aimee McPherson, a popular Pentecostal preacher who faked her own kidnapping in 1926. Beating a retreat, the fundamentalists transformed their churches, schools, and radio stations into the hubs of a separate, parallel society, limiting their exposure to sinners.

······················ **MADE IN AMERICA** ···············

The Art of the Cool

Born in New Orleans around 1900, jazz was the first genre of music to inspire a worldwide mania for all things American (which often meant all things African-American), especially in Western Europe. Drawing from blues and ragtime, the genre also folded the jaunty-yet-soulful marching music of traditional New Orleans' funeral processions into its ingredient list. Before long, jazz spread North, following the wave of African-Americans migrating from the rural South to big Northern cities, and soon it took hold in places like Chicago and New York City, with pioneers like Louis Armstrong, Ferdinand Joseph LaMothe (better known as Jelly Roll Morton), and Duke Ellington.

Jazz was more than just a new kind of music: it was part of a broader style, "American Cool," which quickly became America's top export. And while there's nothing less cool than trying to explain "cool," we'll give it a shot in the interest of the historical record.

Dumping Dixie
African-American Migration, 1900–1930

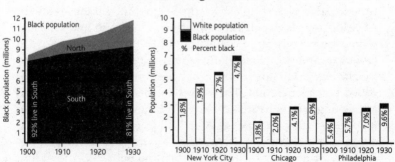

An emotional style focused—paradoxically—on minimizing emotion, "being cool" likely began in African-American culture as a way for individuals to passively deflect the psychological hurt inflicted by white racism. In American Cool, effortless mastery of both oneself and one's context became expressed through verbal and body language, or lack thereof: the cool American is calm, unfazed, even slightly jaded or blasé. This new emotional minimalism was part of a long-term shift in what society modeled as "proper" emotional behavior. In the nineteenth-century Victorian period, individuals were expected to control the extreme feelings raging just beneath the surface; by the twentieth century, they were supposed to be truly, inwardly detached from those feelings, skeptical of any passion except for "natural" urges like hunger and sexual desire.

Along with this general attitude and demeanor, mainstream America also picked up the aesthetic trappings associated with African-American cool: a combination of high and low. This juxtaposition was visible in every area of life, from fashion to art to language, and was particularly true for younger Americans who fought in World War I or came of age shortly afterward—the so-called Lost Generation. These disillusioned and dissolute teens and young adults fixated on all the things their elders tried to ignore, and the "low" part of American Cool manifested in a fascination with illegal or illicit behavior and the renunciation of traditional morality, including tramps and hobos, criminals and private eyes, dive bars and flophouses, drugs and alcohol. (At least, in cities. Rural America remained a bit square, holding fast to traditional values.) One example of this renunciation was the risqué "flapper" fashion embraced by young women of the day. Here's how the *New Republic* described the trend in 1925:

> She is frankly, heavily made up, not to imitate nature, but for an altogether artificial effect—pallor mortis, poisonously scarlet lips, richly ringed eyes . . . Her dress is brief. It is cut low . . . the skirt comes just below her knees, overlapping by a faint fraction her rolled and twisted stockings . . . The corset is as dead as the dodo's grandfather . . . The petticoat is even more defunct . . . The brassiere has been abandoned since 1925.

It Is Never, Under Any Circumstances, Hip to Be Square
A HELPFUL GUIDE TO BEING COOL

WHAT IS . . .	COOL	SQUARE
Music?	Blues, jazz, bebop, rock'n'roll	Gospel, patriotic songs, marches
Transportation?	Trains, planes, and automobiles	Horse & buggy, bicycle, walking
Art?	Edward Hopper, Jackson Pollock	Norman Rockwell
Literature?	F. Scott Fitzgerald, *The Great Gatsby*; Jack Kerouac, *On the Road*	The Bible
Architecture?	Frank Lloyd Wright's "Fallingwater," William Van Alen's Chrysler Building	Queen Anne style, American Foursquare, anything "quaint"
Design?	Art Deco	Arts and Crafts Movement
Work?	Artist, musician, author, poet, architect, bartender, unemployed	Minister, teacher, doctor, banker, accountant, lawyer, maid
Recreation?	Opium addiction, alcoholism, Russian roulette, swing dancing	Sports, crosswords, knitting, square dancing

Originating in the 1910s–1920s and first popularized by jazz idol Lester Young in the 1930s, the idea of "cool" quickly spread through mainstream culture, giving rise to scores of expressions: you can "be cool," "stay cool," "play it cool," "keep your cool," "lose your cool," "cool it," "cool your heels," or "cool your jets." We all want to make a "cool million," and someone can be a "cool customer," "cool cat," "cool as a cucumber," "coolheaded," or just "real cool." Before long (surprise!) the concept was co-opted by corporate America and soon anything could be cool. By the 1950s you could eat Cool Whip, wear Cool-Ray sunglasses, paint your nails with cool Cutex polish, drink cool 7-Up, grill with cool A-1 sauce, or "jazz up" your salad with cool French dressing. For some reason it was extra-cool to spell the word with a "K" in brand names—e.g., Kool cigarettes, Kool-Aid, Dura-Kool fabrics, Kool Krome sunglasses . . . and the list goes on.

Of course, cool wasn't the only new slang being slung in America. "Hip" and "hipster," coined by jazz musicians, referred to the typical position of a supine opium smoker, lying sideways on his or her hip, leading to the coded inquiry: "Are you hip?"

The Original Swine Flu

Proving that things can indeed always get worse, in 1918 the world was devastated by an influenza pandemic that made World War I look like a rowdy soccer match. And it all started in America. Sorry, world!

On March 4, 1918, a deadly influenza virus surfaced among American soldiers in Fort Riley, Kansas—followed by Queens, New York; Charleston, South Carolina; and Detroit, Michigan, later that month. Small and isolated, Fort Riley is definitely the odd man out in this list, prompting an obvious question: why there? Since it's unlikely the flu actually came from Kansas—most flu strains originate in poor countries where peasants live in close proximity to infected livestock—an innocuous precursor was most likely brought to Fort Riley sometime before the first outbreak.

★ *The flu outbreak forced the cancellation of the 1919 Stanley Cup, when so many players fell ill after the fifth game that it was impossible to continue.*

Wherever the disease came from, the events of 1917–1918 were practically designed to spread it, thanks to the global movement of millions of people. After the United States joined World War I in April 1917, the first priority was organizing the greatly expanded U.S. Army. Four million enlisted men were trained and deployed to Europe in waves, beginning with the first draft of 687,000 called up in September 1917. To do this, the Army established 16 regional training centers around the country, each able to accommodate 50,000 men. Like the other centers, Fort Riley brought together large numbers of young men who, for the most part, had never traveled far from home (leaving them vulnerable to strange diseases) and piled them together in drafty barracks. Factor in communal showers, latrines, and dining areas, and you have a pandemic playground. After boot camp, the troops were thrown together in even bigger groups at East Coast ports where they awaited embarkation for Europe. And once in Europe, they were exposed to still more exotic contagions by their foreign allies.

This intercontinental game of musical chairs didn't just move the virus around: it actually may have caused a killer strain, as a result of multiple strains simultaneously infecting the same individual. When that happens, the virus can veer from the script with a "genetic exchange event"—an RNA remix in which different strains combine their characteristics. Somewhere on its European vacation, the virus became even more virulent and deadly: in April 1918, just one month after the Fort Riley outbreak, an epidemic incapacitated French troops at a camp near Bordeaux, followed almost immediately by flare-ups in northern France and across the frontlines in Germany. In May and June of 1918, it killed five out of every 1,000 people in various parts of Europe—but it wasn't until August of that year that it became a super-killer, with three simultaneous outbreaks in Boston, Massachusetts; Brest, France; and Freetown, Sierra Leone.

With the earth encircled by disease, the toll was truly epic: altogether the pandemic infected about 500 million people and carried off 50 million–100 million victims. The death toll was two or three times the total number of military and civilian casualties in World War I, and probably more than those killed by the Black Death in medieval Europe. In the United States alone, the flu killed 675,000 people, about six times the number of American soldiers killed in World War I. And actually, more than half of the 110,000 American war dead—57,000—also died from the flu. This global decimation was especially shocking because most of the casualties were young people, reversing the usual pattern for influenza mortality.

Despite its Midwestern origins, the scourge became known as the "Spanish Flu" because Spain—a neutral country—hadn't instituted wartime censorship, meaning that it was the only place the press could report the actual death toll (260,000).

Frozen Foods
A Birdseye View

It's hard to believe that there was life before frozen food. But in 1924, Birdseye provided a boon to lazy people across the world when it became the anti-Prometheus and brought frozen foods down to earth. Why did such a simple invention take so long to deliver? One obvious challenge was the lack of a method to keep things frozen. This problem was solved in 1911, when a French monk created the first electric-powered refrigerator. By 1919 a modified American design had been acquired by the president of General Motors, William C. Durant, and renamed "Frigidaire." The first freezer-equipped refrigerators hit the market in 1922, but sales were hindered by their great expense—at $714, they cost more than a Ford Model T ($500)!

As prices came down, sales picked up (the new models cost just $275 in 1930), and by 1932 Frigidaire and its two main competitors, Kelvinator and Servel, had total annual sales of 2.5 million units. In fact, the demand continued to grow every year, despite the Great Depression. With refrigerators keeping food fresher for longer, housewives didn't have to make as many shopping trips or worry as much about exposing their families to spoiled milk or meat, which could carry tasty E. coli, salmonella, typhoid fever, and staphylococcus.

> ★ Clarence Birdseye founded his frozen food empire with a $7 capital investment, which he used to purchase an electric fan, buckets of brine, and cakes of ice.

Once the refrigerator had been perfected, the next logical step was refining the art of freezing food. But it turns out you can't just throw fresh meat or vegetables into the freezer: if the freezing process takes too long, water has a chance to form large ice crystals, which rupture the food cell membranes, destroying the food's nutritional value and making it soft and mushy (the technical term is "gross"). Fortunately, in 1916 a Brooklyn taxidermist named Clarence Birdseye realized that this could be avoided with rapid freezing, preserving more of the food's texture, flavor, and nutrients. In following years Birdseye developed a process for "flash-freezing" vegetables in wax-coated cardboard boxes under high pressure; he also figured out that briefly boiling vegetables (blanching) before freezing halted the ripening process, which otherwise resulted in tough, flavorless, discolored vegetables. By 1924 Birdseye had mastered the basic flash-freezing process and opened his own business, the General Seafoods Company, selling flash-frozen fish, vegetables, and rabbit.

In 1929 General Foods—later Kraft General Foods—bought Birdseye's patents and trademarks for the huge sum of $22 million and began selling the first "Birds Eye Frosted Food" in 1930. However, Kraft still faced two big obstacles. On the consumer side, most American housewives remained skeptical that frozen vegetables could taste anything like the fresh version. On the retail side, there was a lack of freezers. Birds Eye tackled the first problem with an advertising blitz in popular magazines, touting the freshness of vacuum-sealed meat and vegetables. To address the second problem, in 1934 Birds Eye began leasing special new glass-topped display freezers to stores for a nominal fee, spurring interest among shopkeepers.

Despite these efforts, sales remained low until rationing during World War II finally forced Americans to give frozen peas a chance. As frozen food sales surged, millions of housewives impressed their picky families with (relatively) fresh vegetables out of season—yet another amazing feature of modern life.

The Rx for Med School

At the end of the nineteenth century, the American medical field was seriously unwell. "Quack" doctors abounded, and many "legitimate" physicians simply apprenticed with an older physician for two years, inheriting all his antiquated beliefs and procedures. While there was some understanding of contagious disease, most doctors failed to take adequate preventive measures and unwittingly became transmission vectors. For instance, obstetricians who failed to wash their hands between deliveries spread puerperal infection ("childbed fever"), killing 20,000 American women a year.

That's not to say there weren't plenty of brilliant minds: from 1881 to 1900, William Stewart Halsted, the first chief surgeon at Johns Hopkins University, pioneered the use of blood transfusions, silk sutures, and rubber surgical gloves. He also developed

THE GREAT WHITE SLOPE

In 1884 William Stewart Halsted established the use of cocaine as a local anesthetic, but during the course of his investigations, he inadvertently became addicted, along with his students and several colleagues. Out of this group, only Halsted and one other colleague eventually recovered … sort of. Physicians at a sanatorium in Providence, Rhode Island, "cured" Halsted's addiction by substituting morphine for cocaine. Unbeknownst to his colleagues and students at Johns Hopkins, Halsted remained a morphine addict for the rest of his life.

surgeries like the radical mastectomy for the treatment of breast cancer and a highly effective procedure for repairing inguinal hernias. And he wasn't alone. The talent was there, mixed indiscriminately with the hacks. The real problem was inconsistency: laymen had no way of knowing whether someone claiming to be a doctor was legit.

That's where Abraham Flexner came in. A teacher from Louisville, Kentucky, Flexner attracted national attention with his new approach to education. He believed in small classes, lots of personal attention, practical demonstrations, and student participation. Flexner's ideas were completely at odds with accepted educational theory, with its narrow focus on rote memorization and recitation of facts, supplemented by corporal punishment as needed. As an agnostic Jew, Flexner also faced anti-Semitic discrimination—which, like racism, was more or less universal in nineteenth-century America. But none of that stopped the Louisville schoolteacher. His experimental prep school became so successful—with most graduates admitted to elite colleges—that criticism soon turned to curiosity.

In 1908 Flexner wrote a critique of American higher education, *The American College,* which attracted the attention of the board of directors of the Carnegie Foundation. The foundation's president, Henry Pritchett, invited Flexner to assess the current state of American and Canadian medical education and draw up a comprehensive program of reform. Despite a complete lack of medical training, Flexner accepted the challenge.

After reviewing German medical schools (then regarded as the most advanced in the world) as well as his alma mater, Johns Hopkins, the top U.S. school, Flexner turned to the other 154 American and Canadian medical schools then in business. At each he reviewed the entrance requirements, faculty qualifications, and the size and quality of lab and hospital facilities. Overall, Flexner found only 16 schools that required at least two years of college education, and only one, Johns Hopkins, requiring four years of college with biology and chemistry. Another fifty required prior education equivalent to high school. The rest—the majority of American medical schools—had no requirements at all besides enough money to pay their fees.

This was about to change: the Carnegie Foundation asked for a candid report, and Flexner—hardly one to mince words in the first place—carried out this directive with vigor. Published with great fanfare in 1910, *Medical Education in the United States and Canada* basically rained fiery death on a large part of the existing system of medical education. Over the next decade, 70 of the establishments Flexner condemned were closed. Meanwhile, philanthropists and state governments raised tens of millions of dollars to revamp the schools that could be saved—most affiliated with universities—in accordance with Flexner's recommendations.

THE QUOTABLE FLEXNER

> Its anatomy room, containing a single cadaver, is indescribably foul . . . Nothing more disgraceful calling itself a medical school can be found anywhere.
>
> —on the soon-to-be-defunct Georgia College of Eclectic Medicine and Surgery located in Atlanta

> The city of Chicago is in respect to medical education the plague spot of the country.
>
> —on Chicago

> Close the medical school, get rid of the student body, build a new medical school on the Johns Hopkins model, get new chairmen and start over.
>
> —advice to philanthropist Robert Brookings on how to improve the Washington University School of Medicine in St. Louis

So what were Flexner's recommendations? Because medicine is a science, medical schools should be integrated into existing academic institutions, giving students and faculty access to libraries and laboratories to support research. They should receive generous financial support from private donors or state governments.

Senior instructors should be tenured professors with a full-time commitment to medical teaching, and instruction should follow a set four-year curriculum, as at Johns Hopkins. Because medicine is also a practice, medical schools should have access to large hospitals where students can participate in all aspects of the profession. To gain a systematic knowledge of medicine, students should be exposed to all its major branches in rotation.

·············· **PROFILES IN SCOURGES** ·····················

"Scarface" Al Capone (1899–1947)

Today Prohibition is regarded as the single biggest failure in the history of American social reform. But on one front, it was a huge success: without Prohibition, we never could have had Al Capone's Chicago Outfit.

When Prohibition was enacted in 1920, it had plenty of popular support. The Christian temperance movement had been calling for legal limits on the sale of alcohol as far back as the seventeenth century, and while proposed bans on tobacco and theaters(!) fell flat, banning alcohol seemed to make more sense. By 1919, 33 states had enacted their own Prohibition laws, bolstered in part by a new surge of women voters showing their muscle at the ballot box.

> The South is dry and will vote dry. That is, everybody sober enough to stagger to the polls.
>
> —Will Rogers, 1926

This was all well and good, but the fact is people like booze. Although there are no statistics on alcohol consumption during Prohibition, the rate of cirrhosis of the liver didn't waver one bit during Prohibition or afterward. So what did banning alcohol accomplish, if people were still drinking just as much? Well, it drove the whole business underground, into the hands of enterprising criminals.

Enter the Sicilian Mafia, also known as *cosa nostra*, "our thing." With massive profits to be made, these shady characters would stop at nothing to protect their business, leading to wholesale corruption and a steady increase in the murder rate from 1920 to 1933. Although the early American Mafia was predominantly Sicilian, non-Sicilian Italians were sometimes given (or just took) important positions. In Chicago, a nascent Mafia was established by Giacomo "Diamond Jim" Colosimo, an Italian immigrant from Calabria (the "toe" in the Italian boot) around the turn of the century. In 1909 Colosimo brought in his nephew Giovanni "Johnny the Fox" Torrio from Brooklyn to serve as his enforcer, and a decade later, Torrio's old second-in-command—an ambitious 20-year-old thug named Al Capone—followed. Like Colosimo and Torrio, Capone was not of Sicilian extraction: his parents were from the area around Naples, and he was born in Brooklyn. But he made up for it with his willingness to employ utmost brutality.

By 1920 it was obvious to Torrio and Capone that Prohibition was a potential bonanza, but Colosimo, an old-fashioned whores-n-numbers guy, was nervous about taking on the federal government. Torrio and Capone had Colosimo "rubbed out," then jumped into the illegal alcohol trade feet first, making the most of Colosimo's network of 200 brothels—a ready-made distribution network for illegal booze with preexisting connections with corrupt cops and politicians.

> This American system of ours . . . call it Americanism, call it capitalism, call it what you like, gives to each and every one of us a great opportunity if we only seize it with both hands and make the most of it.
>
> —Al Capone

From 1920 to 1923, Torrio and Capone saw their business grow by leaps and bounds as the good people of Chicago flocked to speakeasies (the word comes from the barkeep's advice to "speak easy" to avoid police attention). Their network of illegal bars and clubs grew from about 160 in 1920 to about 10,000 by the middle of the decade, when Torrio retired, giving Capone a virtual monopoly. Unlike his Sicilian colleagues, Capone was happy to employ "talented" individuals whatever their background, so the Chicago Outfit was a bit of a rainbow coalition. Capone's gang included plenty of Jews, Irish-Americans, and African-Americans, and at its height in the late 1920s, Capone's Chicago Outfit was said to employ 1,000 people, with a payroll of $300,000 a week, while total annual revenues reached over $100 million a year. According to Capone, about $30 million of his annual revenues went to paying off elected officials, newspapermen, and most of all, the judges and police; by the late 1920s, over half of the judges and cops in Chicago were said to be receiving bribes from Capone.

Alcohol flowed to Capone's establishments from various sources—farmers distilling whiskey in homemade stills, beer and liquor imported from Canada, and rumrunners coming through the Bahamas and Bermuda. Capone's liquor was sold all over the country, from New York City to Omaha, Nebraska, and the mob boss took a personal interest in the management of his regional businesses. In fact, he had at least a dozen luxurious safe houses set up across the country for business travel. Within this vast realm, Capone's influence varied from place to place; while he held absolute power in Chicago and its environs, in other places, like Kansas City and St. Louis, he supplied liquor to local crime families, which then became loosely subordinated to the Chicago Outfit. If ever displeased, Capone could quickly and easily dispatch one of the hundreds of paid killers in his employ almost anywhere in the country to protect his interests.

★ *During the winter months, Model Ts loaded with Canadian booze simply drove across the frozen Detroit River from Windsor.*

Of course you don't keep hundreds of killers on staff if you're not going to use them, which brings us to the "violent" part of "violent crime": beyond "supplying a demand," as Capone innocently described his business activities, what kinds of mayhem was the Chicago Outfit responsible for? Overall, Capone's criminal operation is blamed for about 500 murders—mostly underworld players but also a good number of innocent bystanders. The first wave of murders warranting national attention came during the "Chicago Beer Wars" of 1923–1926, an intermittent series of turf fights that left the Torrio-Capone mob in control of most of the city after 375 gangsters and affiliates on both sides had been murdered. Along the way, in 1924 Capone and Torrio decided to move their headquarters to a quieter spot in the neighboring town of Cicero, Illinois. To ensure a sympathetic government in Cicero, 200 armed hoodlums forced the entire town to vote for their favored candidate; election day ended with the gangsters fighting pitched battles with an equal number of policemen sent from all over Cook County to stop them. Probably the most infamous incident, however, was the Valentine's Day Massacre of seven rival gang members on February 14, 1929. Capone's men, disguised as police officers, pretended to arrest the men but then simply lined them up in a basement garage and shot them. While this succeeded in securing Capone's control of all of Chicago, the brutal execution-style murders—publicized in lurid newspaper photos—sparked a national outcry.

But Capone was never convicted of a single murder or for the illegal sale of alcohol. Rather, his fate hinged on his failure to pay income taxes on all the money generated by the Chicago Outfit. Capone was only able to launder so much of his fortune through reputable businesses, and he was finally caught by Eliot Ness, a former director of public safety for Cleveland, who'd been given a special mission in 1927 to stop Capone. Sifting the Chicago police department for officers not on Capone's payroll, Ness assembled a small team of incorruptible individuals, nicknamed "The Untouchables," who doggedly pursued Capone for three years. (Ness himself survived several assassination attempts.) Capone was finally found guilty on 22 counts of tax evasion in 1931 and sentenced to eleven years, beginning in 1932. In prison Capone's mind began to deteriorate from untreated syphilis, and he was completely demented by the time he was released in 1943. He finally died of late-stage syphilis on January 25, 1947; he was 48 years old.

> If you can't get a drink you aren't trying.
>
> —popular saying in Detroit, 1925

· BY THE NUMBERS · · · · · · · · · · · · · · · · ·

25 million	number of dead in World War I
110,000	number of U.S. dead in World War I
0.4 percent	U.S. dead as a proportion of the total
2,439	number of ships sunk by German U-boats in 1917 (the year with most ships sunk)
6,235,878	total tonnage of ships sunk by German U-boats in 1917
881,027	total tonnage sunk in April 1917 (the worst month of the war, in terms of tonnage losses)
200	number of ships engaged in rum-running during Prohibition
50,000	number of people employed by smuggling in Detroit
$105 million	total revenue of Al Capone's Chicago Outfit, 1930

$32 million	total expenditures on Prohibition by all levels of government, 1930
8	number of murders per 100,000 inhabitants in Chicago, 1918
18	number of murders per 100,000 inhabitants in Chicago, 1925
30 million	weekly movie attendance in 1920
28 percent	proportion of the U.S. population this represented
90 million	weekly movie attendance in 1929
73 percent	proportion of the U.S. population this represented
5,000	nationwide refrigerator sales, 1921
800,000	nationwide refrigerator sales, 1929
8 percent	proportion of the African-American population living in Northern states, 1900
19 percent	proportion of the African-American population living in Northern states, 1930
458,000	number of cars on American roads, 1910
26,750,000	number of cars on American roads, 1930

Superpower Surprise

(1930–1955)

To paraphrase Shakespeare: some countries are born great, some achieve greatness, and some spill something that smells like greatness on themselves after falling asleep on the couch. That last would be America. Having turned its back on international affairs after World War I, the United States had to be roused awake and then dragged kicking and screaming into World War II—after which it ended up a "superpower." Some countries have all the luck.

To be fair, Americans had plenty to worry about on the home front, like the Great Depression. As the plummeting U.S. economy dragged the rest of the world down, ominous developments began abroad. For instance, the fact that authoritarian governments were rising in Germany and Japan would have been worrisome for anyone paying attention, but Americans were too busy wallowing in their misery to take much notice.

America's invitation to the party was delivered on December 7, 1941, with the Japanese surprise attack on Pearl Harbor. The strike plunged the United States into war, not just with Imperial Japan, but also with its allies, Nazi Germany and Fascist Italy. Together the three "Axis Powers" steered the planet into the most destructive war in history—which they almost won. But like all compulsive risk takers, they eventually gambled away their advantage, leaving the war to be decided by brute force and mass production. (Did someone say "American industry"?) Not to give away the ending, but between U.S. industrial output, Soviet manpower, and sheer British stubbornness, by 1945 the Allied Powers—who took to calling themselves the United Nations—completely crushed the Axis, destroying their militaristic regimes and occupying their homelands.

After the war, the United States faced (yet again) the daunting tasks of reviving injured allies and rebuilding defeated foes.

But it also had to deal with a new threat: communist subversion. Sponsored by America's recent ally, the Soviet Union, this brand of communism required a full-court press. And America attacked accordingly with a diverse arsenal of weapons: economic aid, diplomacy, covert operations, and military power, including a whole lotta nukes.

Back at home, American society had emerged from the war as a whole new beast. Perhaps the most important change saw millions of women leave the home to enter the workplace, making up for the critical labor shortage that had resulted from millions of men joining the armed forces. Although many of these women were later fired so employers could give their jobs to returning GIs, a precedent had been established, foreshadowing the feminist movement. Meanwhile, instead of going back to work, many returning soldiers went back to school, thanks to the GI Bill, which paid for millions of young adults to attend college—now an increasingly common part of American education. Finally, another era-defining development saw the 1.2 million African-Americans who fought in the war come home determined to secure the basic civil rights they felt they deserved after their loyal service to their country.

·············· **WHAT HAPPENED WHEN** ····················

October 24, 1929 "Great Crash" of New York stock market.

June 17, 1930 President Herbert Hoover signs the disastrous Smoot-Hawley tariff.

November 8, 1932 Franklin Delano Roosevelt wins first election to presidency.

January 30, 1933 Adolf Hitler becomes chancellor of Germany.

July 5, 1935 National Labor Relations Act lays the groundwork for American union movement.

November 3, 1936 FDR wins second term.

September 1, 1939 Germany invades Poland, beginning World War II.

September 21, 1939	United States establishes "Cash and Carry" policy, trading as neutral power.
November 5, 1940	FDR wins third term.
March 11, 1941	United States drops "Cash and Carry" for "Lend-Lease," openly favoring Allies.
December 7, 1941	Japan attacks Pearl Harbor.
June 4–7, 1942	United States wins Battle of Midway.
November 8, 1942	United States and Britain invade North Africa.
June 6, 1944	"D-Day," the Allied invasion of France.
November 7, 1944	FDR wins fourth term.
December 16, 1944– January 25, 1945	Desperate last-ditch German counteroffensive fails during "The Battle of the Bulge."
April 12, 1945	FDR dies; Vice President Harry Truman becomes president.
May 7, 1945	Germany surrenders.
August 6 and 9, 1945	United States drops atomic bombs on Hiroshima and Nagasaki; Japan surrenders.
March 2–24, 1946	"Iran Crisis" pits America against Soviet Union, until Stalin backs down.
June 24, 1948–May 12, 1949	Soviet forces blockade Western troops in Berlin, but United States circumvents blockade with an airlift.
August 29, 1949	Soviet Union tests its first atomic bomb in Kazakhstan.
December 7, 1949	Mao Zedong's communists triumph in China.
June 25, 1950–July 27, 1953	Korean War rages until an armistice is signed, ending fighting in a draw.

················ **LIES YOUR TEACHER TOLD YOU** ················

LIE: *The stock market crash on October 24, 1929 caused the Great Depression.*

THE TRUTH: Oh, man. There are so many lies about this epic downturn that you need a dedicated staff just to keep track of 'em. First things first: the Great Depression did *not* start with the stock market crash on October 24, 1929–"Black Thursday." At that point, the downturn was already under way, thanks to a combination of credit-happy consumers and reckless lending.

The Federal Reserve Banks, created by Woodrow Wilson in 1913, controlled the money supply by adjusting the interest rate on loans to private banks. When the Fed raised interest rates, private banks had to raise their interest rates too, resulting in less borrowing by businesses and consumers; when the Fed lowered interest rates, it freed up funds and boosted lending. There's nothing inherently wrong with this system, but when politicians got their paws on the Federal Reserve Banks, bad things started to happen. Not really understanding the impact of what they were doing, officials kept interest rates low through the 1920s because it was politically popular. Everyone likes money! The loans sustained short-term economic growth by allowing businesses to invest in new factories and consumers to buy more stuff. Easy credit also "solved" problems caused by tariffs in the United States and Europe. When American exports were too expensive for foreign consumers, the U.S. government simply boosted foreign demand by encouraging American banks to lend the foreigners billions of dollars. The whole system was pumping more and more air into a credit bubble now engulfing the world.

Despite increased production, domestic prices remained high throughout the 1920s, but Americans didn't really notice because there was so much money floating around. With easy access to credit, more consumers bought more goods at higher prices, allowing businesses to hire more employees at higher wages. This gave them collateral to borrow more money and buy more stuff, which . . . you get the idea. Easy credit also led to rampant stock market speculation, with stockbrokers lending investors up to 90 percent of the value of the stocks they'd bought. This too wasn't good for that looming, growing bubble.

At some point, the merry-go-round had to stop. There were already signs of trouble in February 1926, when tire prices started sliding. The trend reflected diminishing auto sales and was followed by rubber in January 1928, cotton and wool in August 1928, and copper in April 1929. Back in July of 1927, with demand starting to sputter, the governor of the New York Federal Reserve Bank, Benjamin Strong, had tried to counter the slide by injecting even more credit into the system. Wall Street kept on partying, but savvy investors were eyeing the exits: something was clearly going on in late 1928, when the Dow Jones Industrial Average climbed to a new record of 295.62 on November 28—then tumbled 13 percent over the following week in a market "correction."

★ *Although the stock market crash popularized the stereotypical suicide image of depressed investors leaping from skyscraper windows, the most common method of suicide during that time was asphyxiation by gas.*

Ironically, it was the Federal Reserve itself that finally pulled the plug in 1929, raising rates after a belated change of heart. Immediately, the wild ride ground to a halt. After growing 15 percent during the previous year, U.S. industrial production stalled in June 1929. By September, the continued standstill triggered the first big slides in stock prices, and October brought panic. Stockbrokers called in loans, speculators started going bankrupt, and many investors were ruined. Then . . . the market recovered: after tumbling from 380 in mid-October to below 200 in November, by April of 1930 the Dow Jones was back above 290.

Okay. So if the United States survived the famous Black Friday crash, what actually kicked off the Great Depression? The truth is, there was *another* crash—the "real" crash—with the Dow Jones plunging from over 270 in June of 1930 to rock bottom at 41.22 on July 8, 1932. Spread out over two years, this vertiginous 85 percent decline was less of a crash and more of a "slow, groaning collapse."

**LIE: Herbert Hoover didn't do anything
to counteract the Great Depression.**
BONUS LIE: FDR saved the day with The New Deal.
THE TRUTH: America might have been better off if Hoover had left some things alone. In June of 1929, Hoover signed the Agricultural Marketing Act, which bought up surplus produce to shore up prices; in October he reversed the Fed's change of heart and

pumped another $300 million into credit markets; in October 1930, he formed the President's Emergency Committee on Employment to coordinate local welfare and work programs; and in January of 1932, he supersized the credit infusion by creating the Reconstruction Finance Corporation (RFC), which distributed $2 billion in emergency loans to banks, railroads, farm mortgage associations, and life insurance companies. Hoover also launched a public works program, including the famous Hoover Dam—at the time, the largest concrete structure in the world. Last but not least, Hoover ordered wage controls, hoping to put more money in workers' pockets and stimulate consumption.

Unfortunately, many of these initiatives simply made things worse. Hoover's biggest domestic policy mistake was insisting that industry continue paying high wages; instead of paying everyone less, bosses simply fired employees. And people struggled to feed their families because prices were kept artificially high by the Agricultural Marketing Act. So everyone spent less, pushing more companies into bankruptcy, and sending unemployment even higher.

★ *Herbert Hoover and his wife spent many years in China and often spoke to each other in Cantonese at the White House to maintain confidentiality.*

In June of 1930 Hoover delivered his economic coup de grâce by signing the Smoot-Hawley Tariff Act (authored by Senator Reed Smoot and Representative Willis Hawley). The move raised duties on 20,000 kinds of imported goods to near-record levels. Predictably, indignant foreign trade partners jacked up their own tariffs, wiping out the American farmers who supplied these markets. As international trade dwindled, Europeans lost faith in the dollar and started cashing in their American currency at U.S. banks for gold. This began depleting the reserves that guaranteed deposits, at which point terrified small-time account holders starting besieging banks to demand their money in gold too. The banks were simultaneously being hit by a wave of bankruptcies overseas—remember all those foreign loans?—and more stock market speculators going belly-up. All told, between January 1930 and December 1933, 10,763 out of 24,970 American banks failed, taking with them deposits worth over $6.8 billion, including the life savings of millions of ordinary people. Basically, over the course of three years, a sum equal to 7 percent of the U.S. gross domestic product in 1930 just evaporated.

Hoover single-handedly took a one-year recession and turned it into an open-ended cataclysm. It's no surprise that voters handed him a pink slip in the presidential election of 1932. But was the new guy—Franklin Delano Roosevelt, the charismatic, eloquent Democratic candidate—really all that different? This is yet another misconception. The truth is, most of FDR's initiatives were simply continuations (or expansions) of Hoover-era policies. The Home Owners' Loan Act of 1933, which distributed more government credit to prevent foreclosures, re-upped the Federal Home Loan Bank created by Hoover in 1932; the Agricultural Adjustment Act of 1933 did Hoover one better by paying farmers not to grow food in the first place; the Emergency Banking Act of 1933 and the Loans to Industry Act of 1934 expanded Hoover's less-than-helpful RFC; and Hoover's Norris-LaGuardia Act of 1932, clearing away legal obstacles to labor organizing, was strengthened by FDR's National Labor Relations Act of 1935. Like Hoover, FDR also reluctantly accepted deficit spending and ordered public works projects, including the Tennessee Valley Authority, created in 1933 to provide hydroelectric power to the rural South. The only real difference was FDR's willingness to distribute relief aid directly to ordinary Americans, which alleviated suffering but did little to end the downturn. Aside from this, their supposed

WAR!

Q: What is it good for?
A: It stimulates production!

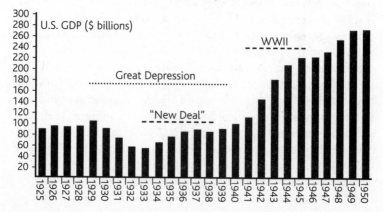

differences are mostly the product of PR spun by both sides during the 1932 election.

So why did a strategy that failed for Hoover work for FDR? Easy: it didn't. In fact, the series of social and economic reforms enacted by FDR (collectively known as the New Deal) may even have delayed recovery by allowing big business to form anti-competitive cartels, raising the price of consumer goods, discouraging hiring by decreeing high wages, propping up failing businesses, and crowding out private investment. What really revived the American economy? War.

LIE: *FDR knew about the impending attack on Pearl Harbor but let it happen to force America to go to war.*

THE TRUTH: FDR did know that the United States was on a collision course with Japan. In fact, he wanted Japan (or Germany) to make the first move so that the United States had a reason for joining the war. But he definitely didn't know that Pearl Harbor was going to be attacked.

The fact is, U.S.-Japan tension had been building for a while. The whole thing started in the 1930s, when a group of fanatical, hypernationalist military officers hijacked Japan's foreign policy. While the rest of the world was distracted by the Great Depression, Japan launched an aggressive campaign of expansion, starting with the occupation of northern China from 1931 to 1936. Then in July of 1937, they picked up the pace. Japanese forces had occupied Beijing by August, Shanghai by October, and Nanjing by December.

Reports of Japanese atrocities during the "Rape of Nanjing" gave FDR the political support he needed to withdraw from the 1911 U.S.-Japan Treaty of Commerce, clearing the way for restrictions on Japanese imports like American coal, metal, and oil. But instead of caving and retreating, the Japanese expanded the scope of their aggression by occupying northern Indochina, a French colonial territory. FDR upped the ante by halting exports of aviation gasoline and scrap iron to Japan. Japan decided to counter by announcing a formal pact with Nazi Germany and Fascist Italy in September 1940. Further incensed by this American "bullying" (can't a guy rape and pillage his neighbors any more?), Japan also invaded southern Indochina in July 1941. Finally, a fed-up FDR countered by halting oil sales, threatening to paralyze the Japanese military, which had only a two-year supply of fuel.

With oil reserves dwindling, the Japanese high command ordered Japan's ambassador, Kichisaburo Nomura (an old friend of

FDR's from World War I) to conduct negotiations. But in fact, Japan had no intention of giving in to American demands: having decided in September 1941 that war was inevitable, the Japanese instead planned to use U.S.-Japan talks as a smoke screen while preparing a surprise attack on the U.S. Pacific fleet at Pearl Harbor. Japan hoped the bombings would put the U.S. fleet out of action long enough to allow them to conquer the oil-rich Dutch East Indies.

By this stage, FDR clearly wanted the United States to join the war, but he believed the only way to get isolation-prone Americans involved was by forcing one of the Axis powers to "shoot first." Like most of his advisors, FDR believed that the first shot would come on the Atlantic side, where German U-boats threatened American ships. On the off chance that it did end up coming on the Pacific side, most people expected the Japanese to attack the Dutch East Indies or the Philippines. Expert opinion held that a sizable carrier fleet simply wouldn't be able to make it from Japan to Hawaii, almost 4,000 miles away, undetected. Furthermore, an airborne attack on Pearl Harbor would require new torpedoes that could be dropped by planes in shallow water—the technology just didn't exist. Except that unbeknownst to the U.S. military, Japan's Imperial Navy had perfected this weapon in the summer of 1941.

Some conspiracy theorists assert that FDR must have known about the impending attack from American intelligence-gathering—but between deliberate Japanese deception and home-grown American incompetence, confusion reigned. For example, U.S. spooks believed shortwave radio broadcasts from Tokyo would be used to deliver coded messages in weather reports, with one phrase, "east wind rain," warning Japanese diplomats of imminent war. After the war, some analysts claimed to remember hearing the code—but it turns out the Japanese never used it. U.S. code breakers did intercept messages to Japanese diplomats instructing them to destroy sensitive documents on December 1, but this was ambiguous: for all they knew, the Japanese were just being paranoid. (The more important Japanese naval code wasn't cracked until the next year.)

★ *Wabun Code is the form of Morse Code used to transmit Japanese text. On December 2, 1941, the Japanese flagship IJN* Nagato *sent the message "Niitakayama nobore 1208" (Climb Mount Niitaka on December 8 Japan Time)."*

In trying to implicate FDR, conspiracy theorists also cite several cloak-and-dagger anecdotes. For example, in June of 1941 British intelligence learned German spies were trying to collect detailed information about U.S. forces in Hawaii, and the Brits supposedly informed J. Edgar Hoover, the head of the Federal Bureau of Investigation. From this, it might have been possible for Hoover to deduce that Japan might attack Pearl Harbor in a war—but let's be realistic: this possibility wasn't a secret, and the intercepts made no mention of specific Japanese plans, let alone dates or times. (The Japanese were unlikely to share such details with even their allies: Pearl Harbor took Hitler by surprise.)

The best argument against these conspiracy theories is common sense: if FDR's goal was defeating Japan, it wasn't very slick to start by sacrificing the majority of the U.S. Pacific fleet. Indeed, if FDR really knew about the impending attack, he could have accomplished the same objective by moving most of the fleet somewhere safe and leaving a few old, obsolete battleships in Pearl Harbor as bait, with their crews enjoying shore leave. But sadly, the truth is that nobody had a clue.

LIE: *America defeated Nazi Germany with help from its plucky British sidekick.*

THE TRUTH: The Soviet Union defeated Hitler—pretty much by itself. While American and British participation did help shorten the war considerably, by the time the United States joined the effort, the Soviet Union had already done most of the work.

Of course, you can also argue that the Soviet Union was just cleaning up its own mess. The Soviet dictator Josef Stalin shared the blame for starting the war, since he helped Hitler with a mutual assistance pact in 1939. The pact freed Hitler to conquer the rest of Europe, while Stalin supplied him with wheat, oil, and other natural resources; in return, Stalin got half of Poland and (he thought) an assurance Hitler wouldn't attack the Soviet Union. Wrong!

Now, your average crazed megalomaniac might decide conquering Western Europe was enough—but Hitler thought *big*. Long diatribe short, the German leader wanted to conquer new territory in the east, kill all the Jews and Slavs, and colonize Eastern Europe with "Aryan" Germans. And he was 100 percent serious about this very, very crazy plan. From the Nazi invasion of the Soviet Union in June 1941 to the end of the war, the number of German troops deployed on the Eastern front never sank below three-quarters of Germany's total strength. As a result, the Eastern front saw mind-boggling casualties: just under 90 percent (3.2 million) of German combat deaths and three-quarters of German tank losses occurred there. On the Soviet side, 11 million soldiers died, including 2 million in German POW camps. Combined with civilian deaths, the total Soviet toll came to an astonishing and horrifying 25 million, compared to 1.3 million combined military and civilian deaths for the United States, U.K., and France.

Responsibility for the horrors of the Eastern front rests with Hitler and his accomplices—but the United States and U.K. didn't seem to be in much of a hurry to help their ally. Stalin brought up the idea of opening up a second front in Western Europe in July 1941, and in June of 1942 the Western Allies assured him that the invasion of France would begin no later than September 1943. When it didn't, Stalin angrily withdrew his ambassadors to the United States and U.K., accusing the Western Allies of delaying so the Germans and Soviets could wear each other out. And he may have been right about that.

The United States did help the Soviet Union with Lend-Lease supplies, including 7,500 tanks, 14,750 planes, and 1,980 rail locomotives—but this aid only accounted for about 9 percent of Soviet wartime needs, as the Red Army lost 61,000 tanks and 26,000 planes from 1943 to 1945 and 15,800 locomotives from 1941 to 1945. The British and Americans also "helped out" by dropping about two million tons of TNT and napalm on Germany, killing over 300,000 civilians, but "strategic bombing" achieved little: the important German factories were moved underground, and war production actually increased from 1942 to 1944.

☞ QUICK'N'EASY WORLD WAR II ☜

War broke out in September 1939 when France and the U.K. finally (belatedly) decided to resist Adolf Hitler's continuing aggression in Europe. It became a global conflict when Hitler forged an alliance with Imperial Japan, which was busily conquering Asia. An American embargo cutting off oil to Japan put the United States on a collision course with the Axis Powers—but the U.S. was already deeply involved in the war. Above all, Allied

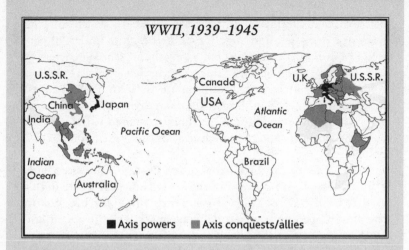

WWII, 1939–1945

■ Axis powers   ■ Axis conquests/allies

victory was due to the combination of enormous Soviet man-power and U.S. industrial production.

Before ever joining the war, the United States was supplying the U.K. under the "Cash and Carry" system, which required the Brits to pay for goods up front and ship them aboard their own vessels to avoid violating neutrality. In March 1941 the U.S. re-placed this with "Lend-Lease," which delivered goods to the Brits and Soviets aboard U.S. vessels in return for IOUs. As in WWI, these ships were targeted by German U-boats in the Atlantic, but U.S. entry into WWII on December 7, 1941 tipped the balance in the "Battle of the Atlantic." In May 1942 the United States began organizing Lend-Lease convoys with naval escorts, and by 1944 the U-boat menace was vanquished—but only after the loss of 3,500 merchant ships and 30,000 crew members.

On land, the U.S.–U.K. strategy in Europe basically called for chipping away at the edges of Axis territory in the south and west while Hitler was distracted by his epic, ill-fated invasion of the Soviet Union in the east. In November 1942 the United States and U.K. invaded North Africa to liberate Morocco, Algeria, and Tunisia from the Vichy regime (the pro-Nazi "collaborationist" government in southern France). From here they invaded Sicily in July 1943, followed by mainland Italy in September 1943. Mus-solini's Fascist government collapsed, but the Germans swiftly occupied Italy in an attempt to halt the Allied advance.

As Allied armies battled their way north to Rome, to the west they launched Operation Overlord, the invasion to liberate France, on June 6, 1944 (D-Day). After landing on the Normandy

Tank production (thousands)
U.S.
Germany
1940 1941 1942 1943 1944 1945

Bomber production (thousands)
U.S.
Germany
1940 1941 1942 1943 1944 1945

U.S. vs. Japanese aircraft carriers in service
U.S.
Japan
1940 1941 1942 1943 1944 1945

peninsula in the face of fierce German resistance, U.S. and U.K. armored columns pushed south and east under the leadership of two daring tank commanders—the American George S. Patton and the British Bernard Law Montgomery. Eager to occupy Germany before the Soviets, the Allies raced forward through France into Belgium—directly into a German trap.

On December 16, 1944 the Germans launched a desperate surprise attack that "bulged out" into Allied territory, cutting off U.S. troops at Bastogne, Belgium. However Patton made a daring counter-attack which broke through enemy lines to rescue the besieged Americans, and a break in winter weather let the Allies use their superior air power again. By January 25, 1945, the Battle of the Bulge was over; three months later, American GIs shook hands with their Soviet counterparts in central Germany.

Meanwhile, somewhere in the Pacific. . . . After the surprise attack on Pearl Harbor, Japanese forces swept out across the western and central Pacific Ocean, conquering the Philippines, Indonesia, and a number of smaller island chains which they turned into air strips and naval bases. U.S. forces had to first stop the Japanese advance, and then roll back the tide—a formidable task, as Japanese conquests ranged across thousands of miles and were defended by soldiers with suicidal devotion to their cause. The United States had a huge advantage in industrial production, however, which allowed it to churn out more ships and weapons than Japan—especially aircraft carriers, which revolutionized naval warfare.

The United States scored a strategic victory at Coral Sea, May 4–8, 1942: although one U.S. aircraft carrier was sunk and another damaged, the U.S.–Australian force halted the Japanese drive to conquer Australia. This was followed by a decisive win at Midway, June 4–7, 1942, where the U.S. Navy turned the tables on a Japanese trap, thanks to cracking the Japanese naval code. Four Japanese carriers were destroyed for the loss of just one

American carrier—a huge blow from which the Japanese never recovered.

Gen. Douglas MacArthur followed up these victories with an attack on Japanese forces occupying the Solomon Islands, from August 1942–February 1943. This provided a base for MacArthur's strategy of "island-hopping"—bypassing less-important enemy strongholds to concentrate on key spots, like atolls within bomber range of Japan. While MacArthur pushed on to liberate the Philippines, U.S. bombers based in the Marianas Islands pulverized Japan with high explosives and napalm. Then in August 1945 two atomic bombs obliterated Hiroshima and Nagasaki. Japan surrendered September 2, 1945.

·········· **OTHER PEOPLE'S STUFF** ··················

Investing in Other People's Stuff

Thanks to wartime production, the United States' economy had been effectively resuscitated. But in a world full of war-ravaged countries, the United States faced a daunting two-fold task. Not only was the nation burdened with trying to revive its traumatized allies, but it also needed to rebuild its defeated foes along (hopefully) democratic lines. Luckily, the United States had a foolproof plan: throw money at the problem.

By the end of the war in 1945, Europe had been totaled. Over 40 million soldiers and civilians were dead and 25 million wounded, while vast areas from the Atlantic to Stalingrad lay in ruins. In Germany alone, 30,000 acres or 36 square miles of built-up urban space had been flattened by British and American strategic bombing. In January 1946 the average German ration was down to 1,500 calories per day and would soon fall to 900 calories per day without swift action.

In addition to simple humanitarian concerns, the catastrophe increased the possibility of a communist takeover of Western Europe. The ideology always played well in times of desperate poverty, and communist cells were now getting covert support from Stalin. A communist revolution in Greece triggered civil war from 1946 to 1949. American officials were even more alarmed by the prospect of communists taking power through legitimate elections. In 1946, French communists won 182 out of a total

627 seats in the new National Assembly, making them the biggest party in France. In Italy in 1948, the communist-led coalition took 31 percent of the vote. *Sacrebleu! Mamma mia!*

The short-term priority—ending hunger in Western Europe—had a relatively straightforward solution: farmers in the United States and Canada went full throttle, while their governments scraped together emergency wheat shipments by diverting grain from livestock feed and alcohol production. Altogether over one billion bushels of wheat were sent to Europe from 1945 to 1952. But while the first crisis had been averted, the long-term goal—steering Western Europe away from communism to a market-based economy—took a little more doing.

★ *The Cooperative for American Remittances to Europe (or CARE, as in CARE package) was formed in 1945 to send Army Surplus rations to starving people in war-ravaged Europe.*

Luckily, the United States had allies in Europe's conservative elite, including businessmen, bankers, aristocrats, and Christian clergy, who were all full of advice about how to combat communism. To convince ordinary Europeans that the market system was the way to go, these advocates said that the Americans had to demonstrate that capitalism delivered a higher standard of living than communism. This meant the free market (literally) had to deliver the goods—bicycles, radios, refrigerators, cars, telephones, children's toys, jewelry, candy, liquor, movies . . . you name it.

Of course some small problems remained, like the lack of raw materials for European factories, money to pay employees, and fuel to transport products. The European Recovery Plan—better known as the Marshall Plan, after U.S. Secretary of State George Marshall—overcame these obstacles by "priming the pump" and doling out grants to businesses, charities, and local governments. From 1948 to 1952, the Marshall Plan disbursed a total of $12.7 billion to rebuild infrastructure, reopen factories, revive banks, and fund small business. Panels of European officials, businessmen, and labor leaders decided how to distribute the money. (Including organized labor in these negotiations was a crucial part of undermining support for communist parties.) Over the same period, the United States also dispensed about $1 billion of aid to Japan. (This was separate from the Marshall Plan.) Not coincidentally, in both places most of the aid was spent on American exports, such as food, machinery, and fuel.

While United States aid to Europe and Japan got the ball rolling, private investment and international trade were leaned on to do the rest. Confidence in the reviving global economy was also bolstered by a new international monetary system created by the U.S. government at Breton Woods, Virginia, in 1944. The Breton Woods system tightened currency controls to avoid a repeat of the roller coaster–like inflation, deflation, and foreign exchange rate fluctuations of the 1930s. Breton Woods also created two new global financial institutions, the International Monetary Fund and the International Bank for Reconstruction and Development (later the World Bank), which supervised exchange rates and provided loans for economic development; both were controlled by the United States and relied on the dollar as their reserve currency.

Thanks in large part to these measures, by the early 1950s the European and Japanese economies were moving again, and the situation looked stable enough for American business to join the action. From 1945 to 1955, total direct investment by American businesses in Europe tripled from $1 billion to $3 billion; meanwhile, in Japan it rose from nothing to $129 million. Overall, the postwar period saw the United States replace Britain as the world's main source of foreign investment.

This also signaled a big change in American attitudes toward the rest of the world. Along with the mantle of "leader of the free world," the United States was now obligated to help protect its allies from the communist threat (or risk seeing them turned into enemies). Meanwhile, Europe was increasingly becoming "Americanized." For example, Germany had turned into a major center of automobile manufacturing, and rates of car ownership, already increasing before the war, surged in the 1950s. On the other hand, some European countries tried to resist the American cultural-economic wave. In February 1950, the French Assembly tried to limit sales of Coca-Cola, arousing the righteous fury of American patriots, but after a great deal of talk and no action, everyone shrugged and forgot about it.

Defending Other People's Stuff

As many a youth sports coach has told their lackluster team: the best offense is a good defense. And a nervous United States was about to storm the world playing field and defend like crazy. As the lines were drawn in early rounds of the Cold War, it became clear that America was going to have to do more than just sell stuff to countries threatened by communism. So in 1947 President Harry Truman laid out a new defense policy promising both financial and military aid to any country threatened by communist forces, internally or externally. To deter aggression, the "Truman Doctrine" emphasized defensive treaties committing the United States to help its allies around the world—a huge change in American foreign policy, which until that point had mostly steered clear of "entangling alliances."

> There will emerge two centers of world significance: a socialist center, drawing to itself the countries which tend toward socialism, and a capitalist center, drawing to itself the countries that incline toward capitalism. The battle between these two centers for command of the world economy will decide the fate of capitalism and of communism in the entire world.
>
> —Josef Stalin, 1927

After the Cold War, it became popular to suggest that American leaders had exaggerated the communist threat. But the threat was real. Communism was a crusading ideology aiming for world domination, and the Soviet version was especially aggressive when compounded with Russian nationalism. The Soviets had demonstrated their pro-expansionist attitude before World War II with the invasion of Finland and the Baltic states, and Stalin began pushing his boundaries again almost immediately after the war was over. And the threat became even more serious when the Soviet Union tested its first atomic bomb in August 1949, canceling out America's main advantage.

> I got very acquainted with Joe Stalin, and I like old Joe!
>
> —Harry Truman, 1948

By June of 1948, Russian-Western relations had turned openly hostile. Stalin set up a year-long blockade of West Berlin in an attempt to force British, French, and American troops out. And while the Western Allies defeated this blockade with the Berlin airlift—delivering 4,000 tons of food per day to the city's grateful inhabitants—the Allies needed a way to guard against further aggression. In 1949, Truman worked to establish the North Atlantic Treaty Organization (NATO), which committed the countries of Western Europe, the United States, and Canada to one another's defense. In truth, this alliance was mostly theoretical for the first few years, because the militaries lacked the ground troops to match up with Stalin's. Instead, the United States relied heavily on the threat of nuclear weapons to make up for a lack of conventional forces: defensive plans like "Reaper" (1949) and "Dropshot" (1950) envisioned dropping over 100 atomic bombs on the Soviet Union. Eventually, NATO decided the best way to respond to Stalin's aggressive tactics was to build up a true military, and that's exactly what it did in the 1950s.

While NATO members were strengthening their alliance, Stalin was busy probing local defenses across the 3,000-mile stretch of Europe and Asia bordering the Soviet sphere. In the late 1940s he put pressure on Iran, Greece, and Turkey, but his bullying backfired, driving these countries into America's arms. In fact, Greece and Turkey joined NATO in 1952. Farther east, however, communism seemed to be taking. Mao Zedong's Chinese communists vanquished the Nationalists in 1949. This was a huge shock to American confidence, spurring recriminations between Democrats and Republicans over who "lost China." After the nation "went Red," Truman couldn't afford to lose another Asian country—but that's exactly what started happening.

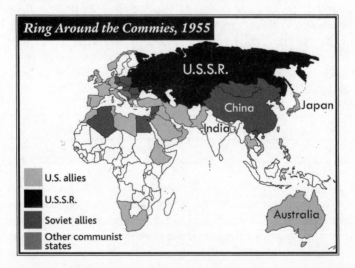

Ring Around the Commies, 1955

U.S.S.R.

China

Japan

India

U.S. allies

U.S.S.R.

Soviet allies

Other communist states

Australia

In the final days of World War II, Soviet forces occupied the northern half of Korea, a former Japanese colony, while U.S. troops occupied the south. Various attempts to reunify the peninsula failed, so in 1949 the Americans set up a pro-U.S. dictator, Syngman Rhee, in South Korea; then they checked out. Bad move: up in North Korea the Soviets were helping communist leader Kim Il-Sung build a formidable army to wage a war of reunification. In June 1950, 231,000 North Korean soldiers poured across the 38th parallel, shredding South Korean forces. To slow the northern advance, General Douglas MacArthur—still supervising the U.S. occupation of Japan—sent over the U.S. Eighth Army. Finally, the North Korean offensive began to stall amid fierce fighting outside the southern port city of Pusan (the "Pusan Perimeter"). At this point things looked pretty bad, with U.S. forces controlling less than 10 percent of the peninsula—but MacArthur was about to flip the script.

Seeing the North Korean armies concentrated in the southeast, in September 1950 MacArthur proposed an amphibious landing on the west coast of the peninsula at the port of Inchon, cutting North Korean supply lines and forcing the North Koreans to fight on two fronts. Many of MacArthur's colleagues expressed alarm, noting that the harbor at Inchon was protected by narrow channels, treacherous currents, and rough, hilly terrain—not to mention the North Koreans themselves. But that was the whole idea, MacArthur argued: the North Koreans would never expect such a crazy move. They'd be totally unprepared.

> I cannot believe that a great nation like the United States cannot give me these few paltry reinforcements for which I ask. Tell the President that if he gives them to me, I will land at Inchon on the rising tide at daybreak on the 15th of September. And between the hammer of this landing and the anvil of the Eighth army, I will shatter and destroy the armies of North Korea.
>
> —MacArthur to Averell Harriman,
> an advisor to Truman, 1950

MacArthur was right. The landing at Inchon was a brilliant success, leading to the total collapse of the North Korean armies. But in the end, he was too aggressive for his own good. He followed up on his initial success by pushing north to the Chinese border, despite repeated warnings that this would provoke Chinese intervention. And—surprise!—that's exactly what happened in late

October 1950, when over 300,000 Chinese troops surged over the border, sending U.S. forces reeling. By early January 1951, the Chinese had recaptured Seoul, and U.S. morale sank to an all-time low.

Embarrassed by his poor judgment, MacArthur wanted Truman to use nuclear weapons against Chinese forces in Korea and northern China. He questioned the president's repeated refusals, and the public breach got him canned. His replacement, Matthew Ridgway, managed to rally U.S. forces and regain some lost territory amid heavy fighting, and the troops stabilized the front around the 38th parallel. In July of 1953, the opposing sides finally agreed to a cease-fire. In other words, everything ended up right where it started, except for the over two million dead, who were distinctly worse off.

Oil Wells (That Ended Well)

Critics often complain (correctly) that America uses its economic and military power to dominate the world's oil supply. But the real question is: who would they rather have in charge?

After World War II, there was no mistaking American designs on foreign oil. Even before the war was over, FDR worked overtime to secure control of the Saudi Arabian supply. In February of 1945, just two months before his fatal stroke, Roosevelt traveled to Egypt aboard a U.S. Navy destroyer to meet with Saudi King Abdulaziz and forge a long-term pact. The promise? American aid and protection in return for oil—lots and lots of oil.

> ★ *King Abdulaziz wanted to bring his own sheep aboard the USS Quincy for his meeting with FDR because, as a Muslim, he only ate freshly killed meat.*

As part of the deal, the U.S. Air Force would expand its base in northern Saudi Arabia, and U.S. Navy aircraft carriers would protect the shipping routes to Europe and Asia. To clear up any confusion about who had priority in the Middle East, FDR shooed the French out of their colonial territories in Syria and Lebanon and bluntly informed the Brits that Saudi Arabia was now off-limits. From day one, U.S. diplomacy was coordinated with private enterprise, and by 1953, the U.S.-dominated oil cartel known as the "Seven Sisters" controlled 87 percent of the world's production, colluding to fix prices and crush competitors.

> **Persian oil is yours. We share the oil of Iraq and Kuwait.
> As for Saudi Arabian oil, it is ours.**
>
> —FDR, to the British ambassador Lord Halifax, 1944

There was good reason to want control of foreign oil: modern industrial societies were completely dependent on oil, both economically and militarily. It's why Japan invaded the Dutch East Indies and Hitler invaded southern Russia. Stalin, realizing that he too could do with more oil, was also looking to expand Soviet influence over oil-rich territories in the Middle East. In fact, American and Western European military planners expected World War III to start with the Red Army lunging for the oil fields of Iran, Iraq, and Saudi Arabia. By protecting Middle Eastern oil fields, the benevolent, kindly United States was also ensuring stable energy supplies for its allies, enabling reconstruction and recovery in Europe and Japan.

Okay, that's the sympathetic interpretation of American actions. There was also a shady side to the whole enterprise. The push to control global oil supplies had started well before World War II, and it involved some pretty questionable (illegal) tactics. As U.S. domestic production increasingly went to support the American love affair with automobiles, U.S. oil companies turned to foreign oil to supply their export businesses. More importantly, they weren't afraid to meddle to protect their interests. This wasn't anything new: when Mexican revolutionaries passed laws in 1925 threatening American oil interests in Mexico, U.S. oil companies plotted the overthrow of the new government. (Eventually the dispute was resolved peacefully.) Likewise, Standard Oil forced its way into Venezuela by threatening to support an independence movement in the oil-rich province of Zulia.

These tactics continued after World War II. When Iran's left-leaning Prime Minister Mohammad Mosaddeq took control of the Anglo-Iranian Oil Company in 1951, the United States saw it as a golden opportunity to replace the Brits. In 1953 President Eisenhower gave the green light for a CIA coup (re)installing the Shah of Iran. And just as the United States had hoped, the shah granted concessions to five U.S. companies—Mobil, Gulf, Standard Oil of California, Standard Oil of New Jersey, and Texaco.

As for America's friendly motives? It's true America helped its allies by protecting the flow of oil against disruption by the

Soviets and other commie bad guys. But this was a double-edged sword: the aircraft carriers that guarded the sea-lanes to Europe and Asia could just as easily close them if the United States became displeased with its allies. In other words, control of oil gave America a stranglehold on the economies of Western Europe and Japan. In this context, it's hardly surprising that the United States encouraged their growing dependence on foreign oil.

THE WIZARD OF OSS

At FDR's request, Major General William Joseph Donovan formed the Office of Strategic Services (OSS) at the height of World War II. Prior to WWII, American intelligence work was conducted by a number of different organizations that didn't coordinate their activities, including divisions of the State Department, Treasury, and the Navy and War departments. Beginning in July 1941, Donovan recruited spies, analysts, and code breakers for a new dedicated intelligence-gathering and covert operations outfit. Formally established by FDR on June 13, 1942, the OSS carried out a number of important missions during WWII, including recruiting a key German spy, the anti-Nazi diplomat Fritz Kolbe, who gave the OSS crucial information about German expectations for D-Day, the V-2 rocket program, new high-tech German jet fighters, and Nazi spies abroad. The OSS worked with French resistance fighters ahead of the Allied liberation of France and also carried out a massive campaign of propaganda, psychological warfare, and disinformation to mislead the Germans about American intentions. Outside Europe the OSS hunted Nazi spies in Africa and Latin America. Meanwhile, in the Pacific theater, OSS agents trained Chinese Kuomintang and communist troops resisting the Japanese, and in Vietnam the OSS made contact with Ho Chi Minh, whose Viet Minh nationalists were also fighting the Japanese. Overall, the OSS employed 24,000 people around the world by the end of the war, including improbable characters like Red Sox catcher Moe Berg and celebrity chef Julia Child. The OSS was disbanded in 1945 but reconstituted as a new group, the Central Intelligence Agency, by President Truman in 1947.

How the CIA and the Mob Became Friends
(and Influenced People)

The end of Prohibition hadn't been the end of the American Mafia. When alcohol became legal again in 1933, Sicilian-American mob bosses took their earnings from rum-running and wisely reinvested in "protection" rackets, loan-sharking, prostitution, gambling, and organized labor. Unions in particular were an ideal new growth opportunity, and by the beginning of World

War II, gangsters controlled an array of them. One that turned out to be especially handy was the International Longshoremen's Association, which represented dockworkers in New York and New Jersey. This meant that, in addition to smuggling, mob bosses could disrupt legitimate shipping by organizing strikes. With the war looming, the U.S. military pragmatically decided it would be easier to play ball with the mob than fight it. Luckily, the mobsters were eager allies motivated by greed, a hatred of Mussolini (who attacked the Mafia in Sicily), and—yes—American patriotism.

The first boss to sign on was Joseph Lanza, who controlled the docks on Manhattan's Lower East Side. He agreed to help the Office of Naval Intelligence (ONI) keep things running smoothly in return for clemency in his 1938 extortion conviction. Through Lanza, the ONI established contact with Charles "Lucky" Luciano and his faithful henchman Albert Anastasia, who controlled the West Side docks. Lanza, Luciano, and Anastasia pledged their assistance in preventing strikes from disrupting wartime shipping and in uncovering spies and saboteurs who threatened dockyard operations. In return for early parole from prison, Luciano also used his connections in Sicily to facilitate the invasion of the island in 1943 by American and British forces. As a thank you, the Americans troops released hundreds of imprisoned mafiosi, put local bosses in charge of dozens of towns, and let them use Army trucks for smuggling. Things got so friendly that some bosses seriously advocated Sicily joining the United States! American diplomats politely deflected this suggestion.

After the war was over, Luciano, who had been freed and deported to Italy by the U.S. government in recognition of his wartime service, started getting involved in organized crime's new high-growth business, drug smuggling, almost certainly with the knowledge—and maybe even help—of the CIA. The postwar Mafia drug-smuggling operation evolved over time, and it was thanks to the mob's BFF, the CIA, that the most profitable network—"the French Connection"—came about.

In 1947, CIA spymasters employed two Corsican brothers, Antoine and Barthelemy Guerini, to break up strikes by communist dockworkers in the port city of Marseilles, France. Once in control of the docks, the Guerinis went into business with Luciano. Beginning in 1951, raw opium harvested in Turkey was smuggled overland to Beirut, Lebanon, refined into morphine base, and then shipped onward to Marseilles, where Corsican drug chemists turned it into heroin. From Marseilles the heroin was distributed all over Europe as well as to the United States via merchant ships sailing from northern European ports. After New York City customs officials caught on, smuggling shifted south under the direction of Santo Trafficante Jr., one of the most powerful mobsters in American history. The boss of the "Tampa family," controlling Florida, Cuba, and the Caribbean, Trafficante established new routes running from Marseilles through Cuba, Martinique, and Guadeloupe, onward to Puerto Rico, and finally to Miami for distribution across the United States.

Whether deliberate or accidental, the CIA's role in reviving the international heroin trade had some rather unfortunate consequences back home. After disappearing almost entirely during World War II, heroin addiction returned with a vengeance in the late 1940s. The Mafia's only concession? They agreed to limit heroin sales to African-American neighborhoods, figuring the government wouldn't care as much about addiction among minority populations. (They were right.)

···············• **MADE IN THE USA** ·····················

The Cult of the Cathode Ray

If there's one American invention that everyone can agree is unambiguously good, except for the huge drawbacks, it's TV. The idea of transmitting images to a display made of a photoconductive element like selenium had occurred to European inventors as early as 1886. French inventors transmitted still images to selenium cells in 1909, and in 1925 a Scottish inventor, John Logie Baird, succeeded in transmitting moving silhouette images to a cathode ray tube. That same year, American Charles Francis Jenkins transmitted moving images of a toy windmill using radio waves, and in 1927 Bell Labs did something similar with synchronized sound. All this science stuff to say: the world was getting closer to its future "Project Runway" addiction, but it wasn't quite there yet.

Enter a red-blooded, technology-obsessed American inventor named Philo T. Farnsworth. Farnsworth developed the first practical electronic (as opposed to electromechanical) television system. While previous inventors had tried using cathode ray tubes as displays, Farnsworth was the first to use a cathode ray tube for the camera. In 1927 he filed a patent for his "Image Dissector" camera, in which light struck a layer of photosensitive material, causing it to emit electron streams that were steered to a positively charged anode, or "detector." In 1931 Farnsworth developed an "electron multiplier" to boost the signal strength, allowing a much clearer image, and in 1934 he demonstrated the complete system at the Franklin Institute in Philadelphia.

It turned out Farnsworth wasn't the only one experimenting with a cathode ray type of camera. In 1923 Vladimir Zworykin, an engineer for Westinghouse Electric Corporation, was doing so too, just not as successfully. Zworykin's camera never produced a clear enough image to warrant further investment. After RCA bought the Westinghouse patent in 1929, it claimed that it superseded Farnsworth's, but the U.S. Patent Office dismissed RCA's claim in 1935, and four years later, RCA agreed to pay Farnsworth the considerable sum of $1 million for the right to use his technology.

Although the Great Depression and World War II hobbled sales at first, the return to peace and prosperity brought a tidal wave of TV to America. It would be hard to exaggerate the TV craze of the late 1940s and early 1950s: the number of television sets in operation in the United States rose from fewer than 7,000 in 1940 to 350,000 in 1948, 9.7 million in 1950, and 42.9 million in 1955. The mania spread socially, as proud owners of new sets invited friends over to watch together; in 1946 the prize fight pitting Joe Louis against Billy Conn was watched by 150,000 viewers gathered around a relatively small number of TV sets, sometimes in groups of 30 or more.

Sensing the huge demand, TV broadcasters rushed to invest in new programming: 1948 saw the debut of "The Ed Sullivan Show," featuring musical performances and variety acts. The year 1951 followed with the pioneering sitcom "I Love Lucy." And 1952 brought NBC's "Today Show," which struggled until host Fred Garroway was joined by a belligerent chimpanzee cohost named J. Fred Muggs.

★ *The first television commercial, for Bulova watches, aired on July 1, 1941.*

TV stations began to organize themselves in networks to offer advertisers greater reach, usually under the umbrella of radio networks. And before long, the leading radio broadcasters dominated TV too. By the early 1950s, there were four main broadcast networks—NBC, ABC, CBS, and DuMont—with dozens of station affiliates around the country. The advertising dollars started pouring in too. Total TV ad revenue jumped from $207 million in 1951 to $750 million in 1955, surpassing radio.

But it wasn't all chimps and beer ads. In 1951 Edward R. Murrow launched America's first TV news program, "See It Now," which gave viewers an up-close look at the sacrifices of U.S. soldiers in the Korean War. In 1954 Murrow helped undermine support for Senator Joseph McCarthy, whose communist witch hunts ruined the reputations of hundreds of innocent people. And it was TV that enabled McCarthy to deliver his own coup de grâce during a live broadcast of his House Un-American Activities Committee hearings on communists in the military. Infuriated by McCarthy's attack on one of his junior staffers, Joseph Welch, a lawyer for the Army, delivered a verbal pistol-whipping witnessed by millions of Americans, which shattered McCarthy's aura of authority and invincibility. Three years later he died of alcoholism.

> Until this moment, Senator, I think I never really gauged your cruelty or your recklessness. Let us not assassinate this lad further, Senator. You have done enough. Have you no sense of decency, sir? At long last, have you left no sense of decency?
>
> —Joseph Welch, to Senator Joseph McCarthy, June 1954

Fissile Missiles

They're nothing to brag about, but nuclear weapons were the single biggest factor shaping the postwar world. Just think about what would have happened if someone else (say, the Nazis) invented them first. In fact, that's the whole reason the American bomb program got rolling in the first place. In 1938 the German chemists Otto Hahn and Fritz Strassmann reported their discovery of a new element, barium, which they created by bombarding uranium with neutrons. It was the first fission reaction observed in an experimental setting. Then in 1939, Enrico Fermi, an Italian physicist, and Leo Szilard, a Hungarian Jew, conducted further experiments at Columbia University confirming that uranium could sustain a nuclear chain reaction.

Fermi and Szilard had only a tiny amount of uranium isotope U-235 for their experiment, but their research showed that with a large enough concentration of "fissile" material, the splitting of trillions of atoms releases a huge amount of energy in what is technically termed a really big explosion. Putting 235 and 235 together, Fermi and Szilard realized that the Nazis could possibly be developing a super-bomb. To get the attention of the U.S. government, Szilard recruited the most famous scientist in the world as a spokesman: Albert Einstein. As a German Jew, Einstein was equally unnerved by the prospect of a "Nazi bomb," and he wrote to FDR, warning him of the potential consequences and urging him to develop an American bomb first.

In 1941 FDR gave the job to the newly created Office of Scientific Research, where a team headed by Nobel-Prize-winning physicist Arthur Compton and fellow physicist J. Robert Oppenheimer produced the first self-sustaining nuclear chain reaction in a reactor beneath the University of Chicago's Stagg Field in December of 1942. The group also determined that in addition to U-235, plutonium (formed by adding a neutron to U-238) would work as a bomb fuel. Now Compton and Oppenheimer just had to refine sufficient quantities of the nuclear fuel and design an actual bomb. Easy enough!

Or not. The scale of the work required a leader who knew how to move mountains. So in September of 1942, control of the "Manhattan Engineer Project" was transferred yet again, this time to the U.S. Army, under the command of Leslie Groves, a brigadier general with a reputation for pushing huge projects to completion under strenuous deadlines by being very unpleasant, if necessary. Concerned for the project's secrecy, Groves relocated the key work to a derelict boys' boarding school in Los Alamos, New Mexico, where the scientists lived and labored in complete seclusion. They even slept in the refurbished dormitories and held conferences in dusty classrooms.

Despite some technical glitches, by August of 1945 the weapons design team at Los Alamos had constructed three plutonium bombs and one uranium bomb. The slender uranium bomb was nicknamed "Little Boy," while the rotund plutonium bombs were called the "Fat Man" (or "Fat Men," technically).

Outside of Los Alamos, the world was changing pretty fast. FDR died in March, Germany surrendered in May. Only the war in the Pacific continued, with Japan appearing determined to hold out to the bitter end. At a conference on May 10–11, a "Target Committee" led by Oppenheimer recommended a list of targets to Groves. With two atom bombs ready to use, on July 26

Truman joined the other Allies in issuing the Potsdam Declaration, calling for Japan's unconditional surrender. When Japan rejected the Declaration on July 29, final preparations for an attack on Hiroshima began.

At 8:15 in the morning on Monday, August 6, 1945, the B-29 *Enola Gay* dropped Little Boy on Hiroshima. Detonating 2,000 feet above the city, the bomb exploded with a force equivalent to 13,000 tons of TNT, destroying five square miles of the city. Seventy thousand inhabitants died instantly, followed by another 70,000 in subsequent weeks and months—all told, the bomb killed 40 percent of the city's population. Three days later, at 11:01 in the morning on Thursday, August 9, the B-29 *Bockscar* (accompanied by one other plane) dropped one of the Fat Man bombs on Nagasaki—a secondary target selected because the first target, Kokura, was obscured by cloud cover. The bomb detonated 1,540 feet above the city, producing an explosion equivalent to 21,000 tons of TNT. The bomb completely ravaged three square miles of the city and killed 40,000 people instantly, followed by another 40,000 in subsequent months—35 percent of the city's total population.

★ The Enola Gay *was named after the mother of the aircraft's pilot, Paul Tibbets.*

Questions about the decision to use the bombs have lingered: Was it really necessary? Was it morally right? Didn't the Japanese try to surrender between Hiroshima and Nagasaki, making the second bomb unnecessary? On the last question, at least, facts indicate that the Japanese were not interested in surrendering: the Japanese high command made no attempt to do so before the bombing of Nagasaki. Indeed, after Hiroshima was destroyed, Japan's top brass asked the nation's nuclear scientists if they could make a similar bomb in six months, indicating they were determined to fight on. Further, the war minister and chiefs of staff of the Imperial Japanese armed forces still refused to surrender after the *second* bomb was dropped. It was only through intervention by Emperor Hirohito on August 14 that the issue was finally settled.

As for the necessity of the bombing, Truman believed he was saving thousands of American lives that would be lost invading

Japan: in the months before the bombings, kamikazes and bloody battles for control of small islands like Iwo Jima and Okinawa indicated that U.S. forces would face plenty of suicidal, last-ditch attacks. American commanders anticipated up to a quarter million American casualties, to say nothing of Japanese deaths. In any event, the atomic bombs could be considered the logical conclusion of America's long campaign of "strategic" bombing with napalm and high explosives. Before Hiroshima and Nagasaki, U.S. bomber fleets had destroyed half of the built-up urban areas in scores of Japan's largest cities; in one attack on Tokyo on the night of March 9-10, U.S. pilots dropped 1,700 tons of bombs on the city, causing a firestorm that killed 100,000 civilians and destroyed 16 square miles—and this was just one of a dozen attacks on the Japanese capital in 1945. Overall, conventional bombing killed 300,000 Japanese and a similar number of German civilians, while leaving more injured or deformed for life.

From Magnetron to Microwave

The same year that saw the invention of the atomic bomb also gave the world another hot device: the microwave oven. The principle behind microwave cooking was discovered by Percy Spencer, an engineer who worked on radar installations for defense contractor Raytheon. After noticing that a chocolate bar melted after being accidentally placed in front of a new "magnetron" vacuum tube, Spencer experimented with other foods, including popcorn (which worked perfectly) and an egg (not so much). After these experiments, Spencer deduced that the food was being heated by low-density microwave energy that could penetrate solid objects. Using those principles, he designed his first primitive oven in 1945, and by October of 1946, Raytheon had filed a patent for a microwave based on Spencer's idea. Excited about the new invention, the company even installed an experimental version in a restaurant in Boston to demonstrate its convenience . . . but there was still a long way to go.

★ *The code name Percy Spencer used for the microwave oven while it was still in the developmental stage was "Speedy Weenie."*

The first oven intended for commercial sale—the Radarange, manufactured in 1947—wasn't particularly practical: almost six feet tall, it tipped the scale at 750 pounds and cost $5,000 (that's in 1947 dollars). The second version, produced in 1954, was better but still needed work: it gobbled electricity and cost $2,000–$3,000, at a time when the average cost of a new car was about $1,700. Figuring a home appliance manufacturer might have better luck than a defense contractor, Raytheon licensed the design to the Tappan Stove Company in 1952, but at $1,295, Tappan's 1955 model still fell flatter than a microwave soufflé . . . at least, where housewives were concerned.

The food service industry was quicker on the uptake. Postwar America had become all about speedy service and convenience, and microwaves allowed the new generation of fast-food restaurants to thaw, cook, and sell large amounts of perishable food quickly, without violating health codes. Before long, manufacturers were employing microwaves to roast coffee beans, nuts, and potato chips. Factories even started using the ovens to treat nonfood items like leather, tobacco, and cotton cloth. Housewives didn't come around until 1967, with the unveiling of a relatively low-energy model costing just $500 by Amana Refrigeration, a Raytheon subsidiary.

·············· **TRENDSPOTTING** ····················

Women Be Workin'

American women have always worked—even harder than men, if you believe 'em. But traditionally, female labor took place in the home, out of public view. In the nineteenth century, girls and young women worked in textile mills and other industrial establishments, but this employment was supposed to be temporary, ending when they got married. Aside from housework (which was of course unpaid), the only work readily available to most women was still domestic—i.e., child care, laundry, sewing, or serving as a maid in an upper-class household. This began to change in the 1880s, when some young women worked outside the home as shopgirls, public school teachers, and nurses. The upper ranks of the business world remained closed to women, but growing numbers began to work in administrative capacities: by 1900, three-quarters of the stenographers and typists in the United States were women, as were many corporate secretaries, telephone switchboard operators, and librarians.

And that's more or less how it was until World War II turned the American workplace and the role of women upside down. From 1941 to 1945, a total of 16 million men served in the U.S. armed forces. This translated to about a quarter of the total American workforce in 1940. The result was a huge shortfall in labor, even after factories sponged up the jobless from the Great Depression. The solution was obvious: housewives. Responding to a concerted propaganda campaign by government and business (think: "Rosie the Riveter"), about seven million women entered the workforce between 1941 and 1945, boosting the share of women from about 25 percent of the total to 36 percent in 1945.

Of course the captains of industry—all men—took advantage of the situation, paying women just $0.65 where male workers earned $1.00. But Pandora's lunch box had been opened: not only had women proved they were just as capable as men, many found they actually enjoyed working outside the home, savoring the sense of accomplishment and camaraderie they got contributing to the war effort. And though these same patriotic women would soon face open discrimination by employers (businesses were under pressure to hire returning GIs), millions of women continued to work after the war.

Picket Fences

Automobiles transformed American society by allowing the growing middle class to live outside cities—particularly after Eisenhower expanded the interstate highway system in the 1950s. From 1920 to 1960, the proportion of Americans living in the 'burbs doubled from 16.7 percent to 33.3 percent—meaning 17.7 million to 60 million people! One of the first car-centric suburbs was located in Westchester County, north of New York City: here the town of New Rochelle saw its population almost quadruple from about 15,000 people in 1900 to 54,000 in 1930. Another New York suburb, Levittown, was the archetypal planned community of the postwar era: a prefabricated suburb of about 17,500 homes, it was built from 1947 to 1951 by William Levitt, a building magnate who embraced streamlined mass-construction methods picked up from the U.S. government during World War II. Levittown provided affordable middle-class homes to factory workers, making it a symbol of American postwar prosperity.

Farther west, on the shores of Lake Michigan, Chicago's suburbs grew to include Evanston, Wilmette, Kenilworth, Arlington Heights, Cicero, Palatine, and Skokie. Within a wider 200-mile radius—an area nicknamed "Chicagoland" by the *Chicago Tribune* in 1926—whole cities came to be considered suburbs of Chicago, including Aurora, Joliet, and Naperville. Around the junction of the Mississippi and Missouri rivers, the St. Louis metropolitan area expanded to include Alton, Brentwood, Concord, Kirkwood, Lakeshire, Webster, and St. Charles.

LIFE IS A SUPERHIGHWAY

The first American interstate highway system, created in the 1920s, was a pretty bare-bones transportation network: many of the "highways" were just local roads given the grand title without much in the way of new pavement or extra lanes to justify it. The real deal came in the 1950s, courtesy of President Dwight D. Eisenhower, who on June 29, 1956, signed a bill ordering the construction of four-, six-, and eight-lane "superhighways" crisscrossing the country. Fittingly titled the Dwight D. Eisenhower National System of Interstate and Defense Highways, the network was a huge gain in personal mobility for Americans who owned cars—but as the name indicates, it also served a strategic military purpose by making it easier to move troops and supplies.

Eisenhower was motivated by a couple of personal experiences in the U.S. Army. As a colonel in 1919, he had accompanied a convoy of military trucks across the country, remarking that the trucks hit dirt roads in Illinois "and practically no more pavement was encountered until reaching California," with many sections in Western states "almost impassable." (In Nevada the road was "one succession of dust, ruts, pits and holes.") Over two decades later, as the supreme commander of the Allied Expeditionary Force in Europe, Eisenhower admired the German *autobahn* highways constructed at Hitler's command in the 1930s and noted their advantages for military mobility.

The most extreme example of car-centric suburban development is southern California, where Los Angeles became a "city" composed entirely of suburbs, with no real city center. In 1920 the original City of Los Angeles, measuring about 500 square miles, was already fairly huge by the standards of the day—but the sprawl was just beginning! As cars became the dominant mode of transportation, more and more people settled in surrounding Los Angeles County, an area measuring about 3,500 square miles (excluding the city) stretching from Long Beach in the south to Palmdale in the north and Malibu in the west. Los Angeles County came to include a total of 88 separate cities and towns. And L.A. *still* wasn't done stretching out. In the second half of the twentieth century, this "urban agglomeration" absorbed four neighboring counties—Orange, Riverside, San Bernardino, and Ventura—forming a metropolitan area measuring 34,000 square miles, with a total population approaching 20 million!

WATER WARS

The huge increase in L.A.'s population—from 1.25 million in 1930 to 2.5 million in 1960—was only possible because of epic efforts to provide the desert metropolis with water, begun by William Mulholland, the all-powerful boss of the city's water department. Mulholland didn't shrink from unethical tactics. From 1898 to 1905, he bought strategically located plots of farmland in the Owens River Valley 250 miles north of L.A., without telling the locals he intended to divert the water south for irrigation as well as domestic use. In 1913 a 233-mile aqueduct began bringing water from the valley to L.A.—but demand grew so quickly that the L.A. water department eventually diverted the Owens River, causing 100-square-mile Owens Lake to dry up. This led to the California Water Wars, in which local farmers dynamited the aqueducts, forcing L.A. to negotiate. (The city settled by buying the rest of their worthless land.) Meanwhile, Mulholland was forced to resign in disgrace after another project, the St. Francis Dam, collapsed on March 12, 1928, leaving 450 dead.

Degrees for Free

Until the middle of the twentieth century, most Americans never contemplated attending a college or university after graduating from public high school. But this all started to change with the emergence of a large, upwardly mobile middle class who viewed education as the key to further social advancement—especially after living through the Great Depression. Of course, World War II played a big part in this attitude shift. Among the rewards offered to young adults for serving in the armed forces was a free college education, courtesy of the Servicemen's Readjustment Act of 1944, better known as the "GI Bill." By the time the legislation had run its course in 1956, it had sent 7.8 million veterans to school.

But the GI Bill wasn't just about recognizing service. For politicians, it became a savvy way to ease the reintegration of millions of young men back into the economy. Political leaders feared that the return of all these soldiers, coinciding with a big reduction in jobs created by defense spending (think of all the factories that had been supplying goods to the troops), could trigger serious economic headaches. By sending some of these veterans to school, the GI Bill kept them off the labor market for a couple years, giving the economy more time to absorb the surplus workers.

While all returning servicemen (including 350,000 women) were eligible for financial assistance under the GI Bill, they didn't all have the same opportunity to attend the school of their choice. American higher education remained segregated by race and gender, and most colleges and universities were closed to African-Americans and women. Although they could attend separate schools, the institutions for blacks and women typically lacked the financial and educational resources available to white men.

★ *Before four years became the norm to earn a college degree, first-year students were called "freshmen," second-year students were "junior sophists" and third-year students were "senior sophists."*

·············· **PROFIILES IN SCOURGES** ··················

Murderous-Minded Perverts

There are documented cases of serial killers in America going back to the eighteenth century, but there was definitely an uptick in the first part of the twentieth century: from January 1911 to April 1912, there were 49 axe murders in Louisiana and Texas, all unsolved, including whole families massacred as they slept. Henry Lee Moore was implicated in 20 axe murders across the Midwest in 1912; Loving Mitchell in 30 more in 1915. Things got even crazier from the 1920s to the 1940s, with more high-profile cases and increasingly detailed reporting of the disturbed psychology of serial killers. Thus the celebrity serial killer was born.

EARLE NELSON (AKA "The Gorilla Killer" and "The Dark Strangler") Nelson murdered at least 22 women in eight states and one Canadian province from 1926 to 1927. After losing both parents to syphilis at the age of two, Nelson underwent a change in personality at age 10 after being hit by a streetcar. At 21 he tried to rape a 12-year-old girl but was thwarted when she screamed for help. Nelson committed his first murder in February 1926, two weeks after being released from a California mental hospital. He targeted middle-aged women who rented rooms in boarding houses, inquiring about lodging and setting them at ease by appearing to study his well-worn Bible . . . before strangling them with his bare hands and stashing the bodies under their beds. Nelson committed acts of necrophilia with the corpses of most of his victims, and on one occasion slept in the same bed with a mutilated body for three days. His physical strength earned him the nickname "The Gorilla Killer." Nelson was caught after killing a landlady in Winnipeg, Canada. After a short-lived jailbreak, he was recaptured, tried, and finally hung on January 13, 1928.

★ *A note in Nelson's Napa State Mental Hospital file indicated that the 18-year-old was "not violent; homicidal; or destructive."*

ALBERT FISH (AKA "The Gray Man," "The Brooklyn Vampire," and "The Werewolf of Wysteria") A real horror show, Albert Fish was convicted of three verifiable child murders, though he claimed the total was closer to 100—all involving molestation and cannibalism. Born Hamilton Fish in 1870, Fish took to calling himself "Albert," the name of his dead brother, after his mother sent him to live in an orphanage. There, young Albert came to derive sexual pleasure from regular beatings. At the age of 12, he had a homosexual relationship with an older boy who introduced him to coprophagia (eating feces), and he started hanging around public baths, where he could watch naked boys. In 1890, Fish moved to New York City, where he became a male prostitute and child rapist, and in 1898 he married a woman (chosen by his mother), who eventually bore him six children. After his wife left him in 1917, Fish began piercing his groin with needles. X-rays later revealed that Fish had 29 needles in his pelvis. He also began hearing voices commanding him to kill and mutilate children.

> I have no particular desire to live. I have no particular desire to be killed. It is a matter of indifference to me. I do not think I am altogether right.
>
> —Albert Fish, 1935

Fish was undone by his own need to brag and torment the families of his victims. In 1928 he abducted and murdered a 10-year-old girl named Grace Budd; six years later he sent a letter to her mother recounting how he had choked her to death and then cooked and ate her over the course of nine days. Police traced the stationery back to a boarding house where Fish had been staying and arrested him on December 13, 1934. At his trial the jury somehow declared Fish "sane" and sentenced him to death. Fish was executed on January 16, 1936, after proclaiming that electrocution would be "the supreme thrill of my life."

JOE BALL After serving in World War I, Ball became a bootlegger and later the proprietor of a small tavern, the Sociable Inn, outside the town of Elmendorf in south Texas. Ball was also the proud owner of five alligators, which he kept in a pool behind the bar as an added attraction—entertaining customers by feeding the creatures live cats, dogs, possums, and raccoons. From 1930 to 1938, Ball hired a procession of young, pretty, maybe not-so-bright women as waitresses, who tended to disappear after a few months. Oddly enough, so did several of his wives and girlfriends. At long last, suspecting Ball was up to no good, local law enforcement made several inquiries that turned up nothing: Ball, an intimidating sort, was able to keep his activities cloaked in mystery by scaring the bejeezus out of nosy neighbors. (One was so terrified he moved out of town.) But in 1938 Ball started pushing his luck: a 23-year-old woman went missing after working for him for just a few months, followed by two more employees. Then the frightened neighbor finally came forward, returning from California to tell the sheriff that Ball had threatened his life. Apparently, the neighbor had seen Ball dismembering a body next to the alligator pit. When deputies went to the Sociable Inn to question Ball again, he offed himself with a shot to the heart. In the end, lawmen guessed Ball killed at least 22 women and a teenage boy but never found any evidence for most of these crimes. Or for the hypothesis that he fed the bodies to his pet alligators.

> ★ *Joe Ball's alligators were donated to the San Antonio Zoo, where they became a popular tourist attraction.*

························ **BY THE NUMBERS** ·················

380.33	Dow Jones Industrial Average in mid-October, 1929
41.22	Dow Jones Industrial Average in mid-July, 1932
$104.4 billion	U.S. GDP, 1929
$56.4 billion	U.S. GDP, 1933
10,763	banks closed from 1929 to 1933
1.5 million	U.S. unemployed, 1929
3.2 percent	U.S. unemployment rate, 1929
14 million	U.S. unemployed, 1933
25 percent	U.S. unemployment rate, 1933
2,402	U.S. servicemen killed in the surprise attack on Pearl Harbor, 1941
12,513	U.S. servicemen killed in the battle of Okinawa, 1945
110,000	Japanese soldiers killed in the battle of Okinawa, 1945
140,000	number of people killed in the Hiroshima bombing
80,000	number of people killed in the Nagasaki bombing
100,000	number of people killed in the firebombing of Tokyo, March 9–10, 1945
1,700	tons of bombs dropped on Tokyo in this raid
623,418	tons of bombs dropped by the U.S. Eighth Air Force on Germany in World War II
$50.1 billion	value of material supplied to Allies under Lend-Lease program, 1941–1945
$7.2 billion	U.S. direct investment in foreign countries in 1945
$19.2 billion	U.S. direct investment in foreign countries in 1955
$1,300	average cost of a new car in 1947
$1,900	average cost of a new car in 1955

Sex, Drugs, and Mocking Roles

(1955–1975)

THE STATE OF THE UNION

The curtain rises on a victorious nation bestriding the world in seersucker shorts, penny loafers, and a tennis sweater, humming "Zip-A-Dee-Doo-Dah"—rich, powerful, confident, downright cocky. When the curtain falls, the United States is limping offstage wearing nothing but a dazed look and a tie-dye robe, muttering the lyrics to "Helter Skelter." Even people who saw it all had to wonder: what the hell just happened?

It's one of history's strange ironies that a society enjoying unprecedented prosperity should suddenly tear itself apart, and there's no simple explanation for why it happened. The most important factor was the huge number of children born to returning GIs after World War II. The "baby boom" was fueled by a new feeling of optimism, economic expansion, and welfare guarantees from the New Deal. Average American families enjoyed higher incomes and a better standard of living than any group of people, anywhere, at any time in history, including new housing, better nutrition, and more educational opportunities.

With everything looking swell, people started doing what people do best and popping out babies by the millions—make that tens of millions. From 1945 to 1965, an incredible 80 million new Americans were born, increasing the total population by 62 million. The number of Americans under the age of 20 rose from 45 million in 1940 to 69 million in 1960, increasing from 34 percent to 39 percent of the population; the 1960 figure included 39 million children under the age of 10—or 22 percent of the population.

In short, the United States became a youth culture. The baby boomers were doted on by parents determined to give them all the things they'd missed growing up in the Great Depression—from bikes and baseball gloves to college and cars. The boomers displayed astounding creativity, energy, and sheer precocious self-confidence.

As teenagers and young adults, they voiced concern about nuclear weapons, pollution, and racial discrimination. But their larger-than-life qualities could also be weaknesses: self-assurance could turn to arrogance, self-expression to self-destruction. As a result, movements that began with good intentions often ended up far from their original goals. Maybe free love and psychedelic drugs weren't the solution to the world's problems after all?

It wouldn't be fair to pin all of America's problems on the boomers. Their parents—"The Greatest Generation"—let America's leaders steer the country into Vietnam, resulting in the worst military defeat in U.S. history. On the other hand, these older adults shared their children's concern about the nuclear arms race and also proved surprisingly supportive of the African-American civil rights movement—at least outside the South.

·············· **WHAT HAPPENED WHEN** ··················

May 17, 1954 Supreme Court rules segregation of public schools illegal in *Brown v. Board.*

January 10, 1956 Elvis Presley records his first RCA single, "Heartbreak Hotel."

October 4, 1957 Soviet Union launches Sputnik I, world's first artificial satellite.

November 8, 1960 Massachusetts Senator John F. Kennedy narrowly beats Vice President Richard Nixon in a presidential election marred by accusations of voter fraud.

December 5, 1960 Supreme Court desegregates interstate bus facilities in *Boynton v. Virginia.*

April 12, 1961 Soviet cosmonaut Yuri Gagarin becomes the first man in space.

May 4, 1961 First "Freedom Ride" leaves Washington, D.C., to test Supreme Court desegregation ruling in Southern bus facilities.

May 5, 1961	Alan Shepard becomes first American in space.
October 14–October 28, 1962	Cuban Missile Crisis brings world to brink of nuclear war.
November 22, 1963	JFK is assassinated in Dallas, Texas; Lyndon Johnson becomes president.
January 11, 1964	Surgeon General releases report showing smoking causes lung cancer.
February 9, 1964	First performance by the Beatles on the Ed Sullivan show.
July 2, 1964	LBJ signs Civil Rights Act, outlawing segregation in public places.
February 21, 1965	Malcolm X is assassinated in New York City.
March 7–21, 1965	Martin Luther King Jr. leads three marches from Selma to Montgomery, Alabama, demanding voting rights for African-Americans.
August 6, 1965	LBJ signs Voting Rights Act, banning obstacles to voting based on race.
December 31, 1965	There are 180,000 U.S. troops in South Vietnam.
January 31, 1968	Communists launch surprise attacks across South Vietnam: the "Tet Offensive."
March 31, 1968	LBJ announces he will not run for reelection in November 1968.
April 4, 1968	MLK is assassinated in Memphis, triggering a wave of riots nationwide.

June 5, 1968	Democratic presidential front-runner Robert F. Kennedy is assassinated in Los Angeles.
November 5, 1968	Republican Richard Nixon elected president with 43.4 percent of the vote.
December 31, 1968	There are 536,100 U.S. troops in South Vietnam.
July 16–24, 1969	The Apollo astronauts travel to the moon and return.
August 15–18, 1969	Some 400,000 people gather in Woodstock, New York, for an epic rock concert.
June 30, 1971	Twenty-sixth Amendment lowers voting age from 21 to 18.
February 21–28, 1972	Nixon's historic visit to China leads to better relations.
October 10, 1972	FBI uncovers massive political espionage involving Nixon officials.
January 27, 1973	Paris Peace Accords end U.S. military involvement in Vietnam.
June 25, 1973	White House counsel John Dean implicates Nixon in Watergate cover-up.
August 9, 1974	Facing conviction on impeachment charges, Nixon resigns from office.

·············· **LIES YOUR TEACHER TOLD YOU** ················

LIE: *The sixties were all about peace and love.*

THE TRUTH: People who maintain that the 1960s were groovy and mellow were either so addled with drugs they didn't notice what was going on, or so fried that they forgot about it later. The sixties brought violent upheaval, including assassinations, domestic terrorism by the KKK and crazy left-wing groups, clashes between anti-war protesters and police, and race riots that left hundreds dead. Not exactly "groovy."

One reason for the violence was the civil rights movement, in which African-Americans struggled to secure basic legal protections and political rights that were still denied to them by Southern states. The movement began with African-American veterans who'd been encouraged by the desegregation of the U.S. military in 1948. Seeking recognition of their service in World War II, they hoped that the nation was on the cusp of change. But attempts to gain full equality were rejected by many Southern whites, who had no interest in disrupting the traditional social order enshrined by Jim Crow laws.

One of the first steps came in 1944, when Irene Morgan, an African-American woman, refused to move to the back of a Greyhound bus traveling from Richmond, Virginia, to Baltimore, Maryland. Her protest resulted in a 1946 Supreme Court decision ending segregation on interstate buses. Morgan's case—argued by Thurgood Marshall, an NAACP lawyer and future Supreme Court justice himself—helped inspire Rosa Parks, whose refusal to give up her bus seat sparked the municipal bus boycott in Montgomery, Alabama, in 1955.

Another blow to the extremists was delivered by the Supreme Court's 1960 decision banning segregation in restaurants and waiting rooms in interstate bus facilities. This led to the "Freedom Rides" of 1961, when African-Americans challenged illegal segregation by riding interstate buses through Southern states, visiting lunch counters along the way.

The activists were highly successful in their quest to gain press coverage, which baited violence from angry whites and unwarranted crackdowns from Southern officials. From 1955 to 1968, at least 45 people were murdered for participating, or appearing to participate, in the civil rights movement, including at least 13 killed by Southern lawmen or legislators. The most notorious incident was a bomb attack on a church in Birmingham, Alabama, on September 15, 1963, a few days after city schools were desegregated. The event killed four young girls and wounded

The Freedom Rides and Montgomery bus boycott were instigated in part by African-American activists from the North and their white supporters, including leftist Jews. (Southern whites had a few choice labels for these folks, including "carpetbaggers," "atheists," and "communists.") But the movement's most important leader was a Baptist preacher from Atlanta. Still in his teens when Marshall helped integrate interstate buses, Martin Luther King Jr. was impressed by the power of non-violent civil disobedience to bring about social change, especially if it led to publicity or legal action (ideally both). In fact, King had paid careful attention to Mahatma Gandhi's successes in undermining British rule in India, and he came away believing that peaceful action—designed to provoke violent reaction—could strip government of its legitimacy.

After earning degrees in sociology, divinity, and theology, in 1954 King (just 25 years old) took a traditional leadership role as the pastor of a Baptist church in Montgomery, with the goal of advancing civil rights. He knew he could count on the support of millions of African-Americans who had migrated to Northern cities, where they formed a powerful new political bloc; his main challenge would be winning white support. Organizing marches and boycotts through his Southern Christian Leadership Conference, King's advocacy of non-violent resistance resonated with Christian doctrine and was basically guaranteed to win the sympathy of a religious society—provided there was media coverage.

And King made sure there was. Leveraging the national reach of newspapers, magazines, radio, and especially the brand-new medium of TV, civil rights leaders first built support among non-Southern whites, winning over the majority of the U.S. population. (For example, support for school integration among Northern whites increased from 40 percent in 1942 to 60 percent in 1956 and then 75 percent in 1963.) King then drove a wedge between moderate and extremist Southern whites, isolating and politically marginalizing the latter. Moderate Southern whites rejected vigilante violence by the Ku Klux Klan and also ended up opposing the strategy of "massive resistance" proposed by diehard segregationists who wanted to close public schools rather than accept integration. Although most moderate Southern whites still objected to integration, they placed greater importance on their kids learning to read, and sensibly decided to compromise.

> When you give witness to an evil you do not cause that evil but you oppose it so it can be cured.
>
> —Martin Luther King Jr., 1965

14 other children arriving to hear a Sunday sermon. If the Klu Klux Klan thought bombing churches and killing kids was somehow going to win people over, they were sorely mistaken. These kinds of attacks were the beginning of the end: Klan violence alienated moderate whites, who might oppose integration but were even more appalled by the attack on children at a place of worship.

> They are not the first Negroes to face mobs, they are merely the first Negroes to frighten the mob more than the mob frightens them.
>
> —James Baldwin, August 1960

While African-American protestors did the heavy lifting, forcing confrontations "on the ground" at risk of injury and even death, many of the key legal decisions and enforcement came from Washington, D.C. Of course, the measures were just as much about asserting authority over the states as they were about guarding liberty. The Supreme Court, still dominated by FDR's left-wing appointees, was especially aggressive: after integrating interstate transportation in 1946, it followed up with *Shelley v. Kraemer* (1948) banning "restrictive covenants" in home sales, *Brown v. Board of Education* (1954) declaring "separate but equal" school segregation unconstitutional, and *Loving v. Virginia* (1967) overturning laws against interracial marriage. Congress spiked Jim Crow—now approaching its hundredth birthday—with the 1964 Civil Rights Act, thus banning segregation in public places, work, and government.

Throughout this process, entrenched Southern opposition provoked more and more assertive action by the federal government. For example, when Arkansas Governor Orval Faubus vowed to prevent nine black students from enrolling at Little Rock High School in 1957, President Eisenhower personally warned him that he intended to see the Brown ruling enforced. Grandstanding for white voters, Faubus ignored Ike and sent the Arkansas National Guard to prevent the "Little Rock Nine" from entering the school. Bad move. Provoked, Eisenhower took the extraordinary step of "federalizing" the National Guard, removing it from the governor's control, and sent the Army to escort the students into the school.

At times civil rights activists and the federal government seemed to be working almost hand in hand. In one classic example, Martin Luther King Jr. met with President Lyndon Johnson on February 9, 1965, to urge voting rights for African-Americans—but it seems like the meeting was basically a strategy session. One month later, from March 7 to 21 King led thousands of protesters attempting to march from Montgomery to Selma, Alabama, where they planned to register to vote. As expected, the marches provoked a brutal crackdown by Alabama state troopers, who attacked the marchers with clubs, police dogs, and fire hoses. Images of these attacks, televised nationally, gave President Johnson the congressional support he needed to get the Voting Rights Act passed in March 1965.

> Even if we pass this bill, the battle will not be over. What happened in Selma is part of a far larger movement which reaches into every section and state of America. It is the effort of American Negroes to secure for themselves the full blessings of American life. Their cause must be our cause, too, because it is not just Negroes but really it is all of us who must overcome the crippling legacy of bigotry and injustice. And we shall overcome.
>
> —President Johnson, March 15, 1965

It's important to keep in mind that most Southern whites were not card-carrying KKK ghouls, and from early on "progressive" Southern whites, numbering about 5 percent–20 percent depending on the locale, supported the push for integration. Though outnumbered, their public support was important in encouraging African-American activists and persuading moderate whites to join the desegregationist camp. While 80 percent of white Southerners said they opposed their children going to school with African-Americans in 1956, this number dropped with remarkable speed to 62 percent in 1963, 38 percent in 1965, and just 16 percent in 1970.

Meanwhile, there were definite limits to Northern white support—especially when activism turned radical. Some African-American leaders had always rejected compromise with whites, advocating self-sufficiency or even separation. Marcus Garvey's "African Redemption" movement in the 1920s inspired Wallace Fard Muhammad to found the Nation of Islam, an unorthodox racist sect, in Detroit in 1930. W.F. Muhammad's successor, Elijah Muhammad, encouraged African-Americans to leave Christian churches and adopt new names, with an "X" to denote their long-lost African heritage. But the Nation of Islam truly entered the spotlight when Elijah Muhammad's most talented disciple came to prominence. Born in 1925 in Omaha, Nebraska, Malcolm Little started out a petty criminal. By 1948, he'd joined the Nation while in prison and adopted the surname X. After his release in 1952, the charismatic orator gained notoriety for fierce denunciations of white injustice and justifications of self-defense "by any means necessary"—a thinly veiled call to arms. While Malcolm X did adopt a more conciliatory tone shortly before his assassination in February 1965, the radical banner was taken up by others, including Huey Newton, who founded the militant Black Panthers in 1966.

The white majority found the idea of a black uprising alarming, and scores of violent outbursts in the 1960s did little to ease fears. In the week following the assassination of Martin Luther King Jr. in April 1968, 125 riots resulted in 46 deaths, 1,300 injuries and 20,000 arrests. But those only scratch the surface. From 1963 to 1969, there were 166 riots, which left 188 people dead, 5,000 injured, and 40,000 under arrest. Some infamous events include the 1965 Watts riot in Los Angeles, with 34 dead; the 1967 Newark riot, with 27 dead; and the 1967 Detroit riot, with 43 dead. Although most of the casualties were African-Americans, these events undermined white support for civil rights activism.

LIE: *The president needs permission from Congress to undertake major hostilities.*

THE TRUTH: That's just, like, the Constitution's *opinion,* man. The president can totally send hundreds of thousands of U.S. troops overseas to fight America's enemies for years at a time without an official declaration of war by Congress. Because it's not "war," it's a "police action." See the difference? Most people don't.

> In no part of the Constitution is more wisdom to be found, than in the clause which confides the question of war or peace to the legislature, and not to the executive department.
>
> —James Madison, 1793

The origins of this classic constitutional sleight of hand go back to 1798 and the Quasi-War with France, also called the Undeclared War or the Half War. But the first really egregious dodge came in 1950, when President Harry Truman sent a total of 480,000 U.S. troops to Korea without bothering to get a declaration of war. The presidential power grab (and congressional abdication of responsibility) got even bigger with President Lyndon Johnson. The 1964 Tonkin Gulf Resolution authorized the commander in chief to order whatever military action seemed appropriate in Southeast Asia after North Vietnamese forces (allegedly) took a couple of potshots at U.S. Navy ships. This open-ended resolution basically gave Johnson a blank check to escalate the conflict in Vietnam, setting in motion a textbook example of how not to conduct a war—er, that is, "police action."

For one thing, it had nothing to do with America. Led by the charismatic Ho Chi Minh, the Vietnam war began as a nationalist uprising against French colonialists. It wasn't until 1959 that it morphed into a civil war between Ho's communist North Vietnamese (Vietminh) and pro-U.S. forces in South Vietnam. The sides were being led by two vastly different personalities. While Ho was both experienced in guerrilla warfare and widely revered as "the father of the country," South Vietnam's Ngo Dinh Diem was a devout Catholic who considered becoming a monk or priest before settling on the civil service. Nevertheless, U.S. officials psyched themselves up, convincing each other that Diem was a strong leader with popular support. Overall, the odds looked pretty good—in one corner, the most powerful nation on earth; in the other, North Vietnam, a poor, backward country with almost no industrial base.

Well, the odds looked good on paper. But in the ring was a different story. For over a decade, pro-communist Viet Cong guerrillas in South Vietnam staged surprise attacks on American and South Vietnamese military and civilian targets. Facing (or rather, failing to face) this elusive foe, U.S. forces were supposed to defend South Vietnamese villages, cut off Viet Cong supplies, and somehow, eventually, find and destroy the guerrillas. This proved much more difficult than it seemed from the comfort of Washington, D.C., especially since the guerrillas were sustained by a continuous flow of weapons, fuel, and reinforcements from North Vietnam, via the "Ho Chi Minh Trail."

Because the trail snaked through the jungles of neighboring Laos and Cambodia, Johnson decided to expand the "police action" to Laos, triggering a cycle of failure and escalation that came to be known as "mission creep." Under Kennedy there had been, at the highest, 16,300 troops in 1963. When relatively small deployments failed to stop communist infiltration, Johnson upped the ante. In 1964, there were 23,000 U.S. troops stationed there. In 1965, troop strength rose to 184,000, and it finally peaked at 536,000 in 1968. But the enemy just kept growing stronger and stronger, no matter how many troops America deployed. What went wrong?

BONUS LIE: *Old people supported war in Vietnam, while young people opposed it.*

This is one of the most enduring misconceptions about Vietnam. It turns out younger Americans (under the age of 30) were consistently more likely to support the war in Vietnam than those over the age of 49, with middle-aged folks falling somewhere in, well, the middle. In August of 1965, a Gallup poll found 76 percent of adults under 30 supported U.S. intervention in Vietnam, versus 51 percent of adults over 49. By July 1967, when 62 percent of the under-30 crowd still supported intervention, the over-49 crowd was down to 37 percent; and in January 1970 the numbers fell to 41 percent and 20 percent, respectively.

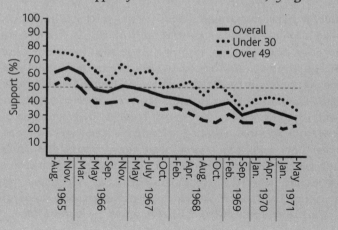

Public Support for Vietnam Intervention, by Age

The fact is, the United States misread almost everything about the war. To begin with, U.S. officials didn't realize that many Vietnamese saw America as an imperial power, and Diem as its puppet. Worse, Diem alienated South Vietnam's Buddhist majority by persecuting monks, touching off civil unrest. So in November 1963, the CIA changed its mind and organized a coup that toppled Diem, whose equally unpopular replacement was ousted in another (non-CIA) coup three months later. U.S. officials also failed to grasp that the North Vietnamese were truly fighting for their homeland's independence, rather than just acting as pawns of Moscow or Beijing, so they underestimated the morale of the North Vietnamese—especially their ability to absorb casualties. Finally, U.S. advantages didn't count for much in Vietnam: tanks couldn't maneuver in the jungle, so "grunts" had to fight on foot against adversaries who knew the terrain much better.

> You can kill ten of my men for every one I kill of yours, but even at those odds, you will lose and I will win.
>
> —Ho Chi Minh, to a French official, 1946

But perhaps the biggest factor was that U.S. commanders weren't allowed to send ground troops into North Vietnam—the enemy homeland—for fear of provoking a "real" war with China or Russia. In addition to basically guaranteeing defeat, this led to over-reliance on air power in the form of vicious bombing campaigns. Operations like "Rolling Thunder," pulverizing North Vietnam from 1965 to 1968, failed to stop the enemy but did manage to convince civilians the United States wanted to exterminate them. Laos was also bombed mercilessly in a failed bid to cut the Ho Chi Minh Trail—and this paled in comparison to the bombing of South Vietnam, America's ally. Altogether from 1964 to 1973, the United States dropped an incredible seven million tons of bombs—twice the total tonnage dropped by U.S.

forces in World War II—on a region about half the size of Peru. The United States also sprayed 18 million gallons of the defoliant Agent Orange to expose enemy hideouts. Around 500,000 birth defects in Vietnam have been attributed to the spray campaign, and an unknown number of cancers in U.S. veterans.

★ *Agent Orange was so named for the colored markings on the barrels in which it was shipped. Other similarly named herbicides were called Agents Purple, Pink, and Green.*

Nonetheless, there were always enough successes to justify hopes for final victory: whenever the Viet Cong came out to fight pitched battles, they were annihilated, as in the Tet Offensive of 1968. But perversely, Tet became a psychological victory for the North Vietnamese, showing Americans that Pentagon "progress reports" were baloney. American support for the war waned, and privately Johnson's advisors told him Vietnam was unwinnable. In March of 1968 the president—overwhelmed by the police action he'd made—announced he wouldn't seek reelection that year. That November, Democratic Vice President Humphrey was defeated in the presidential election by Republican Richard Nixon, who won with the vague, improbable vow of "peace with honor."

This turned out to mean "bomb the bejeezus out of Vietnam, Cambodia, and Laos, while making nice with the Soviets and Chinese." The idea was to isolate North Vietnam and give South Vietnam a fighting chance, and it did allow Nixon to withdraw U.S. troops and turn over most of the fighting to South Vietnam. Knowing that South Vietnam wasn't up to the task, Nixon tried to help out with air power, which stopped a big North Vietnamese push for Saigon in 1972.

> We should declare war on North Vietnam....We could pave the whole country and put parking strips on it, and still be home by Christmas.
>
> —Ronald Reagan, 1965

However, Nixon's "secret bombing" of Laos and Cambodia from 1969 to 1972 failed to halt communist infiltration of South Vietnam. It simultaneously outraged anti-war Americans—even in the pre-Internet era, you still couldn't drop two million tons of bombs without someone noticing. Protests erupted on college campuses nationwide, including Kent State, where the Ohio National Guard shot and killed four unarmed protesters on May 4, 1970, galvanizing anti-war sentiment.

True, Nixon's 1972 bombing of Hanoi in "Linebacker I & II" helped bring the North Vietnamese to the negotiating table, but the resulting Paris Peace Accords, signed in January 1973, were really just a fig leaf to let America retreat from Southeast Asia with a shred of dignity. Everyone knew the communists were biding their time before crushing South Vietnam and reunifying the country, completing their decades-long quest. Of course, that last shred of dignity was stripped away by the spectacle of South Vietnamese civilians desperately clinging to departing American helicopters during the final evacuation of the U.S. embassy in Saigon, as North Vietnamese forces closed in on April 29–30, 1975.

LIE: *Technology makes life better.*

THE TRUTH: Okay, this is definitely true if you're rich. If you're poor, well . . .

In the mid-1950s, the United States was still the largest industrial power on earth, but its dominance was being eroded by postwar recovery in Japan and Europe and new industrialization in Latin America and Asia. The U.S. share of global production fell from 35 percent to 25 percent between 1955 and 1975, with its share of steel output tumbling from 39 percent to 16 percent, and car production plunging from 70 percent to 27 percent. In other words, America now had competition. This was good for consumers (hooray for choices!) and workers in foreign countries (hooray for relatively high-paying jobs and a higher standard of living!)— but it was bad news for Americans who depended on factory work. With foreign labor cheaper than American labor, foreign manufacturers could offer comparable goods at lower prices, forcing American companies to lower prices too. To stay competitive, American companies had to make more stuff at lower cost. The solution? Robots.

Automation began during World War II, as companies worked to fulfill government contracts with a smaller workforce. At the time, labor was tight. In fact, the war period was the best time to be an unskilled worker. But after the war, companies like GM and Ford continued to up their automation. After all, they were facing significant foreign competition from hugely popular models like the Volkswagen Beetle and Toyota Corona.

To keep up with the low foreign prices, U.S. manufacturers turned to a combination of two things: automation and layoffs. When it came time to cut positions, less-skilled, low-paying jobs were the first to go—these jobs were less likely to be unionized and were simply easier for machines to do. Adding insult to injury, laid-off workers had a hard time finding new jobs because automation was spreading from industry to industry like a robot plague. For example, beginning in 1956, hundreds of thousands of dockworkers lost their jobs after the introduction of container shipping and automation, which allowed shipping lines to consolidate cargo traffic in a couple of big ports.

These advancements in technology were especially devastating to African-American workers, who often lacked the education and skills for higher-paying jobs. The result was mass unemployment beginning in the 1950s, growing to crisis proportions by the 1960s. Poverty was accompanied by a wave of crime, drug addiction and—most ominously—the breakdown of African-American families. Faced with spiraling crime and plummeting property values, everyone who could afford it fled big cities for the suburbs. The resulting collapse of the tax base brought

UNIONIZE ME

The decline of manufacturing led to the decline of unions, at least in the private sector. The high wages dictated by unions weren't sustainable in the face of foreign competition, and the remaining manufacturing jobs began moving from heavily unionized states in the North to nonunionized states in the South—or out of the country altogether.

From 1965 to 1975, the Northeastern United States lost over a million manufacturing jobs, while the South picked up 860,000—usually nonunion and at substantially lower wages (on average 20 percent less than Northern wages for comparable work). U.S. companies also began outsourcing simple manufacturing work to developing countries.

Overall, the proportion of American workers who belonged to a union fell from about 40 percent in 1955 to 30 percent in 1975—in the private sector. However, the situation was different in the public sector (meaning government jobs), thanks to JFK, who encouraged federal workers to unionize, setting the precedent for state and county employees not long after. From 1955 to 1975, the proportion of public employees who belonged to unions jumped from 12 percent to 40 percent. Insert jokes about the DMV here.

sharp declines in education and public services like mass transit, sanitation, and policing. Millions were trapped in a vicious cycle of poverty and social breakdown. In short, the inner cities had become ghettoes.

WHAT'S SO GREAT ABOUT THE GREAT SOCIETY?

Lyndon Johnson's hero was Franklin Delano Roosevelt, and it shows in his policies. Believing that poverty contributed to crime and civil disorder, Johnson devoted his presidency to expanding the welfare system first introduced by FDR. As a follow-up to the New Deal, Johnson's "Great Society" program was breathtakingly ambitious: it established an Office of Economic Opportunity to organize job training, created Medicaid and Medicare to help poor and elderly Americans pay for health care, provided federal funds to the states for poor school districts, established the U.S. Department of Housing and Urban Development (HUD) to finance low-cost housing, created a permanent Food Stamp Program, and provided preschool for low-income children through Head Start.

Johnson and his Democratic allies in Congress clearly had a thing for legislating, and the Great Society became the high-water mark of Democratic power after World War II. But critics say many of their well-intentioned reforms backfired. Federal assistance intended to lift people out of poverty instead fostered economic dependency, with welfare accepted as an ordinary part of life—the exact opposite of the original goal. The number of U.S. citizens receiving welfare skyrocketed from six million in 1967 to 18 million in 1974. What's more, the (white) news media—always ready to pander unhelpfully—created the false impression that most welfare recipients were African-American, when in fact the majority were white, reinforcing prejudices among whites and negative self-image among African-Americans.

★ *White recipients, Aid to Families with Dependent Children, 1975: 5.7 million*
Black recipients, AFDC, 1975: 4.9 million
White households receiving food stamps, 1975: 2.8 million
Black households receiving food stamps, 1975: 1.6 million

Getting It On

Nothing says "I love you" like a sexually transmitted disease, except maybe an illegitimate child. And during the era of "free love" from 1965 to 1975, these tokens of affection became more and more common. But what caused the sudden increase in fooling around?

The twentieth century had brought big social changes: the extended family gave way to the nuclear family, everyone became more mobile thanks to new modes of transportation, and more women worked outside the home. Meanwhile, religious belief was coming into conflict with the new cults of science and technology. All of this, combined with the widespread availability of condoms—legalized in 1918—enabled people to control their sexual reproduction. As a result, traditional sexual mores gave way to more permissive attitudes post-World War I. In the 1940s, the U.S. military entertained no illusions about the virtue of enlisted men: by the end of World War II, the armed forces were distributing a remarkable 50 million condoms per month along with a short "educational" film popularizing the slogan, "Put it on before you put it in."

★ *Hoping to stop the spread of venereal diseases, in 1935 Connecticut became the first U.S. state to require premarital blood tests.*

After the war Americans were pleasantly scandalized by the first large-scale sex studies. From 1948 to 1953 Alfred Kinsey, a University of Indiana zoologist, conducted pioneering surveys documenting American sexual behaviors and attitudes. Though his methodology and data were later questioned, Kinsey certainly succeeded in getting Americans to talk about sex, especially since his findings suggested widespread sexual deviance. According to Kinsey's research, 37 percent of American men had at least one homosexual experience, 50 percent of married men had at least one extramarital encounter, and 22 percent of men and 12 percent of women reported themselves aroused by sadomasochism. Not coincidentally, Hugh Hefner's scandalous and highly successful *Playboy* launched the same year as Kinsey's last study, with early issues devoting a great deal of attention to Kinsey's kinky findings. Then in 1957 William Masters and Virginia Johnson began their physiological studies on subjects like sexual arousal, male impotence, female frigidity, and a host of other naughty subjects. Their findings—based on observations of about 10,000 sexual acts involving a total of 694 subjects in a laboratory setting (382 women and 312 men, never all at once)—were summarized in the best-selling *Human Sexual Response*, published in 1965, and the best-selling follow-up, *Human Sexual Inadequacy*, which appeared in 1970.

With all this academic activity, it's not surprising that the "sexual revolution" began on college campuses, just as female coeducational students ("coeds") were gaining admission to previously all-male bastions. Still, collegiate sex remained fairly conservative at first: although 40 percent of male students reported having premarital sex in the late 1950s, it was often with prostitutes. Only one out of five college women reported having premarital sex—and usually only if she was engaged or in a long-term relationship. Young women (and to a lesser degree, young men) who regularly had premarital intercourse were considered "low class." But by the time the sixties rolled around, everything was about to change, thanks to "The Pill."

Developed by an American biologist named Dr. Gregory Pincus, the combined oral contraceptive pill quickly emerged as the most important advance in birth control since the condom, with an estimated failure rate of only 0.3 percent without human error, compared to 2 percent for condoms. The Food and Drug Administration approved The Pill for contraceptive use in 1961, and indeed, it's hard to overstate its popularity: the number of American women taking The Pill surged from 400,000 in 1961 to 10 million in 1975, making it the most popular form of birth control. In 1973 there was a temporary dip in sales after studies confirmed that the drug caused blood clots in a small number of users, but for most, the benefits still outweighed the risks. The only real problem with The Pill stemmed from its success. It was so effective as birth control that people stopped using pesky, inconvenient condoms. As "full-contact" premarital sex and promiscuity increased, so did the rates of sexually transmitted diseases.

With all of this promiscuous sex going on, there were plenty of other things to worry about too . . . like the decline of marriage. In 1969 California became the first state to allow "no-fault" di-

The Pill Is a Thrill!

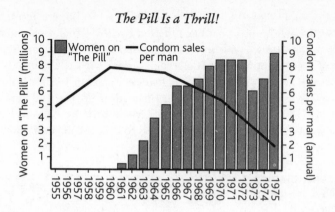

vorces, and by 1975 all but five states had some kind of no-fault divorce statute. As the divorce rate doubled from 1955 to 1975, the number of people getting married in the first place declined by 15 percent, reflecting a new skepticism about the purpose and benefits of matrimony. During the same time period, the number of children born out of wedlock jumped from 4.5 percent of all births to 14.2 percent. Despite the availability of The Pill and other forms of contraception, there was also a huge increase in the number of legal abortions, facilitated by a handful of states adopting more liberal laws. In 1973 the Supreme Court made abortion legal in *Roe v. Wade*, overturning laws banning abortion in 30 states and touching off a bitter ideological conflict that still rages today.

Happy Meals

Like many gifts from America to the world, McDonald's is a mixed bag: on one hand, it's gloriously greasy and delicious junk food that isn't so good for you; on the other hand, it's gloriously greasy and delicious junk food that isn't so good for you.

Richard (Dick) and Maurice (Mac) McDonald opened their first restaurant in San Bernardino, California, in 1940. Initially, the McDonald's Bar-B-Que was a pretty standard drive-in joint with waitresses serving guests who ate in their cars. But the brothers soon elevated the humble burger to an art form. In 1948 they revamped the restaurant as a self-service drive-in—losing the waitresses, replacing silverware with plastic, and ditching most of the menu to focus on their nine best sellers, especially the 15-cent hamburger. The next year, they replaced potato chips with French fries, another instant classic, and started offering milkshakes.

The McDonald's Bar-B-Que remained a local operation until 1954, when the brothers were visited by Ray Kroc, a restaurant equipment salesman who was impressed by the restaurant's efficiency and popularity. Kroc struck a deal with the brothers to turn McDonald's into a national franchise, and in 1961 he bought them out for $2.7 million. Under his leadership, the McDonald's Corporation expanded like the American waistline: from 9 restaurants in 1955, the number jumped to 710 in 1965 and 3,076 in 1975.

★ *The Big Mac was added to McDonald's national menu in 1968. It was intended to compete with the popular Big Boy double-decker burger. Similarly, the Filet-O-Fish was tacked on to lure Catholics who purchased Big Boy fish dinners and sandwiches.*

The chain's success was due largely to Kroc's obsessive management style. He standardized everything from the length and width of French fries to the architectural finishes of restaurants, including the iconic Golden Arches. Franchises got uniform ingredients from Kroc's central supply and distribution system, and in 1956, he established control over new restaurant locations with a commercial real estate business, the Franchise Realty Corporation. This new corporation not only acted as a landlord for new branches, but it also provided a new corporate revenue stream. But Kroc was hardly done. In 1961 he established "Hamburger University," a professional training program in Elk Grove Village, Illinois. Kroc also encouraged enterprise on the part of franchise managers—giving them free rein with local marketing while supporting their efforts with national advertising campaigns. And through a new series of television ads in 1966, a character named Ronald McDonald joined the cultural lexicon.

As the popularity of fast-food joints skyrocketed, American diets began to change. Per capita consumption of soft drinks surged from 11 gallons per year in 1955 to 30 gallons per year in 1975, the annual intake of red meat jumped from 107 pounds to 130 pounds, and "added fats" (like cooking oil, margarine, and butter) went from 45 pounds to 53 pounds. Unsurprisingly, the proportion of obese Americans increased from 10 percent in 1955 to 15 percent in 1975. Luckily, medical advances helped limit the damage as the number of fatal heart attacks decreased from five per 1,000 people in 1955 to four per 1,000 in 1975.

Ad Men

Science is great and all, but apparently, it's got nothing on ad campaigns. When the U.S. Surgeon General finally confirmed in 1964 that smoking cigarettes—wonderful, stimulating, relaxing, sexy cigarettes—greatly increased the risk of dying of lung cancer, heart disease, and emphysema, tobacco companies responded with more sophisticated advertising. And Americans responded by lighting up.

The ill effects of tobacco, including its association with cancer and respiratory diseases, were suspected as soon as Europeans began using it regularly in the sixteenth century. But there was no way to measure the precise impact: most people didn't live long enough for the effects of chronic tobacco use to show up, and the medical profession was only beginning to apply scientific methods to understanding disease. In the twentieth century, however, longer lives and the growing popularity of machine-rolled cigarettes led to an increase in tobacco-related disease.

After German researchers conducted pioneering investigations at the urging of Adolf Hitler (who hated cigarettes, on top of everything else) more than a dozen studies in the 1950s by the American Cancer Society (ACS) and others demonstrated a connection between smoking, lung cancer, and heart disease. But the American news media mostly neglected to report these findings—maybe because tobacco advertising revenues were the single biggest ad category in print and broadcast, ahead of automobiles. Meanwhile, tobacco companies mounted a furious counterattack, playing up tobacco's patriotic association with American history and funding studies that blamed the rising prevalence of lung cancer on other plausible culprits, like increasing air pollution. In 1953 the industry came together to create the Council for Tobacco Research, which sought to win over the scientific community with generous research grants, followed in 1958 by the Tobacco Institute, whose main mission was neutralizing negative PR. Beginning in 1954, the industry also trumpeted the cigarette filter, which supposedly made tobacco "safe" (it didn't).

In 1957, U.S. Surgeon General Leroy E. Burney publicly stated the U.S. Public Health Service's belief that smoking causes lung cancer. But the ACS and the American Heart Association—dissatisfied with media coverage—demanded stronger statements and regulation. Encouraged by a scathing report from Britain's Royal College of Physicians in 1962, U.S. Surgeon General Luther L. Terry convened an expert committee, which reviewed thousands of scientific studies and in 1964 concluded, again, that smoking indeed causes lung cancer. This time, however, there was no way the media could dodge the news: the report made newspaper headlines and was the lead story on every broadcast news program. Among other things, the report warned of a 20-fold increase in the risk of lung cancer for heavy smokers, but also noted greatly diminished risk if they quit.

The report certainly got people's attention, but that doesn't mean everyone took it to heart. In 1966 one Harris Poll found less than half of adults believed smoking was a "major" cause of lung cancer. Meanwhile, the tobacco industry opened the advertising floodgates even further, with total ad spending jumping from an already huge $115 million in 1955 to a whopping $263 million in 1965. Thanks to its efforts, total cigarette sales soared from 386.4 billion to 521.1 billion over the same period. Shameless as always, tobacco companies became especially effective at marketing the cigarettes to women, touting cigarettes for weight loss and positioning them as part of women's liberation (really).

★ *Babe Ruth, Lucille Ball, Ronald Reagan, The Flintstones, and even Santa Claus all appeared in cigarette ads on television.*

In 1964 the Federal Trade Commission banned deceptive advertising by tobacco companies and called for mandatory warnings of tobacco's health effects in advertising and on cigarette packaging—but tobacco industry lobbyists were able to derail this legislation with help from pro-tobacco legislators, delaying the new warnings and watering down the wording. Congress finally mandated stronger wording in 1969 and banned TV and radio ads for tobacco products in 1970. But the industry still enjoyed free rein in print media and billboard ads and managed to come up with ingenious substitutes for broadcast advertising, including sponsorship of sporting events, concerts, contests, sweepstakes, and point-of-sale promotions (like eye-catching posters and displays in stores). By 1975 the ad spending on marketing campaigns was at nearly $500 million.

Once again, it was money well spent: from 1965 to 1975, cigarette sales increased steadily from 521.1 billion to 603 billion. Of course, there were terrible human consequences. The death rate from lung cancer more than doubled from 17 per 100,000 people in 1955 to 37 in 1975, and this was just part of the total toll; overall 1955–1975 saw seven million tobacco-related deaths in the United States. Meanwhile, during the same period, total industry revenues almost tripled, from $5.3 billion to $14.8 billion, for total revenues of over $200 billion or about $28,500 per fatality.

This Is Your Country on Drugs

As if gonorrhea, cheeseburgers, and cigarettes weren't unhealthy enough, Americans also experimented with a colorful cornucopia of illegal drugs in the 1960s and 1970s, breezily disregarding the fact that many of them were illegal for a reason. While a lot of people had a good time, and some even "expanded their minds," there were also thousands of cases of fatal overdoses, nasty blood diseases, and terrible accidents, and God only knows how many bad trips (literally: he was there for many of them).

The most popular illegal drug in the United States, hands down, was and is marijuana—also known as pot, bud, Buddha, cheeba, chronic, dank, dolo, dope, endo, ganja, grass, green, hay, herb, jive, kaya, leaf, lobo, loco, Mary Jane, reefer, rope, sess, skunk, smoke, sticky icky, tea, weed, and whacky tobaccky. After being introduced to America by Mexican laborers, who passed the pipe with poor blacks in New Orleans around 1910, the herbal cigarette use followed jazz musicians to Chicago and then radiated to Eastern cities in the 1920s–1930s, where it was a popular alternative to alcohol in the Prohibition era.

During this period, marijuana use was limited almost exclusively to African-Americans and Mexican immigrants, who made easy targets for a law enforcement apparatus left idle by the end of Prohibition. Newspapers helped whip white fears into a frenzy with lurid, largely fictional reports of "crazed Mexicans" and "wild-eyed Negroes" raping and murdering unsuspecting victims while in the thrall of the drug's "delirious hallucinations." While this makes strange reading juxtaposed with the current "stoner" stereotype, most readers didn't know the first thing about the drug (or Mexicans, for that matter). The result was a federal law banning marijuana in 1937, which conveniently gave the newly created Federal Bureau of Narcotics something to do.

Marijuana use didn't cross over to white America until the late 1940s, when it was adopted by members of the emerging "Beat" subculture, and it remained fairly uncommon until the 1960s, when it became ubiquitous almost overnight in the hippie sub-culture. The number of first-time users tripled from 1960 to 1965 to 600,000, then surged to 2.5 million new users in 1969 and nearly 3.5 million in 1972, and continued at that rate for the rest of the 1970s. In total, from 1960 to 1975 over 28 million Ameri-cans experimented with marijuana, equaling 13 percent of the population in 1975, with a good number—around 14 million—returning for follow-up experiments.

That same period saw a 10-fold increase in the number of her-oin addicts in the United States, from about 55,000 to 550,000. While the majority of users lived in poor urban areas, with espe-cially high rates of addiction among inner-city African-American populations, heroin also made inroads in the white middle class, particularly among teenagers and young adults, who experi-mented with the drug on college campuses. Popular Beat writers like Jack Kerouac gave heroin cultural cachet as a cool, glamorous drug. Hundreds of thousands of young men were also exposed to cheap, high-grade heroin in Vietnam, with one study estimating that 15 percent of U.S. troops were regular users in 1971. Though most returning soldiers kicked the habit, some hard-core addicts introduced it to friends back home, especially in the ghettoes, where heroin use was already established. By 1971 the U.S. govern-ment estimated that American heroin addicts were spending over $2.7 billion a year on the drug. Heroin-related deaths in New York City (home to almost half the country's addicts) soared from 199 in 1960 to a peak of 1,409 in 1972, thanks to a spike in overdoses and also increasing prevalence of two dangerous new diseases, hepatitis A and B, which spread by junkies sharing needles.

★ *The CIA helped a former Chinese Nationalist, Khun Sa, carve out an opium-growing empire in Burma and transported his high-grade heroin to local markets aboard the agency's secret air force, "Air America." The CIA used its share of the profits to fund off-the-books covert operations across Southeast Asia.*

The most emblematic drug of the 1960s had to be lysergic acid diethylamide, or LSD. While marijuana and heroin were about feeling good, LSD transformed people by "opening their minds." The effects of this man-made hallucinogen can only be described as bizarre, including vivid visual and auditory hallucinations, novel corporeal sensations, out-of-body experiences, synesthesia ("hearing colors" or "tasting sounds"), and heightened sensitivity to time and space. People took LSD in the hope of grasping profound truths, and some reported success, relating feelings of union with nature, revelations of their own individuality, and healing of old emotional traumas.

Awesome, right? Well, except for the plethora of terrifying "bad trips"—seemingly endless waking nightmares characterized by paranoia, despair, alienation, and the loss of sense of self. This wasn't a rare occurrence: there were so many bad trips at Woodstock the organizers set up a row of tents where doctors and volunteers could take care of hundreds of people who were "freaking out" (including one of the organizers). Some doctors have also suggested that psychedelic drugs can trigger full-blown schizophrenia.

Facing a rising tide of illegal drug use, in 1971 Richard Nixon declared "war on drugs," calling the abuse "public enemy No. 1." In 1973 he created the Drug Enforcement Administration, the successor to the Federal Bureau of Narcotics, to coordinate the efforts of Customs, Treasury agents, the FBI, and local law enforcement to stop the flow of drugs into the United States from abroad. But the feds were no match for the huge demand and profit potential of illegal drugs: while marijuana seizures along the Mexican border soared from 6,432 pounds in 1963 to 451,800 pounds in 1973, the latter figure represents just 2.5 percent of the estimated 8,750 tons of marijuana consumed in the United States that year.

★ *Illegal drugs weren't the only substance being abused by Americans in the 1960s: the number of Valium prescriptions written per year in the United States rose from 4 million in 1964 to 61 million in 1975.*

All the Single Ladies

Although the 1950s and early 1960s are usually thought of as a dormant period in the women's rights movement, they saw an acceleration of the trends that began during World War II. Where 19.3 million women worked in 1955, making up 33 percent of the U.S. workforce, by 1965 the number rose to 28 million, or 39 percent of the workforce. The number of women who attended college also rose sharply, thanks to the integration of previously all-male universities: female undergrads more than doubled from 900,000 in 1955 to 2.15 million in 1965—increasing from 35 percent to 39 percent of the total.

These trends set the stage for yet another social upheaval. As working women enjoyed greater economic independence, giving them more say in their relations with men, they couldn't fail to notice the barriers to professional advancement and economic discrimination—on average women made just 61 percent of what men earned for comparable work in 1960. Likewise, women who graduated from college were certainly better-educated, but with little hope of landing higher-paying jobs or academic positions.

The first salvo in this new feminist movement was fired by Betty Friedan, the daughter of a jeweler in Peoria, Illinois. Friedan, who experienced anti-Semitism as a young woman, was first swept up by radical leftism. After attending Smith College and Berkeley in the 1930s–1940s, she wrote for a left-wing union publication but was fired in 1952 because she was pregnant. At loose ends, in 1957 she organized a survey of female college graduates from the University of California system and found a deep current of dissatisfaction with their lives as housewives. This outpouring of unhappiness inspired her groundbreaking work, *The Feminine Mystique*; published in 1963, the book criticized modern society for confining women to the home when their education and ambition would allow them to do much more, and let women in this position know they weren't alone. Friedan also attacked theories of "penis envy" and other notions as proposed by Sigmund Freud, then the dominant thinker in American psychology.

> The problem lay buried, unspoken, for many years in the minds of American women. It was a strange stirring, a sense of dissatisfaction, a yearning [that is, a longing] that women suffered in the middle of the twentieth century in the United States. Each suburban wife struggled with it alone. As she made the beds, shopped for groceries . . . she was afraid to ask even of herself the silent question—"Is this all?"
>
> —Betty Friedan, *The Feminine Mystique*, 1963

Meanwhile, women had been paying close attention to the civil rights movement, which provided a model for organized action to combat widespread discrimination. In 1966 Friedan became co-founder of the National Organization for Women (NOW), which lobbied for legislative reforms. Some of the reforms piggybacked on bills first proposed by black civil rights activists, including a clause prohibiting discrimination on the basis of gender added to the Civil Rights Act of 1964. But like the civil rights activists,

NOW lobbyists found that legislative reforms that looked good on paper were often difficult to enforce: the 1963 Equal Pay Act, which aimed to abolish wage discrimination based on gender, didn't have a visible impact for more than 20 years.

Frustrated by the limited success of legislative reform, the feminist movement became increasingly radical over the course of the 1960s, again paralleling the civil rights and anti-war movements. In fact, many feminist leaders experienced their "political awakening" pursuing these other causes: Gloria Steinem, another Smith alum turned freelance journalist, became involved in politics in 1968 while working on the Democratic primary campaign of George McGovern. In 1969 Steinem won fame as a feminist leader with her uncompromising defense of abortion rights, now at the center of the "Women's Liberation" movement. She also testified to Congress in support of the Equal Rights Amendment (ERA), which stated, "Equality of rights under the law shall not be denied or abridged by the United States or by any state on account of sex."

Although the ERA was never ratified by all the states, feminists won a huge victory in 1973 with the Supreme Court's decision in *Roe v. Wade*, effectively legalizing abortion in all 50 states. In its wake the National Abortion Rights Action League partnered with the ACLU to bring lawsuits forcing public hospitals to offer abortions—but *Roe v. Wade* remains very controversial, bitterly opposed by "pro-life" activists and conservatives who argue that the Supreme Court overreached.

★ Roe v. Wade *didn't pass quickly enough to help Norma McCorvey, aka Jane Roe. She gave birth to a baby girl, who was given up for adoption. McCorvey, who later accepted baptism and communion in the Catholic Church, is now a pro-life advocate.*

Otherwise, progress during this period was slow but significant, as women came to occupy more management and academic positions. But there were still blatant disparities: in 1975 women earned just 62 percent of what men were paid—and men still expected working spouses to handle traditional duties like housework and raising kids.

Hooray for Race Wars

Not that kind of race war, silly! Because the Cold War never involved direct armed conflict between the rival superpowers, the United States and the Soviet Union sublimated their aggression into "races" that gave them an excuse to spend lots of money, while allowing them to measure "progress" with enough ambiguity that both sides could claim to be winning.

The Arms Race

If you can't actually declare war and whup on your enemy, the next best thing is accumulating colossal military power and loudly declaring that if there were a war, you would totally whup them worse than they could whup you. The great thing about this strategy is you never have to find out if it's true or not.

The idea of the "arms race" is as old as hating your neighbor, but with its long history of isolationism, the United States was a relative newcomer to the concept. On those few occasions that the United States had previously faced a serious military challenge, like World War I, it quickly assembled formidable armed forces that were then dismantled when peace returned. But World War II and the ensuing Cold War—where the global march of communism seemed to repeat the pattern of Axis aggression— changed this mindset forever. From now on, the United States would have to maintain a large standing army, navy, and air force to keep "the Reds" from getting any ideas.

The centerpiece of the "deterrence" strategy was a large nuclear arsenal, and we do mean large: from six fission bombs in 1945, the U.S. stash grew to include 3,057 fission and fusion warheads by 1955 and 31,642 by 1965. The number of high-yield (multi-megaton) devices peaked around 1960; supposing 500 high-yield bombs could wipe out human life on earth, it seems the U.S. nuclear arsenal had enough firepower that year to destroy civilization five times over, give or take an apocalypse.

> In 1951 President Truman announced the launch of CONELRAD, or the Control of Electromagnetic Radiation system of emergency notification. If Russia homed in on American radio signals to use them as beacons for its atomic missiles, all radio stations would cease broadcasting after an alert from the White House.

Part of the reason for this absurd overproduction was the American military's fear that the Soviets might try to take out the U.S. arsenal with a surprise attack. This paranoia led the Strategic Air Command (SAC) to carry out the "Airborne Alert," one of the most remarkable logistical operations in history. From 1958 to 1968, long-range jet-powered B-52 bombers flew from SAC bases in the Midwest over Canada to the North Pole. In the event of war, they were to continue onward to targets in the Soviet Union. To ensure that the United States was always prepared to strike, from 1958 to 1968 several waves of B-52s were continuously taking off, flying as far as the North Pole, and then turning around and heading home. There were always at least a dozen bombers in the air at any time of night or day for 10 years.

By the early 1960s, the Americans and Russians had come up with an even better way of delivering horrific mass destruction: long-range ballistic missiles. Werner von Braun's team of ex-Nazi rocket scientists (relocated to Huntsville, Alabama, by the U.S. military after World War II) designed a series of progressively more impressive nuclear missiles: the short-range Redstone deployed by the U.S. Army in 1958 was limited to targets within a 200-mile radius, but by 1962, the Minuteman I had a range of 8,100 miles. By the end of the 1960s, most of the SAC's nuclear strike capability had shifted to intercontinental ballistic missiles (ICBMs), which could reach Soviet targets from missile bases in the United States in 30 minutes. The United States also deployed

A GOVERNMENT BY THE PEOPLE, FOR THE PEOPLE, HIDDEN VERY FAR BENEATH THE PEOPLE

In case the Soviets pulled off a first strike, the U.S. government had plans to carry on the fight. Presuming they had enough warning, senior officials would be evacuated by helicopter from Washington, D.C., to top-secret bunkers equipped with their own power plants and stockpiles of food, water, and fuel, to direct the continuing war and reconstruction. The Pentagon had plans to relocate to "Site R," a 700,000-square-foot complex beneath 650 acres of rolling hills at Raven Rock in Pennsylvania's Blue Ridge Mountains. Meanwhile, the president, his cabinet, and the Supreme Court would be flown to "High Point," a 600,000-square-foot bunker under Mount Weather, Virginia, equipped with a hospital, TV studio, and five-foot-thick, 34-ton steel blast doors, completed in 1958. As for the U.S. Congress, members were to be evacuated to "Casper," a 112,000-square-foot bunker located beneath the exclusive Greenbrier resort in White Sulphur Springs, West Virginia, where precise replicas of the House and Senate chambers were completed in 1962.

Jupiter and Pershing intermediate-range missiles in Western Europe and the submarine-based Polaris. In keeping with the arms race mentality, however, the U.S. Air Force retained a large fleet of B-52s, because you can never have too many ways to kill everyone five times over.

Of course nuclear weapons were only part of the arms race: both sides also prepared to fight good old-fashioned "conventional" wars with each other or with each other's proxies (pawns) as in the Vietnam War But the Vietnam disaster eroded public support for the U.S. armed forces, leading to a decrease in defense spending, especially after Congress cut off all financial support for military operations in Southeast Asia in 1971. By 1970, Soviet defense spending had passed U.S. defense spending, although the Kremlin's notorious secrecy meant American analysts didn't figure this out until later that decade.

The Space Race

The arms race wasn't the only U.S./Soviet pissing contest. The space race was another great excuse to spend boatloads of taxpayer money to demonstrate to the world how much bigger and manlier the United States was.

The Soviets kicked off the space race by delivering a series of humiliating defeats that wounded American pride. In 1957 they launched the first man-made satellite, Sputnik, and put the first living creature in orbit (the space dog Laika). But their greatest triumph came on April 12, 1961, when a 27-year-old test pilot, Yuri Gagarin, became the first human being in space. The U.S. news media freaked out over every Soviet victory: Orbiting nukes! Russian moon bases! Communist dogs in space! America couldn't afford to have the universe go Red. There was some serious catching up to do.

★ Space dog Laika bravely gave her life for the people's revolutionary cause. The first Soviet space dog to return to Earth safely, Strelka, later gave birth to six "pupniks." Nikita Khrushchev gave one of them to First Daughter Caroline Kennedy in 1961.

The first move was the 1959–1963 Mercury Project, in which the new National Aeronautics and Space Administration (NASA) carried out the first manned American spaceflights. Astronauts recruited from the U.S. Air Force and Navy were carried into outer space in small capsules lifted by Redstone rockets. Alan

Shepard became the first American in space, with a brief flight on May 5, 1961, and on February 20, 1962, John Glenn became the first American to orbit the Earth. Separately, in December 1962 the Mariner 2 probe became the first spacecraft to visit another planet with a flyby 22,000 miles from Venus (in solar system terms, that's a visit).

All this was a preamble to the main event, 1960–1972's Apollo Program, which fulfilled the ancient human quest to travel to the moon. This epic effort required nine years of intensive research and development, which produced hundreds of useful inventions, including the flight computer (boasting a massive 36K of memory), computer-controlled machine manufacturing, the first practical electrolytic fuel cell, water purification and dialysis, flame-retardant synthetic fabrics, radiation shielding, and freeze-dried food. But the most formidable engineering achievement was the Saturn V rocket. Standing at 36 stories tall and 33 feet wide, and weighing in at 3,350 tons, the Saturn V was actually three stacked rockets, which fired in sequence before dropping back to the planet's surface. The first stage alone was powered by five engines with a total 160 million horsepower, equivalent to about 300,000 big rigs.

After various test missions, on July 16, 1969, the first two stages of the Saturn V rocket lifted the 32-ton Apollo 11 command and lunar landing modules (named Columbia and Eagle) into Earth orbit with astronauts Neil Armstrong, Michael Collins, and Edwin "Buzz" Aldrin aboard. The third stage pushed the spacecraft beyond Earth's immediate gravitational field to arrive in orbit around the moon on July 19. Over the next 60 hours, while Collins remained in Columbia making photographic surveys, Armstrong and Aldrin descended to the lunar surface in Eagle to collect moon rocks, set up equipment for seismic measurement and laser telemetry from Earth, and observe the effects of the low-gravity environment. During the 2.5-hour moonwalk, they also left behind an Apollo 11 mission patch, a gold olive branch, a silicon disk with messages of goodwill from world leaders, a memorial plaque, and—perhaps most importantly—an American flag.

★ *Neil Armstrong's astronaut application arrived almost a week past the June 1, 1962, deadline. A friend of his who worked at the Manned Spacecraft Center slipped the tardy form into the pile before anyone noticed the postmark.*

The lunar landing was a foreign policy triumph. At a time when televised images of the losing battle in Vietnam were broadcast around the world, Apollo 11 provided undeniable proof of American wealth, power, and technical skill in the form of a riveting broadcast event. The event was watched live by about 600 million people around the world.

Havana Terrible Decade

The United States gets blamed for a lot of things it didn't do, but in the case of Cuba, the accusations are almost all true. Like, putting the mob in charge of an entire country. That's pretty much what happened under the rule of General Fulgencio Batista, an ex-president of Cuba who seized power in 1952 with the backing of both the U.S. government and the powerful Jewish mob financier Meyer Lansky. Batista appointed Lansky "minister of gambling" and offered to match any outside investment of $1 million or more in the hotel business (read: casinos), while police turned a blind eye to prostitution and drug smuggling. From 1952 to 1959, Havana was a Mafia playground, with Batista taking a 10 percent–30 percent "skim" off the brothels (which employed 10,000–12,000 prostitutes), the 13 mob-controlled casinos, and the various allied criminal enterprises.

If you're wondering what was going on in the rest of Cuba in this period, you've already shown more initiative than the mobsters, who displayed a remarkable lack of curiosity about everything outside of their Havana fiefdoms. This was shortsighted, because what was going on was revolution. Outside the cities and towns, Cuba remained backward and divided, with large numbers of peasants exploited by a small group of landowners. Basic services in the countryside were primitive or nonexistent. Three-quarters of the children in rural areas didn't attend school, and 43 percent of agricultural workers were illiterate. Three-quarters of rural dwellings lacked running water.

The spread of communism in the 1920s added an incendiary new element to the already volatile mix. But the figure most associated with Cuban communism, Fidel Castro, didn't embrace the ideology until late in his revolutionary career. In fact, Castro's political mentor, Eduardo Chibas, was a staunch anti-communist, whose Ortodoxo Party simply advocated reforms against corruption and an end to U.S. domination. As for Castro, he married the daughter of a rich family who lavished money on him, funding a long trip to New York—which he seemed to enjoy without qualms—and he was also happy to receive gifts from his friend Batista.

But when Batista's 1952 coup frustrated Castro's political ambitions, Castro turned against his friend and was forced into exile in Mexico. When he returned to Cuba with the veteran guerrilla fighter Che Guevara in December 1956, there was still no trace of communism in his revolutionary program. As Castro's guerrilla army battled Batista's troops in 1957, he benefited from favorable coverage by the American media, who were encouraged by his 1958 promise not to seize foreign investments. After several rebel victories, Batista fled the country on January 1, 1959, taking with him an astounding $300 million. Oh, and he made sure his old friend Lansky got out safely too.

> I don't agree with communism. We are democracy. We are against all kinds of dictators ... That is why we oppose communism.
>
> —Fidel Castro, 1959

In the first half of 1959, Castro still presented himself as a nationalist rather than communist revolutionary—but when President Eisenhower rebuffed the new Cuban government's requests for aid, Castro turned to the Soviets, who were only too happy to get a foothold right off the coast of the United States. Although cooperation was limited at first, Soviet aid to Cuba set off alarm bells in Washington, D.C., and Eisenhower responded by breaking off diplomatic relations in February 1960 ... which of course pushed Castro further into the Soviet camp. In June of 1960, the United States imposed a trade embargo; Castro retaliated by seizing American businesses in Cuba. He also started receiving weapons from the Soviet Union. With the rift now unbridgeable, in April of 1961 President John F. Kennedy gave the green light for a CIA-created army of Cuban exiles to invade the island with the goal of toppling Castro. The far-fetched plan ended in debacle: it turned out the spot selected for the landing, the Bay of Pigs, was Castro's favorite fishing spot. Big mistake. The "secret" incursion was discovered immediately, and JFK sealed its doom by withholding critical air support. The tiny invasion force was mopped up by the Soviet-armed Cuban military in three days.

Kennedy scrambled to contain the public outcry over this defeat (it was especially embarrassing in light of a pledge he'd made just five days earlier not to invade Cuba), but things were only going to get worse. Distrusting the United States more than ever, in September of 1962 Castro allowed the Soviet premier, Nikita Khrushchev, to secretly station medium-range nuclear missiles on Cuba, where they threatened the entire American East Coast. Ironically, Castro believed this would deter future invasions.

On October 15, 1962, an aerial reconnaissance by a U-2 spy plane revealed the existence of the missiles, and it quickly became clear that Cuba had miscalculated. Already humiliated, Kennedy was not going to tolerate another communist affront in "America's backyard." The Cuban Missile Crisis was now in full swing, and for two weeks in October 1962, the world teetered on the brink of nuclear war. On Sunday, October 21, Kennedy ordered a naval blockade to prevent Soviet ships believed to be carrying nuclear weapons from reaching the island. He also ordered a general mobilization in preparation for a full-scale invasion. As follow-up U2 flights revealed the presence of Soviet fighter planes, bombers, and cruise missiles in Cuba, and the U.S. Navy prepared for a standoff with Soviet ships in the mid-Atlantic, Kennedy and his advisors weighed their options.

On Monday, October 22, Kennedy advised the American public of the unfolding crisis in a televised address. This triggered mass hysteria as Americans mobbed supermarkets to stock hastily improvised fallout shelters. On Tuesday, new reconnaissance showed some of the Soviet missiles were ready to launch, but Kennedy decided to pull the naval blockade back, giving Khrushchev more time to negotiate. On Wednesday, most of the Soviet ships slowed down or reversed course, in a small matching concession.

On Thursday, Kennedy sent a letter to Khrushchev blaming Soviet actions for creating the crisis and demanding the removal of all offensive missiles from Cuba. On Friday, Khrushchev appeared ready to compromise, offering to withdraw the missiles from Cuba in exchange for a public pledge from Kennedy never to invade Cuba. Forcing everyone to keep working all weekend, on Saturday Khrushchev also demanded removal of American Jupiter nuclear missiles from Turkey as an added condition. Kennedy sent a letter to Khrushchev in which he agreed to the first condition (promising not to attack Cuba). Finally, on Sunday, October 28, Khrushchev announced in a radio broadcast that he would remove the missiles from Cuba. A few months later—without much commotion—American Jupiter rockets were quietly withdrawn from Turkey as well.

Coup and the Gang

Oh, the leaders you'll shoot. Since both the United States and the Soviets were sure that the fate of the world depended on them, they felt justified in using pretty much any methods they pleased. Here are a few of the CIA's lowlights:

★ **Congo, 1960.** The Belgian Congo was led to independence in June 1960 by 34-year-old Patrice Lumumba, a democratically elected leader whose socialist rhetoric alarmed U.S. officials. President Eisenhower told CIA chief Allen Dulles that Lumumba should be "eliminated." Dulles sent two teams of assassins to Congo, armed with guns and poison. Neither team got a shot at Lumumba, but the CIA still got their man. In September of 1960, he was overthrown by Colonel Joseph Mobutu with help from the CIA. He fled but was captured and murdered in January 1961 by Belgian troops at the behest of the CIA. Mobutu (who took the name Mobutu Sese Seko) went on to be one of the most brutal and corrupt dictators of the twentieth century, which is saying a lot.

★ **Iraq, 1963 and 1968.** This is a twofer, with two CIA-backed coups in Iraq in just five years. First to go was General Abd al-Karim Qasim, who overthrew Iraq's pro-American monarchy in 1958. The last straw was his move to nationalize Iraq's oil industry. Totally unacceptable. In February of 1963, he was overthrown by the new anti-communist Ba'ath Party, supported by the CIA and British intelligence, which embarked on a bloody purge, killing 5,000 communists. But then a countercoup in November of 1963 brought Abdul Salam Arif to power. Arif angered the United States by nationalizing foreign-owned businesses. After his death in 1966, his brother Abdul Rahman pushed Johnson's buttons by siding with Egypt, Syria, and Jordan in the 1967 war with Israel. So in 1968, the CIA supported another Ba'athist coup by Ahmed Hassan al-Bakr and his protégé, Saddam Hussein.

★ **Brazil, 1964.** The United States took a dislike to Brazil's President Joao Goulart after he made a political alliance with Brazil's leftist trade unions and declared his intention to trade with communist countries. On Johnson's order, the CIA provided weapons, supplies, and funding to coup plotters led by General Humberto de Alencar Castello Branco. Johnson also dispatched an emergency airlift of 110 tons of ammunition, as well as a U.S. Navy squadron, sent to cruise off Brazil's northern coast. Branco moved swiftly to ban trade unions and attack Brazil's communists, inaugurating over 20 years of military rule in Brazil—but on the bright side, no communism!

★ **Indonesia, 1965.** Ever since declaring independence in 1945, Indonesia had been ruled by Sukarno, who led the wars of independence against Japanese occupiers and Dutch colonialists. But his ideology—an idiosyncratic mix of moderate Islam and Marxism—simply didn't sit well with the United States (especially in light of Indonesia's abundant oil resources). After supporting a failed coup attempt in 1957–1958, the CIA kept a low profile for a few years. But when Sukarno nationalized U.S. businesses and accepted Soviet military aid in 1965, the United States decided to give it another shot. This time it succeeded. To celebrate, the CIA's new man in Indonesia, General Suharto, launched—you guessed it—a bloody anti-communist purge, which claimed at least 300,000 lives.

★ **Chile, 1973.** Richard Nixon and his national security advisor, Henry Kissinger, loathed Chile's Marxist president Salvador Allende, who took power in 1970 after a close three-way election and steered Chile down a far-left economic path. The CIA favorite to replace Allende was a conservative army officer named Augusto Pinochet. In 1970 the CIA orchestrated the assassination of the commander in chief of the Chilean armed forces and also worked to destabilize Chile with inflation, a collapse of foreign trade, and crippling strikes. Amid this growing chaos, in August 1973 the Chilean parliament asked the military to restore the "rule of law." Pinochet, the new commander in chief, clearly interpreted this as an invitation to stage a coup, which he did after consulting with the CIA on September 11, 1973. Defiant to the end, Allende was killed when Pinochet ordered planes and tanks to attack the presidential palace.

·············· **MADE IN AMERICA** ··················

We Love Rock-n-Roll

While mainstream musical tastes were still dominated by jazz, in the 1950s African-American musicians created a new kind of music to get hearts racing and hips shaking.

Although no one person "invented" rock-n-roll, one of the first musicians to hit it big was Chuck Berry, the son of a construction contractor and school principal from St. Louis, Missouri. Berry considered a few different career paths: photographer, beautician, minor criminal. But in the end, his true love was music. After learning to play blues guitar as a teenager, Berry also picked up country music, switching back and forth to entertain black and white audiences in St. Louis nightclubs. Berry's first hit, "Maybellene," was an old country tune. "Ida Red," which he updated by replacing the fiddle with an electric guitar, revved up to a jumpy blues tempo. The single sold a million records, rocketing Berry to fame and blowing open the rock-n-roll era. In 1956 Berry had another hit, "Roll Over Beethoven," followed by "Rock and Roll Music," "Sweet Sixteen," and the epochal "Johnny B. Goode." As noted, Berry wasn't alone: a number of musicians working in similar musical styles scored hits around the same time, including Riley B. King (B.B. King), Ellas Othat Bates (Bo Diddley), Antoine Dominique (Fats Domino), and Richard Wayne Penniman (Little Richard).

Chuck Berry first demonstrated his trademark "duck walk" as a child, when he used it (to his family's amusement) to retrieve a ball from under the kitchen table.

Like jazz, rock-n-roll crossed over to the white mainstream with remarkable speed, aided by radio, TV, movies, magazines, and newspapers. Not coincidentally, the pioneering white rock-n-roll musicians all grew up in the rural South, where they were exposed to African-American music despite racial segregation. The first and greatest, Elvis Presley, was born in 1935 in a two-room shotgun shack in Tupelo, Mississippi, where he grew up with white gospel and "hillbilly" music, but also black gospel, blues, and boogie-woogie. When he was a teenager, his mother moved the family to Memphis, Tennessee, where he enjoyed the burgeoning country and blues scene and perfected his guitar playing. But Presley remained a shy, withdrawn "mama's boy" until his senior year of high school in 1953, when he performed in a music contest in downtown Memphis. Around this time he established the persona that would make him the world's most famous performing artist—combining unerring musicianship with an unreal singing voice and an unsafe amount of sex appeal. His stage presence was made all the more charming by his approachable, "aw shucks" country boy demeanor when not performing.

Elvis and other white musicians like Buddy Holly and Jerry Lee Lewis made rock-n-roll safe for the white mainstream but naughty enough that it was sure to enrage the older generations. (Lewis, whose first big hit was subtly titled "Great Balls of Fire," scandalized the country by marrying his 13-year-old cousin.) Youthful rebellion remained the hallmark of rock-n-roll, reflecting the broader upheaval in society resulting from baby boomers coming of age. But there was no mistaking its popularity, and "adults" in the entertainment business learned to play along: Ed Sullivan wisely rescinded a ban on Elvis, whom he'd dismissed as unfit for a "family show," and his debut on September 9, 1956, drew 60 million viewers—over one-third of the U.S. population.

The shockwaves from America's collision with rock-n-roll spread out in different directions, leading to an amazing variety of subgenres. On the West Coast it was adopted by the beach-going youth subculture in the form of "surf music." Traveling across the Atlantic, rock-n-roll triggered a musical revolution in Britain. Having embraced and absorbed American rock music, the Brits took it to the next level, emphasizing musicianship, lyrics, and songwriting and experimenting with different tones, rhythms, and composition styles. Also, they turned the volume way up.

Suddenly, the trans-Atlantic dynamic was reversed by the "British Invasion." "Beatle-mania" swept America (74 million viewers tuned into their first performance on the Ed Sullivan Show), followed by the Rolling Stones, the Animals, Manfred Mann, Donovan, and the Kinks. While these bands made their fortunes in the United States, the British rock scene continued innovating, with a second wave of "hard rock" bands featuring virtuoso guitarists playing—incredibly—at an even higher volume. This next wave of bands included The Who and the Yardbirds, some of whom went on to found a second generation of hard rock bands, including Cream and Led Zeppelin.

> ★ George Harrison would later recall nervously thinking during the Beatles' first flight to the United States: "They've got everything over there. What do they want us for?"

But America wasn't about to give up the amps. The flood of British talent was answered by a prodigy from Seattle, James "Jimi" Marshall Hendrix, who became perhaps the greatest rock guitarist ever. Inspired to take up guitar after seeing Elvis perform in 1957, Hendrix started out in conventional R&B bands like the Velvetones and King Kasuals, with a break in 1961–1962 for a very undistinguished stint in the Army. After kicking around Nashville and New York City and touring as backup for the Isley Brothers and Little Richard, in 1966 Hendrix moved to London at the suggestion of Chas Chandler, the bassist for the Animals, where he formed a new band, The Jimi Hendrix Experience.

It was in Britain that the nascent guitar god finally hit it big. At this point both sides of the Atlantic were awash in a sea of psychedelic drugs, and Hendrix was particularly well-lubricated in this regard. In this state he experimented with radical new techniques and sounds. Among other things, Hendrix is remembered for pioneering the use of shrieking feedback—previously avoided as an unpleasant mistake—the "wah-wah" pedal, and "whammy" bar to produce startling effects (for example, making his guitar sound like it was talking). Returning to America, where he headlined Woodstock in 1969, Hendrix transformed the sound of rock-n-roll before his untimely death from a drug overdose in 1970 at the age of 27.

More Things That Go "Boom!"

After the invention of the atomic bomb in 1945, naturally everyone's first thought was: surely there must be some way to make this thing bigger. And sure enough there was: in 1951 two Eastern

European physicists living in the United States—Hungarian Edward Teller and Pole Stanislaw Ulam—designed the first fusion or "hydrogen" bomb. Where the atom bomb had produced energy through fission (splitting atoms), the fusion bomb produced it by pushing atoms together. The largest H-bomb ever built had an explosive power of 100 megatons, equal to 100 million tons of TNT. Or 5,000 times the Nagasaki bomb.

Once this apocalyptic weapon was in hand, naturally everyone's first thought was: we gotta set this thing off somewhere. Thus began a fairly insane marathon of nuclear testing, involving scores of explosions on a scale that made the 1945 Trinity shot look like a small, damp firecracker. After trying out "just" six nuclear devices from 1945 to 1950, the U.S. government tested an incredible 901 fission and fusion bombs from 1951 to 1975, for an average 36 explosions per year. First place goes to 1962, with 170 explosions, and 1958 gets runner-up with 78. The vast majority of these explosions took place at the Nevada Test Site, a 1,350-square-mile swath of desert 65 miles northwest of Las Vegas—but all the really big ones took place outside the continental United States, on remote island chains in the Pacific Ocean.

The most alarming thing about these tests is that they really were tests: the bomb makers had a general idea what was going to happen (loud noise, bright light) but were surprised by a number of duds, or "fizzles," and less frequent but far more unsettling instances of "over-delivery." Take, for example, 1954's "Castle Bravo" test on the Bikini Atoll in the Marshall Islands—the first test of a practical fusion bomb. No question, Castle Bravo was certainly a success: where Teller expected a yield of about 5 megatons, or 250 Nagasakis, the device actually produced an explosion equal to 15 megatons!

After the early 1960s, the United States for the most part stopped testing multi-megaton "strategic" nuclear weapons intended to destroy cities and countries, and in 1963 President John F. Kennedy and Soviet Premier Nikita Khrushchev signed a treaty agreeing to limit weapons testing to underground explosions to, you know, contain the radiation. After that, the United States moved testing away from islands in the Pacific and restricted it to Nevada.

Credit Cards (and the Great Charge Forward)

Sure, getting into debt seems like a long-standing American pastime, but it was a whole lot harder before 1958, when American Express introduced the first modern credit card.

There had been an earlier generation of "credit cards" issued by gas station chains, which allowed consumers to buy gas at stations in different places without carrying cash. And in 1949, Frank McNamara created the Diners' Club credit card after forgetting to bring his wallet to a business dinner. But these early credit cards, usually made out of cardboard, were inconveniently limited to purchases at certain kinds of businesses (gas stations, restaurants, and entertainment). In 1958 there was a breakthrough: American Express produced a card that could be used for purchases at a variety of establishments, and in 1959, the company replaced the cardboard cards with one word: plastic.

Competitors cropped up immediately, and companies gained market share by allowing consumers to maintain a "revolving balance"—meaning you could run up credit card debt. In 1958 Bank of America introduced the BankAmericard, which was then licensed to other banks outside California and branded as Visa in 1970. Meanwhile, in 1966 a group of California banks came together to form the Interbank Card Association, which in turn partnered with a New York bank in 1969 to create a new card called Master Charge (renamed MasterCard in 1979).

The national scope of these bank consortiums and licensing deals allowed them to offer their services to businesses across the country, which in turn helped recruit cardholders who liked the efficiency and ubiquity of the cards. Additional innovations, like the introduction of magnetic stripes in 1970, allowing electronic transmission of purchase and credit information, made credit cards even more convenient and secure. Meanwhile, BankAmericard and Master Charge took a very aggressive approach to marketing, sending out millions of functioning credit cards, unsolicited, to households in their customer databases.

As a result, the number of bank-issued credit cards in circulation soared from just 1.1 million in 1959 to 75 million in 1975. Of course there were some setbacks, as might be expected when inviting millions of people to spend money they don't have: BankAmericard, in particular, had a rather rough launch in 1958–1960, with tens of thousands of customers defaulting. But Bank of America salvaged its product, and Americans have happily put it on credit ever since, with the total amount of credit card debt held by American households increasing from $400 million in 1960 to $9.5 billion in 1975 and almost $1 trillion in 2009!

Charging Ahead

Legend:
- Total # of credit cards
- Total credit card debt

Left axis: Credit cards in circulation (millions) — 5 to 75
Right axis: Credit card debt (billions) — 0.5 to 9.5
X axis: 1958–1975

Richard Nixon (1913–1994)

Born into a poor, pious Quaker family in Yorba Linda, California, on January 9, 1913, Richard Milhouse Nixon was shaped by an austere childhood with parents who forbade alcohol, tobacco, and gambling. His fierce work ethic was paired with enormous ambition, which became all-consuming after the tragic loss to tuberculosis of his two brothers. In 1930—the height of the Great Depression—poverty forced Nixon to turn down Yale and Harvard and enroll at Whittier College, a local Quaker school. After earning his law degree from Duke University, he headed back to California to practice law. In 1938 he met Thelma "Pat" Ryan in a community theater production, and in 1940 they were married.

While serving in the U.S. Navy, Nixon won a large amount of money in poker games (he had some skills, despite his Quaker upbringing), which funded his first campaign for the U.S. House of Representatives in 1946. Over the next six years, first in the House of Representatives and then in the Senate, he won national fame for fighting against communism. In 1952 Dwight D. Eisenhower chose Nixon as his running mate, stifling his personal dislike for the younger man (whom he found arrogant and abrasive) because he needed Nixon's anti-communist credentials.

As the campaign heated up, Illinois Governor and Democratic presidential candidate Adlai Stevenson accused Nixon of accepting cash from rich donors in return for favors. Nixon took to the airwaves to rebut the accusations in a live TV broadcast watched by 60 million Americans. With his wife next to him, Nixon gave an accounting of his finances and then—in a brilliant twist—disclosed the one gift he'd ever accepted: his family's dog, Checkers. The "Checkers" speech, which generated an outpouring of sympathy, was a masterful use of the emerging medium of TV.

> You know what it was? It was a little cocker spaniel dog ... And our little girl—Tricia, the six-year-old—named it Checkers ... and I just want to say this right now, that regardless of what they say about it, we're gonna keep it.
>
> —Richard Nixon

But eight years later, after losing his 1960 run for the White House to John F. Kennedy amid accusations of voter fraud in Illinois and Texas, Nixon retired from politics to write his memoirs and practice law. A failed 1962 bid for governor of California seemed to seal his fate, until the crisis in Vietnam and domestic upheavals gave him a new lease on life, as an anti-communist stalwart and advocate of "decency and order." With his competition falling one by one (Johnson declined to run, Robert Kennedy was assassinated, and Vice President Hubert Humphrey was tainted by the Democratic Convention protests), in November, Nixon won with 43.4 percent of the popular vote.

If it weren't for Watergate, Nixon would rank as one of America's greatest presidents. On the domestic front he signed new civil rights legislation, created the Environmental Protection Agency and signed the Clean Air Act of 1970, boosted spending on social services, passed pioneering consumer protections, and mandated the first fuel efficiency rules. In foreign policy he made the best of a bad situation in Vietnam, withdrawing troops while continuing to support the South Vietnamese with air power. Then in February 1972 he shocked the world by visiting China for a historic meeting with Mao Zedong. Nixon exploited tension between China and the Soviets to turn the communist powers against each other while improving U.S. relations with both—a clever gambit that National Security Advisor Henry Kissinger called "triangular diplomacy." And Americans were fans: in 1972 Nixon won reelection with 47.2 million votes—equal to 60.7 percent of the popular vote.

Still, "Tricky Dick" could hold a grudge, and as president he grew paranoid about "traitors" leaking unflattering secrets. So in July 1971 he ordered his domestic advisor, John Ehrlichman, to organize a covert group, "the Plumbers," to "plug leaks" in the White House by figuring out who was talking to the press. Ehrlichman put his friend Egil Krogh in charge, who in turn recruited a CIA agent, Howard Hunt, and an eccentric ex-FBI agent, G. Gordon Liddy.

Before long the Plumbers were engaged in political espionage. On May 28 and June 17, 1972, they broke into the headquarters of the Democratic National Committee at the Watergate Hotel in Washington, D.C. The second time they got caught. In January 1973, seven men, including Hunt and Liddy, were found guilty of conspiracy, burglary, and illegal wiretapping. The FBI then followed a financial paper trail linking them to a political group, the Committee to Re-elect the President (CREEP, to their foes), whose members included White House counsel John Dean and former Attorney General John Mitchell.

At this point two reporters for *The Washington Post*, Bob Woodward and Carl Bernstein, began reporting that knowledge of Watergate and other illegal activities went much higher than previously suspected, citing an unnamed source with the bizarrely inappropriate codename "Deep Throat" (identified in 2005 as William Mark Felt, Sr., the former deputy director of the FBI). Felt implicated scores of people in the FBI, CIA, and Justice Department. In February 1973, acting FBI director L. Patrick Gray told senators he gave FBI files on Watergate to Dean—implying the White House was secretly undermining the investigation.

With the scandal exploding, Nixon scrambled first to pin responsibility on Dean, Ehrlichman, and White House Chief of Staff H.R. Haldeman, then pretended to cooperate by appointing a new attorney general, Elliot Richardson, and special prosecutor, Archibald Cox. But in May of 1973, the Senate opened its own inquiry. In June, Dean testified that he'd paid "hush money" to the Watergate burglars, implicating Nixon in the cover-up. Then in July, Haldeman's assistant, Alexander Butterfield, disclosed the existence of a secret White House recording system installed at Nixon's order. (Why you'd want to record criminal acts is unclear.)

With the entire country in an uproar, Cox subpoenaed the tapes—but Nixon refused, citing executive privilege. He tried to have the special prosecutor quietly canned, but Attorney General Richardson refused to fire Cox—so Nixon fired Richardson. When Richardson's deputy, William Ruckelshaus, also refused to fire Cox, Nixon fired him too. On his third try he found someone willing to fire Cox—Solicitor General Robert Bork—but it was a Pyrrhic victory: the "Saturday Night Massacre" just made Nixon look guiltier than ever.

> **I'm not a crook!**
> —Richard Nixon, November 17, 1973

Nixon was forced to appoint a new special prosecutor, Leon Jaworksi, and agreed to release transcripts of the tapes—one of which had an 18.5-minute gap in the middle. As Congress prepared three charges of impeachment—obstruction of justice, abuse of power, and contempt of Congress—the missing tape was finally made public. In it Nixon and Haldeman discussed having the CIA block the FBI investigation by (falsely) claiming it involved national security.

The jig was up: this super-incriminating conversation, which could be summarized "screw the Constitution," made a guilty verdict unavoidable. On August 8, 1974, Nixon became the only president in U.S. history to resign from office. A month later his successor, Gerald Ford, gave him an unconditional pardon. Altogether, 40 other federal officials were indicted during Watergate.

·················· **BY THE NUMBERS** ··················

58,202 U.S. troops killed in Vietnam War
223,748 South Vietnamese troops killed in Vietnam War
1.1 million approximate number of North Vietnamese troops killed in Vietnam War
4 million civilians killed in Vietnam War, in North and South Vietnam
14 percent proportion of total Vietnamese population killed in the Vietnam War
10.6 percent proportion of U.S. military personnel in Vietnam who were African-American
13.5 percent proportion of African-Americans in the U.S. population during this period
19 average age of U.S. GIs in Vietnam

$68.4 billion U.S. government spending, 1955

17.3 percent proportion of total U.S. gross domestic product this represented

$332.3 billion U.S. government spending, 1975

21.3 percent proportion of U.S. GDP this represented

9 number of McDonald's restaurants, 1955

3,076 number of McDonald's restaurants, 1975

4.5 percent proportion of U.S. births out of wedlock, 1955

14.2 percent proportion of U.S. births out of wedlock, 1975

145 new cases of gonorrhea reported per 100,000 Americans, 1955

468 new cases of gonorrhea reported per 100,000 Americans, 1975

57,115 number of foreign automobiles imported by the United States, 1955

1.3 million number of foreign automobiles imported by the United States, 1975

3 billion barrels of oil consumed by the United States in 1955

10 percent proportion of this that was imported

6 billion barrels of oil consumed by the United States in 1975

33 percent proportion of this that was imported

90 calories in the largest McDonald's soda, 1955

250 calories in the largest McDonald's soda, 1975

Morning in America?

(1975–1992)

············ **THE STATE OF THE UNION** ············

After the disastrous 1960s and 1970s, Americans were disillusioned by defeat in Vietnam, dishonesty in Watergate, and disco on the dance floor. But things were about to turn around. Exhausted by the honest, earnest pessimism of Jimmy Carter, in 1980 Americans elected the sunny, congenial Ronald Reagan, who told them, "It's Morning in America." Like his Republican predecessor Richard Nixon, Reagan was short on details but long on optimism . . . and it worked: Reagan promised that whatever problems the country faced, Americans had the strength and spirit to overcome them.

> They say that the United States has had its days in the sun, that our nation has passed its zenith. They expect you to tell your children that the American people no longer have the will to cope with their problems, that the future will be one of sacrifice and few opportunities. My fellow citizens, I utterly reject that view.
>
> —Ronald Reagan, 1980

As president, Reagan managed to restore America's dwindling mojo, lift the economy out of the doldrums, and revitalize its damaged, demoralized military, all while soothing partisan rancor with his folksy personal style. He won the votes of "Reagan Democrats" by reminding Americans of the continuing Soviet threat to the "free world" (something of a misnomer, since it included many pro-American dictators) and by advocating for a strong, unapologetic role for the United States in world affairs. Reagan massively increased the American defense budget and mounted overt and covert interventions to reverse communist gains. Some of these were of questionable legality—okay, they were illegal—but with his avuncular charm and bad memory, Reagan never seemed to get caught. Just his subordinates.

This isn't to say everything was peachy at home: the 1980s will be remembered for some of the worst social problems in American history, including a wave of crime associated with the drug of the moment—cocaine, first in powdered form, then as smokable "crack" rocks. Crack contributed to the continuing disintegration of inner cities, which reached "rock" bottom in this period. The end of this period also brought a sharp economic downturn and the most costly episode of urban mayhem in American history—the L.A. riots—which revealed deep rifts in American society. Meanwhile, a terrifying new disease, HIV-AIDS, emerged in America's gay subculture before migrating to the heterosexual mainstream, spreading through sexual contact, shared needles among IV drug users, and (in the early stages of the epidemic) blood transfusions.

On the other hand, there were amazing technological advances that transformed the American economy and then the world. The most important by far was the personal computer, pioneered by Apple in 1976 and extended to the masses by PCs equipped with Microsoft Windows. The personal computing revolution paved the way for the later expansion of the Internet—a new technology that remained a relative rarity in this period. In foreign affairs the United States was more powerful than ever, winning the First Gulf War and then—quite unexpectedly—the Cold War, with the shocking collapse of the Soviet Union in 1991.

··············· **WHAT HAPPENED WHEN** ··················

April 4, 1975 Microsoft founded by Bill Gates in Albuquerque, New Mexico.

April 1, 1976 Apple I, the first personal computer, unveiled.

May 1976 Hard rock band Blue Öyster Cult releases "Don't Fear the Reaper."

July 4, 1976 United States celebrates bicentennial.

January 21, 1977 President Carter pardons Vietnam draft dodgers on his first day in office.

September 5–12, 1978 Carter presides over historic Camp David peace accords between Egypt and Israel.

January 17 and February 1, 1979	Shah Pahlavi flees Iran; Ayatollah Khomeini returns from exile to lead country.
November 4, 1979	Iranian students storm U.S. Embassy in Teheran, hold workers hostage.
December 24, 1979	Soviets invade Afghanistan to crush U.S.-backed *mujahedin*.
July 19–August 3, 1980	United States boycotts Summer Olympics in Moscow.
September 22, 1980	Iraqi dictator Saddam Hussein invades Iran.
November 4, 1980	Republican Ronald Reagan unseats incumbent President Jimmy Carter.
January 20, 1981	U.S. embassy hostages are released hours after Reagan is inaugurated.
August 12, 1981	IBM launches first PC.
September 25, 1981	Sandra Day O'Connor becomes first female U.S. Supreme Court justice.
June–July 1981	First reports of gay men dying from AIDS in New York, L.A., and San Francisco.
August 1, 1981	MTV launches.
January 24, 1984	Apple Macintosh debuts.
January 28, 1986	Space shuttle Challenger explodes on liftoff, killing seven.
October 19, 1987	U.S. stock market crashes; stock values dive 508.32 points, or 22.6 percent.
November 8, 1988	Vice President George H.W. Bush beats Massachusetts Governor Michael Dukakis in race for president.
November 9, 1989	Berlin Wall falls.
August 2, 1990	Iraq invades Kuwait.
January 16–February 27, 1991	United States leads international coalition to liberate Kuwait in Operation Desert Storm.
November 7, 1991	Earvin "Magic" Johnson announces he has HIV.

December 8, 1991 Soviet Union collapses.

April 29–May 4, Not-guilty verdict in Rodney King beating case
1992 triggers L.A. riots.

LIE: *The Republicans got evangelical*
Christians involved in politics.

THE TRUTH: It was the Democrats—specifically, Jimmy Carter—
who politicized evangelical Christians during the 1976 presidential
race. The Dems just couldn't hold on to them.

Before 1976 neither party had a real claim on evangelical Protestants. In 1964 moderate Southern Baptists voted for Lyndon
Johnson out of regional loyalty, but evangelical support was fleeting. Horrified by the wave of drug use, casual sex, and "heathen
cults" that swept the country in the late 1960s, in 1968 they
switched to Republican Richard Nixon, a pious Quaker, who ran
as the champion of decency and order. But then in 1974, they were
shocked by Nixon's dishonesty in Watergate (not to mention the
unrelenting stream of profanity on White House tapes that surfaced during the scandal). Evangelicals were further angered by
Gerald Ford's pardon of the ex-president, contrary to their ideals
of personal responsibility.

History suggested the disillusioned evangelicals would join
fundamentalists in withdrawing from politics altogether, but
there was a new activist impulse at work, inspired by moral issues:
in 1969 evangelicals in Anaheim, California, drew national attention with protests against a sex education curriculum planned
for the city's public schools, followed in 1974 by a similar protest
against sex ed in Kanawha County, West Virginia. Then the Democrats surprised everyone by nominating a "born-again" Southern
evangelical to run for president in 1976.

Georgia Governor Jimmy Carter hit all the right issues, la-
menting "the loss of stability and loss of values in our lives,"
which he blamed on "the steady erosion and weakening of our
families." He promised to tackle divorce, illegitimacy, and drug
abuse, but his most important promise was also the simplest: "I
will never lie to you." This stance won him the support of televan-
gelists like Pat Robertson, who told millions of viewers "we have
an unprecedented opportunity for America to fulfill the dream of

the early settlers . . . that this land would be used to glorify God."
Bailey Smith, a prominent figure among Southern Baptists,
opined, "This country needs a born-again man in the White House.
And his initials are the same as our Lord's."

Overall, Carter took about half the evangelical vote in 1976, a
huge increase from the 20 percent who voted Democrat four years
before. He also took 59.1 percent of the Southern Baptist vote
versus 37.6 percent for Ford, helping secure his victory in Southern states. Up north, born-again evangelicals favored Carter 58
percent–33 percent, giving him the margin of victory in important swing states like Ohio and Pennsylvania. Of course, Carter's
narrow win was also due to strong support from other constituencies, including over 90 percent of the African-American vote.
But 1976 marked the first time a presidential candidate had targeted evangelicals as a distinct political bloc, and they responded
with dramatic results. Little wonder, then, that *Time* and *News-
week* both declared 1976 "The Year of the Evangelical."

When Carter failed to deliver on his promises, however, the
powerful forces he summoned turned against him. He admitted
(in *Playboy*, no less) to having "lusted in his heart" for women besides his wife, put no evangelicals in high-ranking positions, sidestepped issues like abortion and school prayer, and supported the
hated Equal Rights Amendment backed by feminists. Indeed it
looked like he'd broken his most important promise—not to lie.
Meanwhile, the fundamentalists reemerged onto the scene, shocked
by the "decay" of American society and disillusioned with Carter,
exploiting evangelical anger to take leadership positions in once-
moderate organizations. Before long evangelicals and fundamentalists had recombined forces in a broader political movement,
which eventually included even Catholics—a complete revolution
for American Protestants, who had long viewed the Vatican as
Public Enemy No. 1.

> In reality, there is little difference theologically between
> Fundamentalists and Evangelicals . . . We Fundamentalists
> have much to offer our Evangelical brethren that they need.
> We preach the Bible with authority and conviction. Where
> they hesitate and equivocate, we loudly thunder,
> "Thus saith the Lord!"
>
> —Jerry Falwell, 1981

In 1978 fundamentalists rallied the troops to protest an IRS decision revoking the tax-exempt status of Bible colleges like Bob Jones University that practiced de facto racial segregation. Media continued to be a crucial organizational tool: James Dobson drummed up support via his radio program "Focus on the Family," launched in 1977, while Falwell used his TV pulpit and national speaking tours to raise awareness. At the same time fundamentalist leaders also moved quietly to seize power in key organizations: during the annual meeting of the Southern Baptist Convention in Houston in 1979, fundamentalist Baptists implemented a secret plan to purge the organization of liberals over the next decade. (By 1988 fundamentalists had complete control.)

When Carter failed to affirm his opposition to abortion in 1979, an ultraconservative Catholic, Paul Weyrich, helped Falwell found the Moral Majority, a lobbying group whose first project was campaigning for Ronald Reagan (not an evangelical, but he seemed to hold their views on abortion, school prayer, and taxes). The Moral Majority claimed it registered 2 million–4 million fundamentalist voters for the 1980 presidential election, giving Reagan 63 percent of the evangelical vote, including 61 percent of the white born-again vote and half the Southern Baptists. In the end, Reagan didn't actually do much for evangelical causes, but he did restore battered American self-confidence, and everyone likes a winner. Evangelicals have voted Republican ever since.

LIE: *The United States supported Osama bin Laden in the 1980s.*

THE TRUTH: While the United States historically has supported an awful lot of awful people, this one is a blatant conspiracy theory. The story goes like this: in the 1980s the United States supported Afghan guerrilla fighters resisting the Soviet invasion of their country. Osama bin Laden also supported the resistance fighters; therefore, the United States supported Osama bin Laden. And that's it. But there is no evidence, none, that the United States had anything to do with bin Laden before, during, or after the war of resistance in Afghanistan.

U.S. involvement in Afghanistan began on July 3, 1979, when President Jimmy Carter ordered the CIA to provide covert support to guerrilla fighters (*mujahedin*) opposing the communist regime in Kabul. This followed a series of American diplomatic victories in the region: in 1978–1979, the United States had coaxed Iraqi leader Saddam Hussein into friendlier relations, reconciled with Turkey after the controversy over Cyprus, and brokered a peace agreement between Israel and Egypt. Fearing another American victory in the global checkers game that was the Cold War, in December of 1979, Leonid Brezhnev—the senile premier of the Soviet Union—ordered the Red Army to occupy Afghanistan and prop up the hated communist regime in Kabul. Of course, this just ended up making things a thousand times worse, which was the American plan all along.

> It was on July 3, 1979 that President Carter signed the first directive for secret aid to the opponents of the pro-Soviet regime in Kabul . . . That secret operation was an excellent idea. It had the effect of drawing the Soviets into the Afghan trap.
>
> —Former U.S. Secretary of State Zbigniew Brzezinski, 1998

It worked like a charm. Before you could say "Zbigniew Brzezinski," the Soviet invasion triggered an international outcry, turning world opinion against the Kremlin. Meanwhile, the Red Army waded into a deep pile of guerrilla feces in Afghanistan, noted for its rugged terrain and national pastime of killing strangers. Better still, in all the indignation the rest of the world (temporarily) forgot about the U.S. debacle in Vietnam.

Toward the end of the Carter administration, the CIA initiated "Operation Cyclone," delivering money and weapons to the Afghan guerillas via Pakistan, an American ally since the 1950s—but at this point the level of funding ($20 million–$30 million in 1980) was too low to have any real impact on the course of the war. That changed when a U.S. congressman from Texas named Charlie Wilson took an interest in the Afghan resistance and—at the urging of CIA Director William Casey and CIA Afghan task force chief Gust Avrakotos—persuaded Congress to funnel more and more money and weapons to the mujahedin, reaching about $600 million per year by the mid-1980s. Congress also agreed to send billions of dollars in aid to Pakistan to keep things running smoothly, including emergency relief for millions of Afghan refugees. Meanwhile, American allies, led by Saudi Arabia, also poured billions of dollars into the resistance.

So where was Osama bin Laden during all this? To hear him tell it, bin Laden—who was studying economics at Saudi Arabia's King Abdul Aziz University—dropped everything to fly to Afghanistan just a few weeks after the Soviet invasion in December 1979. Other accounts say he didn't head north until more than a year later. Either way, bin Laden was definitely in the area by 1981. In the area—but not in Afghanistan. Bin Laden spent most of the war in Pakistan, where he used the personal fortune he inherited from his father, a Saudi construction tycoon, to build roads for bringing in supplies and to set up camps and religious schools (*madrassas*) where new mujahedin could train, safe from Soviet attack.

Since the entire system of foreign support technically didn't exist, there was no official oversight or coordination between the CIA and the other foreign intelligence agencies. And that's how they wanted it: the chaotic situation allowed the agencies to cooperate when necessary, but also try to outmaneuver each other by forging secret alliances with their favorite mujahedin leaders. The CIA secretly backed a warlord named Abdul Haq, while bin Laden channeled Saudi funding to a handful of Afghan mujahedin leaders who subscribed to Wahhabism, Saudi Arabia's particularly strict and militant brand of Islam. Bin Laden followed orders from Saudi intelligence chief Prince Turki, who insisted that all contact with foreign agencies be handled by headquarters in Riyadh—not field operatives. This is important because it means bin Laden never had contact with the CIA.

The closest the CIA ever came to bin Laden was through its relationship with Abdullah Yusuf Azzam, a former teacher of bin Laden's who worked with him in Peshawar, Pakistan. The organization Azzam founded in 1984, *Maktab al-Khadamat,* or "Services Office," played a key role in recruiting young Muslim men from all over the world to fight in Afghanistan, and it was definitely supported by the ISI (Pakistan's intelligence service) with funds from the CIA and Saudi intelligence (the GID). But there's no evidence for CIA contact with bin Laden through Azzam, who tried to keep the agency in the dark about the extent of his Saudi support.

So no, it looks like the United States didn't support bin Laden in Afghanistan. But does that really matter? While the CIA may not have had contact with bin Laden specifically, it unquestionably helped turn Islamist extremism into the global threat it is today. When the Afghans fell to fighting each other in the mid-1980s, the CIA and its allies decided to focus on recruiting foreign Muslim fighters, who were felt to be more committed. To rally Muslim support, they portrayed the Afghan resistance as a *jihad* (holy war) pitting Islam against the Soviet infidels, and created a global network of Islamist charities to raise funds and recruit new jihadists.

Not everyone thought this was such a hot idea: in 1989 Benazir Bhutto, the prime minister of Pakistan, warned President George Bush, "You are creating a Frankenstein." But by then it was too late.

LIE: *Al Gore said he invented the Internet.*

THE TRUTH: Gore's political rivals said he said this, to make him look silly during the 2000 presidential election. Shocking, we know.

Gore made the now-infamous statement on March 9, 1999, during an interview with CNN's Wolf Blitzer, who asked the vice president and aspiring presidential candidate what qualities and accomplishments distinguished him from his main competitor in the Democratic primary, Senator Bill Bradley. As part of a longer answer (no one ever said he invented brevity) Gore said: "During my service in the United States Congress, I took the initiative in creating the Internet. I took the initiative in moving forward a whole range of initiatives that have proven to be important to our country's economic growth."

While this is a bold claim, "took the initiative in creating" is not the same as "invented." The latter summons up a cinematic montage of Gore writing equations in a white lab coat, laying fiber-optic cable in a hardhat, and sharing a cup of tea with a housewife while explaining how to use e-mail; the former suggests that he played a key role in a broader congressional effort to formulate policies that enabled other people (engineers and computer scientists) to make the Internet what it is today. And that is pretty close to the truth.

Indeed, Al Gore was well aware that the "Internet" was already in existence when he was first elected to Congress in 1977. The groundwork for the Internet was laid in the late 1960s by researchers at leading California universities who invented a way to transmit information by breaking large amounts of data into smaller "packets," which could be sent to multiple computers simultaneously. This pioneering digital network was organized and funded by the Advanced Research Projects Agency (ARPA), the Pentagon's cutting-edge research and development division, as a way of sharing information between research sites: ARPANET's first four routers were located at UCLA, UC Santa Barbara, Stanford, and the University of Utah. As more schools and labs were added, the network grew from four routers in 1969 to 40 in 1972. In 1975, when there were 57 routers (including some in Europe), ARPA handed the Net over to the Pentagon, which planned to use it as a back up in case other communications were knocked out by a Soviet first strike.

★ *The first spam e-mail was sent out via ARPANET in May 1978 by a marketing rep at Digital Equipment Corporation. Quite accidentally, he'd sent out an invitation to an open house to every person in the ARPANET directory instead of just his intended recipients.*

Al Gore played an early, central role in making the growing network available for nonmilitary use. One year after the Pentagon separated the military and civilian parts of the network in 1983, Gore supported initiatives by NASA, the Department of Energy, and the National Science Foundation to build new "wide area networks" (WAN). To speed this process, in 1986 Gore authored the Supercomputer Network Act, which funded research to expand connections between universities and federal research facilities using high-capacity fiber-optic cables.

In 1988 the Pentagon announced it would phase out ARPANET by 1990, prompting universities, industry, and other civilian users to expand the nonmilitary network. At the urging of these groups, in 1988 Gore authored legislation allocating federal funds to connect 1,000 academic and other civilian networks to form an "information superhighway." This evolved into the National High-Performance Computing and Communications Act, a $1.7 billion project linking universities, libraries, government facilities, and industrial labs in a common network. The NHPCCA—otherwise known as the "Gore Bill"—also funded computer scientists at the University of Illinois at Champaign-Urbana who developed Mosaic, the first graphic Web browser, which inspired successors like Netscape Navigator and Internet Explorer.

The 1992 expiration date set for funding from the National Science Foundation raised the question of how to finance further expansion. Again, Gore was instrumental in getting Congress to pass the Information Infrastructure and Technology Act of 1992, which allowed businesses and individuals to use the Internet for commercial purposes. There was no question Gore understood the broader implications of his policies: rallying support for the NHPCCA in the House of Representatives in 1989, he told committee members, "I genuinely believe that the creation of this nationwide network will create an environment where work stations are common in homes and even small businesses."

Some years later, Gore's colleagues and leading computer scientists stepped up to defend his claim that he "took the initiative in creating the Internet." In September 2000, Newt Gingrich, a former GOP Speaker of the House, said, "Gore is the person who, in the Congress, most systematically worked to make sure that we got to an Internet." Meanwhile Vinton Cerf—who played a key role in designing the basic architecture and core protocols of the Internet and is sometimes credited as the "father of the Internet"—recalled that "Al Gore was the first political leader to recognize the importance of the Internet and to promote and support its development . . . long before most people were listening."

···················· **SPECIAL REPORT**···············

Riot Here, Riot Now

After the civil rights movement, whites were eager to turn the page. After all, the country had finally dealt with the legacy of 300 years of racist oppression of African-Americans. Phew!

Actually, the optimists were half right. From 1950 to 1975, the number of blacks living in poverty dropped from 75 percent to 31 percent as per capita income rose from $810 to $2,980 ($7,150 to $10,800 in 2008 dollars). Adult illiteracy fell from 10 percent to 2 percent, and the number of African-Americans enrolled in four-year colleges increased fivefold to 665,000. And the numbers don't lie, right? Well, it turns out these gains weren't shared evenly by the community: as things got better for the rising African-American middle class, they got worse for an increasingly destitute and desperate "underclass." While there had always been an African-American class hierarchy, beginning around 1970, the internal divisions became increasingly pronounced,

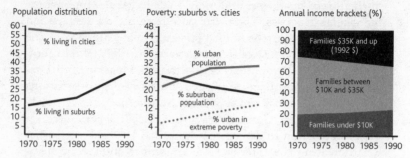

Middle Class on the Move
Socioeconomic polarization in the African-American community

Population distribution

% living in cities

% living in suburbs

1970 1975 1980 1985 1990

Poverty: suburbs vs. cities

% urban population

% suburban population

% urban in extreme poverty

1970 1975 1980 1985 1990

Annual income brackets (%)

Families $35K and up (1992 $)

Families between $10K and $35K

Families under $10K

1970 1975 1980 1985 1990

forming two distinct communities that continued to drift further apart.

Following the earlier pattern of "white flight" from cities to suburbs, the African-American middle class left ghettoes for suburban neighborhoods with lower crime rates, better schools, and higher property values. From 1970 to 1990, the number of African-Americans living in suburbs jumped from 3.6 million to 10.2 million. However "black flight" contributed to an even greater concentration of poverty in central cities. The total number of African-Americans living in poverty in the ghettoes increased from 2.9 million in 1970 to 5.3 million in 1990, from 13 percent to 18 percent of the African-American population.

In many cities the tax base tumbled to new lows, inevitably sending public education, transportation, law enforcement, and sanitation into a nosedive. Although the phenomenon was widespread, some cases stand out for sheer awfulness. From 1970 to 1990, the unfortunate city of East St. Louis, Illinois, saw its population dwindle from 70,000 to 40,000, while tax revenues plunged from $175 million to under $50 million. Thirty percent of the city's buildings were abandoned, and garbage collection simply ceased from 1987 to 1992. As mountains of stinking garbage piled up, the city pumps broke, backing up raw sewage into schools and forming a sewage "lake" in the courtyard of one housing project. Police and firefighters went on strike for unpaid wages, city hall was sold to pay down the debt, and traffic lights were turned off because of overdue bills.

As if things weren't bad enough, the arrival of crack in 1984 took U.S. urban blight to the next level, transforming ghettoes into burned-out, postapocalyptic war zones in just a few short years. By 1990 half a million people reported using crack in the previous month, almost all in urban areas. Crime rates surged, with the number of young African-American men murdered each year tripling between 1985 and 1992. From 1975 to 1992, the number of African-American men in prison almost quadrupled, to 425,000, or 50 percent of the total prison population. In 1991 the Justice Department estimated that an African-American male born that year had a 28 percent chance of going to prison someday.

Most Americans did their best to ignore deteriorating conditions in inner cities. But there were occasional updates in the form of eruptions of civil disorder: clear expressions of discontent within this crushing urban poverty. The most spectacular outbreak occurred in Los Angeles in 1992. Racial tensions were already running high following news broadcasts of a videotape showing six white LAPD officers beating an African-American motorist, Rodney King, who they pulled over after a high-speed chase on the night of March 3, 1991. The police later testified that King—whose blood alcohol limit was twice the legal level—hit one of the officers, lunged for another's gun, and didn't stop after two shocks from a Tazer, leading them to conclude he was on PCP.

All this allegedly occurred before George Holliday, a resident in a nearby apartment block, began videotaping the incident; the video showed King being kicked six times while receiving 56 blows from nightsticks, attempting to crawl out of the circle of police officers, and on one occasion rising to his knees before being knocked over again. King was treated for a broken ankle, a facial fracture, and many cuts and bruises; a nurse later testified she heard the officers joking about the beating.

After the LAPD declined to investigate Holliday's complaint, he took the video to a local TV station, KTLA, which aired it on the local news. The video was soon picked up by CNN and other national news outlets. The resulting outcry prompted L.A.'s district attorney to charge four of the officers with using excessive force. At first, a guilty verdict seemed like a foregone conclusion—until the trial venue was moved to Simi Valley, a white, conservative suburb northwest of L.A. There, a jury composed of 10 whites, one Asian, and one Latino acquitted the officers of almost all charges.

The verdicts were handed down at 3:10 p.m. on Wednesday, April 29, 1992, and by 3:45 p.m. an angry crowd of several hundred had gathered in front of the L.A. County Courthouse; the first reports of looting came around 6:15 p.m. LAPD helicopters took fire from rooftop snipers (who also forced LAX air traffic control to reroute planes until flights were canceled), but TV news helicopters went unmolested, and for the first time ever, Americans could watch a riot unfold, live, with a bird's-eye view of the action. The first report of arson came at 7:45 p.m., and soon south central L.A. was ablaze. By nightfall, there were over 500 fires ravaging the city. L.A.'s African-American mayor, Tom Bradley, declared a dusk-to-dawn curfew in south central L.A., and California governor Pete Wilson ordered the mobilization of 2,000 National Guardsmen.

> Gangs in earlier years were rather benign. They settled their differences with chains, baseball bats, and knives; guns were comparatively rare. In 1992 they had literally thousands of guns, many of them better than ours.
>
> —Major General James Delk,
> California National Guard

On Thursday, April 30, the sun rose over a paralyzed city, as all public transportation in L.A. was suspended and all public schools were closed. The second day of rioting brought more arson and looting, and on Friday, May 1, President George H .W. Bush mobilized federal troops to restore order. Still, the violence continued unabated until Saturday, when 8,000 local law enforcement officers were reinforced by 10,000 National Guardsmen, 3,500 Army soldiers, 1,500 Marines, and 1,000 U.S. Marshals.

By Monday evening the riots were over, leaving 53 dead, 2,400 injured, and 12,100 in jail. Seven thousand fires had destroyed 613 buildings and damaged another 960, while looters robbed and vandalized 2,700 businesses, many of which never reopened. The total cost of the damage was $1.5 billion, almost all in African-American neighborhoods. As in previous riots, most of the victims were also minorities: the death toll included 25 African-Americans, 16 Latinos, 8 whites, 2 Asians, and 2 immigrants from the Middle East.

Shirt Happens
The Shirt Off Men's Backs

Men have always enjoyed looking at women, but ogling had mostly been a one-way street in the modern era. Hollywood had acknowledged women's appreciation of male physical beauty in the first decades of the twentieth century, when audiences swooned for movie stars like Rudolph Valentino and Douglas Fairbanks. But displays were still fairly modest, focusing on handsome features accentuated by well-tailored suits (or in Valentino's case, flowing robes), which only hinted at the body underneath. Likewise in the 1940s, leading men like Clark Gable and Cary Grant built careers on a handsome smile, while Humphrey Bogart was admired more for his cool demeanor than good looks. By contrast, female stars like Marilyn Monroe, Betty Grable, Doris Day, Deborah Kerr, and Debbie Reynolds showed a lot of skin in an endless parade of movies set near beaches or swimming pools.

> ★ *Clark Gable's dazzling smile was the result of a full set of porcelain dentures; he'd had most of his teeth extracted in 1933.*

In the 1960s actresses like Liz Taylor, Julie Christie, and Bridget Bardot graduated to bikinis, but men still didn't show much skin—which was strange, considering the very positive audience reactions when movies did stray into beefcake country: the famous surf kiss between Burt Lancaster and Deborah Kerr in "From Here to Eternity" (which also featured a shirtless Montgomery Clift), Marlon Brando doffing his shirt in "A Streetcar Named Desire" in 1951, and a young Paul Newman doing the same—repeatedly—in "Cat on a Hot Tin Roof," in 1958. Also, anything starring James Dean.

Nevertheless, it wasn't until the 1970s that male beauty emerged as a subject of public discussion, thanks to feminists (who were on one hand reluctant to declare their appreciation for anything man-related, but at the same time determined to even the score in the objectification game). In 1972 Burt Reynolds posed for his famous centerfold in *Cosmopolitan* magazine, 1973 brought the debut of *Playgirl*, and in 1975 *Ms.* magazine published a "Men's Issue" with Robert Redford's lats on the cover. *New York* magazine noted, "Women are admitting to being turned on by male cheesecake, a situation inconceivable until now."

The 1980s brought more open ogling of the male form, focusing on a new generation of male "sex symbols." In 1980 Richard Gere started things off with a bang in "American Gigolo," causing a minor uproar with a few moments of blurry full-frontal nudity, and 1982's "Rambo: First Blood" featured a muscle-bound Sylvester Stallone. In 1983 Tom Cruise hit it big with his role as a young basketball player in "All the Right Moves," heralding a career built on beefcake, including "Risky Business" (1983) and "Top Gun" (1986). In 1987 "Dirty Dancing" centered on Patrick Swayze's sweaty torso, and Mel Gibson won critical acclaim for walking around bare-bottomed in "Lethal Weapon."

But men had one more step to take before catching up with women in the objectification game: nudity for the sole purpose of selling consumer goods. This proud moment finally came in 1982, when fashion designer Calvin Klein began plastering bill-

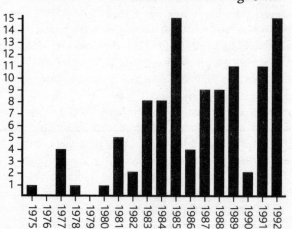

Number of Times "Hunk" Is Used in Reference to a Man in Time *and* New York *Magazines*

boards and magazines with artfully titillating underwear ads. In 1992 Klein catapulted to national prominence with ads showing 21-year-old Mark Wahlberg, still known by his stage name, Marky Mark, wearing Klein's iconic boxer briefs. Finally, gender equality—at least, on the nearly naked front.

Losing Our Shirts to Pay for Health Care

In 1975 Americans spent $133 billion, or $590 per person, on health care, including prescriptions, surgery, and hospital bills. In 1992 health-care spending totaled $839 billion, or $3,288 per person (which is $1,256 per person in 1975 dollars). What the health happened?

In fact, the increased cost of health care was (partly) a positive trend, reflecting the improved quality of health care available to ordinary people. After taking the lead in medical research in the 1950s, America generated a flood of new medications, surgical techniques, and devices to prolong and improve the quality of life. From 1975 to 1992, average American life expectancy rose from 72.6 to 75.8, thanks to advances on multiple fronts, with the death rate for heart disease falling 16 percent and the five-year survival rate for cancer increasing from 48 percent to 60 percent. This included big gains in five-year survival for breast cancer (from 75 percent to 85 percent), melanoma (67 percent–88 percent), childhood leukemia (50 percent–85 percent), and prostate cancer (67 percent–97 percent). Go America!

Many of these improvements were made possible by expensive new technologies or medicines that cost a lot of money to develop—in 1992 alone, pharmaceutical companies spent an average $500 million on research and development for each new drug. Higher survival rates were also due to Americans getting more regular checkups and screenings, which also cost more money. At $100 per mammogram, for example, breast cancer screenings cost about $2 billion per year in the early 1990s. Last but not least, the fact that Americans were living longer raised costs in areas like nursing home care and prescription drugs. In short, as with most goods and services, as people wanted more and better health care, they had to pay more for it.

But unfortunately, not all the money was going to corresponding increases in the quality or quantity of health care. The publicly funded health-care plans established by Lyndon Johnson—Medicaid and Medicare—had billions of dollars of waste resulting from fraud and inefficiency. The congressional General Accounting Office estimated that from 1975 to 1992 10 percent of Medicare spending was lost to fraud and abuse, for a total $110 billion over that period. In 1996 the Inspector General for the Department of Health and Human Services revised the estimate up to 14 percent of all Medicare costs—over $23 billion per year! And in 1991 alone, Medicaid supposedly paid $5.5 billion in fraudulent prescription drug fees—about 7.7 percent of its total spending.

> ★ Fraud investigators have turned up all kinds of absurd schemes to bilk Medicare and Medicaid. One elderly woman's medical care required 12.5 miles of tape; a dentist claimed to see 500 patients a day; a 19-year-old football player was treated for diaper rash; and comatose patients were prescribed birth control pills.

This is a mind-boggling amount of fraud, but it's plausible considering that only 17 percent of all Medicare claims received any kind of review in 1989. Meanwhile, because Medicaid was set up in a way that positively encouraged more spending (the federal government provides matching funds to states for health-care expenditures, essentially paying states to spend more), states also learned how to "game" the system; one creative scheme involved raising taxes on health care providers, refunding their tax payments, and counting the refunds as "spending." Between rising legitimate costs, pork barrel, and massive fraud, federal spending on Medicare jumped nine-fold from $15.5 billion in 1975 to $136.3 billion in 1992, while Medicaid spending increased 10-fold from $6.6 billion to $66 billion. That compares to a mere six-fold increase in total health care spending over the same period. Somehow, the math just doesn't seem to add up.

Of course, it's not all Uncle Sam's fault. The private sector had its own issues, like the always fun practice of suing doctors. During this same period, the number of medical malpractice lawsuits soared from 2.5 per 100 physicians in 1975 to 14.1 per 100 in 1992. Some of these were doubtless justified, but profit, as always, was a major factor. And why shouldn't it have been? Payouts were bigger than ever: the average verdict of malpractice lawsuits increased from $220,000 in 1975 to $1.2 million in 1990. And while most plaintiffs who brought frivolous medical malpractice lawsuits didn't actually end up winning any money, the mere fact that physicians were sued for malpractice triggered automatic rate hikes in their medical malpractice insurance premiums. Of course, doctors simply passed these costs along to the public.

So what did Americans do about spiraling health-care costs? For the most part, nothing. During this period, attempts to reform Medicare and Medicaid failed miserably, for the simple reason that people like free stuff from the government. In 1981 Ronald Reagan dropped the idea of reforming Medicare payments like a hot potato after realizing he was on the wrong side of public opinion. As for malpractice lawsuits, some states passed legislation modeled on California's 1975 Medical Injury Compensation Reform Act, which lowered malpractice insurance premiums by limiting malpractice verdicts for "pain and suffering" to $250,000—but congressional efforts to reform malpractice law were derailed by lobbyists representing trial lawyers.

AIDS AND ADVOCACY

In June–July 1981, the Centers for Disease Control in Atlanta reported that gay men in New York, Los Angeles, and San Francisco were being hospitalized with the same mysterious set of symptoms, including pneumonia, Kaposi's sarcoma—a rare skin cancer usually seen in elderly patients—and oral thrush, an indication of immune failure. Ominously, 26 of the 29 patients were already dead. By the end of 1981, 241 people had died—almost all gay men—with the annual toll rising sharply to 853 in 1982, 2,304 in 1983, and 4,251 in 1984.

At a loss, doctors dubbed the new disease "gay-related immune deficiency" (GRID) and speculated it might be caused by drug abuse or some other element of young gay men's "party lifestyle." By 1982 CDC researchers had linked the disease to bodily fluids and speculated it was transmitted by homosexual anal intercourse, which causes small tears and bleeding in the rectal lining. That same year the CDC dropped GRID in favor of a new name, acquired immune deficiency syndrome, indicating it wasn't intrinsically gay-related. But health officials still failed to anticipate it might cross over to heterosexuals—an egregious oversight, which helped the epidemic get a foothold in the general population. The disease probably spread to heterosexuals via bisexual men, shared needles among intravenous drug users, and tainted blood transfusions. (After linking AIDS to blood in 1982, it took another year for the CDC to warn that blood banks might be contaminated.)

With evidence of epidemics surfacing in Europe and Africa, in 1983 the Pasteur Institute in Paris, France, said it had isolated the human immunodeficiency virus, which causes AIDS. In 1984 Dr. Robert Gallo, a researcher at the U.S. National Cancer Institute, claimed (incorrectly) to be the first to discover the virus; however, techniques developed by his lab in the 1970s had been crucial to the Pasteur Institute's isolation of the virus a year earlier. In 1985 the U.S. Food and Drug Administration introduced the first antibody test and finally began screening blood supplies. The year 1985 also saw the first celebrity AIDS death—Rock Hudson, a Hollywood heartthrob from the 1950s and 1960s who never publicly revealed his homosexuality. He was one of 5,636 U.S. AIDS deaths that year.

The first effective treatment for AIDS, AZT, was introduced in 1987, and in 1988 U.S. Surgeon General C. Everett Koop mounted a publicity blitz promoting the use of condoms for safe sex, including the mailing of 107 million pamphlets titled "Understanding AIDS." Nonetheless, the number of AIDS deaths continued climbing sharply to 14,544 in 1989 and 18,447 in 1990—including Ryan White, a teenage hemophiliac infected by a tainted blood transfusion. In 1991, 20,454 people succumbed in the United States, and basketball player Irvin "Magic" Johnson revealed he had HIV. In 1992, 23,411 died and one million Americans were estimated to have HIV.

The U.S. death toll would continue to climb until the mid-1990s, when the first protease-inhibitor drugs were introduced in 1995–1996. Overall, from 1981 to 2009, at least 600,000 Americans died from AIDS, and 1.2 million Americans are currently living with HIV. Worldwide, total deaths topped 25 million, and at least 35 million people are currently living with the virus. AIDS has orphaned 14 million children in sub-Saharan Africa.

Ironically, the AIDS epidemic resulted in greater visibility—and ultimately, acceptance—for "alternative sexualities" in American society (lesbians, gays, bisexuals, and transgendered people, or LGBT for sort-of-short). This was partly the work of new advocacy organizations formed to publicize the effects of the AIDS epidemic and put pressure on public officials and pharmaceutical companies for swift action. These included the Gay Men's Health Crisis, formed in 1982, the American Foundation for Aids Research (AmFAR) formed in 1985, ACT UP, formed in 1987, and the AIDS Memorial Quilt project, also started in 1987.

Cable TV On, Women's Shirts Off

Before the Internet became a limitless font of pornography just a mouse-click away, late-night premium cable TV was pretty much the best thing ever invented, as far as teenage boys were concerned. And, okay, all those hundreds of other cable channels weren't bad either.

Cable TV actually started way back in the late 1940s as a way of getting television to remote rural areas: receiving towers picked up distant broadcast signals and distributed them to local subscribers via cable—a less costly alternative to "repeater" towers, which used a lot more power to boost faraway broadcast signals. Because the receiving towers could pick up local broadcasts from hundreds of miles away, by the 1950s many cable subscribers actually had more viewing choices than households limited to plain old "bunny ears" broadcast TV. Local broadcasters supported by the Big Three Networks—NBC, CBS, and ABC—complained about the new competition, prompting the FCC to clamp down on cable in the 1960s, with limits on what kind of content cable networks could carry, and from where.

But it's hard to stop a good idea, especially when it has the potential to deliver pornography to private households. 1972 brought the beginning of cable deregulation (thanks, Nixon!), and that same year, Charles Dolan and Gerald Levin of Sterling Manhattan Cable launched the first premium pay cable company, Home Box Office, which they envisioned as a local cable network allowing wealthy Manhattanites to watch movies in the comfort of their own luxury apartments—a revolutionary concept. After being bought by magazine publisher Time Inc. in 1973, HBO went national in September 1975 by leasing bandwidth on satellites, which allowed it to deliver the signal to local cable receiving towers all over the country. Once again, cable subscribers were getting more viewing options than regular broadcast-only households—and this time there was nothing the broadcasters could do about it.

In December of 1976, HBO was followed into orbit by WTCG, a local Atlanta-based cable network whose owner—an aspiring media mogul named R.E. "Ted" Turner—wanted to use satellite to achieve national reach for his programming. Ted's channels were dominated by sitcoms, cartoons, old movies, and sports (including the Atlanta Braves and Atlanta Hawks, which he also owned). But unlike HBO, Turner distributed his content for free, making money by selling advertising at cheaper rates than the broadcast networks. By 1981 Turner Broadcasting System reached 2.5 million households around the country, with annual advertising revenues of $95 million, growing to an incredible $1.77 billion by 1992.

But back to the seventies. The late part of the decade brought a flurry of new national cable networks, both free and premium, and couch potatoes couldn't have been happier: Viacom's new Showtime channel debuted in March 1978, The Movie Channel in January 1979, and the Entertainment and Sports Network in September 1979. In June 1980 Ted Turner revolutionized TV (again) with the launch of the Cable News Network, CNN, providing 24-hour news coverage. Two months later HBO launched Cinemax to compete with The Movie Channel and Showtime. Before long, the intensifying competition pushed all four movie channels to switch to round-the-clock programming.

Around this time, big media companies like Time Inc., Warner Cable Communications, and Viacom expanded from cable programming to cable infrastructure, tying together local networks to form regional and then national distribution systems. And in 1984 they got a boost from Congress, which cleared away legal obstacles to further expansion, triggering a byzantine series of mergers, acquisitions, joint ventures, and spinoffs.

The most important thing to remember, though, is that these vast media empires were built to a considerable degree on smut. As media historians Thomas Baldwin and D. Stevens McVoy wrote in 1983, "It has always been accepted that uncut, R-rated movies are a major appeal of the big pay networks." HBO Chairman Michael Fuchs himself told a new employee that "randy guys are a major part of our demographic." In the early 1980s, The Movie Channel enjoyed rapid growth as the only premium movie channel to show R-rated movies in daytime, prompting Showtime and Cinemax (aka "Skinemax") to begin doing the same. In 1982 the Playboy Channel launched with 340,000 subscribers, which jumped to 750,000 by 1985—but when execs foolishly tried to take the channel more "mainstream" (it's *Playboy*, people!), subscribers tumbled to 400,000 by 1988. Meanwhile, competitors clearly understood the formula for Playboy's success: in 1984 Bridget Potter, the head of original programming for HBO, issued a directive that Cinemax would focus (even more) on classy softcore porn. Her exact instructions? "Spicy but not obscene."

·············· **MADE IN AMERICA** ··················

Computers Get Personal

It's difficult to imagine, but once, long ago, personal computers *didn't exist*. Let us journey back to this strange, semi-mythical time, when the world was full of legend, wonder, and superstition.

Before personal computers, all computing was handled by "mainframe" computers, which were shared by teams of people.

Mostly used by scientists, mathematicians, and government officials, these behemoth computing machines performed complex calculations that would take humans weeks, months, or years. The first mainframes were built during World War II to calculate ballistic trajectories, and in the 1950s, Remington Rand built mainframe computers for the U.S. Census Bureau and the Internal Revenue Service.

By the early 1970s, most big businesses and academic institutions had computers. But the costs were exorbitant. In fact, researchers had to share computers, with people waiting their turn to perform all their calculations in scheduled windows of availability—a system that inevitably led to accusations of computer hogging and arguments about whose research was more important.

Everything was about to change. In 1976 two computer science geeks in Palo Alto, California, Steve Jobs and Steve Wozniak, designed and sold the Apple I—the first low-cost, preassembled computer circuit board, incorporating 30 microchips, which users (pretty much computer geeks exclusively) could easily hook up to a television monitor and electronic keyboard. The next step was the Apple II, the first complete, "out of the box" personal computer in 1977. Where the Apple I sold about 200 units total, the Apple II sold at least five

BEFORE THERE WAS IPAD . . .

1944: The Electronic Numerical Integrator and Calculator (ENIAC) weighs 30 tons and sucks up about 200 kilowatts of electrical power to determine the feasibility of the first hydrogen bomb.

1951: The Census Bureau's UNIVAC I weighs "just" 15 tons and uses 125 kilowatts of electricity.

1955: International Business Machines (IBM) introduces its first commercially successful mainframe, the 705, weighing 17 tons, occupying over 1,000 square feet, and using about 100 kilowatts.

1957: IBM ships the 608, which dramatically reduces the size and energy consumption of computers by replacing vacuum tubes with transistors.

1960–1963: MIT engineers develop the first integrated circuits, which concentrate huge numbers of transistors on very small pieces of silicon substrate, called microprocessors or microchips. The first practical integrated circuits are incorporated into the Apollo guidance computer by MIT engineers, with design and production improvements lowering the cost from $1,000 in 1960 to just $25 in 1963.

million over the next 10 years. Apple was soon joined by IBM, which rushed its own pioneering personal computer, the IBM 5150, to market in 1981.

With the scale and marketing resources of a huge company behind it, IBM's desktop seemed poised to crush Apple and dominate the PC market. But in 1984 Apple hit back with the Macintosh, a $2,000 console with a graphic interface that was more accessible than IBM's PC. Apple paid film director Ridley Scott $1.5 million to create an iconic TV ad invoking the imagery of George Orwell's novel *1984*, with a female athlete (Apple) throwing a sledgehammer and shattering a huge television screen filled by a propaganda-spewing dictator (IBM). The ad aired during Superbowl XVIII on January 22, 1984, and is generally considered one of the most effective television ads in history, drawing a line between Mac and PC fans that remains to this day.

Both Apple and IBM continued improving their personal computers, offering more memory and capabilities at lower prices in a fierce battle for market share. Ultimately, IBM and Apple took different approaches to personal computing products, which ironically ended up marginalizing both companies, although for different reasons. IBM followed a policy of "open architecture," incorporating processors built by third-party technology companies that were compatible with a variety of operating systems. Meanwhile, Apple prohibited users from installing any operating system besides the proprietary Mac system and also refused to license the Mac graphical interface for use in PCs.

As a result of these decisions, both companies created an opening for a new generation of personal computer manufacturers to join the fray. On one hand, IBM's open architecture meant rival manufacturers could produce cheaper PC "clones" that functioned just like IBMs. For its part, Apple's refusal to license the Mac operating system failed to prevent Seattle-based Microsoft, founded by Bill Gates in 1975, from introducing Windows—an operating system featuring a graphic interface that bore an uncanny resemblance to the Mac—in 1985. (Anyway, Mac's system actually borrowed heavily from an earlier prototype interface developed by Xerox.) At this point the focus shifted from hardware to software, and Microsoft quickly became the dominant force in personal computing.

Gold on the Silver Screen

After inventing the movie camera and the movie star, America's next big contribution to the movie business was the blockbuster—

an epic movie, released simultaneously at movie theaters nation-wide (usually during the summer), which becomes a huge hit, rakes in hundreds of millions of dollars, and dazzles the news media into giving it additional free publicity.

In previous eras, hit films built their success gradually, moving from limited distribution to nationwide distribution as "buzz" built in the press. This was partly due to the fact that the U.S. movie business was divided among literally hundreds of independent theaters and small chains, mostly the result of court-ordered breakups of the "big five" movie chains in the late 1940s and 1950s. But in the 1960s, a new round of consolidation was aided by the rise of the "multiplex"—a group of theaters under one roof connected to a mall. As the total number of movie screens rose from 10,335 in 1970 to 22,774 in 1990, the number of screens owned by the four largest chains also rose, from about 800 (8 percent) to about 8,000 (35 percent) over the same period.

Increasing concentration of movie theater ownership made it easier to coordinate the simultaneous release of movies across America. At the same time, by the early 1970s movie theater owners were desperate for something to reverse a long-term slump in audience numbers resulting from competition from television. True, there had been some big hits, which showed cinema still had a hold on the American imagination: in 1972 Francis Ford Coppola's "The Godfather" eventually achieved nationwide distribution, raking in $135 million in U.S. box office sales, and two years later "The Exorcist" also succeeded the old-fashioned way, attaining national distribution and box office sales of $193 million.

It was Sidney Sheinberg, the president and chief operating officer of MCA, who first hit upon the idea that "wide release" could generate enough buzz—and sales—to offset bigger initial expenses for marketing and promotions. As a bonus, the studio could actually save money in the long run, since the marketing spending would all be front-loaded in the first couple of weeks (rather than spread out, piecemeal, as the film gradually penetrated new markets). Of course, Sheinberg also realized he needed a larger-than-life movie to justify this gamble.

Luckily, Sheinberg had wisely supported an enterprising young director, Steven Spielberg, who had taken on an unconventional project: a big-screen adaptation of a best-selling novel about a 25-foot great white shark terrorizing a summer tourist spot. On June 20, 1975, "Jaws" opened amid a publicity feeding frenzy at almost

The years following "Jaws" saw more epic movies opening with equally epic national distribution and ticket sales: "Star Wars" (1977, $461 million), "Superman" (1978, $134 million), "The Empire Strikes Back" (1980, $290 million), "Raiders of the Lost Ark" (1981, $245 million), "E.T." (1982, $435 million), "Return of the Jedi" (1983, $309 million), "Ghostbusters" (1984, $238 million), "Indiana Jones and the Temple of Doom" (1984, $179 million), "Beverly Hills Cop" (1984, $234 million), and "Back to the Future" (1985, $210 million). The combined box office receipts of these blockbusters—totaling $3 billion— exceeded the 1985 GDPs of 65 sovereign nations, including Iceland and Nicaragua.

500 theaters nationwide. The result was the largest movie debut in history (to date), earning $7 million in its first weekend (or $28 million in 2008 dollars). "Jaws" went on to make $260 million in U.S. ticket sales. In some cities, crowds of moviegoers formed ticket lines that stretched all the way around the block; the era of the "blockbuster" had begun.

Hip-Hop Hooray

For like the hundredth time in U.S. history, musical innovation by African-Americans in the 1970s and 1980s led to the creation of a whole new genre of music—hip-hop—which swept white mainstream American youth culture before taking over the rest of the world. Sound strangely familiar? Well, it's pretty much the exact same sequence of events that catapulted first jazz and then rock-n-roll to global dominance.

Like its predecessors, hip-hop's origins are a bit mysterious because it emerged in a poor, marginal community. It was pioneered sometime in the mid-1970s by street-corner artists in the Bronx, who delivered impromptu vocal performances, sometimes in the form of contests, where participants improvised rhythmic, lyrical "spoken word" monologues. Known as rapping, this practice incorporated other folk traditions, like the ritualized exchange of insults, boasting and intimidation, and comical narrative, all mixed together with a healthy dose of word play.

By the late 1970s, some rappers joined forces with DJs who were experimenting with turntable techniques at dance parties, looping short stretches of funk and disco records where the other instruments "break" to showcase the bass and percussion. By repeating these breaks again and again, they created a totally new, infectious, and highly danceable sound. The DJs paired up turntables, allowing them to extend the break beats or pair them in novel ways with bits of blues, jazz, rock, and Motown, and also experimented with "scratching"—the feedback-like sound produced by pulling a record backward to loop the break beat.

Before long, rappers were part of the performance, accompanying DJs at dance parties as "masters of ceremonies" or "MCs" who improvised "disco raps" over the break beats. Rival rappers developed followings who packed clubs to hear them compete in (relatively) friendly contests displaying verbal prowess and rhyming skills. Between their feuds, flamboyant costumes, and sexy backup dancers, it wasn't hard for MCs to steal the spotlight from the DJs, but the MC-DJ relationship remained central to the new musical genre known as "hip-hop."

As party music, early hip-hop was mostly about dancing and having a good time: the archetypal example is the Sugar Hill Gang's "Rapper's Delight," which sampled the hit disco song "Good Times" by Chic and became the first hip-hop song to break through to mainstream audiences in 1979–1980. However, the tone and subject matter took a decidedly negative turn as conditions in inner cities deteriorated over the course of the 1980s, especially with the arrival of crack cocaine in 1983–1984. The mid-1980s saw the emergence of a new subgenre of hip-hop, "gangsta rap," created by rappers who took the criminal underworld as their subject matter. In fact, some of the most famous hip-hop stars of this period started out as crack dealers, including Eric Lynn Wright, aka Eazy-E; Shawn Corey Carter, aka Jay-Z; and Christopher Wallace, aka Frank White, aka The Notorious B.I.G., aka Biggie Smalls, aka Big Poppa.

·················· **PARTISAN PROFILES** ·················

Ladies of the Right

While left-leaning feminists tended to dominate women's political involvement in the 1970s, feminism and related social movements for abortion and gay rights triggered a backlash by conservative women who stood up for "traditional" values. Predictably, they met with an extremely hostile reaction from feminists—but they did succeed in letting the world know American women held a wide range of political views.

PHYLLIS SCHLAFLY (b. August 15, 1924). The uber-grandma of female conservative activism, Schlafly was involved in politics before feminism even hit the scene. Her principle concern was the global threat of communism, and she even joined the hard-core John Birch Society for a brief time. (She left because she disagreed with its paranoid focus on domestic communist threats.)

However, Schlafly was soon drawn into the domestic upheavals that divided America in the 1960s. She opposed liberal Republicans like Nixon as too moderate on social issues, and in 1964 she tore into the Northeastern liberal GOP for selling out its principles. That same year she also supported ultraconservative Republican presidential candidate Barry Goldwater—distinguished by his opposition to the New Deal and his hawkish foreign policy views.

When feminism emerged in the early 1970s, Schlafly was having none of it: her activism was now devoted to sticking up for women who opted for traditional roles as wives and mothers (although she herself was a working professional). Schlafly achieved national prominence with her campaign against the Equal Rights Amendment proposed in 1972, and she played a key role in defeating the amendment. She founded an activist group, Stop Taking Our Privileges (STOP), which argued the ERA would actually undermine women's social position by freeing husbands from the obligation to support their wives, making it harder for widowed housewives to collect Social Security, and making women eligible for the draft. Whether or not these warnings were accurate, they helped turn public opinion against the ERA, which failed in June 1982 after being ratified by 35 out of the required 38 states.

ANITA BRYANT (b. March 25, 1940). Bryant is best remembered for her failed attempts to roll back gay rights—oh, and for a string of saccharine hit songs in the 1950s and early 1960s, including "Til There Was You," "Paper Roses," and "Step By Step, Little By Little."

After achieving moderate success as a singer, in 1969 Bryant became the spokeswoman for the Florida Citrus Commission, appearing in TV commercials where she exhorted the audience to "Come to the Florida Sunshine Tree!" In 1977, however, Bryant suddenly threw herself into politics with her campaign to reverse a local gay rights ordinance in Dade County, Florida, which would have prohibited discrimination on the basis of sexual orientation. A Southern Baptist, like other conservative evangelicals Bryant viewed the gay rights movement as an assault on morality itself. With encouragement from Jerry Falwell, Bryant founded an activist group called Save Our Children, which managed to repeal the gay rights ordinance in Dade County (until 1998, when it was finally reinstituted).

> **If homosexuals are allowed to change the law in their favor, why not prostitutes, thieves, or murderers?**
>
> —Anita Bryant, 1977

Bryant's initiative inspired similar (but less successful) campaigns to repeal gay rights ordinances across the country. Meanwhile, a national boycott of orange juice prompted the Florida Citrus Commission to drop Bryant in 1980; she was also shunned by the liberal entertainment business, leading to bankruptcy, and conservative Christians turned on her following her divorce in 1979. She currently leads Anita Bryant Ministries in Oklahoma City.

JEANNE KIRKPATRICK (November 19, 1926–December 7, 2006). Although she started out as a Democrat, America's first female ambassador to the United Nations ended up as a prominent female figure in the GOP.

The daughter of an Oklahoma oil prospector, Kirkpatrick displayed a formidable intellect at an early age and then pursued a career in academia with all the usual liberal credentials. In 1968 Kirkpatrick supported Democratic candidate Hubert Humphrey—but over the course of the 1970s, she became increasingly disillusioned with the foreign policy of Democrats like Jimmy Carter, who mostly steered clear of confrontation with the Soviets after the defeat in Vietnam. Kirkpatrick warned that as a totalitarian regime, the Soviet government was fundamentally untrustworthy and would secretly find a way around the arms control agreements (she was right). For Kirkpatrick and other hawks, Carter's moves to increase military spending and aid rebels in Afghanistan were too little, too late.

In 1980—while still a registered Democrat—Kirkpatrick became a foreign policy advisor to Republican presidential candidate Ronald Reagan, encouraging his hard-line position against the Soviets. After he became president, Reagan appointed Kirkpatrick U.S. ambassador to the United Nations. Kirkpatrick became notorious for her ultra-hawkish foreign policy views, including support for Argentina's far-right military dictatorship and the secret scheme that became known as the Iran-Contra Affair. In 1984—*still* a registered Democrat—she delivered the keynote address to the Republican National Convention, lashing out at

Democrats who "blamed America" for the world's problems instead of recognizing Soviet aggression for what it was.

As Reagan adopted a more conciliatory approach toward the Soviet Union in his second term, in 1985 Kirkpatrick resigned her ambassadorship and returned to academia as a professor at Georgetown (in 1985 she also finally joined the Republican party).

> Russia is playing chess, while we are playing Monopoly.
> The only question is whether they will checkmate us
> before we bankrupt them.
>
> —Jeanne Kirkpatrick, 1988

SANDRA DAY O'CONNOR: NOT DOWN WIT' GOP

Born in El Paso, Texas, in 1930, Sandra Day O'Connor was one of the first female students to graduate from Stanford University Law School and was a trailblazing female attorney before serving as an Arizona state senator and then an elected judge in Maricopa County, Arizona. A Republican, she nonetheless failed to conform to the views of "pro-life" Republicans, who publicly opposed her nomination by President Reagan in 1981. Reagan brushed off their criticism, and O'Connor was approved by the Senate with a world-beating 99–0 vote, making her the first female Supreme Court justice in U.S. history.

·········· **OTHER PEOPLE'S STUFF** ·················

Persian Gulf, Part I
Ayatollah There'd Be Trouble!

Shah Mohammad Reza Pahlavi had been America's BFF in the Persian Gulf since 1953, when President Eisenhower ordered the CIA to overthrow the democratically elected prime minister of Persia, Mohammad Mossadeq, and replace him with Pahlavi. The shah was a loyal American ally, crushing Middle Eastern communist movements, supporting Israel, and keeping the oil flowing from Iran and its Arab neighbors. He also bought billions of dollars of American arms. But he failed to make friends with one crucial interest group—his people. Over the course of his 26-year reign, Shah Pahlavi managed to systematically alienate all the important constituencies.

To keep the lid on dissent, the shah resorted to increasingly brutal repression by secret police, whose agents were trained in "domestic espionage and interrogation techniques" (torture) by CIA advisors. Washington bent over backward to avoid mentioning the shah's human rights abuses until 1977, when it finally started publicly pressuring the shah to ease up on political repression—at the exact wrong moment. The shah's belated political reforms backfired, allowing the opposition to overthrow the government. And instead of ushering in a more democratic regime, U.S. intervention helped to create a new regime that was even worse (whoops). In January 1979 the shah fled Iran, and Ayatollah Khomeini—a preeminent Shiite cleric famed for his unflinching opposition to the shah—returned from exile.

Khomeini preached a new political philosophy based on Shiite tradition called *velayat e-faqih,* "the guardianship of the clerics," which called for Shiite *mullahs* to "guard" the power of the state from misuse. This included imposing *Sharia* (Islamic law), censoring the media, and creating an ultraconservative Council of Guardians, which could invalidate political candidates. Some of Khomeini's fiercest supporters were radical anti-American university students, who stormed the U.S. embassy and took 53 Americans hostage on November 4, 1979.

Under growing public pressure, President Carter approved a multistage (aka absurdly ambitious) plan code-named "Eagle Claw" to free the hostages. Eight U.S. Navy helicopters were to fly from aircraft carriers in the Arabian Sea to a desert landing strip in eastern Iran, where they would meet up with four transport planes carrying fuel and U.S. special forces, and would refuel before carrying the special forces to a spot outside Teheran, where they would hide out overnight before boarding trucks driven by Iranian CIA operatives, sneaking into downtown Teheran, freeing the hostages, and then heading to a nearby soccer stadium for pickup by the helicopters, which would fly them back to the carriers. It was perfect—nothing could go wrong.

The plan didn't even make it past the first stage: three of the Navy helicopters malfunctioned when sand got stuck in their rotors, forcing the mission to abort after the various aircraft met up in eastern Iran. Worse, as the aircraft prepared to withdraw, one of the helicopters collided with a transport, killing eight servicemen and destroying both aircraft. During the panicked evacuation, the other helicopters were abandoned, so the Iranians actually came out ahead by five helicopters. Although it was an embarrassing failure, Eagle Claw raised public awareness about the decline in American military power, leading to reform and revitalization in the 1980s. Meanwhile, the hostages were finally released a few hours after Ronald Reagan's inauguration (prompting unproven allegations that his campaign had a secret deal with the Iranians). The hostage crisis lasted 444 days from November 4, 1979, to January 21, 1981.

★ *Upon their return to the United States, each of the hostages received a lifetime pass to any Major League Baseball game.*

Persian Gulf, Part II
Revenge Is a Dish Best Served a Thousandfold

The hostage crisis was a huge escalation of the conflict between the Islamic Republic and the United States, which left Americans feeling humiliated and angry—and eager for payback. The chance for revenge came when Saddam Hussein, the dictator of Iraq, invaded Iran in September 1980. When the tide of war turned against Hussein in June of 1982, President Reagan decided he couldn't allow Iraq to be defeated. We needed the oil! (Okay, and good ol' revenge too.)

The United States started off helping behind the scenes, passing along weapons, ammunition, vehicles, bank loans, military advice and intelligence, chemical weapon ingredients—basically, anything dangerous that could be covertly passed along. But when Iranian attacks on oil tankers in the Persian Gulf threatened global price stability, the gloves came off. In April 1988 Reagan ordered Operation Praying Mantis, which destroyed the better part of the Iranian navy and Iranian oil platforms in the Persian Gulf. Then on July 3, 1988, the

I SAY HEROISM, YOU SAY HIGH TREASON

After Marxist *Sandinistas* overthrew the Nicaraguan dictator Anastasio Somoza Debayle, the United States forged an alliance of anti-Sandinista elements, the "contras." Beginning in July 1985, members of Reagan's National Security Council raised money for the contras "off the books" by selling weapons to Iran, still a bitter U.S. enemy—which constituted high treason, since Congress had specifically forbidden this. Rear Admiral John Poindexter was found guilty of multiple felonies, and Secretary of Defense Caspar Weinberger was indicted on charges of perjury and obstruction of justice, but President Bush pardoned them before Weinberger faced trial. Somehow Colonel Oliver North, who arranged the payments to the contras—the treason part—came out of this an "American hero." As for Reagan, he couldn't recall his role. Oh well!

guided missile cruiser USS *Vincennes* shot down Iran Air Flight 655, killing 290 civilian passengers and crew. The United States claimed this was a mistake, but Khomeini believed it was deliberate and feared it might presage escalating American involvement. This persuaded him to finally agree to a U.N.-brokered armistice. The eight-year war was especially destructive for Iran, which lost about 800,000 soldiers and civilians versus 300,000 Iraqi dead—due in large part to American support for Iraq.

Persian Gulf, Part III
With Friends Like These . . .

America had wreaked vengeance on Iran, but nothing is ever simple: now it had to deal with Iraq, which it had just armed to the teeth. Irony!

The U.S. government was never exactly a fan of Saddam Hussein, who snuggled up to the Soviet Union in the 1970s and portrayed himself as the leader of Arab opposition to Israel. The State Department had publicly condemned Iraq's use of chemical weapons during the Iran-Iraq War (despite the fact that American companies were providing some ingredients), and everyone was nervous about his clear interest in nuclear weapons. The last straw was Hussein's invasion of neighboring Kuwait, a tiny, defenseless country that just happens to be sitting on about 7.2 percent of the world's proven oil reserves.

Hussein had borrowed billions of dollars from Kuwait during his war with Iran, and when Kuwait refused to cancel his debts, Hussein decided to cancel Kuwait, confident the United States wouldn't stop him. He had good reason to think this, because that's what he was told by April Glaspie, the U.S. ambassador to Iraq. It's not clear how much of Glaspie's disclosure was directed by President Bush and how much was just a gap in communications (or, for the conspiracy theorists, how much was a deliberate plan to trick Iraq into invading Kuwait so the United States could be on the side of good).

> We have no opinion on the Arab-Arab conflicts, like your border disagreement with Kuwait . . . the issue is not associated with America . . . All that we hope is that these issues are solved quickly.
>
> —April Glaspie

After Iraq invaded Kuwait on August 2, 1990, the U.N. immediately imposed economic sanctions on Iraq, and in November of 1990, the U.N. Security Council gave Iraq a deadline of January 15, 1991, to withdraw its troops. President Bush hurried U.S. troops to Saudi Arabia to protect America's key ally and oil supplier from Iraqi aggression (Operation Desert Shield, August 7, 1990–January 15, 1991), and he began assembling a global coalition to liberate Kuwait. Altogether, almost a million troops converged on the Persian Gulf region, of which 543,000 were U.S. personnel.

The liberation of Kuwait (Operation Desert Storm, January 16–April 11, 1992) was a massive, high-tech turkey shoot, opening with one of the most devastating aerial bombardments in history. Although fewer bombs were dropped than in previous wars, a larger proportion were "precision munitions," equipped with laser guidance systems that allowed attacking aircraft to destroy their target the first time—doing with one "smart bomb" what previously took 10 or 100 "dumb bombs." In the first two weeks alone, coalition planes flew 37,000 missions, targeting the Iraqi air force and air defenses, followed by Iraqi Republican Guard and Iraqi Army formations in Kuwait and Iraq. After wiping out most of these targets, the air campaign moved on to SCUD missile launchers, production labs for weapons of mass destruction, oil refineries and port facilities, the Iraqi navy, roads and bridges in Iraq, and the Iraqi power network.

After this deluge, the ground campaign was almost an afterthought, if not a foregone conclusion. On February 24, 1991, U.S. Marines crossed from Saudi Arabia into Kuwait, taking thousands of prisoners. Tens of thousands of Iraqi troops tried to flee along the main highway to Iraq but were slaughtered by U.S. air power in such numbers it was dubbed the "Highway of Death." By February 27, Kuwait was liberated, and the following day the Iraqi commander agreed to meet for cease-fire negotiations.

After the war, America was on top of the world again, with President Bush enthusing, "We finally beat the Vietnam syndrome." The United States had flexed its muscles, protected its allies, and showed that it was a team player in the U.N. Even better, the United States just happened to end up with a vastly expanded military presence in the Persian Gulf, with troops in Bahrain, Kuwait, Oman, Qatar, Saudi Arabia, and the United Arab Emirates. And no one could have a problem with that, right?

DIRTY LITTLE WARS

Between all the dirty, hit'n'run wars and the well-intentioned but ill-fated peace-keeping missions, America had its fair share of scrapes. Here are a few of the notches we added to the old ammunition belt:

Invasion of Grenada, October 1983: One of the more "comic opera" wars in U.S. history. Reagan ordered the invasion of the wee Caribbean island nation of Grenada when an internal quarrel in the ruling communist regime presented a chance to flush the whole miniature Marxist misadventure into the sea. In 1984 Grenada held its first elections in almost a decade.

Lebanon, 1982–1984: In 1975 the small eastern Mediterranean nation of Lebanon descended into civil war, and in 1982 the U.N. organized a multinational peacekeeping force. However, not all the Lebanese factions wanted peace. On October 23, 1983, a Hezbollah suicide bomber detonated a truck full of explosives in front of barracks housing foreign troops, killing 241 U.S. Marines and 58 French soldiers. The U.N. force withdrew soon after.

Libya, Operation El Dorado Canyon, April 15, 1986: After Libyan intelligence was implicated in the bombing of a West Berlin nightclub popular with U.S. servicemen, Reagan ordered punitive air raids that killed 45 soldiers and officials and 15 civilians, including the adopted daughter of the Libyan leader, Muammar Qaddafi. The strike is believed to have provoked the Libyan bombing of Pan Am Flight 103 over Lockerbie, Scotland, killing 270.

Panama, Operation Just Cause, December 1989: In the 1970s and early 1980s, Panamanian dictator Manuel Noriega was an important U.S. ally, but he also got in bed with cocaine smugglers. On December 20, 1989, 28,000 U.S. troops descended on Panama, and Noriega was extradited to the United States, where he was eventually tried and convicted of racketeering, drug smuggling, and money laundering.

Pulling the Rod Out of the Iron Curtain

The single most important U.S. diplomatic victory in recent history is also the least understood. In the early 1980s, the Soviet Union was the "Evil Empire"—a huge, powerful adversary, oppressing tens of millions of Eastern European vassals and spinning nefarious anti-American plots. Then, in the early 1990s, it simply ceased to exist. What happened?

In the early 1970s, Richard Nixon warmed to the idea of détente, or a "thaw" in the Cold War—but in the second half of the decade, a group of "neoconservative" analysts unearthed evidence that the Soviets tricked the United States: while reducing their long-range ICBMs as agreed, they more than made up for it with new medium-range missiles. Soviet aggression in Afghanistan (un)sealed the deal, wrecking détente and sending relations to their lowest point since the beginning of the Cold War.

In response, Reagan basically reopened the arms race, eliminating the Soviet advantage and forcing the Kremlin to increase spending as well. But the Politburo realized it had a problem: with a smaller economy, the Soviet Union was already devoting a large proportion of its gross national product to defense, and the only way to spend more was by lowering the population's standard of living. U.S. and European trade sanctions in response to the invasion of Afghanistan made the situation even worse. Soviet trade with Western Europe fell sharply as a result, decreasing from 22 percent to 15 percent of Soviet exports from 1980 to 1988. Likewise, from 1981 to 1983 Reagan convinced Congress to enforce trade sanctions against Poland (a key Soviet ally) which eventually forced the communist regime in Warsaw to recognize Solidarity, a new democratic reform movement led by Lech Walesa, the boss of the dockworkers' union.

As the standard of living declined behind the Iron Curtain, popular discontent increased, but there was also a glimmer of hope in Mikhail Gorbachev, a reformer who took power in 1985. Gorbachev decided the only way to sustain military and social spending simultaneously was by seeking renewed foreign trade with Western Europe—especially sales of abundant Soviet oil and natural gas. But NATO allies in Europe—Margaret Thatcher in Britain, Helmut Kohl in West Germany, and François Mitterrand

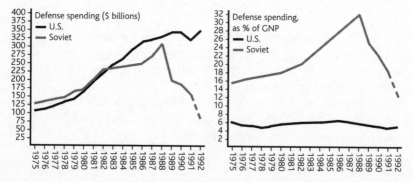

Spending Habits, U.S. vs. Soviet Union

in France—mostly supported Reagan (well, sort of), giving him leverage over Gorbachev. Not coincidentally, beginning in January 1984, Reagan also indicated he would be receptive to new negotiations for nuclear and conventional arms control agreements—a classic "carrot and stick" approach.

★ *While Raisa Gorbachev dazzled the Western world (she was often referred to as "the Princess Di of the Soviet Union"), she wasn't very popular at home. Soviets derided everything from her designer wardrobe to the apparent influence she had on her husband.*

Reagan and Gorbachev met in person for the first time in Geneva, Switzerland, on November 19, 1985, to discuss nuclear arms control and Soviet objections to Reagan's provocative plan for space-based missile defense (the Strategic Defense Initiative). Thus commenced a very unusual friendship between the American and Soviet leaders. Reagan was surprised to discover that Gorbachev was a genuine reformer who wanted to open up the Soviet Union and give its citizens more freedom, while Gorbachev was pleased to find that Reagan was hardly the bellicose, trigger-happy cowboy that some of his official remarks seemed to suggest.

> **My fellow Americans, I am pleased to tell you today that I've signed legislation that will outlaw Russia forever. We begin bombing in five minutes.**
>
> —Ronald Reagan, whose "joke" was accidentally broadcast on the radio during a live on-air mic check, August 11, 1984

A subsequent meeting in Reykjavik, Iceland, on October 11, 1986, didn't produce the hoped-for arms control agreement—but at least the rival superpowers were still talking. Moreover, Gorbachev's dealings with Reagan gave him the credibility he needed at home to implement *perestroika*—political and economic reforms—over the objections of hard-liners on the Politburo. At this point Reagan ratcheted up the rhetoric again, strengthening Gorbachev's hand at the expense of the hard-liners. On June 12, 1987, Reagan visited Berlin's famous Brandenburg Gate—then divided by the Berlin Wall—and challenged Gorbachev to carry out his promises of liberalization behind the Iron Curtain.

> General Secretary Gorbachev, if you seek peace, if you seek prosperity for the Soviet Union and Eastern Europe, if you seek liberalization: Come here to this gate! Mr. Gorbachev, open this gate! Mr. Gorbachev, tear down this wall!
>
> —Ronald Reagan, at the Brandenburg Gate in Berlin, June 12, 1987

In December 1987 Gorbachev came to Washington, D.C., where the two leaders negotiated the first (mostly symbolic) nuclear arms reduction agreement—signed by Reagan over the protests of foreign policy hawks in his administration. In return, April 1988 brought Gorbachev's biggest concession yet, with his announcement that Soviet troops would begin withdrawing from Afghanistan. This in turn cleared the way for Reagan's visit to Moscow in May 1988, where he was allowed to meet with political dissidents—a sign Gorbachev was sincere about reform.

While Gorbachev never intended to bring about the dissolution of the Soviet Union, the reforms he implemented quickly spun out of control—beginning with his new policy of non-interference in the internal affairs of Warsaw Pact allies. In April 1989 Poland agreed to democratic reforms. In early 1989, the Hungarian government allowed non-communist political parties, followed by the dissolution of the communist Party in October. In May of 1989, the Hungarians opened the border with Austria, leading to an exodus of citizens from other Warsaw Pact countries through Hungary to the West. In November–December 1989, the communist regime in Czechoslovakia resigned under public pressure, leading to free elections. In the first weeks of 1990, the communist regime in Bulgaria collapsed, and the Berlin Wall fell. In December 1989, the brutal Romanian dictator Nicolae Ceausescu was overthrown and executed, and finally, the Soviet Union itself collapsed after a failed coup attempt against Gorbachev by hardliners in August 1991. After two years of upheaval that no one could have predicted, the Cold War was suddenly over.

·················· **BY THE NUMBERS** ··················

31.3 percent African-American poverty rate, 1975
33.4 percent African-American poverty rate, 1991
360,000 African-American men in prison, 1992
310,000 African-American men in college, 1992

4KB standard amount of memory preinstalled on
Apple II computers, 1977

4MB standard amount of memory preinstalled on
Apple Macintosh Quadra 900s, 1991

99,900 percent increase in standard preinstalled
memory over this 14-year period

16 million number of households subscribing to cable TV,
1980

57 million number of households subscribing to cable TV,
1992

$5 billion–$6 billion estimated revenues of the Medellin Cartel,
mid-1980s

$24 billion Pablo Escobar's personal fortune, as estimated
by *Forbes* magazine, 1989

13,309 total U.S. AIDS deaths, 1985

206,000 total U.S. AIDS deaths, 1992

4 million total world AIDS deaths, 1992

31 percent proportion of Americans identifying as
evangelical or born-again Christians, Gallup,
1976

39 percent proportion identifying as evangelical or
born-again Christians, Gallup, 1998

38 percent proportion who said they interpret the Bible
literally, Gallup, 1980

32 percent proportion who said they interpret the Bible
literally, Gallup, 1992

18 percent proportion who said flooding was divine
punishment for the sins of inhabitants of the
Mississippi River Valley, Gallup, 1993

120,000 number of Iraqi troops occupying Kuwait,
1990–1991

960,000 total number of coalition troops participating
in the First Gulf War 1990–1991

543,000 number of U.S. troops in this total

35,000 number of Iraqi dead

379 number of coalition dead

3 million+ sorties flown by U.S. Air Force, Navy, and
Marine Corps pilots in Vietnam

94,000 sorties flown by U.S. Air Force, Navy, and
Marine Corps pilots in First Gulf War

4 percent Iraqi electricity production at the end of the
war, as a proportion of prewar production

88,000 tons of bombs dropped in First Gulf War
7 million tons of bombs dropped in Vietnam conflict
$61 billion cost of the First Gulf War
$48.2 billion total contribution from coalition allies
4 percent proportion of American children who were obese in 1975
11 percent proportion of American children who were obese in 1992

10

America the Decider

(1992–2010)

If you follow history long enough, eventually you get to right now, the very moment you are reading this sentence.

And there's some good news to report: lots of things are better than ever. In the twenty-first century Americans are, on average, living longer and enjoying a higher standard of living, with more leisure time and more disposable income than any previous period in history. After a nasty upswing in the 1960s–1970s, all types of crime have decreased steadily since the early 1990s, and the high school dropout rate has gone down across all races and income groups.

Technological advances that began in the United States have transformed the personal and professional lives of billions around the globe, with the rise of the Internet as the single most important communications revolution since the invention of the telephone. Some of America's oldest and bitterest divisions appear to be fading, albeit slowly and unevenly. Race relations have improved to a degree previous generations would probably have considered impossible, as symbolized by the 2008 election of the first African-American president, Barack Obama (not to mention the first African-American Secretaries of State, Colin Powell and Condoleeza Rice, appointed by Obama's predecessor George W. Bush).

But it ain't all roses and perfume. In the first decade of the twenty-first century, the United States and the world received a shocking wake-up call about the threat of global Islamist terrorism with the terrorist attacks on September 11, 2001. Osama bin Laden's declaration of war on the United States drew America, and the world, into another decades-long struggle that will dominate U.S. foreign policy for the foreseeable future. This won't always be pretty, as demonstrated by the subsequent U.S. invasion of Iraq. America also gave the world not one but *two* economic downturns, both resulting from completely idiotic behavior on the part of people who should have known better. The second downturn is turning out to be rather epic—in fact, as of press time, it's still going on.

·············· **WHAT HAPPENED WHEN** ····················

February 26, 1993 World Trade Center bombed by Islamist terrorists.

January 1, 1994 North American Free Trade Agreement (NAFTA) takes effect.

November 1995 President Bill Clinton begins a furtive affair with intern Monica Lewinsky.

January 23, 1997 Madeleine Albright becomes first female secretary of state.

July 1997 Mars Pathfinder lands on Mars on July 4; Camel drops its cartoon mascot, Joe Camel, over allegations it targets children on July 27.

August 1998 Al Qaeda bombs U.S. embassies in Dar es Salaam, Tanzania, and Nairobi, Kenya, killing 223; Bill Clinton admits to his relationship with Lewinsky on national TV.

December 1998 U.S. bombs Iraqi weapons of mass destruction (WMD), government sites in Operation Desert Fox.

February 2000 Dot.com stock bubble bursts, sending stocks into nosedive.

November 2000 Ambiguous ballots in Florida lead to a dispute over the results of the 2000 presidential race between Vice President Al Gore and former Texas Governor George W. Bush.

September 11, 2001 Terrorists attack World Trade Center and Pentagon.

October 7, 2001 The United States invades Afghanistan.

March 20, 2003 The United States invades Iraq.

December 13, 2003 Saddam Hussein is captured.

February 2004	CIA admits prewar WMD assessments were wrong.
August 29, 2005	Hurricane Katrina destroys a large part of New Orleans.
October 15, 2005	Iraqis vote to approve a new democratic constitution.
October 2006	The U.S. population passes 300 million.
January 2007	President Bush announces a "troop surge" for Iraq.
September 2008	The worst global financial crisis in decades begins.
October 3, 2008	The U.S. Congress approves a $700 billion emergency bailout.
November 4, 2008	Barack Obama is elected the first African-American U.S. president.
December 2009	President Obama announces a 30,000-troop surge for Afghanistan.

·················· **LIES YOUR TEACHER TOLD YOU** ··············

LIE: *Bill Clinton cut welfare.*

THE TRUTH: Kind of, but not really. During Bill Clinton's presidency, a bunch of welfare was redistributed from one of the federal welfare programs to various other federal programs. The total amount of welfare spending never decreased—in fact, it kept going up.

Ever since Lyndon Johnson launched the Great Society in the 1960s, politicians have gotten votes by playing on middle class resentment of welfare, which is condemned as "free handouts" to the poor. Politicians and media portray welfare recipients as unwilling to work, and they warn that welfare programs encourage dependence on the government (which may be true). They also appeal to white racial prejudice by implying that most recipients are African-American (which isn't true).

If anyone ever wanted votes, it was Bill Clinton, the Democratic governor from Arkansas who won a long-shot bid to unseat President George H.W. Bush in 1992, in the middle of a deep recession.

Sensing antagonism toward welfare recipients, Clinton made welfare reform a Democratic issue, promising to "end welfare as we know it"—a complete reversal of his party's previous stance. But did Clinton really end welfare as we know it? Maybe at first glance: in 1996 he signed the Personal Responsibility and Work Opportunity Reconciliation Act, better known as the Welfare Reform Bill, which phased out a federal welfare program, Aid to Families with Dependent Children (AFDC) and replaced it with a new, more limited program, Temporary Assistance to Needy Families (TANF). TANF capped the amount of time a family could spend on welfare to three years and the amount of money that the federal government distributed to states for this assistance. It also cracked down on deadbeat dads who fell behind on child support payments. However, the most important reform as far as public opinion was concerned was that welfare recipients were required to work (which could include job training).

Setting aside the fact that the bill was authored by Republicans, and the fact that Clinton had vetoed a practically identical bill under pressure from liberal groups not long before, *and* the fact that he just happened to reverse himself a few months before the 1996 presidential election—the fact remains that the welfare reform bill didn't achieve any long-term cost savings or reduce the number of people on federal welfare. It just shuffled the people and numbers around.

True, the number of individuals receiving family assistance from the federal government through AFDC or TANF decreased dramatically from a high of 14.4 million in 1994 to just 4.1 million in 2006. There was nothing magical about this: the number dropped primarily thanks to economic growth, which picked up halfway through Clinton's first term. This fortunate coincidence allowed Clinton and the Republican Congress to take credit for moving millions of people "off welfare" (succeeding before the bill was even passed, which is especially impressive).

So did "cutting welfare" actually save any money? In a word, no. Crunching the numbers, there were 38.1 million people receiving food stamps or family assistance in 1996; in 2009 the number is back up to 40.4 million. Total federal food aid more than doubled from $28 billion in 2000 to $57.5 billion in 2008, while federal housing assistance increased from $28.8 billion to $41 billion over the same period.

LIE: *America is divided into red and blue states.*

THE TRUTH: We look purple from space. Americans get good and worked up over politics, an admirable quality taken advantage of by two groups: politicians and the media. Both do a great job of stirring up rivalry by vilifying the opposition, composed of "those other people" who live "over there." "Red state" TV viewers can fulminate about the godless perverts sipping lattes and marrying their dogs "on the coasts," while their "blue state" counterparts can heap scorn on all the stupid hicks who think dinosaurs are a U.N. hoax in "flyover country."

★ *The late Tim Russert of NBC News is credited with popularizing the terms "red and blue states" during the 2000 presidential election.*

But the red-blue distinction is hardly black and white. While someone has to win the election in each state, we tend to forget how close those margins can be. During the presidential election in November 2000, Florida's vote in the electoral college—for the win!—was decided by 537 ballots in the popular vote, or less than 0.01 percent of the total six million ballots cast in the state. Even the most extreme cases display a great deal of diversity. In 2004 the population of Utah—the "reddest" state that year—still voted 26.4 percent for John Kerry, meaning one out of every four people was secretly "blue." Fast forward to the 2008 election, and the most pro-Obama state, Hawaii, still voted 26.6 percent for McCain.

And let's not forget that red and blue aren't the only two crayons in the box. Check out the 1992 election, when a third-party candidate, Ross Perot, took an astounding 19 percent of the popular vote, stealing an equal balance of voters from both parties. Basically, one out of five Americans was so fed up with both "red" and "blue" politicians that they voted for a rich, ornery gnome from Texas who promised to balance the federal budget and expand the war on drugs (usually Republican talking points) but also supported protectionist trade measures, gun control, environmentalism, and abortion rights (Democratic touchstones).

In other words, America is a lot more complicated than the red vs. blue setup. A look at county-level results more accurately reflects the political landscape: it turns out blue states like New York and California are mostly red outside their metropolitan areas, while seemingly solid red states in the Midwest and South have unexpected pockets of blue along major river valleys. But county-level results can also be misleading, as even small towns are often evenly divided. In 2008 the Missouri popular vote went for McCain by 49.4 percent to 49.3 percent—but would have gone the other way if just 2,000 people had voted differently in counties like Adair (which split 49.6 percent–48.3 percent for McCain) or Clay (49.7 percent to 49 percent). Meanwhile, in solidly blue New York City, a map of political donations in the 2004 presidential election showed the Upper East Side favoring Republicans and the equally rich Upper West Side supporting Democrats. In other words, we aren't divided into red and blue states or even counties, but neighborhoods and streets.

Of course ideological divisions really do exist on issues like abortion, taxation, redistribution of wealth, and foreign wars. Such disagreements are a natural part of any functioning democracy—in fact, they're the whole reason for democratic government.

But at some point the national dialogue started breaking down, as media sources have become more and more partisan. In the 1980s–1990s, many Americans believed national newspapers and TV news were pushing liberal opinions on the rest of the country, and their alienation was reflected in the growing popularity of conservative commentators like Rush Limbaugh, who by 1990 had the largest audience of any radio talk show host in the United States. It also contributed to the success of Fox News, a 24-hour news channel with a right-wing slant founded by Rupert Murdoch's News Corp. in 1996. Fox News has in turn provoked more politically biased coverage from left-leaning new outlets.

The media bias certainly shows. For example, it's probably not a coincidence that Fox News called the 2000 election for George W. Bush before any other news organization—or that the call was made by Bush's cousin John Ellis, a former *Boston Globe* reporter who was working as a freelance political analyst for Fox News during the election. On the other side, CBS News anchorman Dan Rather was clearly eager to discredit Bush in the final months before the 2004 election with a report that Bush was AWOL from the Texas Air National Guard in the 1970s, based on documents that turned out to be forgeries—a discovery first publicized by a conservative blog, Powerline. (Indeed, Rather had pursued something of a vendetta against the Bush dynasty: in January 1988 he ambushed Bush Sr., the presumptive GOP presidential candidate, with questions about his involvement in Iran-Contra after promising not to bring up the subject.)

YOUR TIRED, YOUR POOR,
YOUR UNDOCUMENTED MASSES————————————————

Always a popular immigration destination, the United States' biggest immigrant group of recent years, hands down, consists of Spanish-speaking people from Latin America, particularly Mexico, which shares a long, not-so-policed border with the United States.

Of the 35 million immigrants living in the United States in 2008, the total number of foreign-born Spanish speakers constituted just over half—nearly 18 million. With the United States exerting this kind of attraction, it's not surprising that Hispanics also constitute the largest population of illegal immigrants: 55 percent of the Mexican immigrants, or about seven million people, are living in the United States illegally, along with similar percentages from other Spanish-speaking countries.

Still, foreign-born Hispanics only represent about 40 percent of the American Hispanic population. Adding up native-born citizens, naturalized citizens, legal immigrants, and illegal immigrants, the total number of U.S. Hispanics topped 45 million in 2008, or about 15 percent of the U.S. population, making it the largest Hispanic population in the world outside Mexico. Overall, the Hispanic population is following the pattern of economic assimilation established by earlier immigrants, with the median income of Hispanic households nearing $39,000 in 2008, up 15 percent from $34,000 in 1992 (in 2008 dollars). Where 51 percent of the adult Hispanic population had a high school diploma in 1990, the number rose to 59 percent by 2005, while the number holding college degrees increased from 5.5 percent to 8.5 percent. Still, parts of the Hispanic community continue to face some serious challenges: in 2008 the high school dropout rate for Latinos was 17 percent, compared to 9 percent for African-Americans, 6 percent for whites, and 4 percent for Asians. This in turn affects progress in areas like learning English, which correlates directly with employment opportunities and income levels. About 16 million Hispanics, or 35 percent of the total population, have limited or no English.

Like other immigrant groups, the influx of Hispanics has triggered a xenophobic backlash, based partly on cultural difference and partly on fear of economic competition. Both political parties have pandered to anti-immigrant sentiment, with Republicans taking the lead in fighting immigration reform in 2005. But the rapid growth of the Hispanic electorate makes this a risky proposition, especially as the fastest-growing populations are in important states like Florida, Texas, and California.

LIE: *Bankers are good with money.*

THE TRUTH: Bankers like money, but that doesn't mean they're any good with it. If anyone needed convincing of that fact, the ongoing financial catastrophe that began in 2007 should remove any lingering doubts. Of course, bankers weren't the only culprits: like most good financial disasters, this one began with well-intentioned government policies that totally backfired.

Tinkering with interest rates has always been an accepted way of softening "down phases" during economic cycles. So when the recession hit in 1991–1992, the Federal Reserve lowered interest rates to get banks lending more money. The low rates and general prosperity of the mid-1990s, particularly in the housing sector, encouraged the growth of mortgage companies specializing in "subprime" and adjustable-rate mortgages—new kinds of loans for would-be homebuyers with bad credit histories. These mortgages were equipped with special features intended to help people with almost no money acquire property. During the boom years, millions of people plowed money into real estate, seduced by the prospect of getting rich quick. Everyone assumed property would continue increasing in value, paying for itself.

This wave of speculation drove real estate prices higher, attracting more speculators to the market, which raised prices even more—a classic bubble. Easy credit made it all possible, with new subprime and ARM loans jumping from $25 billion in 1993 to $140 billion in 2000. The real estate bubble began growing even faster following the Federal Reserve's decision to lower interest rates again during the recession of 2001–2002. From 2000 to 2006, the total appraised value of residential real estate rose from $21 trillion to $30.5 trillion. As in any bubble, the apparent expansion in value was fueled by frantic deal-making, giving ordinary investors the impression of a solid trend—and the feeling that they might be missing out on a good thing. Mortgage debt more than doubled, while real estate agents cleaned up, with annual commissions jumping from $36 billion to $55 billion over the same period.

Were there warning signs? Of course. Alarmed financial analysts pointed to history, which showed that between 1890 and 1990, real estate prices had only increased 10.2 percent in inflation-adjusted terms. From 1990 to 2006, they soared an astounding 85 percent. Meanwhile, beginning around 1995 real estate prices started to eclipse their rental earning potential at an alarming rate. In other words, the value of residential real estate was no longer linked to its utility; instead, prices kept going up because, well, prices kept going up.

What's that old expression about everything that goes up? From 2006 to 2009, the total appraised value of U.S. residential real estate fell from $30.5 trillion to $24.7 trillion, and if it continues falling in 2010, it could wind up right back where it started in 2000. This would have been bad if it had only affected the millions of Americans who took an ice-cold bath on real estate. But it was worse. It turned out banks had built an entire financial universe on the unworthy foundation of subprime mortgages. Although the deals were incredibly complicated, the basic story is pretty straightforward, involving—once again—some ill-advised moves by the U.S. government.

★ *In 2010, there were 19 million vacant homes in the United States—enough to house the population of France at 3.4 people per home.*

The first ill-advised move came after a 1992 study by the Boston Federal Reserve Bank revealed continuing discrimination against low-income homebuyers, including minorities. In 1994 President Clinton pushed the Department of Housing and Urban Development to draw up new guidelines for banks issuing mortgages in its National Homeownership Strategy, loosening lending standards and establishing quotas determining the number of low-income mortgages banks had to offer. To encourage banks to lend more to homebuyers, the government offered positive incentives for more subprime mortgages, urging the Federal National Mortgage Association, nicknamed "Fannie Mae," and the Federal Home Mortgage Corporation, "Freddie Mac," to buy more and more subprime securities packages (investment products resembling mutual funds) from banks.

In 2000 Fannie and Freddie increased their quota of low-income mortgage-backed securities from 42 percent to 50 percent of all purchases—then again to 52 percent in 2005 and 55 percent in 2007. Meanwhile, investment bankers complained that they were missing out on all the fun. So in October 2004 the Securities and Exchange Commission agreed to waive regulations on five of the biggest—Goldman Sachs, Merrill Lynch, Lehman Brothers, Bear Stearns, and Morgan Stanley—allowing them to invest more in these risky mortgage-backed securities.

All this gave a huge boost to the risky securities market, which in turn gave private lenders a big incentive to offer more risky loans. Following the lead of Countrywide Financial, a big subprime lender, in 2004 many subprime mortgage corporations began using automated loan approval systems, meaning loan applicants were (barely) screened by computers, with scant human supervision. By 2007 a total of $1.5 trillion in subprime mortgages were held by 7.5 million homebuyers—13.4 percent of all outstanding home loans.

At the same time, the volume of risky mortgage-backed securities issued annually rose from $87 billion in 2001 to $450 billion in 2006, with private investors taking a bigger and bigger slice. Thus when the real estate market began declining in the second half of 2006, a lot more was riding on it than most people understood—but everyone was about to get a quick tutorial. Large numbers of subprime mortgages began going into default, and by August 2008, 9 percent of all U.S. mortgages were in default. The first wave of failures hit subprime mortgage corporations, with more than 20 of these specialized lenders collapsing in 2006–2007. Now all of those securities based on subprime mortgages were basically worthless too, and from 2007 to 2008, it became increasingly obvious that trillions of dollars that banks believed to exist, in fact, didn't.

Fall 2007 brought revelations of giant losses on subprime holdings across the industry. The losses were so huge that everyone started clamping down on loans to other financial institutions (a little late, guys!), making the situation even worse. As credit markets froze, banks started selling shares to anyone with money in a desperate effort to raise cash. This included "sovereign investments" from the governments of Singapore, Saudi Arabia, Kuwait, and South Korea.

And it was about to get *even worse*. For 2007–2008, there were hundreds of billions of dollars in write-downs from the main players, with Merrill Lynch taking the biggest hit at a total of $60 billion, followed by Citigroup with $46 billion. Frantically trying to stave off total financial collapse, the Federal Reserve and U.S. Treasury rushed from emergency to emergency, forcing banks into hastily conceived and comically mismatched marriages. With their perfunctory blessing, from January to October 2008, Bank of America bought Countrywide Financial Corp. and Merrill Lynch, JP Morgan Chase got Bear Stearns and WaMu, and Wells Fargo acquired Wachovia. Unfortunately, not everyone made the cut: U.S. officials peddled Lehman to any and every possible suitor, to no avail. With $50 billion of subprime securities, Lehman was stuck, and in September 2008, it flat out folded triggering the feared financial crisis.

From January to December 2008, total subprime losses in the financial sector almost quadrupled, from $218 billion to $800 billion, rippling outward from the original subprime culprits. Adding up the failures and government-brokered fire sales, bank shareholders lost $7 trillion. Meanwhile, global stock markets lost an incomprehensible $30 trillion in value—yes, that's $30,000,000,000,000. For comparison, that's the net worth of Green Bay, Wisconsin, if every resident was Madonna; alternatively, it's like winning the Powerball lotto jackpot 300,000 times in a row.

The staggering losses made a government bailout funded by the public (hello, you!) unavoidable. In July of 2008, President Bush signed a bill providing $300 billion in new loans to keep the mortgage market from freezing up completely. As panic set in following the Lehman Brothers failure in September, the U.S. government took control of Fannie Mae and Freddie Mac (setting aside $200 billion to cover their subprime securities losses), poured another $295 billion into domestic financial markets, loaned $330 billion to foreign central banks to stabilize overseas financial markets, and ponied up $125 billion to bail out American International Group (AIG), an insurance giant that lost tens of billions. In October, President Bush signed a bailout bill allocating $700 billion to buy risky mortgage-backed securities from banks, while the Fed provided another $150 billion in short-term loans to U.S. banks and $540 billion in loans to keep money markets functioning. The government also bailed out major U.S. automakers, ultimately investing $130 billion in Chrysler and GM.

American taxpayers were none too happy about bailing out irresponsible bankers, or taking ownership of AIG and GM (which turned over majority control to the U.S. government in exchange for bailout funds). As of 2010, the general American view of bankers might be characterized as a mix of resentment, jealousy, and distrust. How could bankers screw the pooch on such an epic—nay, cosmic—scale?

★ *The $5.8 trillion decline in the value of residential real estate was more than twice China's 2006 GDP of $2.7 trillion.*

Although it would be impossible to recount them all, the financial meltdown was made possible by mistakes and deceit at various levels. At the bottom, unqualified or under-qualified homebuyers were approved for sketchy loans through unethical (or plain illegal) practices by subprime mortgage corporations. Then brokers deliberately mixed bad loans with good loans in securities, making the securities appear less risky than they actually were. Some subprime mortgage corporations simply altered information on bad mortgages before selling them to banks. And it was easy to trick banks because credit-rating agencies gave high ratings to risky securities based on the (inaccurate) information provided by the subprime mortgage corporations.

Basically, no one did any research checking where all this (imaginary) money was coming from, even though a perfunctory examination of lending practices would reveal that an alarming number of subprime loans were bound to default. Why didn't bankers or regulators check? They were lazy, and it was easier to believe everyone could get rich by helping poor people buy houses.

If you're looking for political culprits in the financial disaster of 2007–20??, you won't be able to pin it on one political party. The Democrats helped lay the groundwork with President Clinton's 1995 decision to allow Fannie Mae and Freddie Mac to count subprime securities purchases as aid to low-income homebuyers, followed by congressional Democrats pushing the mortgage agencies to increase their subprime purchase targets in 2000 and 2005. For their part, in 2004 the Republicans poured gasoline on the fire by pressuring the SEC to let investment banks purchase more subprime-backed securities. Unlike nearly everything else to come out of Washington in the early 2000s, the financial crisis was a true bipartisan creation.

·········· **OTHER PEOPLE'S STUFF** ·················

Two Towers and the Morning of 9/11

On the clear, sunny morning of September 11, 2001, fifteen Saudis, two citizens of the United Arab Emirates, one Lebanese, and one Egyptian armed with box cutters commandeered four airliners, and then crashed two into the twin towers of New York's World Trade Center and one into the Pentagon in Washington, D.C. The fourth airliner—possibly intended for the U.S. Capitol or the White House—crashed in rural Pennsylvania after passengers tried to overpower the hijackers. Besides the 19 hijackers, the attacks claimed the lives of 2,740 Americans and 236 foreigners, including 2,605 at the World Trade Center, 70 civilians and 55 military personnel at the Pentagon, and 246 passengers and crew aboard the planes; among the Trade Center dead were 411 emergency workers, including 341 firefighters.

Americans responded to the murderous attacks with shock and fury, as sympathizers abroad held candlelight vigils to express solidarity. By the end of the day, the U.S. government had identified the culprit as Al Qaeda, a terrorist organization formed by Osama bin Laden after his involvement in the *Maktab al-Khidamat* (MAK), founded to help Afghan mujahedin fight Soviet invaders. In fact, Al Qaeda had demanded that the United States withdraw all of its troops from Saudi Arabia, because the Americans defiled Mecca by their very presence. The terrorist group also wanted America to cease interference in any internal affairs of Muslim countries. The attack on America was Al Qaeda making its threat heard.

While the civilian death toll was lower than initially feared (up to 50,000 people worked in the World Trade Center on a typical day), it was still shocking—and completely outside any accepted rules of warfare. A decisive military response was inevitable. While President George W. Bush vowed to wage a wide-ranging war on terror, the first logical target was Afghanistan, where the ultra-Islamist Taliban regime had harbored bin Laden since 1997. On the evening of September 11, the leader of the Taliban, Mullah Omar, begged the United States not to attack Afghanistan, but he subsequently refused to give up bin Laden, citing Islamic rules of hospitality. On September 12, NATO invoked Article 5 of the Alliance treaty calling for collective defense, making European and Canadian forces available for the U.S.-led response. Within 24 hours of September 11, three aircraft carrier battle groups set sail for the Arabian Sea, and U.S. planes and ground forces began gathering in friendly countries around the Persian Gulf. Under U.S. pressure, Saudi Arabia and Pakistan renounced the Taliban, whom they'd previously supported, and Pakistan opened its airspace to U.S. warplanes. Even Iran, still a bitter U.S. enemy, agreed to rescue any American airmen forced down in its territory.

The attack on the Taliban regime commenced October 7, 2001, with bombardments focused on breaking the stalemate in northern Afghanistan, where Taliban and Northern Alliance troops faced each other from networks of defensive trenches. The results were dramatic and, by all accounts, terrifying: low-flying B-52s carpet bombed the Taliban trenches, annihilating entire divisions in a single pass, while C-130 transport planes dropped 15,000-pound BLU-82 "Daisy Cutters"—the largest nonnuclear explosive in the U.S. arsenal, obliterating an area measuring 260 feet in diameter. The Taliban broke and ran, loading everyone in pickup trucks and beating a retreat for the capital, Kabul. But this was a mistake: trained to destroy tank armies, U.S. air power specialized in picking off vehicles moving across open terrain. Kabul fell to the Northern Alliance on the night of November 12-13, 2001, bringing overjoyed residents into the streets, with men publicly shaving their beards and young people dancing to music from radios (all forbidden by the hirsute, fun-averse Taliban). In December the remaining Taliban abandoned their southern stronghold, Kandahar, and returned to the remote, ungoverned mountain ranges of southeastern Afghanistan from which they'd emerged a decade earlier.

But this spectacular success didn't translate into lasting victory. Osama bin Laden managed to elude the U.S. dragnet, while his Taliban allies regrouped in southeastern Afghanistan and Pakistan, protected by rugged terrain and their Pashtun ethnic kinsmen. In December of 2009, President Obama increased the U.S. troop commitment by 30,000, but if history is any guide, force alone won't be sufficient to "fix" Afghanistan, let alone "win" the War on Terror.

FILE UNDER "COUNTERPRODUCTIVE"

Sadly, terrorism is almost certain to continue, despite the fact that it has never, ever worked. The record of nineteenth-century anarchist terror was one of complete, unmitigated failure. In the twentieth century, Gerry Adams, the leader of *Sinn Fein* (the political arm of the Northern Irish independence movement) admitted that IRA bomb attacks against civilians were a "mistake;" the Basque separatist movement in Spain, ETA, is almost *terminado*; and the PLO, Hamas, and Hezbollah have gained nothing from decades of violence against Israel. In fact, terrorism historically has been inherently self-defeating: random acts of violence against civilians only succeed in making the survivors angry.

The Case of the Missing WMDs

The invasion of Iraq in 2003 is America's most controversial foreign war since Vietnam. While it's too soon to make any big historical judgments, there are a couple of aspects of the story that aren't quite as straightforward as they seem.

Iraq's dictator, Saddam Hussein, was universally condemned for using chemical weapons in both the Iran–Iraq War and against his own people during the *Anfal* Kurdish genocide. He was universally re-condemned for invading Kuwait in August 1990, and after his defeat in the First Gulf War, Hussein remained a bitter foe of the United States and its allies. He was also viewed as a threat to regional stability because of his support of Palestinian terrorist groups opposing Israel and his dogged pursuit of weapons of mass destruction.

Official American policy toward Iraq emphasized the need to halt Hussein's nuclear, chemical, and biological weapons programs. After the First Gulf War, the U.S. Navy enforced U.N. sanctions intended to deprive Iraq of materials needed for weapons of mass destruction (WMD). And in December of 1998, President Clinton ordered Operation Desert Fox, a bombing mission targeting Iraq's WMD sites, government, and infrastructure after Hussein refused to allow U.N. weapons inspectors access to some suspected sites. It wasn't until Clinton's signing of the Iraq Liberation Act in October 1998, however, that the United States also officially sought Hussein's overthrow. The Iraq Liberation Act was mostly symbolic. But the terrorist attacks on 9/11 completely transformed the American political landscape, allowing Bush to pursue regime change much more aggressively than Clinton had been able to.

This is where the controversy comes in, with opponents of the war leveling a number of criticisms regarding the Bush administration's handling of the WMD issue, its true intentions in going to war, and its conduct of the invasion and occupation.

In keeping with previous U.S. policy, the Bush administration presented Iraqi WMD as the main justification for war. But when Hussein allowed U.N. weapons inspectors to return to Iraq in November 2002, they didn't find any evidence of WMD stockpiles or production. Yet the White House chose to ignore these findings in favor of much more alarming assessments from "working groups" in the Pentagon and CIA who were ordered to err on the side of suspicion. Critics point to this pattern as proof that administration officials only wanted to hear analyses that confirmed their suspicions; some even accuse the administration of deliberately lying about Iraqi WMD to swing public opinion behind the war.

★ *Yet another new term emerged from the Iraq war in 2003—"embedded reporters," journalists who are attached to military units engaged in armed conflicts.*

There's no question the administration painted an alarming picture of Iraq's WMD progress to make the case for war, including many claims that turned out to be untrue. But that doesn't necessarily mean administration officials knowingly deceived the public. The U.N. and CIA had both been hoodwinked about WMD in the past. Hussein was a champion liar, and Iraq is a big country—170,000 square miles, the size of California—with lots of hiding places. It remains something of a mystery why Hussein didn't allow inspectors in earlier if he really had nothing to hide; one theory is he wanted everyone to think he had the weapons to deter other countries from invading Iraq (ah, the irony).

> **At the time I was preparing that presentation it was presented to me as being solid.**
>
> —U.S. Secretary of State Colin Powell, on his inaccurate February 2003 address to the U.N. about Iraqi WMD

But none of this proves that they *didn't* knowingly deceive the public. The basic WMD premise didn't make much sense at all. It was extremely unlikely that Hussein would have used the WMD himself against civilian targets in the United States, since that would have basically ensured his own destruction. And the suggestion that Hussein might hand off WMD to Al Qaeda is even more ridiculous, considering that Osama bin Laden had on several occasions called for the overthrow of Hussein, whom he condemned as a secular tyrant, "a bad Muslim" and "an infidel."

And then there's that 18.5-billion-ton gorilla in the room: Iraq's massive oil reserves. According to the conspiracy theory, Bush and company used Hussein's alleged WMD as an excuse to grab Iraq's oil. Critics point to a number of nefarious connections between the administration and oil interests, including Vice President Dick Cheney's connection with Halliburton, an energy services firm that performed emergency repairs on Iraqi oil infrastructure after the invasion. It's true Cheney was in a position to direct business to Halliburton (where he served as CEO from 1995 to 2000), but it would be hard to prove charges of favoritism, as Halliburton is the largest energy services company in the world and had already won several contracts from the U.S. Army Corps of Engineers during the Clinton administration.

But the fact remains that successive U.S. administrations have sought to control global energy supplies since before the Second World War—especially oil. So the idea that the invasion had *nothing* to do with Iraq's oil is obviously pretty implausible. The focus on oil was evident in the planning and execution of the war, when special forces parachuted in to protect Iraq's oil fields, while armories, power plants, and other government buildings were left open to looters and saboteurs. After the war, U.S. advisors helped draw up new contracts dividing up oil development between five Western energy companies, including America's largest oil companies, Exxon-Mobil and Chevron. Mission accomplished?

Not exactly. Clearly, the invasion of Iraq didn't turn out quite as hoped. So what happened?

The mistakes began with the size of the invasion force. As the Bush administration worked to rally support for the invasion of Iraq, it needed to persuade the American public that the war wouldn't be enormously expensive. By using a smaller invasion force, the administration intended to burn through less money. Initially, Secretary of Defense Donald Rumsfeld proposed an invasion force of just 75,000 U.S. troops, but General Tommy Franks eventually persuaded him to allocate 125,000 U.S. troops to the invasion of Iraq (together with 45,000 British troops). Even then, Rumsfeld's aide Paul Wolfowitz estimated the total cost of the invasion and reconstruction at less than $95 billion (by the end of 2009, actual expenditures topped $700 billion).

★ *Donald Rumsfeld was both the youngest and oldest person to serve as Secretary of Defense in U.S. history, at age 43 in 1975 and age 74 in 2006.*

In March of 2003 the Iraqi military collapsed before the initial U.S. combined air and ground onslaught—but there were early signs of trouble. As the Marines pressed forward toward Baghdad, rear areas came under attack by Iraqi guerrilla fighters. In the end, the Marines were able to crush most of this early guerrilla activity—but the mere fact of continuing resistance was a bad sign, foreshadowing a long postwar insurgency that the Pentagon failed to anticipate.

> As we know, there are known knowns. These are things we know that we know. We also know there are known unknowns. That is to say, we know there are some things we do not know. But there are also unknown unknowns, the ones we don't know we don't know.
>
> —Donald Rumsfeld, February 12, 2002

These problems were multiplied by some profoundly ill-advised U.S. policies. The first wrong move was the disbanding of the Iraqi army in May 2003 by L. Paul Bremer, the civilian governor of Iraq appointed by the Bush administration. Bush later tried to push blame for this disastrous decision on to Bremer, who fired back that he was following the wishes of the president. It's amazing that we still don't really know who decided to disband Iraq's army, but we do know that it was a really bad idea. The U.S. occupiers basically told a quarter-million angry young men: "Sorry, you're out of work—but you can keep your gun!"

The same goes for the Bush administration's decision to purge all former members of Hussein's Ba'ath Party from positions of responsibility—effectively firing most of Iraq's clerks, police officers, engineers, bank managers, factory bosses, teachers, doctors . . . basically anyone with any sort of experience and authority. Firing them was a double whammy, since it provided even more unemployed, embittered potential recruits for the insurgency.

While it's still way too soon to say, despite all the mistakes, it appears that the American invasion and occupation of Iraq may actually succeed, thanks to a combination of delayed common sense and good luck. On the American side, common sense prevailed when the Pentagon adopted a "surge" strategy committing 20,000 more troops to help stabilize the war-torn country in 2007–2008. Common sense scored another victory with the decision by most Shiite groups to embrace the democratic process, as free, fair elections were virtually guaranteed to give the country's oppressed majority the upper hand. Last but not least, the political landscape was transformed by the emergence of the Sunni *Sahwa*

Iraq: Fatalities per Quarter

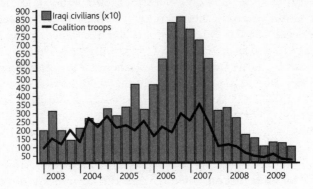

or "Awakening" movement, led by tribal sheiks who succeeded in rooting out at least some of the foreign terrorists inspired by Al Qaeda.

···················· **PROFILES IN URGES**····················

Politicians have always engaged in extracurricular hanky-panky, but before the late twentieth century, the press usually chose to politely ignore their various dalliances, peccadilloes, rendezvous, and seraglios. Why, it seems almost quaint now, doesn't it? Here's a quick review of just a handful of the bigger political sex scandals.

GARY HART (b. November 28, 1936). The handsome senator from Colorado was considered a front-runner for the Democratic presidential nomination in 1988 until revelations in *The New York Times* and *The Miami Herald* that he was having an extramarital affair with a 29-year-old model named Donna Rice. Not long after, the *National Enquirer* published a photo of Rice seated on Hart's knee aboard a yacht (the aptly named *Monkey Business*). The scandal was devastating to Hart's political prospects: literally overnight, his support in the New Hampshire Democratic primary dropped from 32 percent to 17 percent, leaving Massachusetts Governor Michael Dukakis the front-runner. On May 8, 1987, Hart dropped out of the race; interestingly, a Gallup poll found 64 percent of Americans thought Hart's treatment by the media was unfair.

CLARENCE THOMAS (b. June 23, 1948). After Thurgood Marshall retired in 1991, President George H.W. Bush stirred controversy by nominating Clarence Thomas, a conservative

African-American judge from the U.S. District Court of Appeals in Washington, D.C., to the Supreme Court. Liberals criticized Thomas for opposing abortion rights and affirmative action, while legal scholars questioned his qualifications (he was 43, compared to an average age of 54 for new justices). Then a female professor from the University of Oklahoma, Anita Hill, told the FBI that Thomas sexually harassed her when she was his assistant in 1982–1983. Among other things, Hill said Thomas recounted pornographic movies depicting orgies, rape, and bestiality; discussed the endowment of a pornographic film star, "Long Dong Silver"; and joked about what appeared to be a pubic hair on a soda can. Dividing along partisan lines, the Democrats looked for more dirt on Thomas, while the Republicans did their best to discredit Hill with rumors and innuendo. Thomas angrily accused Hill (who is also African-American) of participating in a "high-tech lynching" orchestrated by the white news media. He was finally confirmed by a party-line vote of 52–48.

BOB PACKWOOD (b. September 11, 1932). Before his downfall, the Republican senator from Oregon was considered "one of the nation's most powerful elected officials," because of his senior position on several key Senate committees. Respected by liberals for his views on the environment and women's rights—especially on abortion—Packwood wasn't quite so enlightened in his private life. In November 1992 *The Washington Post* published shocking allegations of sexual misconduct from ten women, including lobbyists and former female staffers. The Senate Ethics Committee demanded Packwood turn over his diary, which was said to include incriminating details of his sex life, but Packwood stonewalled, vaguely threatening to expose misconduct by other members of Congress. The Senate Ethics Committee finally recommended Packwood be expelled from the Senate—an extraordinary measure last used during the Civil War—prompting him to resign on September 7, 1995.

BILL CLINTON (b. August 19, 1946). Clinton was dogged by allegations of sexual harassment and extramarital affairs before he was even elected, beginning with Gennifer Flowers, who claimed she had an affair with Clinton when he was governor of Arkansas. After he won election, in May 1994 Clinton was accused of sexual harassment by a former Arkansas state employee, Paula Jones, who said she'd been lewdly propositioned by then-governor Clinton three years before. In 1997 a judge ruled that Jones's lawyers could subpoena other women to testify about their relationships with Clinton, including Monica Lewinsky, a 22-year-old former White House intern. Clinton and Lewinsky both denied any sexual relationship, and Clinton eventually settled with Jones out of court with a payment of $850,000.

But it turned out one of Lewinsky's coworkers, Linda Tripp, had secretly taped phone conversations in which she discussed her affair with Clinton. In January 1998 Tripp turned the tapes over to a special prosecutor, Kenneth Starr, appointed by the Republican-dominated Congress to investigate Clinton's other alleged misdoings. After the Drudge Report Web site broke the news on January 17, Clinton gave a press conference where he famously insisted, "I did not have sexual relations with that woman, Ms. Lewinsky."

In July Starr agreed to give Lewinsky immunity for her perjury in the Jones case in return for testifying about her affair with Clinton and the subsequent cover-up. This included turning over a blue dress with a semen stain, which DNA testing showed to be Clinton's. In August 1998 Clinton admitted the relationship with Lewinsky in grand jury testimony, opening himself to charges of perjury and obstruction of justice—both impeachable offenses. Congress voted to impeach him on December 19, 1998, but he was acquitted by the Senate on February 12, 1999.

···················· **SPECIAL REPORT**··············

We've Got New Issues
The Gay Marriage Debate

Homosexual activity used to be illegal in most states, under statues prohibiting "sodomy," which includes any sexual contact between two people of the same gender. However, most of those laws were repealed voluntarily by the states in the second half of the twentieth century, and in 2003 the Supreme Court overturned all remaining sodomy laws in *Lawrence v. Texas*. The next logical step, to many gay rights activists, was gaining the right to marry. While most state laws have defined or presumed marriage to be the union of a man and a woman, gay marriage advocates point out there's no particular reason it shouldn't be modified to allow any two consenting adults to marry.

No surprise, there is more than a little disagreement on this point. Many opponents object on religious grounds, while gay marriage advocates point out that religious laws as set forth in holy books are not identical with the laws of the United States (the whole separation of church and state thing). Similarly, some opponents warn that same-sex marriages will "undermine the sanctity of marriage" although some of the sanctity-free marriages coming out of Hollywood seem a rebuttal in their own right. Others equate marriage with "natural law," arguing that it brings a man and woman together for the purpose of biological reproduction . . . which would also seem to exclude straight couples who are infertile or don't want children. Then there's the "slippery slope" argument, i.e., "if two men can get married today, somewhere down the line a man will be able to marry his dog/ Gila monster/emu." (Of course, the obvious difference here is that—unlike two consenting human adults—the animal of choice is not able to give verbal consent, let alone demand a pre-nup.)

★ *In 2004, 30% of U.S. high school students said they had a close friend who was gay.*

At this point, each side is digging in its heels, and the argument goes on. As of 2010 gay marriage was legal in five states— Connecticut, Iowa, Massachusetts, New Hampshire, and Vermont— as well as Washington, D.C. Meanwhile, New York, Rhode Island, and Maryland recognize same-sex marriages performed in other states, but don't grant them in state. On the other hand, the 1996 Defense of Marriage Act signed by Bill Clinton prevents the federal government from recognizing same-sex marriages, and 30 states have passed amendments to their state constitutions banning same-sex marriage, including California, which passed Proposition 8 in 2008. (Many of these laws resemble anti-miscegenation laws prohibiting interracial marriages in the early twentieth century, which should tell you something.)

But the big story is at the national level, where the halfhearted attempt by Republicans in Congress to amend the U.S. Constitution to prohibit gay marriage failed in 2006. Without a constitutional amendment, gay rights activists can challenge the state laws before the U.S. Supreme Court on the grounds they violate the Fourteenth Amendment, which guarantees "equal protection." Meanwhile, the overall trend seems to be one of gradually increasing acceptance. Where Gallup found that 68 percent of American adults opposed gay marriage in 1996, that number gradually dropped to 61 percent in 2003 and then 57 percent in 2009.

Hurricane Katrina

The worst U.S. natural disaster in over a century, Hurricane Katrina killed more people and caused more damage than any natural event since the Galveston Hurricane in 1900. After originating as a tropical depression over the mid-Atlantic on August 23, 2005, Katrina passed over southern Florida into the Gulf of Mexico on August 26, where it absorbed more energy from the warm tropical waters. By the evening of August 28, Katrina was a Category 5 hurricane with sustained winds of 175 miles per hour and gusts up to 215 miles per hour. It weakened to a Category 3 hurricane by the time it made landfall south of New Orleans early on August 29, 2005, but the storm surge was still devastating to coastal towns. At around 8 a.m., a levee on the east side of New Orleans was breached by rising water in the Industrial Canal. Within minutes the National Weather Service issued a flash flood warning, and less than an hour later, there were over six feet of water in the city's impoverished Ninth Ward.

> ★ The Galveston Hurricane on September 8, 1900 completely destroyed the low-lying port city, killing 8,000 people. Afterwards, the entire city was raised by 17 feet to prevent a repeat of the disaster.

On August 30 a second levee broke, and by the next day, 80 percent of New Orleans was underwater. As the city's low-lying areas were submerged, residents who'd ignored earlier warnings to evacuate (or were unable to comply) found themselves stranded on their rooftops waiting for rescue by Coast Guard helicopters. And they were the lucky ones: around 400 people drowned, while another 360 died of injury and illness in New Orleans—including many old and infirm people who couldn't move to safety—contributing to almost half of Katrina's total death toll of 1,836 in Louisiana and Mississippi.

Twenty-five thousand people took shelter in the New Orleans Superdome, where they were protected from the elements but lacked food, water, or medical treatment for several days. Cut off from the outside world, conditions at the Superdome became increasingly squalid as the displaced people overwhelmed the trash receptacles and bathrooms. By the time the last people were evacuated to the Houston Astrodome on September 4, 2005, six had died—including four from "natural causes," one from a drug overdose, and one from suicide. Although the news media was filled with reports of rape and murder in New Orleans and the Superdome, virtually all these turned out to be baseless rumors. There was, however, widespread looting in New Orleans.

> I don't want to go to no Astrodome. I've been domed almost to death.
>
> —Janice Singleton, at the Superdome,
> September 3, 2005

The disaster also led to widespread criticism of the city, state, and federal governments for allowing the better part of a large American city to be destroyed. While local and national officials are still trading accusations, there is plenty of blame to go around. The director of the National Hurricane Center advised the governments of New Orleans and the state of Louisiana to issue a mandatory evacuation order on Saturday, August 27, but New Orleans Mayor Charles Nagin delayed until the following day—then failed to enforce the order. (He finally authorized police and National Guardsmen to remove residents by force, if necessary, on September 6.) As a result emergency response personnel were forced to improvise, including housing 20,000 people in the New Orleans Convention Center; no one knows who made this decision.

> Brownie, you're doing a heckuva job.
>
> —George W. Bush, to FEMA director
> Michael D. Brown, September 2, 2005
>
> It was beyond the capacity of the state and local governments, and it was beyond the capacity of FEMA.
>
> —Brown, January 18, 2006

It was popular to blame the Federal Emergency Management Administration for its belated intervention, and it seems safe to say its performance didn't justify praise it received from President Bush. On the other hand, some of this criticism was spin from local officials trying to dodge blame for their own mistakes. There's no question, however, that the federal government shared responsibility for failing to strengthen and maintain the levees around New Orleans. Flood control is partly a federal responsibility because New Orleans was made more vulnerable by navigation improvements on the Mississippi River intended to facilitate interstate commerce. However, flood control improvements planned in 1965 still weren't finished—40 years later!—due to lack of funds. Complicating the situation, in the 1970s some proposed flood protection measures were blocked by environmental lobbyists. Meanwhile, studies by the U.S. Army Corps of Engineers, which built the levees in the 1960s, repeatedly warned that they were vulnerable to storm surges—as did some of the contractors employed by the Corps, as well as the *New Orleans Times-Picayune*, which published a multipart series on the threat in 2002.

None of this talk resulted in any action, however, and New Orleans paid a spectacular price for the negligence. In addition to the deaths, the city suffered $20 billion in damage, contributing to the total price tag of $100 billion for a 93,000-square-mile swath of the Gulf Coast. Indeed, even without the flooding, Katrina was a Grade-A catastrophe. Altogether the hurricane and flooding destroyed 300,000 homes, generated 120 million cubic yards of debris, and displaced 770,000 people, many of whom never returned. The population of New Orleans dipped from 461,600 in 2004 to just 210,768 in 2006; by 2008, it had rebounded to 311,853.

·················· **TRENDSPOTTING** ················

Debt Row

Americans are practically addicted to addiction: alcohol, tobacco, caffeine, gasoline, pornography, reality TV, etc. But, possibly thanks to too many hours playing Monopoly as kids, Americans' most American addiction is something that doesn't exist at all: imaginary money.

For most of its history, the U.S. government borrowed very little money. In emergencies (wars), the government was authorized to borrow money from the people by selling "war bonds." But then during the Great Depression, Presidents Herbert Hoover and Franklin Delano Roosevelt attempted to "prime the pump" of the economy with an innovation—large-scale peacetime deficit spending, peaking at $4.3 billion in 1936. Anathema to old-fashioned fiscal conservatives, deficit spending became linked with economic recovery in the popular imagination, changing American public finance forever. In fact, every administration since LBJ has turned to deficit spending at some point: from 1970 to 2010, there have only been four years when the U.S. government *didn't* run a deficit (1998–2001).

You may be wondering—if the country did just fine without deficit spending for its first 150 years of existence—what are we spending all this money on now. Well, a whole bunch of "mandatory" social spending like Medicare and Medicaid, for one thing. Combined spending on these two programs alone came to $511 billion in 2006 and is projected to increase to $1 trillion *annually* by 2020 (down from an earlier projection of $1.5 trillion, thanks to the health-care reform bill passed amid much acrimony in March 2010).

Despite the supposed cost reductions contained in the bill, the fact remains that both political parties have embraced increasingly reckless financial policies. From 2000 to 2008, the Republican Party threw its small government ideology to the wind, with deficit spending growing to $460 billion in 2008. And that's nothing compared to the deficits that followed during the Obama administration, as the government borrowed to stimulate a shell-shocked economy and escalate the war in Afghanistan—sending the annual budget deficit to $1.41 trillion in 2009, $1.56 trillion in 2010, and a projected $1.27 trillion in 2011. At this rate, the total U.S. debt is projected to increase from $12 trillion in 2009 to $20 trillion in 2020.

Those figures are enough to make economists very nervous. One of the most commonly used measures of a country's financial health is the ratio of its total debt to its annual gross domestic product. From about one-third of GDP in the mid-1970s, the U.S.

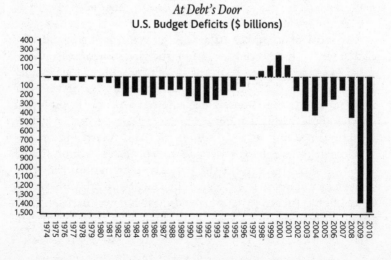

At Debt's Door
U.S. Budget Deficits ($ billions)

government debt gradually increased to about 50 percent of GDP in the late 1980s, before zooming to 94 percent of GDP in 2010.

Will there be any negative consequences from owing this much dough? No one knows, because the United States is entering mostly uncharted territory in terms of its debt. What we do know is that so far, 2010 is turning out to be an anemic recovery at best, with most economists forecasting low growth rates for the next decade or so—meaning the debt is just going to sit there and fester.

CASH OR CREDIT?

In addition to the national debt and the mortgage debt, Americans have piled up an impressive amount of consumer debt—mostly in the form of credit card debt. From 2006 to 2008, total U.S. credit card debt increased from $770 billion to $973 billion. That comes to $8,316 per household. By contrast, Chinese consumers owe a total $114 billion, equaling $325 per household. What's more, from 2010 to 2014, U.S. credit card lenders expect to write off $395 billion in bad loans—up from $275 billion from 2005 to 2009.

> When it's $100,000 of debt, it's your problem. When it's a million dollars of debt, it's the bank's problem.
>
> —Robert D. Manning, author of *Credit Card Nation*

Going Green

Americans have been concerned about the impact of human activity on the environment at least as far back as the conservationist movement in the late nineteenth century, which resulted in the establishment of the National Park System, beginning with Yellowstone in 1872. In the second half of the twentieth century, books like Rachel Carson's *Silent Spring,* published in 1962, raised awareness about the effects of man-made pollutants on the natural world and human health, leading to the modern environmental movement. Environmental legislation brought reductions in common pollutants like lead and mercury and combated the growth of landfills through recycling.

The last years of the twentieth century brought a second wave of environmental activism, focused on the threat of global warming (allegedly) caused by man-made "greenhouse" gases, chiefly carbon dioxide. Scientists first proposed the theory of a "greenhouse effect," in which carbon dioxide and water vapor trap reflected solar radiation in Earth's atmosphere, in the late nineteenth century—but their work was largely ignored until 1976, when Stanford University climatologist Stephen Schneider linked the greenhouse effect to a sharp rise in temperatures. In 1988 the United Nations and the World Meteorological Organization formed the Intergovernmental Panel on Climate Change to study and combat the phenomenon of global warming. In 1998, 186 countries signed the Kyoto Protocol, agreeing to reduce greenhouse gas emissions—although it received a setback when the Bush administration refused to ratify it in 2001.

While the U.S. government has been balky about combating climate change, the American people seem increasingly willing to jump on the "green" bandwagon, as reflected in the success of Al Gore's 2006 documentary, "An Inconvenient Truth," and the growing obsession with "carbon footprints." Unsurprisingly, marketers have latched on to the green trend with an array of "environment-friendly" products and services, including food, clothing, cars, houses, appliances, consumer electronics, bathroom fixtures, financial planning, travel bookings, daycare, pet grooming, mortuary arrangements . . . the list is practically infinite.

But America is a contradictory place, and there also seems to be growing skepticism about global warming: in 2009 an opinion poll by Harris Interactive found 51 percent of Americans believed that global warming was caused by greenhouse gases—down sharply from 71 percent just two years before. The cause wasn't helped by revelations that climate scientists at the IPCC had issued exaggerated forecasts of global warming impacts.

In the midst of the worst recession in decades, polls also show that a majority of Americans prioritize economic growth above environmental issues. Still, there seem to be areas where "green" issues and economic concerns overlap. One hot-button issue is fossil fuels, where environmentalists and economists receive additional support from national security wonks who want to discourage dependence on Middle Eastern oil.

★ In 1980 there were about 105 million acres of wetlands in the United States, but by 2010 the number had shrunk almost 10 percent to 95 million acres. The country is currently losing about 80,000 acres of wetlands per year—scientists estimate there were over 220 million acres of wetlands before European settlement.

Better Living Through Medication

The end of the twentieth century brought a huge increase in the number and amount of prescription drugs taken by Americans, both legally and illegally. In 2004 the U.S. Department of Health and Human Services found that half of Americans were taking at least one prescription drug, with one in six Americans taking three or more medications. Some of the most popular—and controversial—prescription drug categories include antidepressants, stimulants to treat attention deficit hyperactive disorder, drugs for erectile dysfunction, and of course those perennial favorites, the opioids.

The antidepressant surge began with Prozac, invented in 1972 and first marketed in the United States for treatment of depression and other mental illnesses in 1988. The number of prescriptions for all kinds of antidepressants surged over 250 percent from 46 million in 1990 to 164 million in 2008. Predictably, the explosion in antidepressant use has caused some alarm: experts point out that no one knows the long-term effects of these drugs, and some critics have blamed Zoloft and Paxil for psychotic episodes in some patients (although these allegations are disputed). Nonetheless, the drugs have proved a godsend for the roughly 20 million Americans who suffer chronic depression, helping them live normal, productive lives.

★ *Even though it seems much longer, we've only been inundated with TV commercials for prescription drugs since 1997, when the FDA relaxed the rules for direct-to-consumer drug advertising.*

You don't hear nearly as many complaints about another new class of prescription wonder drug—medications for the treatment of male erectile dysfunction, including sildenafil citrate (Viagra, invented by Pfizer and approved by the FDA in 1998), vardenafil (Levitra, Bayer-GSK-SP, 2003), and tadalafil (Cialis, Eli Lilly-ICOS, 2003). These drugs represented a revolution in the treatment of impotence—one of the most common and psychologically harmful male sexual complaints—so in that regard, they pretty much sell themselves. However, in the early stages of marketing Viagra, Pfizer still faced the challenge of, heh, raising awareness about the new treatment and overcoming predictable reactions of shame and embarrassment, not to mention general reluctance among older generations to talk about, you know . . . S-E-X. So who better to, er, spearhead the marketing effort than Bob Dole, the former Republican senator from Kansas? After stepping into the national spotlight with his failed campaign to unseat the Democrat President Bill Clinton in 1996, in 1999 Dole lent his folksy humor and respectability to Pfizer's print and broadcast ad campaign promoting Viagra.

ROID RAGE

Another troubling trend is the illicit use of anabolic steroids, which male and female athletes take to build muscle and improve their performance on the playing field. Currently about one million Americans are estimated to take anabolic steroids illegally, about half of whom are adolescents. A 1990 survey found about 4.4 percent of high school students said they had used or were currently using steroids, edging up to 6.1 percent in 2005—and that's just the ones who admitted to it. But it's not just about athletics. Interestingly, roughly a third of male high school students who abuse steroids say they do so solely to improve their appearance, reflecting the steady inflation of expectations for physical beauty among men and women alike.

Steroid users run the risk of quite a few negative side effects, which include increased risks of heart disease, immune suppression, kidney disease, prostate enlargement, and sterility in both men and women. Of course, taking male sex hormones linked to aggression can also have some predictable psychological side effects, like...aggression. The phenomenon of "roid rage," while seemingly less common than other side effects, is potentially the scariest: anecdotal evidence includes stories of mania, paranoia, psychosis, and violence from previously stable individuals...who can now hurl a grown man across the room. What's not to like?

Statistical evidence seems to suggest (but not prove) the existence of an epidemic: for example, the average weight of NFL linemen increased from about 250 pounds to 300 pounds from 1980 to 2005. Meanwhile, the number of home runs per Major League Baseball game jumped from 0.8 per game around 1990 to 1.2 per game in 2000. Baseball players seem especially prone to steroid abuse, as revealed by the investigation into a hormone supplement company called BALCO in 2003–2004. Famous baseball players who admitted using steroids include Mark McGwire, Barry Bonds, Jason Giambi, Alex Rodriguez ("A-Rod"), Ken Caminiti, and Jose Canseco. Canseco estimated that 85 percent of players in Major League Baseball abused steroids, while Caminiti offered a more modest estimate of 50 percent. (The MLB banned steroids in 1991, but for some reason didn't start testing until 2003; from 2005 to 2006, 111 players were suspended.)

A great deal more controversy surrounds the growing use of stimulants like Ritalin and Adderall, in large part because so many medicated people are preteens. Parents and teachers have looked on these drugs as a miracle cure for attention deficit disorder (ADD), characterized by an inability to focus or complete tasks, and attention deficit hyperactive disorder (ADHD), which has the bonus of rambunctious, disruptive behavior in the home and classroom. The total number of prescriptions for Ritalin, Adderall, and related ADD/ADHD drugs rocketed from three million in 1990 to 39.5 million in 2008—a 1,200 percent increase—while the number of children taking these drugs increased from one million to over six million. And many of these kids are *young*: in the mid-1990s, the biggest rate of increase in new Ritalin prescriptions was among children ages 2–4.

All this has elicited a number of criticisms from researchers, doctors, and children's advocates. First of all, they point out that (like antidepressants) the long-term effects of these drugs are still unknown, while studies *have* shown that amphetamines in general can cause permanent changes in brain chemistry. Even if the drugs aren't harmful, many believe they are overprescribed, accusing doctors and parents of being too quick to classify any undesirable behavior or learning disability as ADD/ADHD. They also warn that stimulants are habit-forming, pointing to widespread abuse of Ritalin and Adderall by teenagers and college students: one study found 10 percent of teens admitted to taking Ritalin or Adderall without a doctor's order.

Popping Pills
U.S. Prescriptions Filled (millions)

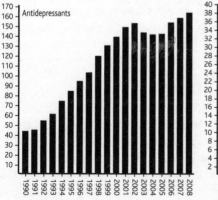

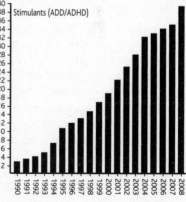

But Ritalin and Adderall ain't got nothin' on the golden oldies of prescription drug abuse—opioid painkillers like codeine, Vicodin, and Percocet, whose appeal has only grown with the introduction of new, more powerful medications like oxycodone (brand name OxyContin). According to the Mayo Clinic, the number of prescriptions written for opioid painkillers increased from 40 million in 1991 to 180 million in 2007. Even factoring in the growing number of elderly people in end-of-life care and an increase in the number of surgical procedures (from 24 million to 33 million in 2006), this 350 percent increase in opioid prescriptions seems a little suspicious. And those numbers don't take into account the drugs that are simply stolen: in 2003 over two million doses of opioid painkillers were filched from pharmacies, with thieves often leaving cash and other valuables untouched. In 2007 an estimated five million Americans were addicted to prescription opioids. The results have been predictable: from 1999 to 2006, opioid overdose deaths more than tripled from 4,000 to 13,500.

·············· **MADE IN AMERICA** ····················

Rise of the Dot.coms

In 1990 about two million Americans were using the Internet— less than 1 percent of the total U.S. population; by 2010, the number had climbed to 200 million, or 63 percent of the total population. This expansion went hand in hand with a tidal surge of online business activity, beginning—where else?—in America.

The groundwork for the commercialization of the Internet was laid by Congress in 1992, effectively ceding control of the Internet to private interests. Also in 1992 the Internet became more accessible to non–computer geeks with the launch of America Online and Mosaic, the forerunner of Netscape Navigator. At the time, big businesses were already using the Electronic Data Interchange, their own proprietary system for business-to-business electronic vending, which anticipated many features of the Internet and proved the viability of e-commerce.

Once business-to-business transactions had paved the way, it was only natural to bring the efficiency of e-commerce to business-to-consumer transactions as well: enter online shopping! In addition to convenience, e-commerce eliminated whole categories of business expense: all you really needed was warehouse space, as demonstrated by Amazon.com, the online book—and now, everything—emporium, which launched in 1995. Soon you could buy anything under the sun (and some things beyond the sun: the International Star Registry will let you name a star for $15).

Inevitably, people got a little *too* excited about the potential for e-commerce, leading to—yes—a financial bubble on Wall Street as stock prices for new "Dot.com" ventures soared, regardless of minor details like profitability and redundancy with other companies with the same idea. The numbers certainly looked good at first glance, as total e-commerce revenues shot up from $4 billion in 1997 to $29 billion in 2000. But startup costs were also huge, with many companies requiring multiple rounds of investment before they could break even. Amazon.com, arguably the most successful Dot.com, had revenues of $1.6 billion in 1999 but still lost $722 million. Across the board, the growth of Dot.com stock values was wildly out of proportion to the actual size of the businesses.

One company in particular, AOL, became an iconic symbol of the Dot.com boom with multi-billion-dollar deals: in 1998 it acquired Netscape for $4.2 billion, and in January 2000, it paid a stupefying $182 billion for Time-Warner, a traditional media company and cable provider. But "irrational exuberance," as Federal Reserve Chairman Alan Greenspan put it, was endemic. That same month—the end of the good times—20 Dot.com startups paid $2 million–$3 million each for 30-second spots during the Superbowl, while the Dow Jones Industrial Average hit a record high of 11,722.98.

★ Pizza Hut was the first restaurant chain to offer online ordering to its customers. The pizza peddler test-marketed the system in Santa Cruz, California, in the summer of 1994.

And just as inevitably, the bubble burst as the Dot.coms dot bombed. From February to November 2000, Dot.com stocks shed about $1.8 trillion in value, sinking to a mere $1.2 trillion. Over this period Yahoo alone lost $102 billion in value. But the most spectacular decline came at newly created AOL-Time Warner, which was slammed by the market-wide shift of Internet users from portal-based subscription access, on the AOL model, to high-speed broadband connections. AOL-Time Warner's total value plunged from $350 billion in January of 2000 to $84 billion in 2004; the companies ended the failed merger in May 2009, and as of 2010, the combined value of the now-separate companies is roughly $50 billion. In other words, in less than a decade, a single corporation saw its value decrease by an amount exceeding the individual GDPs of 180 countries in the year 2000, including Russia, Sweden, Turkey, and Pakistan.

But this was only a bump in the road for e-commerce. The basic concept was sound, indeed irresistible. Total online shopping revenues rose steadily from $30 billion in 2001 to a projected $140 billion in 2010. Meanwhile, whole new growth areas were opened up by the rise in broadband subscriptions, which soared from five million in 2000 to 90 million in 2010, enabling a creative explosion of multimedia content and interactive applications for both good and bad, including blogs, social networks, and photo-, audio-, and video-sharing.

The new king of the Internet (at least for the time being) is Google, the search engine founded in 1998, which took the basic search advertising model established by Yahoo and made it pay, by giving advertisers an opportunity to bid for search-term-based ad placement, greatly increasing the chances of reaching someone interested in their product. From a mere $19 million in 2000, Google's total ad revenues increased over a thousandfold to $23.6 billion in 2009. More generally, the interactive quality of the Web gives online advertising a huge advantage over traditional media, since advertisers can now directly observe which ads and ad placements spark consumer interest and adjust their strategies accordingly. Excluding Google, total online ad revenues increased from under $1 billion in 1997 to a projected $24 billion in 2010.

INTERNET, INTERNET, MAKE ME A MATCH

For once, money is the least interesting part of the story. What's truly fascinating is how the Internet is changing everyday life for billions of people around the planet. The phenomenon is too wide-ranging, varied, and dynamic to ever accurately describe, but just look at personal ads: in the good ol' days, most people frankly viewed personals ads as a last resort, the domain of the antisocial, the ugly, and the generally unmarriageable. Then the Internet changed everything.

One of the first online dating sites, Match.com, was founded in 1993, and by 2004 had eight million active members. It didn't take long before other dating sites joined the party, and by 2010 the sheer number and variety of online personals sites is astounding, with countless "niche" services targeting various identities at the local, regional, national, and global levels. There are online dating sites for Christians, Muslims, Jews, Hindus, Buddhists, and pagans, as well as dozens of sects, confessions, and sacral divisions within these religions—and don't forget the sites for atheists and agnostics. There are ethnic dating sites for African-Americans, Hispanics, Asians, mixed-race individuals, and, yes, white supremacists. There are dating sites targeting gays and lesbians, seniors, gold diggers, single parents, and HIV-positive people. There are even sites and people who market themselves as e-Cyrano de Bergerac's, with the sole goal of polishing up your profile and helping you suave up your e-communications so you can reel in your dream prospect.

And, okay, money's still part of it. Online dating is big business: in 2009 Match .com's revenues came to over $340 million, and the company spent over $50 million on TV advertising in 2008. And the money is well-earned, to judge by the growing number of online romance success stories. While it's hard to judge the company's claims, one of the most popular online dating sites, eHarmony, claimed to have helped facilitate 43,000 marriages in 2007 alone—about 2 percent of the total 2.3 million weddings in the United States in 2007.

Robots vs. Martians

It's hard to top the Apollo Program for sheer technical awesomeness in outer space, but the series of remote-controlled robots built by NASA to explore the surface of Mars come pretty darn close (while going a whole lot farther).

First, there's the robots themselves, which pack a huge amount of sophisticated scientific equipment into an incredibly small package. Sojourner, which landed on Mars as part of the Pathfinder mission on July 4, 1997, weighed just 10.5 kilograms—but this included a computer, solar power panels, several cameras, and a miniature X-ray spectrometer for analyzing soil samples. The two Mars Exploration Rovers that landed on Mars in June and July 2003—Spirit and Opportunity—both weighed 185 kilograms, including solar panels, batteries, computers, communications antennae, cameras, and an instrument arm containing three kinds of spectrometer and a grinder for preparing rock samples. By comparison, the Viking landers sent to Mars by NASA in 1976 weighed 600 kilograms each and carried less scientific instrumentation.

It's even more amazing that all this complex, sensitive equipment actually works, considering the way these robots are delivered to the Red Planet.

In 2003 the MER missions loaded Spirit and Opportunity onto three-stage Boeing Delta II rockets, which propelled them beyond Earth's gravity for their 320-million-mile journey to Mars. Six months later, both Explorer spacecraft entered the Martian gravity field in January 2004 traveling at about 12,000 miles per hour.

After hitting the atmosphere, the entry vehicles were slowed to about 1,000 miles per hour by air braking, with external temperatures rising to 2,637° Fahrenheit—the same as the surface of the sun. Then, about 30,000 feet above the planet's surface, giant supersonic parachutes deployed and rockets fired. The rovers were cushioned from impact on the surface of Mars by pyramid-shaped honeycombs of air bags, measuring 18 feet across, which inflated around the entry vehicles just seconds before impact. After impact, the "bubble-wrapped" landing vehicles bounced four to five stories while rolling about half a mile across the planet's surface.

Once they came to a stop, NASA mission control crew at the Jet Propulsion Laboratory in Pasadena, California, established regular communications via the Mars Odyssey and Mars Global Surveyor orbiters circling the planet; traveling at the speed of light, it took anywhere from 3 to 22 minutes for radio waves from Earth to reach the landing vehicles and rovers on Mars, depending on the relative location of the two planets. Mission control then transmitted commands causing the air bags to deflate and retract—clearing the way for the landing vehicle's "petals" to unfold, revealing the Mars Explorer Rovers. After leaving the landing vehicles, the rovers far exceeded their original 90-day mission, and as of 2009, both were still operational. In those six years, the rovers traveled over 13 miles across the surface of Mars, sent back over 250,000 digital photos, and conducted experiments giving scientists a window into the planet's watery past.

Perhaps most incredible of all is the total cost of the missions to date: just $950 million (which is a rounding error in terms of federal spending in the first decade of the twenty-first century). And of course, one of the best things about robots is that they aren't people, so if you blow them up, no one gets too upset. Which is not to say they're disposable: NASA gave comedians priceless material with the 1999 loss of the $125 million Climate Orbiter, which broke up in the Martian atmosphere after mission control engineers mixed up metric and "imperial" units (centimeters and inches).

·················· **BY THE NUMBERS** ··················

78 acres covered by the Mall of America,
completed in Minnesota in 1992
2,995 number of people who died in the terrorist
attacks on September 11, 2001

450,000 number of troops recommended for an invasion of Iraq by the Pentagon, 1999

125,000 number of U.S. troops in the 2003 invasion of Iraq

75,000 number of U.S. troops originally proposed by Secretary of Defense Donald Rumsfeld for the invasion of Iraq

19,000,000 vacant homes in the United States, 2010

$30,000,000,000,000 decrease in value of global stock markets following the financial collapse of 2008

$1,560,000,000,000 projected U.S. budget deficit in 2010

$22,500,000,000,000 projected U.S. debt in 2020

$300 billion decrease in stock value of AOL-Time Warner from 2000 to 2009

$260 billion gross domestic product of Russia, 2006

13,000,000 Americans taking antidepressants in 1996

30,000,000 Americans taking antidepressants in 2008

70,000,000 acres of developed land in the United States, 1990

120,000,000 acres of developed land in the United States, 2009

1,836 deaths resulting from Hurricane Katrina, 2005

Appendix

44 Presidents in 45 Minutes

1. George Washington. February 22, 1732–December 14, 1799. President 1789–1797. Nicknames and honorifics: "The Father of the Country." Son of a Virginia plantation owner who joined colonial militia as land surveyor, then served as a British officer in French-and-Indian War (displaying average military talent). Married super-rich young widow, Martha Custis. Led Continental Army in Revolution, won final victory at Yorktown. In 1787 presided over Constitutional Convention; later elected first president. Asserted government's authority by suppressing Whiskey Rebellion, set precedent of serving only two terms, warned against political parties and foreign alliances in Farewell Address. Quote: "I walk on untrodden ground. There is scarcely any part of my conduct which may not hereafter be drawn into precedent." Trivia: only Founding Father to free his slaves.

2. John Adams. October 30, 1735–July 4, 1826. President 1797–1801. Nicknames and honorifics: "Atlas of Independence, Atlas of Liberty, Duke of Braintree, His Rotundity, Colossus of Debate, Father of the Navy, Old Sink or Swim, Bonny Johnny, King John the Second." New England lawyer who joined the Revolution because of warrantless searches by British. As first vice-president, founded the Federalist Party with Alexander Hamilton, advocating strong central government, but as president rejected Hamilton's plans for a large army. In 1800 divided Federalists lost to Thomas Jefferson's Democratic-Republicans. But Chief Justice John Marshall achieved Adams' vision by establishing a strong Supreme Court. Quote: "The only maxim of a free government ought to be to trust no man living with power to endanger the public liberty." Trivia: Adams and his family got lost in the woods moving into the new White House.

3. Thomas Jefferson. April 13, 1743–July 4, 1826. President 1801–1809. Nicknames and honorifics: "Man of the People, Sage of Monticello, Long Tom, Mad Tom, The Pen of the Revolution, Apostle of Democracy." Virginia plantation owner, lawyer, architect, inventor, and statesman, in June of 1776 wrote the Declaration of Independence. Strongly supported the Bill of Rights in 1789 (particularly free religion). Fearing Federalist plans for central government, founded the Democratic-Republicans with James Madison, barely won the election of 1800 after bitter dispute with former friend Aaron Burr. Established West Point, beat the Barbary Pirates, and doubled the size of the United States with the Louisiana Purchase of 1803. Quote: "As our enemies have found we can reason like men, so now let us show them we can fight like men also." Trivia: writing his own epitaph, Jefferson neglected to mention that he served as president.

4. James Madison. March 16, 1751–June 28, 1836. President 1809–1817. Nicknames and honorifics: "Father of the Constitution, Father of the Bill of Rights, Jemmy, Little Jemmy, Sage of Montpelier, His Little Majesty." Virginia lawyer, drafted the Constitution in 1787, based on his model of three branches of government balanced against each other. Also wrote the Bill of Rights to reassure anti-Federalists and co-authored the Federalist Papers with Alexander Hamilton and John Jay to encourage ratification of the Constitution. First Speaker of the House, later served as Jefferson's Secretary of State. As president, led the United States into the War of 1812 and called for a standing army and navy to fight the British (reversing earlier position). Wife Dolley saved the only true portrait of Washington when Brits burned the White House. Quote: "All men having power ought to be distrusted to a certain degree." Trivia: at 5'4", shortest president ever.

5. James Monroe. April 28, 1758–July 4, 1831. President 1817–1825. Nicknames and honorifics: "Last Cocked Hat, Era of Good Feelings President." As teen fought in Continental Army and later studied law with Jefferson before entering politics. Presidency called "Era of Good Feelings"—period without partisan strife thanks to total dominance of Democratic-Republicans. Monroe Doctrine, set forth in 1823, stated the United States wouldn't tolerate interference by European powers in the New World. Quote: "Our country may be likened to a new house. We lack many things, but we possess the most precious of all—liberty!" Trivia: Monroe was the last Founding Father to serve as president and the last to wear a powdered wig.

6. John Quincy Adams. July 11, 1767–February 23, 1848. President 1825–1829. Nicknames and honorifics: "Old Man Eloquent, Publicola, The Abolitionist." New England lawyer like his father John Adams. Monroe's Secretary of State, helped acquire Florida from Spain in 1819. Lost popular vote to Andrew Jackson in 1824 but was voted the winner by House of Representatives. Focused on modernizing infrastructure for economic expansion, but alienated Southern voters with 1828 "Tariff of Abominations." In 1841 he won Supreme Court case defending rebel slaves who seized the Spanish ship *Amistad*. Quote: "America does not go abroad in search of monsters to destroy." Trivia: Adams swam nude in the Potomac every morning. To get an interview, a female journalist named Anne Royall sat on his clothes until he agreed to talk to her.

7. Andrew Jackson. March 15, 1767–June 8, 1845. President 1829–1837. Nicknames and honorifics: "Old Hickory, King Andrew, Hero of New Orleans, Sharp Knife." First president from the frontier, born in South Carolina, lost his entire family during the American Revolution. Won fame as military hero in War of 1812. After 1824 loss to Adams, created Democratic Party, exploiting regional tension between Northeastern elite and the rest of the country. Invented "spoils" system, firing all incumbent civil servants and giving jobs to his supporters. Later condemned for deporting "civilized" native tribes from Southeast to Oklahoma in brutal "Trail of Tears." Quote: "To the victors belong the spoils." Trivia: Jackson survived an assassination attempt when both of the would-be assassin's pistols misfired; Jackson beat him senseless.

8. Martin van Buren. December 5, 1782–July 24, 1862. President 1837–1841. Nicknames and honorifics: "The Little Magician, The Red Fox of Kinderhook, Old Kinderhook, Little Van, The Enchanter, The Great Manager, Matty Van." Born in Kinderhook, New York, grew up speaking Dutch. After training as a lawyer, organized New York's first statewide political machine and won election to the Senate in 1821. Curried favor in South with staunch defense of slavery and opposition to tariffs; played a key role in building Jackson's Democratic Party. After serving as Jackson's vice president, he easily won election in 1836 but took the blame for a deep economic depression which began in 1837. Quote: "The less government interferes with private pursuits, the better for general prosperity." Trivia: some historians say the word "okay" comes from van Buren supporters who abbreviated his nickname, "Old Kinderhook," "O.K."

9. William Henry Harrison. February 9, 1773–April 4, 1841. President 1841. Nicknames and honorifics: "Old Tippecanoe, Old Tip, Washington of the West, Old Granny." Military hero for victory over native alliance led by Tecumseh at Tippecanoe in 1811. Barely served a month before dying from a respiratory infection. Quote: "I contend that the strongest of all governments is that which is most free." Trivia: Harrison delivered the longest inauguration speech ever, caught cold, and died, making his the shortest presidency ever.

10. John Tyler. March 29, 1790–January 18, 1862. President 1841–1845. Nicknames and honorifics: "Accidental President, His Accidency, Young Hickory." Virginia lawyer who supported Democrats at first, but jumped to Whigs after Jackson threatened to use force if South Carolina "nullified" the Tariff of Abominations during the "Nullification Crisis" of 1833 (an early dispute over states' rights). First VP to succeed to the presidency on death of predecessor. Wanted to admit Texas as slave state, but was frustrated by Whig anti-slavery faction; succeeded in admitting Florida as slave state in 1845. Later supported Secession and served in the Confederate House of Representatives. Quote: "I can never consent to being dictated to." Trivia: Tyler had 15 children by two wives, the most of any president.

11. James Polk. November 2, 1795–June 15, 1849. President 1845–1849. Nicknames and honorifics: "Polk the Purposeful, Polk the Plodder, Napoleon of the Stump." Son of a Scots-Irish merchant from North Carolina, studied law in Tennessee before getting into politics. Elected to Congress, Polk became Speaker of the House and a key Jackson ally. In 1844 Polk broke pro/anti-slavery deadlock at Democratic convention by promising to admit Texas as slave state and then step down after one term, leaving future expansion up for grabs. Annexation of Texas in 1845 led to the Mexican-American War of 1846–1848; Polk grabbed a huge chunk of land from Mexico including California. Quote: "With me it is exceptionally true that the Presidency is no bed of roses." Trivia: first president to have his photo taken.

12. Zachary Taylor. November 24, 1784–July 9, 1850. President 1849–1850. Nicknames and honorifics: "Old Rough and Ready, Old Zack." Military hero of the Mexican-American War, hailed from Virginia and owned slaves in Louisiana, but alienated South by trying to have California and New Mexico join as free states (in bid to please North). Died of food poisoning after just 16 months in office. Quote: "I have always done my duty. I am ready to die. My only regret is for the friends I leave behind me." Trivia: last president to own slaves while in office.

13. Millard Fillmore. January 7, 1800–March 8, 1874. President 1850–1853. Nicknames and honorifics: "The Accidental President, The Wool-Carder President." Lawyer from upstate New York, chosen as Taylor's vice president to give Whigs broad national support. Ironically pursued opposite approach to nation unity, trying to admit New Mexico and Utah as slave states to please South (alienating North). Supported Compromise of 1850: California joined a free state, New Mexico and Utah as territories with no restrictions on slavery, Fugitive Slave Law said Federal marshals could help capture runaway slaves in North. Quote: "May God save the country, for it is evident that the people will not." Trivia: Fillmore refused an honorary degree from Oxford, protesting he had "neither literary nor scientific attainment."

14. Franklin Pierce. November 23, 1804–October 8, 1869. President 1853–1857. Nicknames and honorifics: "Handsome Frank, Baby, Purse." New Hampshire lawyer and Mexican-American War hero. Northern background and Southern sympathies helped win Democratic nomination and the White House. Major event was the Kansas-Nebraska Act of 1854, scrapping the Missouri Compromise of 1820 and opening territory above the 36°30′ line to slavery, leading to open violence between pro- and anti-slavery settlers. Only incumbent president not re-nominated by his party. Quote: "There is nothing left to do but get drunk." Trivia: first president to have a White House Christmas tree.

15. James Buchanan. April 23, 1791–June 1, 1868. President 1857–1861. Nicknames and honorifics: "Old Buck, The Do-Nothing President, Ten-Cent Jimmie." Pennsylvania lawyer with Southern sympathies nominated by the Democrats in 1856 as a compromise between pro- and anti-slavery factions. Punted slavery to the Supreme Court, which ruled in *Dred Scott v. Sanford* (1857) that Congress couldn't prohibit slavery in U.S. territories, leading to surge by anti-slavery Republicans. When Southern states seceded following Lincoln's election, took position that states weren't allowed to secede, but he also wasn't allowed to stop them. Quote: "What is right and what is practicable are two different things." Trivia: only president who never married.

16. Abraham Lincoln. February 12, 1809–April 15, 1865. President 1861–1865. Nicknames and honorifics: "Honest Abe, Uncle Abe, The

Rail-Splitter, The Great Emancipator, The Liberator, King Lincoln." Born in Kentucky, moved to Illinois because his father objected to slavery. Ferried cargo aboard flatboats on the Mississippi and gained respect as a formidable wrestler. Lost Senate bid in 1858 but won fame for eloquent opposition to slavery in debates with Sen. Stephen A. Douglas. Election in 1860 provoked Southern Secession and Civil War. Turned war into a crusade with Emancipation Proclamation of 1863, freeing slaves in rebel states. Assassinated by an unstable actor, John Wilkes Booth, shortly after Confederate surrender. Ranked one of the greatest presidents for preserving Union and freeing slaves. Quote: "A house divided against itself cannot stand." Trivia: at 6'4', tallest president.

17. Andrew Johnson. December 29, 1808–July 31, 1875. President 1865–1869. Nicknames and honorifics: "The Tailor, Sir Veto." Democrat from east Tennessee, only Southern Senator who didn't resign during Secession. In 1864 nominated as VP to show Lincoln's commitment to postwar reconciliation. Tried to follow Lincoln's moderate approach to Reconstruction but couldn't control Radical Republicans in Congress who wanted to punish South, leading to the rise of Jim Crow. Quote: "I feel incompetent to perform duties . . . which have been so unexpectedly thrown upon me." Trivia: Johnson was buried with his head resting on a copy of the Constitution.

18. Ulysses S. Grant. April 27, 1822–July 23, 1885. President 1869–1877. Nicknames and honorifics: "American Caesar, Unconditional Surrender Grant, Useless S. Grant, Galena Tanner, Butcher Grant." Failed businessman from Ohio who won fame for leading Union armies to victory in the Civil War. As president secured ratification of the Fifteenth Amendment, giving freedmen the right to vote, and mobilized Union troops to combat the Ku Klux Klan, but failed to produce lasting changes in Southern society, leading to renewed oppression under Jim Crow. Also criticized for incredibly corrupt administration, marred by major scandals, and failing to stop the Panic of 1873, leading to a deep five-year depression. Quote: "It was my fortune, or misfortune, to be called to the office of Chief Executive without any previous political training." Trivia: established the first National Park at Yellowstone on March 1, 1872.

19. Rutherford B. Hayes. October 4, 1822–January 17, 1893. President 1877–1881. Nicknames and honorifics: "His Fraudulency, Old 8 to 7, The Great Usurper, Rutherfraud Hayes, President De Facto, Granny Hayes." Born in Ohio, graduated Harvard Law in 1845. Served in the Union army, then elected Republican governor of Ohio. Lost popular vote in 1876 but took White House through shady deal with Southern Democrats in return for promise to end Reconstruction. Declared president by 8-to-7 vote by congressional commission. Withdrew Federal troops from South. Quote: "It is the desire of the good people of the whole country that sectionalism as a factor in our politics should disappear." Trivia: held first White House Easter egg roll.

20. James A. Garfield. November 19, 1831–September 19, 1881. President 1881. Nicknames and honorifics: "Canal Boy, The Preacher President, Boatman Jim." Born in Ohio, worked on riverboats and tried preaching before becoming a high school principal. Later fought for the Union. As Republican member of Congress, helped make Hayes president in 1876. As president unveiled plans to reform the civil service but was assassinated by Charles J. Guiteau, angered by failure to obtain an appointment as U.S. consul to France. Quote: "The truth will set you free, but first it will make you miserable." Trivia: probably died from an infection caused by surgeons probing for a bullet near his spine with bare hands; not the bullet itself.

21. Chester A. Arthur. October 5, 1829–November 18, 1886. President 1881–1885. Nicknames and honorifics: "Gentleman Boss, Prince Arthur, Walrus, The Father of the Civil Service." Born in Vermont, practiced law in New York before joining Republicans. Continued Garfield's anti-corruption crusade with the Pendleton Civil Service Reform Act of 1883 instituting written examinations for civil service appointments. Quote: "I may be President of the United States, but my private life is nobody's damn business." Trivia: wife Nell died 20 months before he became president; vowed not to remarry, but still received four marriage proposals on last day in office.

22 & 24. Grover Cleveland. March 18, 1837–June 24, 1908. President 1885–1889, 1893–1897. Nicknames and honorifics: "Grover the Good, Old Grover, His Obstinacy, Beast of Buffalo, Uncle Jumbo." Only president to serve non-consecutive terms. Son of Presbyterian pastor from Caldwell, New Jersey, practiced law in Buffalo, won election as sheriff in 1871, mayor in 1881, then governor of New York in 1882. First Democratic president since Johnson, rejected "spoils system," used veto 534 times, but failed to institute gold standard or lower tariffs as hoped. In 1888 Republicans exploited dislike of anti-tariff stance to elect Benjamin Harrison, though Cleveland won popular vote. In second term repealed Harrison's silver standard and tried again to lower tariffs without success. Criticized for breaking up railroad strikes in 1894. Quote: "Officeholders are the agents of the people, not their masters." Trivia: only bachelor president to marry in White House, to 21-year-old Frances Folsom in 1886.

23. Benjamin Harrison. August 20, 1833–March 13, 1901. President 1889–1893. Nicknames and honorifics: "Young Tippecanoe, Little Ben, The Centennial President, The Human Iceberg, Kid Gloves Harrison." Grandson of William Henry Harrison, practiced law in Indianapolis then fought in Civil War. Elected to Senate as Republican in 1880, supported high tariffs to protect domestic industries. As president signed the McKinley Tariff (one of the highest in U.S. history) and the Sherman Antitrust Act. Also presided over admission of North Dakota, South Dakota, Montana, Washington, Idaho, and Wyoming. Blamed for worsening economic conditions, leading to defeat in 1892. Quote: "We Americans have no commission from God to police the world." Trivia: first president recorded on phonograph.

25. William McKinley. January 29, 1843–September 14, 1901. President 1897–1901. Nicknames and honorifics: "The Major, Liberator of Cuba, Idol of Ohio, Wobbly Willie." Won praise for courage as junior officer in Civil War, later practiced law in Ohio. Campaigned for his old commander, Rutherford B. Hayes, then served in Congress, later governor of Ohio. Beat populist Democrat William Jennings Bryan in 1896, reflecting shift from rural agrarian to urban industrial economy. Initially opposed Spanish-American War before giving in to public opinion; also oversaw annexation of Hawaii. Assassinated less than a year into his second term by anarchist Leon Czolgosz. Quote: "Unlike any other nation, here the people rule, and their will is the supreme law." Trivia: first president to ride in a car and first to campaign by telephone.

26. Theodore Roosevelt. October 27, 1858–January 6, 1919. President 1901–1909. Nicknames and honorifics: "TR, Teedie, Teddy, Rough Rider, Rough and Ready, Hero of San Juan Hill, Cowboy, Old Four Eyes, Ted the Meddler, The Lion, Trust Buster." From wealthy New York political family, at Harvard alternated academic pursuits with crew and boxing. Dropped out of Columbia Law to run for New York State Assembly. After death of mother Mittie and first wife Alice in 1884, withdrew to North Dakota, where he served as frontier sheriff. After returning and marrying second wife Edith, led civil service reform for Harrison, then became police commissioner of New York City in 1895. Famed for fighting corruption, appointed assistant secretary of the Navy (with a break in 1898 to fight in the Spanish-American War). After war, governor of New York and finally vice president under McKinley. As president focused on trust-busting and consumer protection. Helped create new nation, Panama, as site for Panama Canal. Unsuccessful bid for a third term with "Bull Moose Party" in 1912. Quote: "Speak softly and carry a big stick; you will go far." Trivia: love of nature made him a pioneering conservationist, and in 1903 an admirer sent him a stuffed toy bear, sparking the craze for "Teddy" bears.

27. William Howard Taft. September 15, 1857–March 8, 1930. President 1909–1913. Nicknames and honorifics: "Big Chief, Old Bill, Big Lub." Another Republican lawyer from Ohio. Worked in private practice and then served on the Ohio Supreme Court before being appointed U.S. solicitor general in 1890. Appointed governor-general of the Philippines and later Secretary of War under Roosevelt. Carried on some of TR's initiatives, including trust-busting and civil service reforms, but managed to alienate both big business and progressive reformers, and lost in a landslide to Wilson in 1912. Second public career as Chief Justice of the U.S. Supreme Court, 1921–1930. Quote: "The world is not going to be saved by legislation." Trivia: At over 350 pounds, the heaviest president; on several occasions got stuck in the White House bathtub.

28. Woodrow Wilson. December 28, 1856–February 3, 1924. President 1913–1921. Nicknames and honorifics: "The Professor, The Phrasemaker, The Prince of Peace." Son of Presbyterian theologian from Virginia, first studied law but then switched to history and political science. President of Princeton, in 1910 elected governor of New Jersey as Progressive Democrat, won fame for fighting corrupt political "machines." First term as president focused on antitrust, bank, and currency reforms, including creation of Federal Reserve in 1913. Second term dominated by WWI. Failed to restrain vengeful French at Versailles treaty negotiations, also failed to persuade Republican Senators at home to join the League of Nations, setting stage for WWII. After stroke in September 1919, wife Edith ran the White House for the rest of his second term. Quote: "The world must be made safe for democracy." Trivia: first president to deliver his State of the Union address to Congress in person since John Adams in 1799.

29. Warren G. Harding. November 2, 1865–August 2, 1923. President 1921–1923. Nicknames and honorifics: "W. G., Wobbly Warren." Ohio Republican, newspaper publisher. Administration tarnished by scandals, including Teapot Dome (oil companies bribed Secretary of the Interior for mineral rights). Criticized for relying on untrustworthy friends, collectively known as "the Ohio Gang." Died of a heart attack after less than three years in office. Quote: "I have no trouble with my enemies . . . but my friends, my goddamned friends, they're the ones who keep me walking the floor at nights!" Trivia: wearing size 14 shoes, had the largest feet of any president.

30. Calvin Coolidge. July 4, 1872–January 5, 1933. President 1923–1929. Nicknames and honorifics: "Silent Cal, Cautious Cal, Cool Cal, The Sphinx of the Potomac." Lawyer from Vermont, built his political base in Massachusetts: president of the state senate in 1914, lieutenant governor in 1915, governor in 1919. As vice-president, one of few officials in the Harding administration not tainted by corruption. Presided over rapid economic growth in the "roaring 20s" and Dawes Plan, which staved off European financial collapse with new loans but set the stage for the Great Depression. Quote: "The business of America is business." Trivia: slept more than any other president—ten hours a day.

31. Herbert Hoover. August 10, 1874–October 20, 1964. President 1929–1933. Nicknames and honorifics: "Wonder Boy, Chief, The Grand Old Man, The Great Engineer, The Great Humanitarian." Born in Iowa, orphaned at age nine, went to Oregon to live with an uncle. Studied geology at Stanford, first career as mining engineer took him to Australia and China. Organized humanitarian aid during WW I, saving millions of lives in Europe and Russia. Secretary of Commerce under Harding and Coolidge (who gave him the sarcastic nickname "Wonder Boy"). Won landslide victory in 1928, but was derailed by the Great Depression. Many key policies, like wage and price controls, backfired and made the situation worse. Quote: "With impressive proof on all sides of magnificent progress, no one can rightly deny the fundamental correctness of our economic system." Trivia: said he could never join the Democratic Party because as a boy in Iowa the only Democrat he knew was the town drunk.

32. Franklin Delano Roosevelt. January 30, 1882–April 12, 1945. President 1933–1945. Nicknames and honorifics: "FDR, The Boss, King Franklin, That Man In the White House, The New Dealer." Born into old New York political family (TR was fifth cousin). Served as assistant secretary of the Navy in World War I, then James M. Cox's running mate in unsuccessful 1920 Democratic presidential campaign. In August 1921, contracted polio which resulted in permanent paralysis below the waist. Elected Democratic governor of New York in 1928, then president in 1932. New Deal was credited with helping end Depression, but unclear how much it really helped. Also criticized for trying to stack the Supreme Court in 1937. Nonetheless considered one of the greatest presidents for leading the United States to victory in World War II. After Pearl Harbor, maintained political support for war by explaining complex strategic issues so ordinary people could understand. Coordinated U.S. efforts with Allies (U.K. and U.S.S.R.). Chief architect of the post-war political landscape, setting the stage for the Cold War; also launched Manhattan Project, opening the nuclear age. Suffered a stroke and died just a few months into his unprecedented fourth term. Quote: "The only thing we have to fear is fear itself." Trivia: there are only two published photographs of FDR in his wheelchair.

33. Harry S. Truman. May 8, 1884–December 26, 1972. President 1945–1952. Nicknames and honorifics: "Give 'Em Hell Harry, Haberdasher Harry, High-Tax Harry, Mister Missouri." Small-town businessman from Missouri. After serving as artillery officer in WWI, got involved in local politics, later elected Democratic Senator from Missouri in 1935. FDR's third vice president. As president gave the order to drop atom bombs on Japan, ending WWII. Later presided over difficult postwar period as economy readjusted. Expected to lose in 1948, beat Republican Thomas Dewey by small margin. Launched Marshall Plan to rebuild Europe, helped form NATO, forced Soviets out of Iran, and withstood Soviet pressure by ordering Berlin airlift. Desegregated military and introduced anti-communist screening for government jobs. Repelled North Korean invasion of South Korea in 1950 (but dismissed MacArthur for insubordination). Quote: "The buck stops here." Trivia: the "S." in Truman's name doesn't stand for anything.

34. Dwight D. Eisenhower. October 14, 1890–March 28, 1969. President 1953–1961. Nicknames and honorifics: "Ike, Kansas Cyclone, Duckpin." As Supreme Commander of the Allied Expeditionary Force in Europe, directed Normandy landings and liberation of France in 1944, then invasion and occupation of Western Germany. As president, ended war in Korea by threatening to use nuclear weapons against China. At home, ordered construction of interstate highway system and enforced Supreme Court's decision integrating schools in *Brown v. Board*. Also launched U.S. space program in response to Sputnik. Despite military background, favored smaller military balanced by more nuclear weapons; warned against growth of "military-industrial complex." Quote: "Any man who wants to be president is either an egomaniac or crazy." Trivia: greatest disappointment was not making West Point baseball team.

35. John Fitzgerald Kennedy. May 29, 1917–November 22, 1963. President 1961–1963. Nicknames and honorifics: "JFK, Jack." Son of wealthy Wall St. financier Joseph Kennedy, attended Harvard and served in the Pacific in WWII. Served as Democratic representative and senator from Massachusetts, then won close election over Richard Nixon in shady circumstances in 1960. First Catholic and Irish-American president, supported civil rights and planned to extend New Deal programs. Approved invasion of Cuba by CIA-backed exiles but withheld air support, resulting in debacle at Bay of Pigs in 1961. In 1962, confronted Soviets over nuclear missiles stationed on Cuba in the Cuban Missile Crisis. Assassinated in Dallas by Lee Harvey Oswald. Quote: "And so, my fellow Americans, ask not what your country can do for you; ask what you can do for your country." Trivia: the only president who also won a Pulitzer Prize (for *Profiles in Courage*, 1955).

36. Lyndon Baines Johnson. August 27, 1908–January 22, 1972. President 1963–1969. Nicknames and honorifics: "LBJ, Landslide Lyndon." Taught high school speech and debate in Texas before winning election to Congress in 1937. During WWII he asked for a combat command but was instead sent by FDR to be fact finder in the Pacific. Elected senator from Texas in 1948, lost the Democratic nomination to JFK in 1960, then argued his way into becoming JFK's running mate. Supported civil rights; continued space race; expanded New Deal welfare guarantees with the Great Society, including Medicaid and Medicare. Beat Goldwater by a huge margin in 1964, but anti-communist political pressure from GOP led him to escalate Vietnam War. Chose not to seek reelection in 1968. Quote: "If one morning I walked on top of the water across the Potomac River, the headline that afternoon would read: 'President Can't Swim.' " Trivia: liked the soft drink Fresca so much it was on tap in the White House.

37. Richard M. Nixon. January 9, 1913–April 22, 1994. President 1969–1974. Nicknames and honorifics: "Tricky Dick." After serving as naval officer in WWII, elected to House of Representatives in 1946. Elected senator from California in 1950, won fame for anti-communist investigations. In 1952 chosen as Eisenhower's running mate to bolster Ike's anti-communist credentials. After 1960 loss to JFK retired from politics to practice law, but returned to run as "candidate of order and decency" in 1968. Extricated U.S. from Vietnam, but outraged anti-war protestors with secret bombing of Cambodia. Supported civil rights, increased welfare spending, formed the Environmental Protection Agency, signed groundbreaking environmental legislation, and presided over 1969 Apollo moon landing. Won re-election in 1972 with landslide 60 percent of popular vote, but second term was derailed by Watergate scandal; resigned rather than face conviction by Congress on articles of impeachment. Quote: "I am not a crook!" Trivia: first campaign for Congress was funded by wartime poker winnings.

38. Gerald Ford. July 14, 1913–December 26, 2006. President 1974–1977. Nicknames and honorifics: "Jerry, The Accidental President, Mr. Nice Guy." Born in Nebraska, grew up in Michigan, attended UMich, where he was a college football star. He then took a coaching job at Yale and schmoozed his way into Yale Law. After fighting in the Pacific in WWII, left his legal career behind to run for Republican representative from Michigan, ultimately serving 1949–1973 (1965–1973 as GOP Minority Leader). Became vice president in October 1973, replacing Spiro Agnew, who resigned amid allegations of tax fraud. Enjoyed reputation for honesty and sincerity, but criticized for pardoning Nixon and presiding over worst economic downturn since Great Depression, resulting from high inflation and Arab oil embargo punishing U.S. support for Israel. Quote: "My fellow Americans, our long national nightmare is over." Trivia: only person to serve as vice president and president without being elected to either office.

39. James Earl Carter, Jr. Born October 1, 1924. President 1977–1981. Nicknames and honorifics: "Jimmy, The Peanut Farmer." From rural Georgia, attended U.S. Naval Academy during WWII and served in first nuclear submarines before resigning to take over family farm after father died in 1953. Elected to Georgia state senate in 1961 and governor in 1970, despite refusal to support segregation. Evangelical Christian support helped win the White House in 1976, but alienated conservative Christians by supporting feminist-backed Equal Rights Amendment and failing to pursue anti-abortion agenda. Helped bring peace between Israel and Egypt and initiated support for anti-Soviet Afghan rebels, but foreign policy derailed by Islamic Revolution in Iran and subsequent hostage crisis, leading to defeat by Reagan. Second career as humanitarian and peacemaker earned the Nobel Peace Prize in 2002. Quote: "You cannot divorce religious belief and public service. I've never detected any conflict between God's will and my political duty." Trivia: first president born in a hospital.

40. Ronald Reagan. February 6, 1911–June 5, 2004. Nicknames and honorifics: "The Great Communicator, The Gipper, Gip, Dutch, Teflon Ron." Born in Illinois, moved to L.A. in 1930s to pursue acting career. Elected president of Screen Actors Guild, later became spokesman for General Electric, leading to political career. Joined GOP in 1962, elected governor of California in 1967. As president increased funding to Afghan rebels, advocated space-based missile defense ("Star Wars") and reopened the arms race with the Soviets, pushing USSR to financial collapse. Personal friendship with reformist Soviet premier Gorbachev led to more conciliatory approach in second term. At home, massive defense spending and tax cuts helped revitalize economy, but national debt rose, and lax financial regulation led to recession in 1990–1991. Criticized for probable involvement in illegal Iran-Contra affair. Quote: "The most terrifying words in the English language are: I'm from the government and I'm here to help." Trivia: oldest president, age 69 at first election.

41. George H. W. Bush. Born June 12, 1924. President 1989–1993. Nicknames and honorifics: "Poppy." Son of Massachusetts banker Prescott Bush, served as Navy pilot in WWII (at age 18, the youngest person in the service when he joined), attended Yale, later went into Texas oil business, making millions. Elected to Congress in 1967, appointed ambassador to U.N. by Nixon in 1971, then CIA director under Ford. After unsuccessful bid for GOP nomination in 1980, became Reagan's running mate. As president won praise for decisive victory in liberation of Kuwait in First Gulf War (Operation Desert Storm, August 2, 1990–February 28, 1991); also presided over collapse of Soviet Union, fall of Berlin Wall, and end of Cold War. But took blame for steep economic downturn in 1990–1991. Quote: "I have opinions of my own, strong opinions, but I don't always agree with them." Trivia: distantly related to presidents Franklin Pierce, Abraham Lincoln, Teddy Roosevelt, and Gerald Ford, as well as British Prime Minister Winston Churchill.

42. William Jefferson Clinton. Born August 19, 1946. President 1993–2001. Nicknames and honorifics: "Bubba, Big Chief, Big Dog, Old Bill, The Man from Hope, Comeback Kid, Elvis, Slick Willie." Son of a traveling salesman, he decided on political career after meeting JFK at a reception in White House Rose Garden in 1962. Won Rhodes Scholarship to study at Oxford, then went to Yale Law, where he met future wife Hillary. Later criticized for using political connections to avoid serving in Vietnam. Elected attorney general of Arkansas in 1976, governor in 1978 (at age 32, youngest in the country), winning praise for improving backwards educational system. Surprise Democratic nominee in 1992, presided over economic boom; paid down Reagan-era debt; reformed welfare. In foreign policy, strengthened economic ties to Mexico and Canada; reinvented NATO with humanitarian interventions in former Yugoslavia; and bombed Al Qaeda targets following terrorist attacks on U.S. embassies. Dogged by allegations of corrupt land deals in Arkansas

(Whitewater) and multiple extramarital affairs. Lied under oath about affair with intern Monica Lewinsky, leading to impeachment for perjury, but no conviction. Quote: "It depends on what the meaning of the word 'is' is." Trivia: first Democrat to win two elections since FDR.

43. George W. Bush. Born July 6, 1946. President 2001–2009. Nicknames and honorifics: "Dubya, Bushie, Junior, Tweed." Son of George H. W. Bush, born in Connecticut, attended Yale, then Harvard Business School before joining the family oil business. After a failed run for Congress in 1978, became a co-owner of the Texas Rangers baseball team. Turned to Christian faith to overcome drinking problem in 1986. Unseated Democrat Ann Richards as governor of Texas in 1994, then beat Clinton's VP Al Gore in a close, disputed election in 2000. Responded to September 11, 2001 terrorist attacks with "global war on terror," beginning with invasion and occupation of Afghanistan; formation of new cabinet-level Department of Homeland Security; and far-reaching surveillance, including warrantless wiretaps. Ordered controversial invasion of Iraq on March 20, 2003; criticized for leading U.S. to war on faulty intelligence and for invading without sufficient forces. Also faulted for inadequate federal response to Hurricane Katrina, which destroyed much of New Orleans on August 29, 2005. As second term ended, U.S. economy suffered worst downturn since Great Depression, due partly to lax regulation. Helped avert total collapse of financial markets with massive bank bailout and financial stimulus. Quote: "When I take action, I'm not going to fire a $2 million missile at a $10 empty tent and hit a camel in the butt. It's going to be decisive." Trivia: nickname for chief political advisor Karl Rove is "turd-blossom."

44. Barack Hussein Obama. Born August 4, 1961. President 2009–20?? Nicknames and honorifics: "Barry, No Drama Obama." First African-American president. Born in Hawaii to white mother and Kenyan father, lived in Indonesia from 1967–1971, then worked as community organizer in Chicago before attending Columbia, then Harvard Law. Returned to Chicago as civil rights attorney, elected to Illinois state senate in 1997, junior U.S. senator from Illinois in 2004. Surprise Democratic nominee in 2008, beat Arizona Senator John McCain amid major recession, benefiting from widespread dissatisfaction with GOP. Immediately faced conservative backlash for alleged "socialist" policies, including sweeping health care reform, and unprecedented budget deficits. Ordered troop surge to battle resurgent Taliban in Afghanistan, but repudiating unilateral Bush approach has failed to produce progress toward Israeli-Palestinian peace or halting Iran's nuclear program. Also criticized for alleged failure to respond to massive oil spill caused by BP oil rig in Gulf of Mexico. Quote: "What do you think a stimulus is? It's spending—that's the whole point!" Trivia: won two Grammy awards for spoken-word albums for audio versions of his books *Audacity of Hope* (2008) and *Dreams from My Father* (2005).

Index

A Genius for Every Occasion . . .

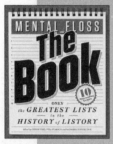

mental_floss: The Book
978-0-06-206930-6 (paperback)

**mental_floss presents
Condensed Knowledge**
978-0-06-056806-1 (paperback)

**mental_floss presents
Forbidden Knowledge**
978-0-06-078475-1 (paperback)

**mental_floss presents
In the Beginning**
978-0-06-125147-4 (paperback)

**mental_floss presents
Be Amazing**
978-0-06-125148-1 (paperback)

**The Mental Floss
History of the United States**
978-0-06-192823-9 (paperback)

**The Mental Floss
History of the World**
978-0-06-184267-2 (paperback)

...also available from...
mental_floss

mental_floss:
Cocktail Party Cheat Sheets
978-0-06-088251-8 (paperback)

mental_floss:
Scatterbrained
978-0-06-088250-1 (paperback)

mental_floss:
What's the Difference?
978-0-06-088249-5 (paperback)

mental_floss:
Genius Instruction Manual
978-0-06-088253-2 (paperback)

mental_floss presents
Instant Knowledge
978-0-06-083461-6 (paperback)

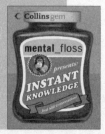